TIBET'S TERRIFYING DEITIES

ART IN ITS CONTEXT

Studies in Ethno - Aesthetics edited by Adrian A. Gerbrands

MUSEUM SERIES: VOLUME I

MOUTON & CO - PUBLISHERS - THE HAGUE - PARIS

F. SIERKSMA

TIBET'S TERRIFYING DEITIES

Sex and aggression in religious acculturation

MOUTON & CO · PUBLISHERS · THE HAGUE · PARIS

THE TRANSLATION OF THIS BOOK HAS BEEN ENABLED BY THE
PRINS BERNHARD FONDS OUT OF THE REIMAN DE BAS FONDS

TRANSLATED FROM THE DUTCH BY MRS. G. E. VAN BAAREN - PAPE

LIBRARY OF CONGRESS CATALOG CARD NO. 66-17948

PRINTED IN THE NETHERLANDS

PREFACE

The original plan of a book on the art of Tibet by two authors was afterwards modified in the sense that the present author was to write a more general introduction in connection with the Terrifying Deities, while in another volume the artistic and iconographical aspects of Tibetan art were to be treated more particularly by an author who has specialized in this field. That is the reason why in this book the context receives considerably more attention than the art itself.

When this monograph was practically finished, R. A. Stein's *Recherches sur l'épopée et le barde au Tibet* appeared. It has been referred to incidentally in some notes, but it was too late to make use of the important results of this research. The latter remark also applies to *Les tribus anciennes des marches sino-tibétaines* and *La civilisation tibétaine* by the same author, which appeared even later, when the present book had already been translated. The author invites the particular attention of insiders to this fact and recommends *La civilisation tibétaine* to the general reader as the best general introduction to the history and culture of Tibet which also provides an excellent background for the present monograph.

With respect to one important subject, however, the present author does not agree with professor Stein. The reader may be referred to his review of *La civilisation tibétaine* in the *Tijdschrift voor Taal-, Land- en Volkenkunde*, vol. 119 (1963), pp. 317-322. The hypothesis is defended there that the influence of the pastoral nomads upon the origin and formation of Tibetan culture was much greater than is assumed by the French scholar. The culture of Tibet's nomad herdsmen is directly related to the other pastoral cultures in the world. For this reference may be made to my 'Two pastoral customs in Tibet', *Man*, vol. LXII (1962), nr. 111, and 'Sacred cairns in pastoral cultures', *History of religions*, vol. 2 (1963), pp. 227-241. The pastoralists have shaped and stamped Tibetan culture. For this the reader may be referred to the above-mentioned review and the present author's article 'Rtsod-pa: the monachal disputations in Tibet', *Indo-Iranian Journal*, vol. 7 (1964), where the historical and psychological connections of Tibetan scholarship with the institutionalized aggression of the ancient pastoralists have been pointed out. Latent and patent aggression can also be found to a marked degree in the biographical data of a contemporary Tibetan theologian which will be published in due time. I am therefore of the opinion that the main thesis of this monograph bearing on the strong pastoral influences in Tibetan culture can and should be maintained.

For help of various kinds I owe thanks to Prof. Dr. M. Draak, Prof. Dr. J. W. de Jong,

Prof. Dr. F. B. J. Kuiper, Prof. Dr. F. Lessing, Dr. A. Wayman, and Prof. Dr. E. Zürcher. I am especially indebted to Dr. P. H. Pott for his iconographical information and his help with the selection of the illustrations. I also have to thank the two Tibetan informants who among other things have made it practically certain that Yami as partner of *gSin-rje* (Yama) is a fable of Western iconographers.

F. Sierksma

CONTENTS

LIST OF PLATES

Foar boerinne, dy't stil har tinzen hat …

Och minskewrâld komt en wurdt wer wei
As tearen fan in stream.

INTRODUCTION

When the New Year was celebrated in Lhasa, the capital of the 'Land of Snows', the Tibetans turned life upside down. In former times this was even done so drastically, that most laymen went out of town for fear of the innumerable begging monks, whom they could not refuse generous alms upon this festival, and whom they also had to receive as guests in their houses. In view of this threatened attack upon their purse and possessions the well-to-do left the sacred city in such numbers as to constitute a veritable exodus. But in more recent times also, when the monks no longer formed a financial danger, it remained evident that the New Year brought about a temporary reversal of all values. Instead of the Dalai Lama and his government of monks and laymen, the monks of the Dre-pung monastery were lords and masters in Lhasa then. The function of a sacred king was fulfilled by the abbot of this monastery, which had once been a considerable power in Tibet, where many monasteries were also fortresses.[1]

A much more remarkable ruler, however, went through the streets at the New Year. Far more of a carnival figure than the venerable abbot of Dre-pung, he played a central part in the festivities. He was the scapegoat, allowed to spend a week among the flesh-pots of Egypt, eating what he wanted and taking whatever he desired, and then sent out into the desert. He was a man from the social no man's land, appointed to play a part in the ritual no man's land between the Old and the New, and in this part much was revealed of that which normally remained hidden under the social, religious and cultural institutions of Tibetan life. That he lived literally between old and new, in the region where normal institutions and customs no longer function, was apparent from his aspect: his face was painted half black and half white. We shall see that every year anew the Tibetan society attempted to exorcize its own inner conflict with the driving out of this ambiguous figure.

After his one week's rule the scapegoat had to stake his power on a game of dice with a monk, who obviously represented the clergy and normal life. It goes without saying that the scapegoat, as representative of all the ancient evil that was to be cancelled, but also of everything that did not match the ideal pattern of society and religion, always lost the game. That was a certainty beforehand. When he had played his game and lost, he was driven out of the city and had to take refuge in the 'abode of demons' of a nearby monastery, where in olden times, according to the stories, he was murdered. That after his temporary rule the scapegoat had to seek refuge with the demons, thus showing to what realm he belonged, is eloquent of his true nature. For one week Evil might roam at will, bearing in the black half of its face the sign of that darkness to which it would inevitably be returned and wherein it would be dissolved – at any rate for one year.

It would not seem hazardous to regard the scapegoat of the New Year as the earthly representative of the demons who, be it said in parentheses, are grouped with the Terrifying Gods who are so important in Tibet. That he may be regarded as such with certainty, however, is clearly evident from the revealing words spoken by him before his enforced departure from Lhasa, when like a true *advocatus diaboli* he said to the monks: 'What we perceive with the five senses is *not* an illusion. All that you teach is untrue.'[2] It would undoubtedly be considered altogether too drastic a sally, if in a Roman Catholic country some figures of the carnival were to address priests and monks with the words: 'The host is *not* the Body of Christ. All that you teach is untrue.' Yet that is more or less how the words of the scapegoat would have to be translated from one culture to the other. If we consider that for the Tibetans nationalism and Buddhism were more or less coincident, and that according to Charles Bell their religion was regarded as the national product of Tibet, then it is clear that the New Year in Tibet had a dark and deep background. The words of the scapegoat attacked the foundations of Buddhism and thus of official Tibet itself. Every year again they must have sounded like an explosion of blasphemy.

Essentially, the New Year festival was indeed an explosion of everything which bid defiance to Buddhism, and which this religion could not suppress either among laymen or monks, especially not among the followers of Tsong-kha-pa. 'At no time do the rules of Buddhism seem to be more heavily transgressed in the holy city than now. The frivolous debauchery of these days forms an unimaginable contrast to the dogma of the church. Unrestricted fornication is countenanced. There is dissipation everywhere. Daily one sees lamas drinking, smoking, gambling. High dignitaries of the church hold orgies with women of the streets' says Schäfer, who also gives examples of conduct 'whereby with sadistic enjoyment cruel aggressive urges are discharged' at the New Year festival.[3]

There are some grounds, then, for supposing that *in the deepest levels of their being the Tibetan people never attached full credence to that strange religion from India, which taught that the world perceived by the senses, in which man erroneously seeks his happiness, is nothing but a fleeting illusion and that man can only find happiness if he breaks all, absolutely all bonds of desire enchaining him to that world with its eternal cycle and succession of reincarnations, by means of ascesis and meditation. The scapegoat may be regarded as the old Adam of the Tibetans, appearing each year over new to prove that he was not dead yet, and always having to be eliminated anew.* This supposition is confirmed by various Tibetan data, and by similar rituals in other cultures. Indeed, all over the world one finds ritual festivities in which the peoples who celebrate them allow free rein for a short period to drives which are frustrated in everyday life by the constraints of nature and the rules of society. Such festivities are safety valves for biological and social tensions.

Indian hunting tribes used once a year to celebrate an 'eat-it-all-feast', when for once they gave no thought to shortage of food and threatening famine, but ate as much as they could. Yet they took good care that their dwellings were so thoroughly closed, that no supernatural

14

power would be able to see their wild indulgence! Other peoples plunge not into oral but into sexual dissipation, ignoring all the rules they can in order to taste the delights of promiscuity. Though in both cases it is a matter of satisfying a physical urge, the social element in these festivals must not be underestimated. The role of the social element was even greater with some African peoples, who once a year turned things so topsy turvy that masters became slaves and slaves masters, or where the king might be mocked and insulted by his subjects. The social character of these festivals has also a historical aspect, for it may be assumed with a fair measure of certainty that institutions such as social rank and kingship originated in the course of history, even if the exact course of events remains unknown.

The Tibetan New Year festival displays other complications, though in essence it is a festival of the above-mentioned type. Its biological element is stronger rather than weaker than the same reversal of all values among most primitive peoples. Just because Buddhism did not preach social regulation and reduction of the natural urges, but the Yellow Caps called for their total extinction, they broke through all barriers in excessive sexuality and aggressivity to reinforce the vocal protest of the scapegoat. The fifth Dalai Lama, who gave this form to the New Year festival, knew what he was doing. He realised that neither the Tibetan people nor most monks were mystics, and that once a year they required full licence to bear witness to that fact. Not only a holiday from themselves, but also a holiday from Buddhism was needed. And the successors of the 'Great Fifth' saw no reason to alter the situation. Schäfer has translated an official answer of government authorities with regard to misconduct of monks at the New Year festival, which makes patently manifest that the high officials of the church accepted such conduct at that time as a matter of course.

From their social and political points of view – and only these concern the cultural anthropologist – this policy was inevitable. In many respects the Tibetans may have become 'good Buddhists', in their hearts they still preferred nature to nurture. A familiar item of the regular equipment of a Buddhist monk is a sieve, for the purpose of clearing his drinking water of the tiny living creatures in it, not from hygienic motives, but because no form of life may be killed. Though a good deal of meat was butchered in Tibet, this prohibition was honoured in principle, and from an exact and lively childhood memory of Norbu[4] we may see that it had an important part in education during the earliest years already. But the prohibition could not wipe out the inborn hunter's aggressivity of many Tibetans. It is not a powerless, but a superior and derisive protest that is voiced in one of the folk songs from A-mdo:

> *Do not fire the gun, speaks the lama.*
> *The word of the honoured lama, indeed, is true.*
> *But full of wild yaks are the rocky, chequered mountains.*
> *To shoot not even one of them – that will hardly do.*[5]

So the scapegoat of the New Year festival was not a solitary rudiment of folklore. He even found a colleague in the sixth Dalai Lama. Owing to various circumstances the very effective education which in other cases succeeded in turning a child into a Dalai Lama, had had no result with him. This fascinating personality was, among other things, a lover of wine, women and song. On the other hand he too had his Buddhist conscience, but to protest against that as a Tibetan one festival a year was not enough for the sixth Dalai Lama. He needed a whole lifetime. He not only took part in many festivals, he also wrote poetry. The theme of one of his poems is the sensory reality of Eve's apple:

> *Lo, the snake gods and the demons*
> *Lurk behind me, stern and mighty.*
> *Sweet the apple grows before me.*
> *Fear leads nowhere, I must pluck it.*[6]

This remarkable High Pontiff, who was by no means unpopular among the people of Tibet, also protested, but he did it in a more subtle manner than the scapegoat and his other subjects. For in a more literal translation the first half of the fourth line of the above poem is as follows: 'Fear is not and non-fear is not'. It seems as if this is a philosophical argument employed to defeat Buddhism with its own weapons. The philosophy of Voidness had many adherents in Tibet. This philosophy is based on the concept, that neither the phenomenal world nor nirvāna have actual existence, but are both annulled in the ultimate reality, which is voidness. It is on these grounds that in Tibetan writings one may repeatedly find that both a concept and its negation are denied, dismissed as unreal. It would appear as if also the sixth Dalai Lama made use of this Buddhist philosophy against Buddhism. Fear does not exist and neither does non-fear, so he has no other choice but to pick the sweet apple. For that matter, the conclusion he drew differed very little from that of many Tantric Buddhists before him: as the world and nirvāna proved to be unreal in any case, they considered that they might equally well achieve the mystical union in a woman's arms as upon the ethereal heights of mystic solitude.

These few examples may suffice for the present to show that the scapegoat was the symbol of the contrast between Tibet and Buddhism, which after all was foreign, and embodied the contrast between the vital urge and the spirit. Cultural anthropology regards such contrasts as closely linked with society and culture. The social aspects are indeed easily recognized in the New Year festival. For when the scapegoat, after having been completely free in his actions for a week, had to play that game of dice with a monk, whose loss was a foregone conclusion, he was an unmistakable representative of the common people, while the monk represented the clergy, and thereby the moneyed and reigning class. According to our ideas a difference in possessions among members of the same society must always lead to envy. Among the Prairie Indians, who are known to be democratic, we find the following ending to a prayer: 'Like a chief, asking help of no one, may I make a good living, may I always have plenty.'[7] Yet one must be careful in judging the social significance of the contrast between rich and poor in a particular society, because this contrast may be regarded as a fact of nature and simply accepted, so that any envy which might be felt remains so far below the threshold of consciousness, that it cannot be regarded as an active factor.

In Tibet there was an evident contrast between rich and poor, and people were very well aware of it. Although the rich cannot be simply equated with the clergy, one may in a general way contrast the propertied clergy and the destitute people, if one considers the fact, for instance, that in the person of the Dalai Lama the 'church' owned all the land in Tibet. Hundreds of thousands of monks formed the great class of the socially privileged, and although the common people certainly did not regard the clergy with negative feelings alone, it is not only mockery of the monks as representatives of the 'spiritual principle' that one comes across in the literature, but also a positive social protest. Significantly, Das speaks of 'the New Year's Day of the working class ... observed by all the people of Tibet, with the exception of the clergy.'[8] And finally information supplied by Hermanns is very important in this connection: in a myth relating the consequences of the Tibetan 'fall of man', which has caused man to degenerate in almost every respect, the contrast between rich and poor is explicitly mentioned.[9] If we remember that the monks in their privileged position were dependent upon the working people, then it is clear that the greed of the scapegoat had a factual background. The meaning of the game of dice between the scapegoat and the monk also becomes clear now: for a week the man of the people could do as he liked and imagine himself a proprietor – a proprietor who did not need to work any more than the monks – but then there was an end of it and the social order had to be restored.

Granting their view of the theocratic state as the ideal form of society, the Dalai Lamas, as we said before, acted like wise politicians when they maintained the New Year festival. Maintained it – for this festival is older than the theocrats and their state, and it has very important aspects from the point of view of cultural history. This was already glanced at in discussing the sacred kingship of the abbot of the Dre-pung monastery during the festivities of the New Year. Tibet has known many conflicts and wars, and when religion became associated more and more with social and political aspects of life, it was not rare for monasteries and religious orders to become involved in a battle for power. In the 17th century the Red Caps were still defending the New Year festival tooth and nail, as their monopoly, against the Yellow Caps. It is true that the Red Caps were also Buddhists, but they were closer to the people, and especially they were far more nationalistic than the Yellow Caps, the sect which gave rise to the Dalai Lamas. In the quarrel referred to the Yellow Caps were simply refused admittance to the New Year festival by the Red Caps.[10] These items show that there was an inner contrast in Tibet, and that the conflict around the New Year festival, regarded by the nationalists as their 'property', was one of the occasions on which it came into the open.

Such contrasts in a culture are always of great importance, and it is fortunate that with regard to the New Year festival as a stake in the conflict between the conservatives and the progressives, various matters are known which cast a clear light upon the nature of this contrast. For Tibet celebrated the New Year twice. As we have seen from the remark of

Das, quoted above, the old New Year was the festival of the working people. The new festival was sometimes called 'the King's New Year'. Now the kings had not only united the separate tribes and groups of Tibet into one people and one state, they were also responsible – perhaps to raise their cultural status as well as to promote political unity – for the introduction of Buddhism and for making it the state religion. Although the importance of Buddhism diminished greatly after the time of the kings, the period of their reign was glorified by the lamas, after the renaissance of their religion around the year 1000 A.D., as the almost mythical period of the coming of salvation. Apart from the fact, that the myths of a people also belong to its history, it becomes evident besides on an occasion like the New Year festival, that this myth has a historical core.

The scapegoat appeared at the old festival, and thus his outspoken protest against the monks gains a historical perspective. He was not just the old Adam of the Tibetans, he was the representative of the old, nationalistic Tibetans, who in spite of all the Buddhist elements which had already infiltrated, defended their own culture and religion against the continually advancing religion, no, the culture of the Buddhists from India. 'What the senses teach us, is *not* an illusion' is in the final instance the protest of Tibet against (Buddhist) India. This thesis may perhaps give rise to objections, in the first place because it is debatable whether Buddhism is a culture, in the second place because this religion was introduced by Tibetan kings, and in the third place because Tibet not only had cultural contacts with India, but also with many other peoples, among whom the Chinese must certainly be named first of all. With respect to this last objection – the other two will be discussed later on – it must be admitted that the influence of China upon Tibet has been very great. Originally this was also the case in religious matters, but a check was already put upon the Chinese Buddhist influence in the time of the kings, at the Council of Lhasa. Like Christian councils, this Council had both religious and political aspects, and there the theologians and the king decided that Tibet would follow Buddhism as it was taught by the teachers from India.[11] As in the end religion set its mark upon the entire society and culture of Tibet, including the social and economic aspects, this decision had far-reaching consequences. The Tibetan Buddhists sought the doctrine of the Buddha there, where it had originated and attained its further development.

Buddhism is too easily and too often regarded exclusively as a religion or a mystic philosophical system, although Max Weber spoke of the sociology of Buddhism in a most convincing manner several decades ago already.[12] Though the examination of complex societies presents even more difficulties than that of primitive communities,[13] there is every reason to regard Buddhism as an Indian sub-culture and to treat it as such. Though the aim of this culture was and is to cancel man and society as visible realities, yet the monastery being the pre-eminent social symbol of this religion justifies the employment of the term culture. For in the monastery a number of individuals live in a regulated society with an ideology of its own, and this society is again linked with, is even dependent on, a number of individuals outside the monastery who support it economically and ideologically in such fashion that they maintain communal relations both with the monastery and with each other. If one may then

18

regard Buddhism on the one hand as one of the ideological aspects of the culture of India, one may on the other hand consider it a more or less independent sub-culture. It was this culture, with its missionary character, which came into contact with the culture of Tibet.

A comparison with 'the Buddhist conquest of China'[14] is most illuminating here. For those interested in the processes and results of culture contact and acculturation, it is fascinating to see how the already greatly differentiated and refined culture of China reacts gently and urbanely – both in the literal and the figurative sense of the word – to Buddhism, how for instance on the one hand in this country Buddhist monks could become literary wits of the drawing-room, and how on the other hand Chinese could label this religion 'barbaric' without more ado. Such things were not possible in Tibet. That was not a country where a reflective landed aristocracy and some more or less eccentric intellectuals had formed an ornamental culture of their own at top level. Tibet was a country of simple stock-herding nomads and farmers, who could fight excellently under a good captain, but who might otherwise be termed 'barbarians' even by less exigent standards than the Chinese. From the historical point of view there is every reason to call Tibet, as it was before the introduction of Buddhism, a primitive culture. For the Tibetans of that time Buddhism, with its accompanying script, literature, science and art, was the very synonym of culture, and they must certainly have regarded it with awe and a sentiment of inferiority. If the Chinese 'gentleman-monk', as Zürcher calls him, in translating the Buddhist writings directed his main endeavour towards elegant phrasing and literary effect, the Tibetan lama, with the deep seriousness of the obedient pupil, aimed at an exact translation, making it as literal as possible. This distinction is typical of their difference.

In Tibet a highly developed religion came into contact, as sub-culture of a large and complex society, with a primitive culture and a primitive religion. This fact is of great importance. There is no need to look down upon so-called primitive cultures in order to realize that in such culture contact there is a chasm to be bridged, and that the resultant processes of acculturation are of an intensive nature, even though they may take place amidst the peaceful coexistence of the cultures concerned. In such a case too one will, for instance, find polarisation of the society around the extremes of progressivity and conservatism, a regular characteristic of acculturation, which is furthermore nearly always accompanied by a strong increase in aggressivity. The main purpose of this book is to display various phenomena of Tibetan Buddhism in their connection with Tibetan art against these and other backgrounds of culture contact and acculturation. From political motives religious connections with the Chinese were almost unanimously rejected, and thus the relationship between India and Tibet is of primary interest in this respect. Furthermore, this relationship affords an interesting study, because there have never been political or military conflicts between the two countries. Yet even in this case we find typical phenomena of acculturation, such as the ambivalent attitude of the weaker party, who feels simultaneously inferior and superior to the stronger – a phenomenon that is generally found among primitive peoples who have come into contact with European civilisation. In Tibet considerable pride is felt at having received a particular teaching straight from India – and indeed it is translated almost slavishly – and at the same time the mountains and trees of India are represented as bowing respectfully in the direction of Tibet to honour the great Tibetan achievements.[15]

How great the difference between India and Tibet originally was, may be set forth in a few examples. In no country have such passion and frankness prevailed in the free expression of love and sexuality, both in life and art and in public and esoteric forms of religion, as in India. The Tibetans, though no strangers to human nature, simply could not afford such luxury in the harsh climate and hard circumstances they lived in. In no country have the practice and theory of mysticism in all levels of the population been so intensely cultivated from so many approaches, as in India. The spiritual life of the farmers and nomad herders of Tibet was nourished by shamanism and magic. Buddhist India brought the message that the world of sense is a fleeting and worthless illusion. The Tibetans were deeply convinced of the reality of mountains, herds, butter, hail, and especially blood.[16] Also in other spheres of life the contrast was very great. In India the ways and wanderings of the spirit could be charted by means of the written word. The Tibetans could not write. To name a final, though by no means the slightest instance, it was from India that the monastery came to Tibet, occasioning quite a revolution in the social, economic, political and religious field. It is no wonder that on the one hand the Tibetans did their best to absorb as much as possible of the new culture, and that they yet opposed the foreign importations for fear of losing their identity, *i.e.* themselves.

It has become a matter of general knowledge by now, that culture contact and acculturation bring tensions which have a disintegrating action. Especially when the gulf between two cultures is so great that the contact between them comes to resemble a collision, these internal tensions are unavoidable. The experiences of primitive peoples have shown that oppression, exploitation, violence and the other characteristics of colonialism considerably strengthen the disintegrating character of culture contact, but all the same such contact exercises a disjunctive effect upon individual and society even without the burden of colonialism. What takes place when two cultures meet may be described as a process of changing over: people are required simultaneously to unlearn some things and to learn others. This must always to some extent cause a disturbance of the individual or the social balance.[17] It is in the period of transition preceding a new equilibrium that symptoms of disintegration appear. That is the reason why also in the case of primitive peoples who are anything but 'underdogs', and who victoriously trample down more complex civilisations, acculturation is accompanied by symptoms of disintegration. In their 'struggle for life' they are the victors, but in their 'struggle for high life' they do not get off scot-free.

The Toltecs and the Aztecs, for instance, were originally primitive peoples who with much dash and ruthlessness 'took over' the highly developed agricultural civilisations of their predecessors and victims. This seems to have been fairly easy in a military way, but the effort it cost them to become cultural *nouveaux riches* can be demonstrated by an analysis of their culture and religion. Undoubtedly the fact must also have been of influence that it must have been difficult for them, comparatively few in numbers as they were, to maintain their occupation of the country they had taken – the initial and perhaps the permanent problem of all despots and rulers – but at the same time for them too the learning and unlearning presented a difficult problem. The hypertrophy of human sacrifice, which made their temple pyramids into religious slaughter-houses, was a symptom of the anxious aggressivity with which the Aztecs tried to prove and had to prove their superiority to themselves and to others. This is directly related to a manifest feeling of cultural inferiority with respect to the peoples they had conquered. In their mythology the vanquished culture is the symbol of a higher civilisation, of luxury and of peace (!), and this symbol finds its most typical expression in the god Quetzalcoatl, who for them was in the first place the legendary king of the conquered culture, a paradise on earth. This paradise, lost to them, was not something the Aztecs hoped upon; on the contrary, they envisaged its return as a menace to their own existence.[18] Quetzalcoatl was the *mauvaise conscience* of the Aztecs, the symptom of inner tension and disintegration. When his reign of peace returned, it would be the end of the Aztecs!

In Tibet we find something of the same kind. The Indian culture of Buddhism was not brought there by force of arms. It was the Tibetan kings – whose power was feared even by the Chinese – who introduced Buddhism to the country. It would be naive to suppose they were desirous of salvation and redemption. 'Man is a status-seeker', as Jules Henry puts it, and there are many examples to show that religion is also regarded as a mark of status. There is little doubt that for the first Tibetan kings Buddhism meant a raise in status for themselves and for their country. They were new rulers, and they also wished to become *nouveaux riches*. A clash between the old and the new, such as is characteristic of acculturation, was unavoidable. In addition, Buddhism could not help evoking more conflicts than any other religion, because unlike most other religions it did not regulate or sanction natural inclinations and institutions, but – in its later forms also – took up a stand against them on principle. Another complicating factor is, that though man is continually linking his spiritual life with his biological, social, economic and political activities, there always prove to be individuals and groups who wish to regard the human spirit as something *sui generis* and make their approach on that understanding. Even one of the Tibetan kings wanted to adopt so demanding a religion as Buddhism in earnest, and tried to make Tibet a Buddhist paradise on earth, one of whose characteristics, curiously enough, was to be equal possession. Extremely important as the vital, social, economic, etc. factors may be, the cultural anthropologist must reckon with the fact that the spiritual and religious factors do not only have a derivative importance, but can also function independently.

In every culture individual behaviour and social institutions show an actual pattern of behaviour which does not tally with the ideal pattern also present in the society. This tension between theory and practice is also found in the underdeveloped, the capitalist and the communist societies of the twentieth century. The question is only, how great the tension is between the two patterns. We have no scientific methods at our disposal to measure these tensions. We cannot take the temperature of a society and its culture to see if it is feverish.

We can be certain, however, that in cases of acculturation the tension is comparatively great, for the simple reason that there are two ideal patterns, the old one and the new one. It has been pointed out that in acculturation the members of a primitive society become more and more conscious of the ideal pattern of behaviour, because they are naturally led to sin against it more and more, which results in abnormal feelings of guilt. On the other hand it must equally be stressed that in such a situation the new ideal pattern also exercises considerable influence, because conduct in conformity with it means 'high life'. Evidence for this is found, for instance, in the fact that also the nationalistic and conservative half of the Tibetan people adopted many of the new Buddhist values and forms, as is also the case with primitive peoples of our own day adopting European values.

Especially when, as in Tibet, a religion like Buddhism takes the lead in the process of acculturation, tension and splitting up are inevitable. All the more so, as it proves to be a general rule that in all striving after new values and forms of behaviour, the old values and forms always show a most tenacious vitality,[19] while a big difference between the old and the new – as in Tibet – will only strengthen the resistance of the old values and forms. From the fact that the socio-political organisation of Tibet finally became an ecclesiastic state of a unique kind, which functioned for centuries in a manner not much better or worse than that of other societies, it may be concluded that a certain synthesis was effected between the old and the new, bringing about a new equilibrium. There is no saying, however, in what relation the disintegrating and the integrating factors stood to one another within that new equilibrium. It must be repeated that we have no scientific means of taking the temperature of a society, neither is it (yet) possible to determine the place of Tibet in the social evolution by comparative research.[20] Comparison with Europe of the Middle Ages, for instance, can for the present merely help to visualize the problem.

Neither can it be denied that in general the available material contains sufficient indications that there were comparatively strong contrasts and tensions in the society and culture of Tibet, only partially resolved in the accepted compromises. Without sharing the conclusions of communist China, one can for instance observe, on the basis of objective data, that there were certain defects in Tibetan economy, and that the myth about the origin of the contrast between the rich and the poor is directly connected with these objective data. In their religion also many signs of tension are to be seen, and sometimes even what might be termed fissures. We must make the reserve here, that of course it is not possible to draw a simple parallel between the religious concepts and the socio-economic conditions. Complementary and other relations are also possible, and only a thorough structural analysis can supply the answer as to the nature of that relationship. As practically no work has been done in this field with regard to Tibet, it is naturally not possible to do more than proffer a few suggestions in a monograph dedicated to certain aspects of Tibetan art.

The nature of our subject, the Terrifying Deities, invites consideration of tension and disintegration rather than of synthesis and integration. Yet these latter factors may by no means be neglected. From the time of the kings until the so-called 'war of liberation' of the Chinese, Tibet has existed as a cultural unity, presenting a culture in many respects unique. Tibet as land of 'mysteries' is largely the product of Western romanticism and Tibetan conservatism and isolation policy. This policy of isolation, however, was unmistakably also a continuation of Tibet's natural isolation. Both biologists and anthropologists are aware, that isolation may lead to strange and unique forms of growth or behaviour.[21] When therefore Buddhism – especially in its tantric, but also in its other forms – comes into contact in the extremely isolated, highest country on earth with a culture of stockherding nomads, farmers and shamans, it is not surprising that a new and unexampled civilisation develops there, and that it has secrets too, though these are often not found where they are usually sought.

In formal structure Tibet stands alone. Both in primitive and in more complex societies one finds a contrast between temporal and spiritual power, and in both cases theocracies may also occur, in the sense of societies ruled by an incarnation or direct representative of a deity.[22] Yet nowhere is there a theocracy to be found like the Tibetan, where both temporal and spiritual power are in the hands of a monk who is the incarnation of a deity, and whose power is principally based on a great number of monasteries, whose inhabitants occupy an exceptional position not only in the religious sphere, but also from the social and economic point of view. As to content also Tibetan Buddhism is unparalleled, though there are many other countries where Buddhism has taken root in its tantric or non-tantric form. A few general remarks on this subject may find a place here.

The constitution of the Tibetan ecclesiastic state shows, that everything is made subordinate to the one religious purpose: the salvation of all mankind. That this purely theocratic principle was not only valid for the ecclesiastic state of the Dalai Lamas, but was already a matter of course for the lamas of the time of the kings, appears from a letter in which the king is given advice by the clergy.[23] In this letter he is not only enlightened as to the unreality of the ego, and not only advised with regard to maintaining and protecting religion and morality, but also instructed in matters pertaining to the aristocracy, the army (!), jurisdiction, and so forth. The writer's disdainful remark, that in former times people in Tibet did not even know what a lama was, casts an interesting sidelight! The mention of the army shows that, inevitably, Heaven was willing to come to terms. It is this conflict between the ideal and reality, which together with the dissension between the nationalists and the progressives dominates the culture and history of Tibet and gives it a character peculiarly its own. The identification of 'state' and 'church' set problems of statecraft before the church and religious problems before the state, which could lead to structural conflicts. In the country that has gained renown both for its mystics and for its robbers it could occur, for instance, that monks went out on a predatory foray,[24] while religious oracles and magic means were employed in matters of state. —

The identification of 'state' and 'church' would, however, even without the tensions between the ideal and actual practice, between the conservatives and the progressives, already have failed through the contrast between lamas and laymen referred to above. As in Buddhism the monasteries are dependent upon the material support of the laymen, the required identification in the sense that all members of the 'state' should also be members of the (monastic) 'church' was of course never possible. Yet in Tibet the inhabitants of the monasteries were not only 'the chief capitalists of the country',[25] but they also had more or less of a monopoly in nearly all important activities. It is illuminating to contrast this with the state of affairs in Ceylon. There, Buddhism was active to educate and elevate the people, thus constituting a positive link between clergy and laymen, while in Tibet the monks kept knowledge and science to a very great extent in their exclusive possession. Ideologically, however, the gulf was bridged in so far as the laymen were to some degree Buddhists, while the lamas had absorbed a not inconsiderable part of the Tibetan religion into their Buddhism. Even the Yellow Caps had, beside doctors of philosophy and of mystic theology, orthodox doctors of magic. And at funerals the Buddhists had to tolerate the calling in, besides one or more monks, of priests of the popular religion of old Tibet – heathen in Buddhist eyes –, without whom the ritual of a Tibetan funeral was unthinkable.[26]

These examples go to show, that by such a give and take both parties came into a mutual relationship with one another upon the basis of a common ideology: the monks rendered spiritual succour to the laymen, and the laymen provided material support to the monks. As the monks always had to be paid for their assistance in money or in goods, while the laymen only received spiritual payment for their contribution, reciprocity was not complete, which is not surprising in a state where it was a principle to set the spiritual above the material. It was precisely in connection with this incomplete reciprocity that the common Tibetan Buddhist ideology had the greater importance. If the interests of monks and laymen had not been the same in this respect and if both parties had not spoken the same language here, Tibet would have entirely disintegrated instead of developing into an ecclesiastic state, notwithstanding all tensions. It was remarked above, that religion was regarded as a national product. Religion could only become so, because in Tibet Buddhism had acknowledged the old Tibetan gods in principle, while assigning them a relative existence, in the same way as it had already done in India with the native gods. The gods exist, but they are not real. Therefore one can call upon them and yet not ultimately believe in their existence, and thus there is room for magic and mysticism.

This curious double meaning incorporated in Tantric and Tibetan Buddhism has led some Westerners to regard the religion of Tibet as degenerated sorcery and empty farrago, whilst others have defended it as a profound philosophy of life. The cultural anthropologist is inclined, like the Tibetan Buddhists, to agree with both parties as far as possible, but he will certainly point out in the first place that it is exactly this ambiguity which made it possible, after all, for monk and layman to live in the context of a common philosophy of life and a world outlook which they shared, and without that circumstance this unique culture could not have existed. A lama and a layman could believe in the gods each in his own fashion, and the difference which remained must be squared by the scapegoat as best he could. Secondly, it must be remarked that in spite of compromise and possible logical inconsistencies (but what place has logic in religion?), the Buddhists did not give up the essence of their religion on essential points. In the now famous Tibetan Book of the Dead, which was intended for high and low, it is always pointed out to the dead man with great emphasis that the gods who appear to him do not really exist, but that they are projections of his own. In another passage of this book it is represented to him that the misery and terror he has to endure are due to nothing else but his own actions and that he can hold no one else responsible for them. For the very reason that the Buddhists held to these principles, they were compelled to apply the adage *audi et alteram partem* in the matter of the scapegoat.

Among these gods, who exist but who are unreal, the Terrifying Deities take a very important place. A number of demoniac gods of Tantric Buddhism had already come to Tibet from India, but now they multiplied and became legion. So it is not a matter of following the fashion or seeking for sensation, to agree with the general opinion that these fearsome, in many respects devilish gods are pre-eminently typical of the religion of Tibet. In the epic of Gesar it is even stated: gods too are demons.[27] The people quaked in awe before the Terrifying Ones. The monks began their day by invoking one of them to keep off the others.[28] And the sixth Dalai Lama felt their devilish menace at his back, when he was about to pick the apples of Eve. On closer examination they will prove on the one hand to form a link between the old Tibet and the new Buddhism, between clergy and laymen, between religion and mysticism, on the other to be so many proofs that the two had not blended into a coherent whole, and that it was not without reason that the scapegoat, as the devil's advocate, was exiled to the abode of the Terrifying Ones, where – as in nearly all Tibetan monasteries – through the half-dark one could discern their grinning figures in sexual union with their *yum*, amidst weapons and trophies of war. In an impressive passage, Tucci writes from his own experience of one of these special 'chapels' of the Terrifying Deities: 'You would think you were looking out over primordial chaos'.[29]

These demoniac gods and their depiction in bronze and on paintings form the subject of the following chapters. To most Western eyes these depictions seem extremely drastic. The way the Tibetans represented the Terrifying Deities in words is, to anyone not devoid of imagination, even more gruesome. One of these gods is described in an iconographical text as follows: 'Surrounded by a protective circle of meteoric iron, stands a large and spacious *gur khang* around which horrible, fierce fires, black wind and whirlwind, these three, are sweeping in succession. Tremendous waves of the wild sea of blood, which is surrounding it, roll into the ten quarters of the world. In the middle of this place, which is filled with various destroyed beings, on top of layers composed of the four elements stands a mound of skeletons; on this peak lies a great and dreadful cemetery. It is an area of the greatest horror and ferocity, it is the land of those whose appearance is of a never changing terror... From the middle of whirling and expanding poisonous vapors flashes terrible lightning. Like thunder sounds the noise of deadly blows. Yellow-flashing meteors and a vehement rain of weapons are falling there... At night fires are blazing there, by day black wind whirls around. A thick mist of pus, blood, and fat falls there at daytime. Ravens, owls, screech-owls, crows and various other demoniacal birds are flying around there with brains of destroyed evil, obstacle-creating demons in their beaks and filling the air with their evil-portending voices. Human corpses – mummified, fresh and in decomposition – are lying scattered around. Waves of blood and fat billow tremendously... In the interior of this gruesome and frightening supernatural abode, in the centre of a vehemently blazing firestorm, emanates from the dark-red syllable *hūm* in a ray the lord of the region, he who destroys all evil-doers, the foes of the religious law and all obstacle-creating demons, who is able to obtain the complete concentration of the mind... He bares his four teeth, sharp like the ice of a glacier, and between them he rolls his tongue with the speed of chain-lightning, causing the three worlds to quake... His forehead is contorted in a terrible anger. His three bloodshot eyes stare full of hatred at the inimical *vighnas*. The yellow-red flames, issuing from his eyebrows and from the hair on his face, burn completely the four kinds of *bdud*. The yellow-brown hair of his head stands on end and in the centre above it resides the lord-protector and king of religion, the great Tsong-kha-pa bearing a placid expression. By moving his two ears vehemently *rDo rje shugs ldan* produces a fierce, devil-destroying wind... From his two nostrils come forth rain-clouds and from these again issue raging thunder and lightning... With his right hand he brandishes towards heaven a fiercely flaming sword... cutting with it the life-roots of all evil-doers... With his left hand he holds in front of his breast, and lifting it to his mouth, a skull-cup filled with the organs of the five senses, heart, brains, and warm blood of the evil-doers... On his head he wears a crown of five dry skulls, from his shoulders hangs a garland of fifty freshly severed, blood-dripping heads... A human skin serves him as a carpet.'[30]

That was how the fearless adventurers and exact cartographers of hell described the god *rDo rje shugs ldan*, one of the numerous Fearful Gods of Tibet. If a human being wishes to attain the perfect concentration of mind this god possesses, then he must imagine this devilish cannibal, standing on a mountain of skeletons in the middle of a sea of billowing blood, just as exactly, 'produce' him in the mind's eye just as minutely in every particular as the text describes him here. To a Westerner, the most curious detail of the whole is perhaps the great religious reformer Tsong-kha-pa, who sits immediately above the flaming hair of this devil 'bearing a placid expression'. The great Mi-la re-pa had built up and lived through a multitude of such visions of hell before he could say:

> *That all the wealth revealed within my mind*
> *And all the circling threefold worlds contain,*
> *Unreal as it is, can yet be seen – that is the miracle.*[31]

The sour stench of mysticism, in which introverts stared upon their navel, has been decried. In Tibet the mystics have obviously inhaled worse smells and stared at more than their navel, before they discovered the ecstatic wonder of the inner world and the outer world, which are unreal and yet existent. Whatever one may think of mysticism, the Terrifying Deities embody a reality, which in Tibet both monks and laity had the courage to envisage.

Tibet is the country where it is a happy omen to see a corpse, and where devils bring salvation. For this reason alone it may be worthwhile to pay a little more attention to the Terrible Ones. 'Gods too are demons', says the epic of Gesar. It is a familiar phenomenon in religious history that a deity is simultaneously possessed of positive and negative qualities, conferring both good and evil. In the final instance, life itself bears the double face of death and life, of devil and god. But this general reflection is insufficient explanation for Tibet with its two New Year festivals, with its Red Caps and Yellow Caps still at logger-heads in 1948,[32] its Dalai Lamas who to the great consternation of a Japanese abbot, far from Lhasa had sheep slaughtered for them,[33] its soldier monks and its blood-drinking devils, who possess and bestow peace of heart.[34] There is something enigmatic in all this, but that is not only due to religious, but also to cultural factors. Something already becomes plainer if we remember that the Terrifying Deities not only bore the official title of 'defenders of the faith', but were at the same time the unmistakable enemies of that faith, who were indeed bound by oath to defend it, but who had to be constantly reminded of that oath! Thus it no longer causes surprise that the blaspheming scapegoat was driven to the abode of the demons. He was the backslider, and his annual relapse a sign that the old gods had not yet renounced their true nature, and were still protesting in the name of flesh and blood. As enemies of the faith these gods signified a line of fissure, as defenders of the faith they stood for the uniting link in Tibet's dualistic culture. That was the reason why their images and pictures were so often seen in monasteries and houses. And bound to that culture, and yet timelessly transcending it, their immaterial forms loomed terrifyingly in the controlled visions of the mystics, who knew that a man can only reach heaven if he has the courage and the strength to go right through hell. Curiously enough, the so-called timeless mysticism was also a unifying element in society and culture. The biography of the absolutistic, but gay mystic Mi-la re-pa was not only read with pleasure by the intellectuals, it was also the most popular book among the common people. The poor had a great love for him as a poor man who followed out his faith to its logical conclusion without any compromise and in whom, saint though he was, they could recognize their own humanity.[35]

INDIA: CORNUCOPIA OF RELIGIONS

1. *Vedic religion and Hinduism*

Buddhism originated in India, the subcontinent of so many religions and sects, gods and goddesses. Although Buddhism expressed detachment from these religions and deities, it was never able to dissociate itself entirely from them, so that 'sous l'habit jaune, le moine demeure l'homme de son siècle et de son milieu'.[36] Furthermore, in view of the essential contribution not only of Buddhism, but also of India in general, to the formation of Tibet's peculiar religious character, a short sketch of the religious development in India is an indispensable introduction.

About 2000 B.C. urban civilisations flourished at Mohenjo-Daro and Harappa. Like all or nearly all urban cultures before the technical industrial revolution of our time, these civilisations were based on agriculture. It is no wonder, then, that in their religion fertility and sexuality were of central importance. Excavations in Harappa revealed an image of a woman lying with legs outspread, a plant sprouting from her vagina.[37] Realistic symbols of male and female sexual organs evidently also played a great part.[38] When the Aryan conquerors, coming from the Indo-Iranian highlands, invaded India, these flourishing urban cultures already belonged to the past, but it is almost self-evident that among other things the ideas and conceptions pertaining to fertility should have continued to live among the autochthonous population. Everything points to their having drastically influenced the subsequent development of Indian religious concepts.[39]

Meanwhile it seemed at first as if the new, foreign rulers were making a clean sweep not only in social, but also in religious matters, and would impress the Aryan mark upon India. In the earliest of their writings preserved to us they show as active and optimistic rulers, developing in the new country their own religion, which was entirely directed towards *this* world. The Rigveda has been described as 'le manuel d'une aristocratie religieuse' in which – and this is not fortuitous if we think of Homer – aesthetic values have great significance.[40] Conscious of their own strength and dignity, these aristocrats applied only contemptuous names to the autochthonous inhabitants, clearly showing they regarded them as barbarians.[41]

For the native gods and goddesses also they seem to have had small respect. Their own gods were strong, virile figures. For them the origin of all things lay in Aditi, the mother of the gods and also the Primeval Mother, from whom in primordial times the whole cosmos was born, so that she was the mistress of cosmic order.[42] But after this grandiose female beginning it were men who ruled and regulated the further course of celestial and terrestrial affairs. The god most often mentioned in the oldest texts is Indra. No wonder, for he was the god of battle and victory, the god of the aristocratic rulers who helped them to conquer their non-Aryan enemies. He was 'le patron des envahisseurs aryens'.[43] His weapon was the vajra, the sign of destructive lightning. Also prominent, and typical of an aggressive male culture of conquest were Mitra and Varuṇa, gods of the cosmic, social and moral order. In history one often finds a relation between the drive towards conquest and (new) order, just as there is also a psychological connection between aggressivity and a sense of order and self-control, in contrast with more peaceable cultures and personalities, who are more inclined to stress that which links and unites, so that they more easily find expression in sexual symbols. Of course in such a culture of conquerors order can only be an ideal if they are able, to some extent at least, to establish, centralise and maintain order.

Two other Aryan gods, Agni and Soma, are also closely connected with these tendencies towards order. Agni, the god of fire, and Soma, the god of the sacrificial liquor, are indeed divinities whose full meaning and significance even an Indologist – let alone a Western intellectual – can barely fathom, but their importance as gods of the continually more exactly ordered and systematised ritual of sacrifice is at least plain to the outsider. As with the Egyptians, the Polynesians and the Aztecs, so too with the Aryans of India the ruling class divided into warriors and priests, and the latter meticulously regulated the intercourse between men and gods, as the temporal rulers established and maintained rule and order in the intercourse between men. The highly complicated ritual of sacrifice was of central significance in religious practice and theory, and from this Agni and Soma – sacrificial fire and sacrificial liquor – derived their high status in the pantheon.

Regulation implies dominance, thus it is in a general way understandable that the tendencies towards magical constraint came to prevail in the ancient Indian sacrifice. In a general way, for in detail the Vedic, *i.e.* the ancient Indian religion of sacrifice is anything but simple. The development from sacrifice to 'means of compulsion', however, is repeatedly seen in the history of religions; only in India it attained gigantic proportions. Though the gods naturally retained a margin of liberty, one may say that the priests – the brahmans – developed the sacrifice into the priestly specialism ensuring the maintenance of the world. A symptom of the same human lust of power is to be seen in the fact that the brahmans formed the highest social class, even above the warriors. Thus the Aryan aristocrats affirmed their power as temporal and as spiritual rulers in the cosmic context of a ritualistic religion of sacrifice.

'That only a very small number of individuals in any group are interested in making an analysis of religious phenomena and that even a smaller number are qualified to do so, is patent.'[44] Among the brahmans too there were these few, who within the framework of the Vedic theory of sacrifice reflected upon the ultimate relation of men, gods and cosmos. Some impression of these trains of thought is conveyed, when we read that on the one hand the primordial mother Aditi was very concretely equated with the primordial cow, and on the other was speculatively identified with the creative word.[45] We are inclined to lay aside such speculations as abracadabra. In ancient India there were individuals who left them behind them, because they found Vedic ritualism too rigid and too arid.[46] It was also too disjointed for them in its compulsion tending towards magic, because they sought unity, the unity of man's essential nature with the essential principle of the universe. Their aim was the aim of all mystics in all time and all cultures.

Brahma, the secret force of the Vedic sacrifice, became for these mystic thinkers the ultimate reality, the primordial source and the principle of all existence. They discovered that he who attains understanding of the nature of Brahma, himself becomes Brahma and is healed of that cleavage in his nature which causes man to suffer. Mysticism is far less determined by time and place, *i.e.* by culture, than other expressions of religion. For this reason the Upaniṣads – the texts in which these mystics have laid down their reflections – have made far more impression in the West and aroused more understanding than the Vedas upon which they are ultimately based. The German philosopher Schopenhauer and the Dutch poet Der Mouw may be mentioned in this connection. For these Indians, however, the mystical union to which they aspired meant infinitely more than for the Westerners influenced by them. For to them it signified the ultimate union of the soul and the 'world soul', liberation from *karma*, the blighting weight of man's actions, determining with an equal inevitability as the law of gravity, his next rebirth in *saṁsāra*, the chain of rebirth. He who both understands and experiences the unity of his own essence with the essence of all which exists – 'thou art that' – has risen above life without end which is nothing but suffering without end.

The technique of this mysticism was called *yoga* in India. But yoga is by no means bound to the mysticism of the Upaniṣads. Because it is a technique of physical and spiritual self-control, it can be adapted to various religious ends and varied accordingly. Indeed, yoga as means to the end is found in most religions of India.[47] For the ancient mystics of 'thou art that' the aim of this physical and mental training was in all probability to empty the mind of all separate contents of thought, that when 'thou art that' sparked over they might pass into Brahma. If we characterise the psychosomatic condition of a mystic at that point as a deep and dreamless sleep, then that is of course nothing but a behaviourist term, only touching the outside and leaving fundamental questions unanswered. To introduce in the Western world, only acquainted with the conscious and the unconscious, a term such as, for instance, the superconscious, merely results in a vagueness which must lead either to overestimation or to undervaluation of mysticism. There will be full opportunity in this book to return to these difficulties, which result from a lack of experience in this field on the part of most Westerners. Here let it only be established that modesty and also sober thinking are prime requirements for a better understanding. We must simply accept the fact that the ancient mystics of India were sometimes able to attain a state of consciousness, which to them differed completely from the effect of a good night's rest. The Greek philosopher and mystic Plotinus wrote that he had only had this experience a few times in his life, but obviously to a mystic such an experience is worth untold gold.

As already stated, the mysticism of the Upaniṣads was a reaction against the ritualism of the brahmans, which on the one hand became smothered in ever multiplying detail, and on the other petrified in the position of social power of the priests, who – be it not forgotten – were and remained the representatives of the Aryan aristocrats and rulers. The mystic reaction only concerned a few individuals. Yet there must also have been a drastic collective reaction against the spiritual supremacy of these intrusive rulers. There must have, for the post-Vedic literature makes most manifest that a spiritual revolution has taken place, the Vedic religion and world view having been crowded into the background to make room for religions rooted in autochthonous India. What happened exactly, what political, social and economic changes may lie concealed beneath this spiritual upheaval is the greatest problem of Indology. No answer being forthcoming, one can only guess.

In the history of the world it has well-nigh always proved impossible for conquerors to maintain their religion and their world outlook untouched and unchanged in the land they have conquered. The Greeks, who for a comparatively long time managed to keep their Olympic pantheon and Olympic mentality relatively pure, yet had to admit therein important autochthonous elements such as the mysteries of Eleusis. The Aztecs, though they pathologically intensified the bloody cult of their war god Huitzilopochtli, offering him ever greater numbers of victims, could not avoid taking over and adapting gods and religious conceptions from the people they had subdued, and they even feared the return of the autochthonous Quetzalcoatl. The Vedas show that at first the Aryans in India continued the development of their own religion practically without 'foreign bodies', but afterwards – probably in the seventh century – unlike the Greeks and the Aztecs they had to abandon the field to the gods of the native population. Apparently some cause or other enabled this people to give notice to the Vedic gods and even to depose them from the thrones they occupied with the Aryan rulers themselves.

That service to the Vedic gods could be renounced at any rate meant in the social field that service was also renounced to the brahmans, or that these could be compelled to acknowledge the native gods. In the epic of the Mahābhārata and elsewhere too it could be explicitly stated that the lower castes no longer considered themselves the subordinates of the brahmans, and no longer supplied them with food as they had been wont.[48] Something of this kind may have taken place in the decisive revolution in this phase of India's spiritual development. On the one hand the influence of the autochthonous inhabitants will have increased in the social and political sphere, on the other hand the Aryan aristocrats will have been overpowered by the seduction of 'going black', which has not only been a danger to the English imperialists. The Aryans maintained their social position in and through the caste system, yet in a great majority they succumbed to the native gods of biological and spiritual sexuality and fertility.

In the late-Vedic period traces of this conflict are to be seen. The contrast between gods and demons became greater, and magic increased.[49] The native gods, especially the yakṣas, whom the Aryans pictured as fierce, pot-bellied and drunken,[50] had to receive more and more recognition, be it in a negative sense. As will appear in greater detail with regard to developments in Tibet, such negative tendencies as demonisation and magic are a general phenomenon in the conflict between two cultures. But the people also produced another very different attitude towards the gods, which was anything but negative. After the great change religious life in India was no longer dominated by the distant ritualistic precision of the brahmans, but by the passionate loving surrender called *bhakti*. However much this outpouring of emotion on the part of the people might differ from the mentality of the mystics, both attitudes have one most important element in common: the search after union and unity instead of detachment. In ancient Greece there was a similar contrast between the Olympic and civic[51] mentality, and the emotional outpour in the cult of Dionysus, in Orphism and the Eleusinian mysteries. The two great philosophers of Hellas, Aristotle and Plato, may be held to personify this contrast. A symptom of the transition in India indicated above, was that the drive towards magic power and the aggressivity of the Aryans, while not entirely disappearing, were yet relegated to the background, making room for the unifying tendencies of sexuality and love. The *bhakti* of popular religions was suffused with loving feeling, not seldom bearing pronounced erotic and sexual aspects. And the mysticism of the Upaniṣads compares the *unio mystica* to the shared delight of man and woman, who 'lose consciousness of what is without and within'.[52]

These social and psychological factors are perhaps part of the background of the revolution that dethroned the Vedic gods and introduced the still continuing period of Hinduism. The powerful members of the Vedic pantheon were degraded to gods of the cardinal points, 'a comparatively insignificant position, ... where the highest purpose they could serve was of a mere accessory character'.[53] One of the principal, if not the most important of the gods who replaced them, was Śiva. In connection with the matters discussed above, it is perhaps not without significance that in origin this great god of Hinduism was a destructive aggressor, who at an early period also became a definitely sexual god, and finally even the great practician of yoga, for – recounts the epic – he had engendered enough, and with an eye to ascesis and yoga castrated himself.[54] One might call Śiva an explosion of repressed popular religion, which would explain both his extreme aggressivity and his sexuality, as well as his energetic adoption of yoga. He is terrifying, yet to his worshippers compassionate and gracious. He is fierce and drunken like the yakṣas (but not pot-bellied, for he is not a despised, but an ideal god!), his symbol is the liṅga, the erect phallus. His votaries worshipped him after a most drastic fashion, but in India it goes without saying that also such a god and his cult were soon spiritualised. The extraordinary success of that operation is apparent from the fact, that it took the Western Indologists a considerable time to discern the original nature of the extremely stylised liṅga. Thus Śaivism included the two extremes of persons who wandered around naked, streaked with ashes and carrying a club, and practised yoga and magic in cemeteries, and of spiritualised theologians and mystics, who designed a differentiated philosophical system explaining the relations between Śiva and man and the world, and whose religious practice aimed at union with their highest god. Both forms of Śaivism have had great influence upon the development of Buddhism, which had arisen

32

earlier and had also been a reaction against the religion of the brahmans, for in spite of all its exclusivity Buddhism could not avoid association with Śaivism and the other children of Mother India.

2. *Buddhism: Hīnayāna and Mahāyāna*

Buddhism originated in the 5th century B.C. in a region of India where the brahmanic religion and the ancient yoga took the lead, and not the religions of Viṣṇu and Śiva, which had already exerted a strong influence elsewhere.[55] It is a great pity that so little is known of the cultural background of the earliest Buddhism. We do know that in common with Śaivism it was opposed to the caste system, so it was also anti-brahmanic.[56] We know too that it was of the nature of an élite, like the mysticism of the Upaniṣads. The social protest against the castes, however, was entirely invalidated by its emphasis upon an élite of individualistic mystics – if that protest was ever strong, as Dasgupta assures us. The Buddha belonged to the warrior caste, and from a social aspect his protest against the brahmans and their caste was not so much a defence of the rights of the people as a demonstration of what a spiritual élite should really be like, in contrast with the brahman élite.

The aristocratic and militant nature of the Buddha and his teaching is clearly set forth in the work of Evola. This author greatly stresses the Aryan character of Buddhism, and his conclusions, tinged with race prejudice, may easily bring the reader to lay the book aside.[57] This would be a mistake though, for the author certainly shows by means of the texts and his own analyses how strongly the earliest Buddhism was characterised by the attitude of the proud aristocrat. Militant comparisons such as the Buddha's word 'Like a bull I have broken every bond'[58] betray once again that no mysticism, even the inexorably logical mysticism of ancient Buddhism, can ever completely free itself from the atmosphere of its milieu and culture. Perhaps too its origin from the warrior caste explains the remarkable fact, that Buddhism, so coolly impassive in mystical theory and practice, proved to be such an active and sometimes almost aggressive missionary religion in the social field.

Psychologically its origin lay – like that of all mysticism – in that intense realisation of the dissociate and fragmentary condition of human existence and its total lack of meaning, which one might also call *taedium vitae* or 'the break-down of the naive joy of living'.[59] This is perfectly legitimate, if it is only realised that after this nauseating cognition true mysticism does not drift along in a *fin-de-siècle* mood, or write tragic verse or philosophies – in the resigned or the rebellious key – but systematically works for deliverance from life and matter through ascesis and contemplation, as far as it is possible for a man to loosen the bonds of life and matter before his death. When the Buddha had once for all deeply sensed and penetrated the completely meaningless pain of living, he left his dwelling to follow the mystic way. That is the way whereby a human being, step by step, slakes all and every bond with the external world, to go in unto himself and – again step by step – attain and realise the Archimedean point of spiritual equipoise where all outward and inward contrasts are dissolved, not into the dark night of a regained womb, but into the white light of consciousness which has transcended itself.[60]

The Buddha had much in common with his predecessors, the mystics of the Upaniṣads. Only he was more practical, more analytical and more logical. The practical turn of his mysticism is particularly evident in the fact that he gained Enlightenment when he no longer directed himself, as former practicians of yoga had done, towards those spiritual spheres that stretch beyond consciousness and above the divine, but when he concentrated his thought upon death, rebirth and the prevention of rebirth.[61] It has repeatedly and rightly been said, that the Buddha is only a sign-post to the Doctrine and that only the Doctrine is important. Yet the Buddha himself – or, if preferred, the mentality of the earliest Buddhists – was so practical, that a saying of his has been preserved to the effect that the Doctrine is the raft on which a man may traverse the sea of life, and once he reaches the shores of beyond, he leaves it lying without a thought, because it is of no further use. Thus the analysis of the inner and outer world, practised with such thoroughness in this practical mysticism, was never able to grow out into a philosophy, but remained an auxiliary on the way of salvation. Analysis only proved the fleetingness of world and life, of matter and mind. Once this conviction had taken root and been assimilated, there was only one watchword: on to the next milestone on the way to the ultimate goal.

The Buddha was especially more logical than other mystics. Once he had dissolved life in understanding, he did not try still to save some morsel or core of that life, and take it with him to the other shore. This appears from the famous four truths he discovered when he directed his thought upon death, rebirth and prevention of rebirth: 1) to live is to suffer; 2) suffering arises from the will to live; 3) this will to live chains us to the fleeting phenomenal world; 4) therefore the elimination of the will to live means liberation from this imprisonment and the end of our suffering. But it is not I that is liberated, for it is the very illusion that we have or are a durable self which binds us to the wold of phenomena, which we then also regard as durable. The incongruence of actual impermanence and the human illusion of permanence causes and *is* suffering. No more than the continually changing constellation of atoms of the phenomenal world has a permanent, settled core, a 'world soul', no more has man a permanent core he might call his soul or his self. Actually, the elimination of the illusion of the self entails the elimination of the will to live and the elimination of suffering. Then one has reached nirvāṇa, *i.e.* 1) a state completely devoid of affects and desires in this life; 2) 'disappearance' at death from the endless chain of rebirth.[62] The earliest Buddhism deliberately avoids discussing the full content of the term nirvāṇa, because it is the negation of life and the world, so that it cannot be formulated, for language has only comparisons and negative terms for that which transcends consciousness and reason.

In a study concerning culture history, it has seemed preferable to attempt to convey the sense of some fraction of ancient Buddhism rather than to embark upon a systematic exposé including its full terminology. Such is available in many books. Omitting Buddhist termi-

34

nology (though this is naturally of supreme importance in other contexts), we may establish here that the Buddha drew the mystical conclusion from what has been formulated in our time by the cybernetic expert Norbert Wiener as follows: 'To be alive is to participate in a continuous stream of influences from the outer world and acts on the outer world in which we are merely the transitional stage'.[63] However, the Buddha did not rest with the abstract comprehension of this concept. He added this insight to the scope of the ancient methods of yoga, whose aim was not to degrade salvation to a matter of words, but to realise it. For the Buddha – and this was the renewed impulse he gave to Indian mysticism – the highest and most absolute realisation was to be found in the combination of yoga or spiritual exercises with insight. This combination was of central importance to him.[64] In the ecstasy, or whatever one wishes to call the spiritual condition resulting from *exercitia spiritualia* and meditation, the insight becomes a direct insight, without medium: thinking becomes being. Therefore, to the ecstatic conditions already known from the practice of yoga, Buddhism added a new and supreme ecstasy,[65] that of nirvāṇa, which is 'to sink back into pure Being, which is nothing but itself' as an ancient text states.[66] 'Opinion – that is remote from the Accomplished One. The Accomplished One has séén', we find in another.[67]

The ideal then might be complete liberation through spiritual exercise and ecstasy acting as two-in-one with insight,[68] either component in itself already demanded a spiritual élite. Who of them was capable of combining both methods in such a way that they would ultimately lead to the identity of thinking and being? It is one of the magnificent and depressing potentialities of man, that he can also discern those possibilities he can not or not completely actualise, or which can only be actualised by a genius. Thus it is not surprising that already in the earliest Buddhism something of a contrast arose between those who sought enlightenment and liberation by the path of ascesis, meditation and ecstasy, and those who attempted the same goal by the path of insight.[69] And as this did not depend upon a difference of opinion, but was simply the recognition of an impossibility, both ways were regarded as equivalent.[70]

One thing both ways had in common, and this common core of Buddhism is insufficiently characterised by the usual label of atheistic mysticism. It is indeed a typical trait of this mysticism, that through rigorously denying an essential core to man and the world it became unnecessary to refute the existence of gods, these gods being simply degraded to entities who were also subject to karma, and could be disregarded by an (expectant) buddha, because they were further off from ultimate liberation than he. A more thorough atheism than this careless indifference in recognising the gods can hardly be imagined. The doctrine that man and the world do not have a lasting constituent principle, but are merely continually changing constellations of atomic particles was, however, of great significance for mysticism itself. The concept of atheism is applicable in describing Buddhism as a religion, but falls short with relation to the *via mystica*, which is characterised by nirvāṇa as the total absence of any affect, even a sublimated affect. The difference with other forms of mysticism is subtle and yet great. In these, enlightenment and liberation are nearly always experienced as the union of two essentially related entities, be they personal or impersonal.

Van der Leeuw describes the *unio mystica* as 'Emptiness finds Emptiness' (Leere findet Leere),[71] *i.e.* man and God disappear in the same Void. This is certainly the ultimate consequence Christian and other forms of mysticism can draw from their premise of the annulment of the polarity between subject and object (Subjekt-Objekt-Spaltung), as Karl Jaspers pregnantly defined mysticism. Yet these mystics are always confronted with something or someone, and it is this relation which affords scope for the sublimated affect of love.[72] This insidious affect occasions a pendulous movement between twoness and oneness. The Buddha on the contrary found nothing in front of him. His aim was nirvāṇa, to be realised without affect and without words. He stood alone, worked alone and disappeared alone.[73] In his cool, almost icily impassive mysticism, there was no place for a mystic union, because there was no place for even the most subtly sublimated affect. He united himself neither with god nor divinity nor voidness. He was an illusion recognising himself as such and so extinguishing.

Meanwhile – this is an ideal. The Orient may have produced a genius or two, as the West afforded an example in Einstein, the complete realisation of this ideal was impossible even to the élite. The fundamental significance of the unattainable religious ideal with its attendant consequences has been completely neglected in the study of religious history, which often describes the ideal as reality. Yet that significance is great. If a man has set himself an ideal and tried to actualise it, a reaction must follow. In religion bourgeois 'accommodements avec le ciel' may still be possible, in mysticism, demanding such intense effort of body and mind, frustration is unavoidable. Two of the possible ways of rendering this frustration tolerable are the following. The discrepancy between the ideal and reality may be rationalised, and once it is reasonably 'explained' one may rest content. There may also be an emotional reaction, for instance pride in what one has attained as compared with other people or – considering the correlation between frustration and aggressivity – a direct or indirect reaction of aggression. Both possibilities are forms of compensation entailing the danger of so-called overcompensation. As rationalising is a seemingly rational proceeding that covers up unconscious motives, it is naturally also possible for both forms of compensation to be combined.

Against this background several developments in Buddhism become understandable. Those who followed the way of insight and found that ultimate enlightenment was not their lot, sought and found compensation in writing books – the sea of Buddhist books is endless as the sea of grievous existence they describe – in which they systematised not experiences, but concepts. Disputes were bound to follow. At first the Doctrine was left untouched and disagreements only concerned monastic discipline, but later on various philosophies arose reinterpreting the doctrine of the Buddha. Thus it was often only too easy for erudition and speculation to replace mystic experience. Though there are no clear indications, it is perhaps to be assumed that especially those who practised asceticism and ecstasy tried to fill the gulf between the ideal and reality by missionary work. It is a peculiarity of human nature to lay the burden one cannot carry oneself upon the shoulders of others. It cannot be sufficiently stressed that after a first period of 'splendid isolation' Buddhism became a typical missionary religion, obtaining conversions by preaching hell and damnation to such an extent[74] that at a later time the Chinese emperor Huan Hsüan said the Buddhists could only convert the barbarians by frightening them.[75]

It has already been pointed out, that the origin of Buddhism from the warrior caste of India may in part explain its militant missionary aspect. The secretly aggressive preaching of hell and damnation by the Buddhist missionaries is also to be explained, however, as the compensation of individuals who faute de mieux transferred their own fear and inadequacy to other people, besides finding the compensation of good works in the conversion of their fellow-men. One need not equate missionary work and aggressivity to be convinced that the mission may be an ideal substratum for sublimated aggressivity, closely connected with the motif of the scapegoat. In a masterly tale, quite eclipsing psychological analyses, Somerset Maugham has given a merciless and yet humane exposure of a missionary attempting to conquer that which he cannot master in himself by converting it in the person of his neighbour.[76] As in the course of its history Buddhism has missionised in many countries, repeatedly giving evidence of a calculating drive for power – for instance, by first converting the ruler of a country, as the Christian missionaries did in Polynesia and elsewhere – these psychological factors should not, in spite of all mysticism, be disregarded.

One may, however, suppose that these symptoms of aggressivity and the urge to power they contain, are foreign to the essential and original Buddhism, and are to be regarded as subsequent foreign intrusions. Apart from the fact that conversion by threats of death and hell was practised quite early, it is important to note two facts which indicate easy points of irruption for aggressivity, not only in possibly degenerate practice, but also in the original mentality and doctrine of Buddhism, without regard to a possible connection with the Buddha's origin from the warrior caste.

In the first place we see, that according to tradition the Buddha entered upon the mystic way from disgust at illness and death, and that he gained enlightenment when he directed his thought upon death and rebirth in a following life, that would again be tainted by death from its inception. It is certainly true to say that Buddhism loathes both life and death, but the repugnance against life proceeds from the repugnance against death, life's inevitable result. Buddhist literature is full of lamentations and exhortations regarding the uncertainty of life and the certainty of death. One may assume with a probability bordering on certainty that when as a young prince he left his home, the Buddha felt not only disgust at death, but also fear. His mysticism did not arise from a positive feeling of infinity, but from a negative sense of nausea and fear. This has remained typical of Buddhism from the very beginning in India until the last phase in Tibet. It is clear, that someone who is unable to conquer death completely in accordance with the Doctrine – the possibility of this in certain cases is not denied here – may react not only with flight, but also with aggression to the unmastered fear. We must remember that for a Buddhist there is no possible hope of heaven, but only the certainty of another life subject to death. Therefore fear of death can very easily be projected upon a scapegoat, who can be conquered by aggression.

In the second place the analytic attitude of the Buddhist mystic can easily lead to aggressive compensation in case of frustration. This factor is of more importance than the one previously mentioned, which is strengthened by it. Other forms of mysticism too include analysis to expose the transience and unmeaningness of unenlightened existence, but they are impelled by the deep longing after union, when man's finite microcosm will blissfully melt into infinity. There is no question of this with the Buddhist mystic, in spite of all comparisons likening nirvāṇa to an abode of peace and salvation.[77] Heiler says with a rather critical undertone, that the Buddhist ideal of salvation lacks all personal warmth, in contrast with the ideal of Christian mysticism and the neo-Platonic mysticism of Plotinus.[78] Voidness he considers the most fitting characteristic, and although non-Buddhist mystics have also used this concept, one can agree with him in this. Indeed, absolute emptiness as an ideal of salvation is completely in harmony with the doctrine that man and the world lack a self or essential core, and the systematic attempts of the Buddhist mystic to destroy every illusion of a self or of inner coherence by means of analysis. The cold, completely indifferent Buddhist mysticism of nirvāṇa can only be compared to the mysticism of Śaṅkara, and indeed he has been said, probably with justice, to be strongly influenced by Buddhism. It is typical, that Śaṅkara too is an abstract and analytical thinker. As there is an element of destructive aggression and lust for power in all analysis, it goes without saying that if nirvāṇa mysticism breaks down half-way, this mental aggressivity can take other forms. It is not without significance that Heiler finds Christian parallels of Buddhist mysticism and methods of meditation with the militant and aggressive Society of Jesus, those who vehemently combated the mysticism of love.

The above analysis, however, can be pursued no further here. It is time to consider the Buddhist attitude towards woman, in which right at the beginning we see the symptoms of fear of death, conversion of that fear into aggression by means of projection upon a scapegoat, and analysis as a weapon in the battle. In principle the victory over sexuality in the person of woman is merely a stage of the *via mystica*, but for those who do not attain the goal the danger is great that they will regard woman as a personal enemy. In an old text woman is succinctly defined as 'the creature to whom lies are as truth and truth as lies'.[79] This formulation is just a little too absolute not to give the impression of misogyny. According to tradition the Buddha himself energetically opposed the admission of women into the order. But even after they had been admitted one searches in vain for great women mystics like Santa Teresa. Before a woman could attain nirvāṇa, she had to be born again as a man.

The ancient Buddhist mystics feared woman, because their own sexuality drove them towards her, fettering them to the world of illusion and rebirth. She was a danger, not because intercourse with her was sinful or dirty, but because she constituted the strongest stimulus for the satisfaction of the strongest form of thirst for life, which the Buddha had discerned to be the cause of all life and suffering and death. She was deadly danger. Attack was the means of defence against this danger. For in order to repress sexual desires meditation upon corpses and skeletons was recommended, and it is noticeable that the subject of this analytical meditation is repeatedly the body or corpse of a woman. A kind of mental dissection was practised. She was analysed into hair of the head, hair of the body, nails, teeth, skin, muscles, tendons, bones, marrow, heart, lungs, liver, intestines, brains, pus, blood, fat, mucus, sweat, saliva etc., into the various openings of the body and the secretions borne out of the body through these openings etc., into the various stages of decomposition of her corpse etc. A story of more recent date shows more explicitly what problems were included in the aggression against woman the enemy. Ananda, who defends the admission of women into Buddhism, is reproached for this and defends himself with the memorable words: 'I know that the women are full of passion, but I thought that if they would see the private parts of the Buddha's Body, they would become deprived of the female organ!'[80]

The little élite of ascetics and mystics, who were indeed organised in a monastic community, but attempted the long and hard *via mystica* as individuals, each for himself, had not only mystical, but also social problems. For as long as they continued in mortal life, they needed food, and as the Buddha or the earliest Buddhists – following the Brahmans? – did not consider it necessary or desirable that the monks should provide for their own requirements by means of agriculture or otherwise, the inhabitants of the monasteries were entirely dependent upon the Buddhist laity. Here the recoil was felt of the attempt to oppose a true spiritual élite to the brahman caste, which had become primarily a social élite. These religious aristocrats considered the layman good enough as a giver of alms, but otherwise looked down on him.[81] It requires little effort to imagine the complaining laity, who had to maintain monks working exclusively for their own salvation. As the fundamental human law of reciprocity was seriously violated here, both psychologically and socially, we have every right to speak of a structural fault in Buddhism which was bound to cause tensions and conflicts. In mysticism, the earliest Buddhists were impressively logical, socially they were as surprisingly inconsequent. He who sets himself outside life and society, should be self-sufficient in every way. Even after the contrast had been softened, the effect of this structural fault could be perceived, and no one less than Lamotte dares say: 'Si l'on ne risquait pas d'être mal compris, on devrait poser l'existence de deux bouddhismes distincts et souvent opposés: celui des religieux et celui des laïques, dont l'interférence, pour ne pas dire la rivalité, conditionne toute l'histoire du bouddhisme indien'.[82] When Lamotte speaks thus, one again wonders whether the Buddha or the earliest Buddhists did not make two mistakes, in trying to organise individualist mystics and in trying to make this *social* organisation into a *spiritualised* aristocratic caste. The laymen desired more in exchange for their gifts than merely the preaching of a doctrine which, even if they understood it, they could not put into practice. In fact, they even entertained some doubt as to whether the monks themselves could realise it, as will presently appear. The disdain of the monks only heightened their feeling that they were having the worst of the exchange. The monks in their turn could not help seeing that they must take account of these feelings of resentment and injury if they did not want to lose their almsgivers. They too had to recognise that mind cannot despise matter with impunity. They proved willing to compromise. For instance, the laity might keep their own gods and continue to worship them.[83] In itself this was no concession, as Buddhism did not trouble to deny the existence of the gods. Yet toleration of the cult of the gods was indeed a small concession, though its value was very much diminished by the addition, that a gift to a future Buddha was more important than the worship of gods. Another concession is to be observed in the remark, that not everyone is equally suited to the Doctrine, so that preaching should be adapted to the comprehension of the audience.[84] More important is, that the latter principle was extended in a striving to become a brahman unto the brahmans.[85] As the monks came from lay families, these little concessions entailed considerable danger of syncretism, and yet they did not satisfy the laymen. If the material ties between them and the monks were so strong, then the spiritual ties should be equally strong. If they were to help the monks to attain the greatest good, then the monks ought to help them to attain a good that would afford them more happiness than a series of rebirths.

In this connection it is curious, that from the very beginning Buddhism knew prophecies announcing the end of the Doctrine.[86] And whenever later on in the course of history the monastic communities were threatened, these prophecies reappeared. It is particularly fascinating to examine the problem, why these negative eschatologies arose so early. In answering it, the fact that Hinduism entertained similar ideas cannot be the decisive factor, because this merely raises the question, why the Buddhists so soon connected pessimistic expectations with their new religion. Various possible causes can be enumerated. One may think of the impossible task the Buddha had laid upon the shoulders of his followers, which could not but make them pessimistic. Then it is by no means unlikely that they saw their existence threatened by the enmity of other religions. Yet the relationship to their own laity may well prove to have been the principal factor in the origin of the eschatology of the end of the Doctrine. The monks must have realised that the high spiritual status they claimed – without reaching nirvāṇa! – made them giants with feet of clay, dependent as they were upon their almsgivers. They must have felt that in preaching the cold and hard Doctrine they were giving the people stones for bread. Nor can one imagine that the obvious thought did not occur to them, that if all laymen became monks, the monks would have nothing to eat. Consciously or unconsciously they must have felt the dilemma: either to risk being left in the lurch, or to attach the laymen by watering down the wine of the Doctrine. The first alternative meant suicide, their aristocratic pride was opposed to the second. The conflict between necessity and pride may easily have led to weary resignation, admitting that times were bad, and that the end of the Doctrine was drawing near, because it was too good for the present.

However that may be, when in the third century B.C. king Aśoka proved willing to protect and propagate Buddhism and to fill the role of royal almsgiver, the security of the monks' subsistence was thereby increased. As a result of the royal support, though, not only the monks but also the lay followers grew in number, causing an increasing influence of lay Buddhism, for with regard to the new monks the rule held good that increase of quantity means loss of quality. The laity were less and less willing to be regarded as second-rate

Buddhists by a small élite, and wished to see their warm-hearted lay Buddhism fully acknowledged beside the cold and haughty Buddhism of the *arhats*, those mystics among the monks who had reached nirvāṇa. The manner in which the laymen fought for their interests shows that they were deeply convinced of the impracticability of the nirvāṇa ideal. They quite simply stated that even the perfected arhats still had seminal emissions at night, so were still not insensible to the charms of fair goddesses![87] Having in this way considerably decreased the distance between themselves and the mystics, they demanded acknowledgement of the way of good works and the assurance, that also a householder could attain to enlightenment and liberation. Just as in former times the Aryan rulers had had to do, so now the Buddhist aristocrats had gradually to give way in their ideology. Recognition of the way of good works as a legitimate path to salvation and of the possibility, that non-monks might attain enlightenment, meant a revolution, but it was only a first revolution.

Matters continued to develop in the same direction, and came to such a pass, that the old ideal of the mystic who liberated himself in accordance with the Doctrine was branded a form of selfishness. Traditional orthodoxy was contemptuously labelled Hīnayāna, the Little Vehicle, and the adherents of Mahāyāna, the Great Vehicle, established a new ideal: the bodhisattva. Their aim was no longer to follow the path indicated by the Buddha. They wished to copy the bodhisattvas, who having travelled the *via mystica* to the end, refrained from nirvāṇa out of compassion with their fellow-men and vowed that they would remain active in the world until all men were liberated. It is perfectly obvious that this was a victory of the masses over the élite, of feeling over the mystical non-affectedness, of the social community over the fundamentally asocial Buddhism.[88] It is most interesting to see how this social and psychological process finds expression in the philosophy of the Mahāyāna School. In early Buddhism there had been a gulf between the phenomenal world of rebirth and nirvāṇa, as there was a gulf between layman and monk. The ideal of the bodhisattva bridged this gulf, it was valid both for monk and layman, and as it were brought heaven – or in Buddhist terms: the Buddha – upon earth. Philosophically expressed: 'Nirvāṇa is not in the least different from birth and death'.[89] This unprecedented statement, quite shocking to a Buddhist of the old school, that the world of absolute detachment and denial does not differ from the world of phenomena and rebirth, becomes clear when it is applied to man. The Mahāyāna teaches that in every human being there is a 'thought of enlightenment', a spark of buddhahood, that with the help of the bodhisattvas could be blown into the pure flame of enlightenment. As the bodhisattva – in contrast with the Buddha, who 'vanished' in nirvāṇa – was a buddha invisibly present upon earth, whose light brightened the darkness, so in everyone glowed the spark of buddhahood.

Quite to fill up the gulf, the Mahāyānist philosophers and intellectuals coined a new concept: the Void, of which the phenomenal world and nirvāṇa were the two aspects. The Void was a similar inexpressible mystery as formerly nirvāṇa. Both were names for an inexpressible condition of consciousness, which was now postulated more as a metaphysical reality. But the former concept had stood at an unbridgeable distance from the everyday world, whereas the new concept linked and reconciled the two separated realities. Besides, it enabled the intellectuals to give a positive evaluation to popular Buddhism as a preliminary stage – differing in externals, but of equal intent – of their own more polished spirituality. As always, here too the philosophy and theology functioned usefully in registering and justifying after the event that which burst forth irresistibly in the hearts of the great mass of the people, and linking it as best might be with the traditions of former centuries. In this case it was the people's longing for warmth of feeling (instead of insight and asceticism) for human solidarity (instead of mystical individualism) and for a religion that might be practised in everyday life by the ordinary man (instead of the asocial mysticism of the élite). Voidness not only philosophically connected the phenomenal world (saṁsāra) and the world of absolute mind (nirvāṇa), making them a dialectical two-in-one, in which thought could reconcile matter and mind, it also linked the masses and the intellectuals, feeling with understanding.

Le coeur a ses raisons... these famous words best fit the transition from Hīnayāna to Mahāyāna. If an élite's doctrine of salvation is to be preached to the people, the élite must put up with the enervation of their doctrine. In principle, this admission was made in the Mahāyāna by the monks, who in their monasteries depended on economic support from outside, besides having difficulty enough with their own doctrine. The former ideals were not destroyed, but theoretically pushed into the background, and practically shelved. Nowadays one might say that they had been put into the deep-freeze, as the Christians have had to do in another, comparable connection with the Sermon on the Mount. For the philosophers, the name of the compromise was Voidness, for the people bodhisattva. The bodhisattvas – for naturally the imaginative faculty, desirous of salvation, created many – were divine figures the people could understand and admire. These humanised buddhas did good works to the advantage of men, who of course were to imitate these good works as best they could. If this was not very successful, however, one could pray for help to the bodhisattvas. For was not their most essential characteristic pity and compassion? Thus Buddhism, in which god and prayer had been unknown, acquired buddhistically tinged gods, to whom one could pray. Whereas the Buddha had declared that he could do nothing in the matter as to which of his disciples reached nirvāṇa and which did not, the bodhisattvas became saviours to be adored and prayed to. Soon they not only helped people in spiritual, but also in material affairs. The bodhisattva Avalokiteśvara protected travellers, sailors and criminals, but at the same time helped them to enter upon a virtuous way of life and to go to heaven. Everywhere in the universe were heavenly paradises, inhabited by innumerable buddhas and bodhisattvas, who were willing to listen to reason, if only they were worshipped and believed in. The philosopher Nāgārjuna both upheld the past and sanctioned the present state of affairs by declaring, that insight and faith led to the same goal.

Formerly everything turned on the élite, now everything turned on the people, while the élite lived on the verges (though it should be borne in mind that most of the inhabitants of the monasteries were laymen in monastic robes). Of recent years a few authors are making

42

convulsive efforts to defend the thesis, that in spite of all changes Buddhism has yet remained essentially the same. They are sometimes more apologists than historians. It is obvious that in the course of centuries some elements of a religion will continue, some will be adapted to new times and circumstances and some will disappear, whilst now and again reformers, active in a small circle or in a larger field, will to some extent purify the central concepts of the tradition. This also applies to Buddhism, which as a result of its unattainable ideal and its economic vulnerability became perverted, though in certain groups and trends the old ideal never entirely vanished. Yet if one wishes to describe the history of this religion as a component part of a society and culture, then a sense of historical proportion demands that already the Mahāyāna – not to mention the later Vajrayāna – should be regarded as a wholesale perversion of the Doctrine. It is the task of the historian of religions to search for the life centre of a religion ('die Lebensmitte einer Religion'),[90] that is the structural centre of gravity, the core, the living heart of a religion which determines and nourishes feeling and thought of its adherents. From the social aspect, this core must be sought not among the élite but with the people when the Mahāyāna is in question. The correctness of this view is proved by the fact, that the élite found themselves compelled to incorporate the popular conceptions in their philosophy. Ideologically, this living core is embodied in the bodhisattva, and it is this figure which betrays the great perversion of the original ideal.

It is not only the transition from the Buddha, who in proud isolation liberated himself, to the bodhisattva who exhausts himself in pity, good works and miracles to help the masses that assiduously honour and worship him, it is also in especial the transition from non-attachment to sentiment verging on sentimentality which characterises the wholesale per-version referred to above. An interminable literature sprang up of long, dull legends, circumstantially recounting the infinite goodness of the bodhisattvas. Before elucidating this thesis, a few things must be established. In the first place there is no question here of a value judgement, but of a psychological observation. As one should distinguish between true and false mysticism, so one should distinguish between sentiment and sentimentality. In the second place the danger of misunderstanding a foreign culture is at a minimum here, if not entirely absent, because the same sentimentality is found in the Christian legends of the saints. The resemblances are truly surprising. Thirdly, no haughty contempt for the masses is expressed here, but understanding for the great majority of the members of a complex society, whose hard existence has shown them, in themselves and others, that man is a wolf to his own kind, that 'goodness, just goodness'[91] is more rare than gold and diamonds, while deep in their hearts they yearn for goodness, so that even a tale about goodness moves them to tears.

The legends of the saints of the Mahāyāna have been remodelled in Tibet into mystery plays with 'moins de longueur... plus de vie et de simplicité',[92] yet even the hardened Tibetans were reduced to tears by them. The shortage of human goodness in daily life was compensated by the extravagant goodness of the bodhisattvas, whose holiness naturally manifested itself already before and at their birth, and in their earliest years. We hear of the Tibetan Tsong-kha-pa that as a child he did not even have a dirty nose, and of course he never told lies.[93] Such trifles, however, were only a preparation for adult charity, such as tearing out one of his eyes as a proof of generosity. Or a bodhisattva cut pieces out of his own body, not to refuse the request of some cannibals. Or a royal bodhisattva gave his beloved wife as bedfellow to an amorous ascetic who wanted her, upon which he had himself sawn into pieces to be able to supply the god Indra with a new stomach.[94] The miracle is the favorite child of faith. One might let this goodness rest, as over-excited wishful thinking on the part of starving humanity, if there was not a small snake in the grass. The sacred legends are not simply popular phantasies, they must have been at least revised by the spiritual leaders, who in this new phase thus demonstrated in a new way the will to power of Buddhism, which is also an aspect of this fascinating and multiform religion.

For the goodness of the bodhisattvas proves to be a form of compulsion and lust of power. The victims of the pity of the bodhisattvas have to be grateful. 'Better is it to take a log out of water than to save an ungrateful person from it!'[95] One bodhisattva is even so pitiful and charitable, that he refuses to be thwarted in his pity and his charity, 'to be thwarted in continuing his giving'.[96] It is clear that by giving himself away the bodhisattva wishes to exercise power. The psychology of the gift as a means of exercising power is well-known and is regularly applied in our world also. Among the North American Kwakiutl this found very open expression when the richest members of the tribe competed with each other in generosity. He who gave most, was the victor. The speeches made at these bitter contests are full of openly confessed lust of power and megalomania.[97] Because the lust of power of the bodhisattvas was not openly confessed, but had to pass for authentic love, the stories about them became sentimental. The correlation between sentimentality and aggressivity is well enough known in other respects. Their aggressive urge to power, though, also betrays itself in megalomania, in that these saints are vividly conscious of their saintliness. Too often one reads: 'Through my goodness I have saved them...' In such sentences, both the possessive and the personal pronoun sound as if spelt with capital letters.

This is the unsound aspect of a Buddhism which did not, in its new aspect, wish to lose its grip upon the laity. Naturally, this religion of good works and compassion also had a brighter side. It gave hope and consolation, and continued to indicate the way to a life of goodness and purity. Hope and consolation were not only granted by buddhas and bodhisattvas, but also by other gods, who had been more and more officially admitted by Buddhism,[98] after the laymen had been permitted to continue the worship of their popular gods in the earliest period. These gods had been listeners and onlookers, in the earliest texts, while the Buddha made known the Doctrine and illustrated it with examples, but they now became powers that were honoured together with buddhas and bodhisattvas.[99] Most laymen will have taken little interest in the matter, but officially these gods were regarded more or less as protectors of Buddhism. It seems not improbable that this theological stratagem was closely connected with the relationship between monks and laity. Just as the laymen, as almsgivers, were the protectors of the monks, so the lay gods became in the Mahāyāna the

1 gŚin-rje gśed (Skt. Yamāntaka) yab-yum. Bronze, some parts polychrome. h.: 13⁷/₈ in. (35 cm)

protectors of the Buddha and the Doctrine. However this may be, the acknowledgement of these gods proves once again the great influence of popular religion, while their function of protectors saved the honour of Buddhist theology. In art, for instance, at an early stage one regularly sees the indigenous yakṣa Vajrapāṇi accompanying the Buddha.[100] One gets the impression that this combination at first represented the association-in-service of laymen and monks, and that later on the god of the people becomes more and more active as a protector. Whatever might have changed in Buddhism, the monks still needed protectors.

They still lived in their monasteries in economic dependence on laymen – or princes – while most of them were more engaged with theology and complicated rituals than with the lonely, laborious *via mystica* of ancient times. In spite of all concessions their position remained vulnerable. One might even say that by giving up pure mysticism and acknowledging the way of good works as an equally valid road to salvation, they had rendered their position even more vulnerable, at least in the eyes of a distrustful people, watching them with critical regard. The simple fact that monks have an assured existence without too heavy work, has at various times and in various places raised the question what use there was in all that learning and all those prayers. Besides this, there were in India the Hindoo religions, which were certainly not unattractive to the people, which could even satisfy the reasoning of critical intellectuals and offer them assurance for heart and mind, and... which did without monasteries. While missionaries spread the Mahāyāna over a large part of Asia, it can cause no surprise that its prosperity at home and abroad required ever new concessions.

3. *Buddhism: Mantrayāna and Vajrayāna*

Some three or four centuries after its inception between 200 and 100 B.C., magical formulas penetrated into the Mahāyāna, which could serve to command good or evil forces. If mysticism is the most international form of spiritualised religion, magic is the most international form of religion directed towards material ends. Spells and magical means of killing an enemy at a distance, finding a treasure, making a woman fall in love, or identifying witches and rendering them harmless, are to be found in practically all primitive or complex cultures. Those who would defend the principle that Buddhism always remained the same, may point out traces of magic even in the earliest texts, but that does not alter the fact that in the third phase of this religion the stream of spells becomes a deluge. Magic became an integral part of Buddhism. In the fourth century A.D. Hsi Ts'o-chih wrote so enthusiastically about one particular Chinese Mahāyāna monastery, where fasting and study was not shirked, and where no magic was performed,[101] that one can only conclude he had discovered an exception to the general rule.

India would not be India, if it had not been attempted to make something of this development also and to raise it to a higher level. The magic spells – *mantras* – were not only used for profane ends such as the death of an enemy or the love of a woman, they were also used in mystic, magic rituals, in which the adept visualised a god in the yogic manner, and then identified himself with him, in order to obtain by the quick way that liberation which in the Mahāyāna could only be procured through moral purification and philosophical knowledge. The text of these rituals is found in the *tantras*, whose magic character forms a contrast with the *sūtras* of the first two phases of Buddhism. This was the origin of Tantrism or Mantrayāna.[102] Thus the vehicle of magic spells includes both the secret formulas for compassing deserving and undeserving profane ends, and the liturgical and yogic texts leading to speedy liberation. For that matter, these two aims were by no means mutually exclusive. That they should be pursued together was extremely characteristic of the great pressure obviously exerted by the people, and remained typical of the third phase right into Tibet. One might say of the Hīnayāna élite, who sought their own salvation and took it for granted that they should be maintained by the laity in the mean time, that they wanted to have their cake and eat it. In the Mantrayāna this could be applied to the people, who wanted speedy and complete spiritual liberation while wishing to obtain material advantages by the same magical mystical way.

This was not yet the end of the concessions. Around the 7th century A.D. the cult of Śiva, already discussed in the first part of this chapter, became a redoutable foe of Buddhism.[103] The adherents of this god attempted to obtain their desire by violent means, as an Indian philosopher puts it.[104] The manner in which they professed their faith is a clear protest against their society, which they confronted in a way calculated to shock: they went naked, carrying a club as a symbol of sexuality and aggressivity, jabbered nonsense, made obscene gestures in the presence of women, drank wine from human skulls, and meditated in cemeteries.[105] Caste was not acknowledged by them, from which one may conclude that their action was a continual protest on the part of outcasts and other victims of India's social organisation. If in the beginning of this chapter Śiva was called an explosion of autochthonous religion, here he must also be termed an outburst of social rebellion. In both cases he is the rude and untutored representative of the natural appetites. The fact that he is also the great yogin, shows that outcasts too are people with their own ideas of human dignity.

Śiva had a female partner, who became increasingly important in this period owing to the influence of Śaktism. The followers of this sect were of opinion, that God was a woman and expressed this by contemplation of the female genital organ, either in effigy or in actuality.[106] This short-cut identifying mind and nature was most probably also a form of social protest, and at the same time a re-activation of autochthonous religion[107] in stirring times of social and political unrest. The sect entered into partnership with Śaivism, bringing Śiva's female companion, the Devī, into high honour. We even find indications that there were differences of opinion as to whether Śiva or his wife was the more important. The later philosophical and mystic Śaivism resolves the matter thus: the Devī is the active *śakti* – *i.e.* creative energy – of the spiritual Creator Śiva who rests in himself, and thus she forms the link between the God and his world and worshippers.[108] The less philosophical and more drastic followers of the god would on occasion solve the problem by copulating with women in cemeteries. The woman was then the śakti of the man. Outside cemeteries also, sacral *coitus* and śakti played a more and more important part in Śaivism as it was popular.

As Śiva was the great, divine yogin and many yogins were to be counted among his followers, the practice of yoga was also influenced by the sexualising tendencies in religious life. But the yogin did not require a corporeal woman, for since ancient times yoga was just as self-sufficient as early Buddhism, which has sometimes been termed pure yoga. 'What need have I of any outer woman? I have an inner woman within myself.'[109] The name of this inner woman is Kuṇḍalinī, and the yogin who practises this form of yoga imagines her as a coiled snake situated in the lowermost 'lotus-centre' of his body, about at the level of the genitals. The uppermost centre is located in the brain, and there Śiva rests in himself. Between these two there are five other lotus-centres. After the physical and mental training indispensable to all yoga, the yogin must now concentrate all his psychical and mental forces on doing what a fakir does with a real snake: 'arousing' the Kuṇḍalinī-snake and inducing it to stretch itself upward.[110] He leads Kuṇḍalinī upwards in such a way that she penetrates the various lotus-centres – in authentic yoga each centre signifies a new and higher state of consciousness – until in the brain-centre she unites herself with her lord and consort Śiva, and the yogin attains the highest enlightenment.[111] A psychological commentary upon this matter would require a separate volume,[112] so that here there is only place for those few remarks strictly necessary to our purpose. A goddess who raises herself up as a snake and pierces lotus flowers, who at the beginning and the end of her 'course' envelops the sweet liṅga of Śiva with her mouth and drinks nectar,[113] is an evident symbol of bi-sexuality. As sexual symbols are not only expressions of sexuality, but not infrequently also express structures and trends of human nature, bisexuality equals autarky,[114] certainly so in this instance, where a man consciously strives to unite nature and mind – phallus and brain, his virility and the woman in himself – within his own body and mind. This will towards autarky is also made evident in the fact, that the yogin's semen or the power of his semen is considered to rise up and descend again transformed into the nectar of Śiva's union.[115] The clearest proof is found in the power obtained by the yogin, to destroy and re-create the world. For as he leads Kuṇḍalinī upwards, he simultaneously demolishes the visible world step by step, so that at the union of Śiva and his consort it vanishes completely. Then as Kuṇḍalinī is led back centre by centre – *i.e.* when the yogin systematically returns to normal consciousness – the world is built up again. If the yogin were to become angry, writes a commentator, he would be able to destroy all the worlds.[116] The difference with mysticism, including Buddhist mysticism, is evident: the mystic comes to non-being or blows out like a flame, the Śaiva yogin seeks power, the power of God himself. Not seldom, he imagines himself to be God.[117] It is significant for our subject that this God in apprehension beholds, in the various states of consciousness he creates, both peaceable and terrifying gods, and that the latter are the 'lords of dissolution', those who preside over the destruction of the world.[118] In this yoga both sexuality and aggressivity serve the lust of power, assuming itself capable of destroying the world and building it anew, like the great god Śiva himself. This means that aggressivity dominates over sexuality in an autism, which recognises mysticism as a danger and conquers it. Yoga and magic often go together. When the Buddha met a yogin who proudly declared that after many years of effort he could walk over the river, the reply was: what a pity to spend so much effort; a little further on they will take you across for a penny. This yoga stands between mysticism and magic, as the latter was described in connection with the Mantrayāna.

The people, themselves fond of employing magic, held the yogins in high honour. Greedy for marvels, their imagination added numerous miracles to the yogins' actual achievements, and so 84 yogins became the legendary 84 Siddhas or miracle-workers. It is significant, that both Śaivism and Tantric Buddhism knew the 84 Siddhas, and that a number of names were the same in both lists.[119] This shows that for wandering yogins and their admirers and followers of that milieu, the line of demarcation between Buddhism and Śaivism was growing faint at that time. Other facts too point in the direction of a syncretism in which particularly Buddhism was the loser. The boundaries between the practices of wandering yogins and the yogic 'communal' rituals in these circles are often not clear either. A tantra translated by Sir John Woodroffe gives a good impression of the spirit and practice of a community of the Śaiva milieu. The symbolism is not only sexual, but also sensual. The tantra breathes an aggressively sectarian spirit. Wine, meat, fish, parched corn and coition have a central role.[120] Wine is very important for the union of Śiva and his partner, and the Praise of Wine, which is sung, contains the obvious and thereby rather dubious argument that it is not the quantity of wine, but its effect upon the drinker that counts.[121] Almost comical is the rule with regard to sexual continence: in the daytime one must abstain, but at night one is free.[122] Intolerance is very great. Whoever practises a different religion is sure of death and hell,[123] and the fierce and terrifying gods are dancing in delight at the thought of the flesh and bones of scoffing unbelievers whom they will devour.[124] The background of this barely sublimated sexuality and aggressivity is evidently of a social nature. A protest against the caste system is clearly audible.[125] No wonder these unfortunate outcasts seek compensation for their sense of inferiority. The members of this church[126] are elevated far above society and its morals.[127] Secrets and secrecy shelter the vulnerability of this proud consciousness of self.[128]

In connection with our subject, two matters claim attention: the Terrifying Gods and the social background of such religious milieus. The terrifying aspect of the god Śiva is the night-side of his aspect of fertility and salvation, and together these form the numinous unity of contrast which characterises every great god, though the stress laid on his demonic activity is probably due to the contempt and enmity the Aryan rulers felt at first for the native god. In Kuṇḍalinī-yoga the lords of dissolution are symbols of the power of the yogin who can destroy the world. Though far more personal than in the case of Śiva himself, this aggressivity is yet sublimated to a very great degree, and is entirely consonant with the system of yoga engaged in. In the sect described above, whose members practised no more than a weak infusion of yoga, the terrifying deities are the signs of an understandable, nevertheless

50

petty-minded hatred. Within their own circle they practised a scantly spiritualised sexuality, externally they ventilated a furious aggressivity. There is no question of any relation between these two forces in human life. One can only think of a hypothesis in child and adolescent psychology, according to which a child can only love certain people if it first hates others. It has to hate these, because otherwise it would simultaneously love and hate its parents and others, and would itself succumb in the conflict.

In social respect we have here the milieu of what Max Weber called 'plebeian religions', which are to be found in various complex cultures. They are the religions of the 'underdogs', who cannot assert themselves and who take their revenge by regarding themselves as the true élite in their religion, 'far better than the rest'. Among themselves they are most fraternal, linked by the same fate, and towards the outside world they are extremely aggressive, in this instance attacking the castes and the monks! Naturally they do not recognise rank and class, any more than the system of values of the existing social order, and this is formulated as being above good and evil. To these characteristics, studied by Weber and set in a wider context by Mühlmann[129] we may add, in a word, that all these religions are dominated by the psychology of resentment. One finds the same thing with non-white peoples under white colonial rule: he who feels inferior wants to eat his cake and have it, wants, for instance, to remain a Papuan and to become white, to remain outcast and to have a religion of a philosophical tint. Much would-be philosophising in the tantras should, I think, be seen in this light.[130] The true proportions are easily seen, when one hears that the tantras, which announce themselves as composed for great minds, are written in an abominable style.

It is not yet certain how things went exactly, but everything points to it that this social protest, manifested in a secret religion with a strong sexual element, also impressed a not inconsiderable part of the Mantrayāna Buddhists. Though fiercely opposed by other milieus of the Mantrayāna,[131] it managed to gain a wide acceptance, and so the Mantrayāna was converted into the Vajrayāna.[132] Tantric Buddhism, then, is a general term for this phase of Buddhism as expressed in the tantras, Mantrayāna indicates more particularly the magical, and Vajrayāna the magico-sexual trend. It is extremely improbable that – as Govinda and others think – the sexually directed magic and the sexual mysticism of the tantras should have originated in Buddhist circles. Already in prehistoric times India, like many other cultures, was acquainted with the zestful and frank adoration of sexual symbols and mother goddesses whose sexual aspect predominated. The Aryan rulers could not in the end prevent this autochthonous religion from reasserting itself, as it did in the religions of Śiva and Viṣṇu.[133] The social underdogs seized upon these indigenous elements to oppose the existing society and to shock it. For evident reasons, the disposition to shock was coupled with a desire for secrecy, so that in Śaivism and Śaktism sex and the sexual act, in themselves capable of filling man with awe and leading him to the numinous, not infrequently acquired a dubious character.[134] The close connection between the two religions also points to a Hindu origin of śaktism in the milieu concerned, while the resistance of Mantrayāna circles to the Vajrayāna rounds off the argument. Sexual conceptions and practices were of indigenous origin, and penetrated into Śaivism and also into that sector of Buddhism where the faithful were sensitive to such a form of rebellion and protest.[135]

The popularity of Śaktism must have compelled the Buddhist leaders to adopt these conceptions, if they did not want to lose their followers to their great competitor, Śaivism. Thus one can read in many texts of the Vajrayāna that buddhahood lies in the vagina. In some places the frontiers between Buddhism and Hinduism must have been very vague indeed at this time, between the seventh and eighth century A.D. The common opposition to the higher classes, to the brahmans and to the Mahāyāna monks with their ritualistic and theological paraphernalia will certainly have carried more weight than religious subtilties.[136] Meanwhile Buddhism, essentially asocial, seems always to have retained something of this character, and to have had a special attraction for those who were asocial by necessity or choice. Only Buddhism produced Zen, profound as it is excentric, and that comes from China, where 'mad monks' were a familiar phenomenon.[137] The Vajrayāna in India did not only draw its adherents from the lowest classes, many Vajrayāna teachers were of good family, but had come down through addiction to wine and women.[138] Perhaps this asocial character – even more asocial, for anti-hindu, than Śaivism – was one of the reasons why Buddhism did not disappear in the sexualistic dark, where all cats are gray. Another factor may have been, that particularly social underdogs fight out group rivalry in the ideological field, because they simply have no other battle-ground and ideology is their only sign of status.[139] However this may be, the Buddhist faithful and, or their yogic leaders managed to keep their identity and in spite of all Hinduistic intrusions they have given the Vajrayāna a clear Buddhist stamp.

Naturally, there was a great resemblance between these Buddhist milieus and the Hinduist, particularly the Śaivan circles. Not an interminable, century-long wrestling after salvation in the endless chain of reincarnation (and social misery!), but liberation here and now by the so-called short path was craved. It was not only dislike of theologians, priests and monks, but also their own religious 'haste' and illiteracy, which caused these people to despise the way of knowledge and insight and give vent to the magical desire for action in the rituals. Tantrism is ritualism. The urgent, intolerable longing after liberation found an outlet in the sexuality of Śaktism. The Mahāyāna theory, that the buddha-spark glows latent in every human being, formed a useful starting-point for the tantric thesis, that salvation and liberation are found in the body. Much stress was laid on *coitus reservatus*, coition without ejaculation, but in the tantric twilight one need not have a 'dirty mind' to suppose that there were two possibilities, and that many of the faithful simply did not have the time and the capacity for strict practice of yoga.[140] Sexually also these people adhered to the magical theory of like by like, the body was to be redeemed by the body. Samsāra = Nirvāṇa! – thus the Buddhist Tantrists. For much the greater part of the faithful, the goal of even seriously practised yoga was not the *unio mystica* but immortality, and magical power in this life was the highest good. Usually yoga was practised more as an attempt, the good intention counting more than the result. When the Hevajra tantra enjoins 'Try it one fortnight with zeal',[141] one can hardly take this seriously, though Snellgrove does. Even an Occidental can see that a fortnight's yoga is too much like the quick courses for this, that and the other that are advertised nowadays. Most results are founded on auto-suggestion. The yoga of the tantric laymen should be regarded in the same light as their conviction that they are the spiritual élite,[142] that the badly written tantras are literature for highly developed minds, etc. Their jealous secrecy alone betrays that they have stuck half-way between actual inferiority and imagined superiority, half-way between natural sexuality and sublimated mysticism, in ritualism and magic. This is not ridiculous or contemptible. Humanly speaking, it is saddening, almost tragic, and completely understandable, like that 'aping the white man' of primitives who have not the possibility and the means truly to follow him. Scientifically, however, it is a phenomenon to be observed and stated. Very convincing are in this respect the following words from a list of tantric code-terms: passion, power, corpse, naked, ejaculation, semen, coition, brain-pan, food, faeces, urine, blood.[143]

Buddhism remained true to its anti-hinduist tradition though, and impressed its own mark upon the new religious forms. Although the Vajrayāna is such a heterogeneous collection of spells, magic, ritualism, yoga, speculation, sexual symbolism and practice that it almost defies definition,[144] they succeeded by holding fast to a few basic concepts. When the rituals were written down, this process was already going on. Indeed, in the tantras one finds gross magic beside Buddhist passages. Later on monasteries and universities produced many commentaries in which this tantrism, which could be taken either way, was interpreted entirely in the spiritual and mystic sense. Although magical elements seldom disappeared entirely, so that it is often to be defined as a mysticism of *illuminati*,[145] Buddhism attained in many of these commentaries to the very heights of religious life. For comparison, the theological and mystical commentaries of Christianity upon the Israelitic eroticism of the Song of Songs may be mentioned, even if the case is not quite the same.

In the first place, the concept of buddhahood was maintained and the idea, that every human being is to become a buddha. Even if this is ultimately a matter of form, it yet remains evidence of deliberate continuity, which made it possible that also the Hinayāna and the Mahāyāna writings were afterwards profoundly studied in Tibet. Then they held to Voidness as the final mystery and the foundation of all that is. Although not an original Buddhist concept, it could fairly often come to sound like the Buddha's anātmatā: the doctrine, that there is no self and no immortal soul. How the cool Buddhist analysis could sometimes revert to keen aggressivity, may be shown in passing by the words of a marginal figure: the spirit which creates the illusory world in which we move, must be killed like a rat.[146] The concept of Voidness was particularly fitted to bring order into the chaos of buddhas, bodhisattvas, gods, rituals and symbols, because thus this chaos was brought *sub specie aeternitatis* and could be recognised as essentially void – a point of view which can also be shared in the 20th century.[147] Tucci very aptly uses the word gnosis for the mysticism and pseudo-mysticism of the Vajrayāna. There are striking resemblances with gnosticism, as also with kabbalism,[148] so that a comparative study might yield interesting results. The symbol of Voidness became the *vajra*, from which this form of Buddhism derives its name. Originally the thunderbolt of the Vedic god Indra, it also appeared in Hinduism as the weapon of Śiva.[149] The Vajrayāna did not simply take over this symbol, but interpreted it anew as the pure, indestructible diamond of Voidness,[150] so that Vajrayāna is best translated as the diamond vehicle. If enlightenment was considered as the mystic union of the male and female principle, the vajra symbolised man and penis, the lotus (in the ritual also a bell) woman and vagina.[151]

Another difference is the Buddhist reinterpretation of the union with the śakti, who in Hinduism symbolised the active energy which created the phenomenal world, while the male god was regarded as the passive spiritual principle, resting in itself. Now whether this mystic union was imagined as a normal copulation, or as a yogic *coitus reservatus*, or as the symbol of a purely spiritual mystic union, in Buddhism the śakti was not active, but passive, and did not symbolise energy, but insight, the supreme wisdom, embraced by the male as a symbol of his desire for insight and good works. Zimmer already drew attention to this reinterpretation,[152] and Snellgrove and Govinda have made it quite a matter of principle.[153] Justly so indeed, for it cannot be denied that the Buddhists usually regarded the union of god and goddess, of man and śakti, as the union of the active impulse towards salvation, manifested in good works and ritual actions, with the passive, quiescent knowledge or wisdom, of *upāya* with *prajñā*. But they were certainly not consistent in this respect. Bhattacharyya speaks here, for instance, of 'Lord Mind and Lady Vacuity', which agrees with the reversal of the active and passive roles, but not with the interpretation of the male as compassion and good works. Besides, in Tibet we shall meet with interpretations that are closer to Śaivism than to Buddhism. Altogether the concept of śakti with its original background does not seem to have entirely disappeared. Not to trespass against the Buddhist reinterpretation of the union of compassion and wisdom, however, the śakti will henceforth be called *mudrā* (= seal), when a woman of flesh and blood is meant, and *yum* (= mother) when referring to a goddess appearing in a vision, in imagination or as a work of art.

In meditation and contemplation the Buddhist also differed clearly from the Śaivite. The latter felt to the last a difference and a distance between himself and his god. In the Buddhist liturgies, the *sādhanas*, the worshipper identifies himself with his god so completely, that one may really speak of identity.[154] Here an essential piece of Buddhism proves to have been preserved. The complete indifference of the Buddha towards the gods, who are illusions like all living beings, has been slightly intensified under the influence of the philosophy of Voidness and the ideas concerning the creative and destructive power of the yogin, and become a unique kind of atheism: the gods exist, in so far as man does not control them. The followers of the Vajrayāna 'conceived of a god in knowledge of his non-existence', as it is formulated in the Hevajra tantra.[155]

Typical of the Buddhism of those who adhered to the diamond vehicle was also the creation of new gods. The Hevajra already referred to is simply the hypostasis of an invocation, upon the principle of *nomina numina*: he vajra. But the scale was turned by their god Yamāntaka,

3 *Vajrapāṇi (Tib. Phyag na rdo-rje). Bronze, Nepal. h.: 6⁷/₈ in. (17.5 cm)*
4 *Tantric magician. Bronze. h.: 5⁵/₈ in. (14,5 cm)*

3

4

who conquered the Hindu god of death Yama, and took his place.[156] Nothing affords better proof of their withdrawal from and hatred of Hinduism, including Śaivism, than the liquidation and complete negation of no one less than the god of death, known and feared by all Hindus. Just as the visualising of a god in knowledge of his non-existence determines the Buddhist character of the Vajrayāna from the religious aspect, so that character is sharply underlined in a social respect by Yamāntaka's liquidation of Yama, who for centuries had ruled as king of the dead, in the Vedic religion, in Hinduism, in Hinayāna and Mahāyāna, with the particular function of judging the dead and inexorably, but justly, determining their next rebirth.

Finally, mention must be made of the work of the theologians. They not only interpreted the sexual and other material symbols and practices mystically in a gnostic fashion – for instance, coition is mystic union, killing an enemy is killing the illusion of the self, one's mother or sister as mudrā means different levels of truth – in their great and flourishing universities they also introduced a systematic order into the continually increasing pantheon of buddhas, bodhisattvas and gods who do not exist, but are real in man as long as he has not transcended himself and thereby the gods. At the head of the five families, to which the gods had been assigned, stood Vajradhara or Vajrasattva, who *is* Voidness. The heads of the five separate families, which correspond to the five components of the human body, are the buddhas Vairocana, Akṣobhya, Ratnasambhava, Amitābha, and Amoghasiddhi. In view of the subject of this book, Akṣobhya calls for particular attention, for his family includes all the terrifying deities (with one exception), and his bodhisattva is Vajrapāṇi. His family is that of the vajra, its colour is blue, the sin assigned to this family and which can be conquered by it is wrath, and the corresponding component of the body is consciousness. These associations will be considered later, for the moment we may point out that, entirely in agreement with the spirit of ancient Buddhism,[157] they are rather of a psychological than of a theological nature. It is at once evident, that *e.g.* the correspondence between components of the body and gods admits of a theory of religious projection, and a mystic way whereby insight can be gained with regard to the non-entity of both body and gods, and the inexpressible Voidness realised.

As it is not possible to give a complete sketch of the Vajrayāna, it will be best to close the chapter with a concrete example, which may convey more than a too summary and too abstract exposé. In Snellgrove's translation of the Hevajra tantra, much praised by specialists, there is a passage which sounds emotional. Here the author of this most important tantra seems to let himself go for a moment, and as people often say more in such a sally than in collected argument, this passage may perhaps be more typical than others. The god Hevajra himself speaks, in part, as follows:[158] 'Without bodily form how should there be bliss? Of bliss one could not speak. The world is pervaded by bliss, which pervades and is itself pervaded. Just as the perfume of a flower depends upon the flower, and without the flower becomes impossible, likewise without form and so on, bliss would not be perceived. I am existence, I am non-existence, I am the Enlightened One for I am enlightened concerning what things are. But me they do not know, those fools, afflicted by indolence. I dwell in the Sukhāvatī, in the vagina of the Vajra Woman, in that place which is symbolized by the syllable E, in that casket of buddha-gems. I am the teacher, and I am the doctrine, I am the disciple endowed with good qualities. I am the goal, and I am the trainer. I am in the world and supramundane. My nature is that of Innate Joy and I come at the end of the Joy that is Perfect and at the beginning of the Joy of Cessation. So be assured, my son, it is like a lamp in darkness. I am the Master with the thirty-two marks, the Lord with the eighty characteristics and I dwell in the Sukhāvatī, in the vagina of the female in the name of semen. Without it – the semen – there is no bliss and again without bliss it – the semen – cannot be. Since they are ineffective one without the other, bliss is found in union with the divinity. So the Enlightened One is neither existence nor non-existence; he has a form with arms and faces and yet in highest bliss is formless. So the whole world is the Innate, for the Innate is its essence. Its essence too is nirvāṇa when the mind is in a purified state. The divine form consists of just something born, for it is a repository of arms and faces and colours, and moreover arises by the normal influence of past actions. With the very poison, a little of which would kill any other being, a man who understands poison would dispell another poison. Just as a man who suffers with flatulence is given beans to eat, so that wind may overcome wind in the way of a homoeopathic cure, so existence is purified by existence in the countering of discursive thought by its own kind. Just as water entered in the ear is drawn out again by water, so also the notion of existing things is purified by appearances. Just as those who have been burned by fire must suffer again by fire, so those who have been burned by the fire of passion must suffer the fire of passion. Those things by which men of evil conduct are bound, others turn into means and gain thereby release from the bonds of existence. By passion the world is bound, by passion too it is released, but by heretical buddhists this practice of reversals is not known.'

This mystical-seeming pantheism of the body, which for a moment appears a pantheism of the semen, makes the impression of a medley of sexuality – of a rather drastic kind in a religious context –, philosophical speculation and comparisons which are clear, but not always delicate. The aggressive sally against the fools who understand nothing of this religious homoeopathy, is characteristic, also in that it is directed against heretical buddhists. Heretics are of course always the others. It is rather piquant, that the later commentators always use the term 'fools' for those who take the tantras literally, whilst here it is those who do not do so, who are called fools. For though a mystical interpretation is certainly possible – one need only think of the commentaries on the Song of Songs – there can be little doubt that here it is the redemption of the body by the body that is preached, and in a high strain. Without the body there is no bliss and, to be exact, this bliss depends on the semen. The world is pervaded by bliss and the god himself is this world. The nature and the essence of the god is the innate joy, which comes at the end of the joy that is perfect, and at the beginning of the joy of cessation. The reader who might find the essential nature of this god obscure, will easily understand the sequence 1) joy, 2) perfect joy, 3) innate joy and 4) joy of cessation, if he considers that it is an analysis of cohabitation as experienced by the male. The commentators interpret these four phases as four yogic conditions of consciousness. They have a perfect right to do so, all the more as they do it subtly and consistently. But it is clear that tantrism is a very different thing in its origin and in its mystical re-interpretation, and that the tantras, which themselves already make the impression of having been worked over, do indeed offer an ambiguous choice. To speak with Snellgrove: it was indeed the razor's edge.

If we turn off the flood-lights of the commentaries, then Hevajra stands before us in this tantra as a tight-rope dancer who slips more than once, and that on the carnal side of his rope. To take an instance, there is his description of a fair mudrā, whose charms include a sweet breath and whose *pudenda* are fragrant as lotus flowers, who is calm and resolute and delightful, and his comment on this description: 'By vulgar men, indeed, she would be classed as first-rank.'[159] The fact that the thought can arise, how vulgar men would judge of the beautiful woman destined for the ritual, is somewhat curious. Many a man will prefer simply to be vulgar in this respect. In the part called the Manifestation of Hevajra, he sinks into the bliss of union with his beloved, whereupon the other goddesses of his court begin calling on him to arise.[160] One of them cries: 'Embrace me in the union of great bliss, and abandon the condition of Voidness'. Even if we leave a very wide margin for the secret language of mysticism, no one familiar with it will believe in this polygamous mysticism, which is a mere projection of the ritual celebrated by a yogin who is provided with a number of so-called tantric assistants. As this tantra also contains directions for a magical rite to gain the favours of a woman, we may with good reason suppose this yoga to carry an uneasy conscience. What is propagated here, is actually a copulating form of religion, either factual or imaginary. The only condition is purification of the spirit. In view of the very sense-bound symbolism and magic, it is to be supposed that in most cases this purity was rather a matter of intention than of fact. The Hevajra tantra is too much impregnated with rankling resentment, sensuousness and sensuality, to give credit to a high level of sublimation. In such cases a secret language is not a sign of profundity, but of ambiguousness.

That there can be no question of mysticism, not even of spurious mysticism or authentic yoga, becomes apparent when Hevajra awakens from his sweet slumber in the lap of Nairātmyā. For then he plants his feet firmly on the ground, and threatens gods and titans in a terrible way, quite without provocation. Mysticism seeks permanent liberation from the self, Hevajra uses sex and aggressivity for the unbounded inflation of his self, in line with the I, I, I, in the quotation given above. This aggressivity is a mixture of the quick anger often manifested by the yogins, so easily offended because their appetite for power is never sated, and the rankling resentment felt by social underdogs, as the tantric Buddhists originally were. Some fortnight's practice of yoga by the faithful will probably have caused both factors to coalesce. It must have been satisfying for outcasts to be able to say: 'One is oneself the Destroyer, the Creator, the King, the Lord'!'[161] Psychologically, this aggressive urge to power is incompatible with sexuality and love, in and outside mysticism. Division and union, destruction and synthesis, maintaining and losing the self, magic and mysticism are unlinked and irreconcilable opposites here. While the Buddha taught, that affective ties with the phenomenal world must be cut, to become free from the illusion of the self, the voluptuous enjoyment of power and sex alternate here, making the ties with the world as thick as cables in magic of mystic pretension, and inflating the ego till it becomes the Lord of Creation himself. So when Hevajra says he is black and terrible, but that peace rules in his heart, one simply does not believe him. One would like to know whether the mystic commentators refer to this, and if so what they said, but most of their work is still unpublished and untranslated. Govinda says the true Buddhist does not seek power,[162] and then Hevajra is a deplorable Buddhist. If Buddhism maintained its identity in essential points, this was not the case in all points. Śiva, the great destroyer and re-creator, had more influence on Hevajra and his followers in point of mysticism than the Buddha. It was necessary to go into this matter, for it was figures like this Hevajra who brought Buddhism to Tibet, figures like one of the 84 Siddhas, who 'makes butter with his śakti', and who flamed into anger like their Terrifying Gods. If the reader, unaccustomed to such material, should be confused by the pluriform content of this chapter, he will at any rate sympathise with the farmers and herdsmen of Tibet, who also had to work through this strange, bizarre world. To put it quite simply, the Tibetans must have been pretty much taken aback, when yogins of the Hevajra type came to preach a new religion to them, a religion in which complicated theories justified men's vagrancy in company with women, and explained as representative of a higher order the commerce of the sexes, which the Tibetans had regarded as belonging to the natural human and animal world (several sexual words in their language refer to humans and animals both, as seems perfectly natural to any herdsman or farmer). Tibet did not easily give in. And afterwards, when the Vajrayāna had gained currency there, it was found that the Tibetans had resolved many dubious matters into their component parts by realistic analysis. However many complications the process of acculturation caused, one's general impression is, that the cool and realistic outlook in Tibet at any rate considerably desexualised the Vajrayāna. Tibet was inclined to call a spade a spade, and to set limits. Much was to happen, however, before this was attained.

6 Mañjuśrī as Dharmadhātuvāgīśvara. Bronze, Nepal. h.: 105/8 in. (27 cm)

6

TIBET: LAND OF HERDSMEN, FARMERS AND SHAMANS

So overwhelming as is the mass of information about India, from which a choice had to be made in the previous chapter, so scarce are the facts known with regard to Tibet before the time of the kings, as both written and archaeological data are practically lacking. Yet there are a few significant facts, which can yield us reliable results through the comparative methods of cultural anthropology. Tibet is the highest country on earth, situated at a height of 5000 metres, in the midst of still higher, majestic ranges. The soil is largely a stony desert. Travellers tell us that grays are the characteristic tints of a landscape which is naturally sometimes modified by near or distant snow. There is little precipitation, and what water does fall not infrequently appears as hail. Unfruitful and inhospitable, it is a thinly populated area, and a few decades ago, for instance, there were three million inhabitants.[163] Its situation also made it an isolated country. Their way of living made high demands on the physique of its people, and this coupled with the rare atmosphere and rocky soil caused them to grow into an extremely hardy race.

From the socio-economic aspect, the Land of Snows belonged to a long range of nomadic cattle-cultures, stretching from North Siberia through Central Asia, Arabia, North and East Africa to the extreme south of Africa.[164] Its religion belonged to the North and Central Asiatic type of shamanism. Shamanism itself was distributed more or less over the whole world, but in the above-mentioned enormous area it acquired a typical form and became a dominant factor in spiritual life.[165] Although cultural anthropology rightly takes the stand, that in the end every culture is unique, yet the fact that a number of cultures may belong to a certain type, is of considerable importance. Various factors may determine such a grouping, the principal factor being usually economic. The introduction of the horse caused a considerable number of strongly differentiated tribes to pour into the Prairie Lands of North America from all points of the compass, and from this contact a rich and fascinating culture resulted in a surprisingly short time, each tribe having its own variant upon the common foundation. Quite another example is afforded by the hunting cultures which were once spread all over the earth, and which show startling resemblances from the social, economic and religious point of view. The great, and so far usually unsolved problem is the question, which of these resemblances are of a structural kind, originating independently, and which are of a historical nature, so that they must be explained by contact, for instance, or by a common country of origin.

What remarkable facts appear in this context – ethnology is full of them – can be shown by an example from these very cultures of nomadic herdsmen. Only insiders are aware, that both among the prehistoric cattle-herding nomads of Ur and the Scythians, and among present-day nomadic herdsmen of Africa (including the very 'pure' Nilotics) and Asia, women would blow with their mouth into the vagina of the cow to increase the milk yield.[166] It was not known before, that exactly the same custom was known and practised all over the country by the nomad herdsmen of Tibet.[167] It is hardly to be supposed that an artifice of this kind could have originated independently among different peoples in different continents. Everything would point to such a detail being a strong piece of evidence in favour of the hypothesis, that the origin of all cattle-herding nomads lies in some region of South-West or Western Asia from which these cultures spread out to West and East. In any case, the example speaks volumes as to the persistence of cultural traditions, and this persistence is the greater, the closer these traditions are to the centre of the economic and religious struggle for life.

It is self-evident, that many resemblances in the cultures of nomad herdsmen arise from their common economy and the directly involved social organisation. With a few exceptions, specialists agree that the nomadic herding of cattle is a specialisation which came after the development of agriculture, not a specialisation of hunters gradually domesticating the animals they were accustomed to hunt.[168] These nomads and their herds are always found in places where agriculture is impossible, or at any rate where it cannot yield enough to live on. On the other hand it is worth noting that most nomad herdsmen have some agriculture as a side-line, or if this is quite impossible, live in the neighbourhood of farming communities from whom they can obtain vegetable food.[169] For Tibet, this conclusion from the comparisons of cultural anthropology was strikingly confirmed by the publication and translation of comparatively very ancient texts, from which it can be inferred that agriculture by means of irrigation was presumably already practised in the marginal areas of Tibet before the time of the kings.[170]

The term of nomads does not mean, of course, that the peoples concerned simply wander about at random. It does mean though, that they have to be constantly moving their herds from one pasture to another, not seldom over great distances, but within one wide area, which they regard as their land. As owing to the infertility of the soil it would be impossible to keep one large herd as the property of the whole tribe, the existence of these herdsmen is not only mobile, but also centrifugal and individualistic.[171] Whether we consider the African Nuer or the Tibetan A-mdo-pa, with them the individual has an importance rarely found in other forms of culture. The permanent social unit and core, indeed, is small.[172] Bacon has given these the Mongolian name of *obok*,[173] *i.e.* family groups of patrilineal descent, definitely patriarchal in spirit, who live more or less separately by themselves and express their common tie by faith in a common ancestor. The women are counted in with the husband's family. Not the least factor in determining the 'masculine' character of these cultures is the handling and care of cattle, which requires muscular force and courage.

Life hinges on the cattle. Cherchez la vache is the key for an understanding of their life in nearly every aspect, as Evans-Pritchard has said of the Nuer.[174] The Frisians – cattle-farmers of old, who resemble nomad herdsmen in many points[175] – have a part-serious joke in which one farmer asks another 'Ho giet it mei it wiif en 't oare fé?', *i.e.* 'How's the wife and the rest of the cattle?'. Outsiders will find it hard fully to understand that owing to the great love for the cattle this can also imply a great love for the wife. The individualism of the nomad herdsmen usually implies a great respect for women as partner and as a personality, also in public affairs. Cattle are not only property, but also a capital of prestige. Apart from its direct importance as food supply, the herd confers status. In spite of the great advantages of a balance in the bank, a South African cattle-farmer would not even consider the sale of his surplus cattle: 'They are so fine to look at'. For the same reason, in their fight against erosion, the Americans had serious difficulties with the Navahos, who would not part with their great flocks of sheep and herds of horses, and were stricken to the soul when forced to relinquish part of them. The nomad herdsman, then, does not regard the quality so much as the quantity of his beasts. A mighty man is a man who has large herds and many sons. Yet this possession, the cattle to which he feels deeply bound and akin,[176] is extremely vulnerable. A single epidemic can make a rich man poor. 'The hazardous nature of herding operations and the social mobility it engenders contribute to another recurrent characteristic of herders: a fierce independence and a military-aggressive character.'[177] They are aggressive, proud and not seldom difficult individualists, who will not be intimidated or impressed by other people or cultures. For a field-worker, indeed, they are often difficult to approach. A great ethnologist such as Evans-Pritchard assures us in one of his three masterly volumes on the Nuer, that they gave him a 'nuerosis'.

In spite of the distances separating the small social units, the militant, individualistic and mobile (horses!) character of nomadic herdsmen sometimes makes it possible for them to found strong states under a vigorous leader, as Genghiz Khan most drastically proved. They only acknowledge the power and prestige of property and character together, so that under a leader who commands respect they may come to found a great, co-ordinated empire, but owing to their individualism the stability of such a state is usually not great.[178] Sometimes they found a real empire of conquest, with the autochthonous farmers at the base and themselves, of course, as ruling class at the top, under a king. Naturally a process of acculturation begins in such a case, which may, for instance, alter the conditions of marriage.[179] This is not without significance for Tibetan polyandry, which has become so famous, for in principle the nomad herdsmen of Tibet are monogamous. This incomplete sketch suffices to show what a world of difference there lies between the nomads of Tibet and the circles where the Vajrayāna was at home in India. To make this difference still plainer, attention must be drawn to a rather neglected phenomenon. In a culture where aggressivity plays a large part, one repeatedly sees that sexuality is crowded into the background, if not repressed. It seems that with agricultural, settled peoples where sexuality already had an important place in life, heightened aggressivity sometimes entails an increase of sexuality also. The question is, however, whether this does not usher in a fatal social development, as van Baal has assumed, rightly I think, with regard to the Marind-anim and Mead with regard to the Mundugumor.[180]

When aggressivity dominates in patriarchal cultures, however, there is little stress on sexuality. Examples that come to mind are the Nuer, the Aztecs, the Israelites and the Tibetans, and three of these peoples are nomadic herdsmen. In the Aztecs' overwrought mode of existence, sex was definitely dirty. The Nuer, Israelites and Tibetans regard sex far more as something self-evident, which is not at the centre of society and culture. In word and deed they pay this fundamental urge due honour, but their values in life have little or no connection with it. Their religion is centred upon heaven, not on earth, or in it. Not sexual virility, but masculine strength, power and prestige constitute their highest values, so that not sexual debauchery, but explosions of aggressive cruelty characterise the dark side of their culture. Still in recent times, the general mentality in Tibet could be described as 'un culte de la force et du pouvoir'.[181] With a certain contemplative trend, this type of character shows positive aspects such as aristocratic self-control, loyalty, and a great awareness of values of the soul and spirit.

That agriculture was carried on in the region of the Koko-nor and in the eastern marginal areas, was already referred to. It was also practised in the central part of Tibet, where in the course of time agriculture gained increasing importance. There is a remarkable, clear difference of build between the nomad herdsmen and the agriculturalists of the central regions. The former are tall and have narrow faces with an aquiline nose, so that their mongoloid features reminded several travellers of North-American Indians; the agriculturalists are short and have the typical, broad mongolian face.[182] It is assumed that there were originally only cattle-keeping nomads in Tibet, in which case the agriculturalists must have come in later from elsewhere. There is no certainty as to this matter. In Central Tibet there seem to be traditions regarding former, tall inhabitants, but on more realistic grounds we may assume that nomad groups concerned themselves with the affairs of the agriculturalists. Those militant gentlemen, who despised every kind of sedentary existence, will certainly have seized their chance.

The matter is of sufficient moment to deserve closer consideration. There are some grounds for the thesis, that kingship lies at the verge of the primitive world, for in principle kingship breaks up the closed character of society.[183] Curiously enough, kingship can hardly be imagined in cultural history without a visible gap between foreign rulers and indigenous agriculturists, and it is remarkable that originally we nearly always find nomad herdsmen in the part of rulers. Rüstow, who has made a deep study of the phenomenon of *Herrschaftsüberlagerung* (establishment of a foreign ruling class) to show that it is the foundation of all *Hochkulturen* (advanced cultures),[184] distinguishes four forms, in three of which nomad herdsmen rule over agriculturalists, while the form of hunters ruling hoe cultivators has far less significance in culture history. Thus the role of nomad pastoralists in the origin of complex urban cultures was very great. Tibet forms no exception. Hermanns' assumption, that the Tibetan nomad herdsmen became rulers over the agriculturalists of the centre[185] is probably correct, if merely because it would be strange if it were not so, on comparative grounds. But Tucci and especially Stein have shown, that the Tibetan aristocrats derived their genealogy from the northeastern regions, those of the nomad pastoralists.[186] This removes all doubt,

66

and we can be certain that the rulers in the central agrarian area of Tibet were nomad herdsmen. This is very important, for one of its implications is that the mentality of Tibetan kingship became the individualistic and aggressive mentality described above, and indeed this was drastically proved in their history. Although of course there must have been mutual influencing and commixture, the kingship of nomad herdsmen exercised a deep influence upon the cultural pattern of Tibet, fixing it for centuries, when even the Dalai Lamas harked back to it. Even though Tibet itself was agricultural, the importance of the nomad pastoralists for its culture can hardly be overestimated.[187] After the time of the kings, too, powerful and influential figures came to Buddhist Lhasa from the East, of whom Tsong-kha-pa is the most famous. A second aspect of the kingship of the nomad herdsmen was, that in this case too social and political inequality was made the principle and norm, because physical force and superior military power, here as elsewhere, formed the basis of the Hochkultur.[188] There were masters and slaves in Tibet, and the social unrest and disintegration occasioned thereby in Tibet's acculturation, still manifested itself in the 10th century in the *hbangs gyen log*, revolts of the slaves and the poor against the ruling classes.[189] That is why the culture of the nomad herdsmen, to whom, after all, the making of Tibetan culture goes back, was stressed in this chapter.

The contrast between the nomads and the agricultural farmers in the little kingdoms remained great. An old biography even used the following terms in describing bad times: 'mauvais cheptel pour les *nomades*, mauvaise récolte pour les *Tibétains*'.[190] Even in recent times the Buddhist monasteries in the marginal areas were called the monasteries in the country of the barbarians. Yet it is permissible to speak of *the* Tibetan culture, as long as this twofold character is kept in mind. The little kingdoms of the centre were confined to the river vales, as agriculture was not possible without irrigation.[191] These valleys being separated by mountains, the warring rulers had little chance of establishing their supremacy. Some reminiscence of these wars has survived.[192] Tradition relates that there were once twelve rulers. In the beginning of the 7th century A.D. one of them succeeded in extending his power,[193] though at first only over the Yar Lung valley. Yet this was the nucleus of the Tibetan kingdom. At the zenith of royal rule, Tibet was feared beyond the frontiers. When the Chinese refused to pay the tribute imposed upon them, a Tibetan army descended and destroyed the Chinese capital, carrying off both tribute and interest.

The establishment of kingship by aggressive nomad herdsmen cannot have left society unchanged. It must have been preceded by bitter fighting, and afterwards too many tensions subsisted, which were certainly not resolved by peaceful means, as the history of the time of the kings plainly shows. In such circumstances a petty king is a primus inter pares, held in enforced respect by the other members of the nobility owing to his power politics, while they keep a sharp eye on him, on the look-out perhaps for a chance for themselves. While trying to extend his territory, he must at the same time maintain the balance in home affairs, which also entails giving his more powerful rivals posts in the government, a course which offers both advantages and disadvantages when he has a set-back or a weak moment. Such times of political change and tensions are unquiet times in other respects too, when life is 'on the move'. It is not only by a show of force that a ruler tries to safeguard his position, he also makes use of various means to enhance his prestige, such as a special costume, great religious ceremonies, and court etiquette. These ways of impressing the people are often copied from abroad, where powerful kings have a long tradition. French as a court language in Europe, and the European uniforms at the court of the Hawaian king Kamehameha, are diverse examples of a general phenomenon, which was undoubtedly also found in Tibet.

There are sparse, but clear indications that religious conceptions and customs also underwent changes. With regard to Tibet it is usual to distinguish between Buddhism from the time of the kings until the present, and the Bon, the national religion before that time. As until recently the Bon received very little attention,[194] so that not much is known about it yet, it goes without saying that practically nothing is known of Tibet's religion before the Bon. It is certain though, that we must distinguish between a pre-Bon religion and the Bon, which seems to have been a modification-under-royal-influence of the earliest Tibetan religion.[195] In general one may say that Tibet's national religion was characterised by the belief in a Sky God,[196] a form of animism with a great many good and evil spirits but few great divinities, a great interest in funeral ceremonies, and last not least by shamanism. Little can be said of the belief in a God dwelling in the sky, but it would not be right to simply put him down as a dieu fainéant, as several authors do. A highest God who does not concern himself with all manner of petty affairs, can yet be of great importance in life as the great, ultimate God in the background. The assiduous popular adoration of the saints in Roman Catholic Europe does not imply that the God in the background[197] is not regarded as the ultimate mystery and the all-decisive power. Besides, traces of the High God in Tibet are plainly confirmed by faith in a High God among other Central Asiatic peoples, where he was not crowded out by Buddhism. Finally, we may note that the belief in a High God is characteristic of most nomad pastoralists; an impressive example, repeatedly recalling the Old Testament, is afforded by the Nuer.[198]

In cultural history Animism means chiefly the belief that 'everything is alive', without everything being reduced to systematic order. Unless brought into relation with the High God – this is not often found – the innumerable spirits of animism make a decentralised impression, perhaps connected with the very little centralised organisation of early societies. Everything in nature and everything in which man finds himself mirrored in the outside world, is experienced as a multitude of living, personal entities.[199] The decentralised character of this belief in Tibet finds striking expression in the conception of groups of identical spirits, which remained alive in spite of Buddhism, and which are to be compared to the Three Graces, the Erinyes, and similar groups. From the texts of Thomas already referred to, it appears that the spirits of Tibetan animism were not only demons, but that there were also definitely benevolent and helpful divine beings among them.[200] The Tibetans had spirits of the sky – the bDud – and also the bTsan, wild red hunters who stormed through celestial space on horseback.[201] Earth too was peopled with spirits, of whom the Sa-bdag, the lords

68

of the soil, were very important.[202] Many of them were mountain gods, who inspired the Tibetans with the deepest awe and respect, as is easily imagined. They were gods to take account of. In our time, a Tibetan in exile cherishes as a profound and moving memory the solemn adoration of the mountain god in his native village in A-mdo, when on the fifth and sixth day of the sixth month all adults climbed the mountain to the ice-cap, to sacrifice there to Kjiri.[203] Then in rivers and lakes there were the *kLu*, in trees and stones the *gNyan*. Finally, it might be suggested that the much discussed and much debated Snowman, the Yeti, is probably no other than the Lord of Animals of the Tibetan hunters, a god found with all hunting peoples, who may easily have been degraded to a mysterious creature in the mountains when Buddhism officially forbade hunting in Tibet, so that in the 20th century Western biologists made scientific search for him.[204] If the above supposition is correct, this biological hunting of a god is certainly unique.

More immediately, everything depended for the Tibetans on whether the Lord of the Cattle, say, or the Lord of the Hearth were well or ill disposed. The nomad herdsmen looked to the Lord of the Tent.[205] Once the rich material provided by Hoffmann and De Nebesky-Wojkowitz has been thoroughly studied, and the Buddhistic coating scratched off a number of gods, those interested will certainly know far more about Tibet's national religion. One would like to know what proportion of well- and ill-disposed spirits there was. There are pre-Buddhist myths telling of cannibal demons who devoured whole families,[206] but when these stories were written the times were already disturbed, and then the demoniac element readily increases. These spirits and demons were not explicitly depicted. Like other primitive Asiatic peoples – another resemblance – the Tibetans represented a god by means of a stick, part of a branch with or without pieces of cloth tied to it.[207] These were mere indications, and references to the divine power which could apparently not be expressed in material form; these 'shorthand-symbols', then, should not always be taken to indicate artistic impotence.[208] All the spirits were venerated and propitiated at the appropriate time or in case of pressing need. The idea of a scapegoat or substitute was prominent: the divine power was offered a replacement,[209] as Abraham sacrificed an animal instead of his son. Bloody sacrifices formed a regular part of the ritual with the Tibetans also.

When one of the kinglets finally managed to become more or less a real king, the sacrifices increased in quantity and quality and the ceremonial became more impressive, in keeping with the king's improved status. Quantity and quality of the victims could not only serve for the better satisfaction of the gods, but also to make a greater impression on the people and on rival nobles. He who strives after power wishes to see it expressed in signs. 'Man is a status-seeker' according to Jules Henry, and it is certainly not only in Tibet that he has made grateful use of the opportunities offered by religion. The influence of the nomad herdsmen was plainly evident from the prepotent significance of bloody victims, sheep, yaks and horses. Thus the religion of pre-Bon times developed into the Bon, a religion in which a central part was played by priests, who changed more and more into specialists of the sacrifice. Seen in the context of the culture of those times, Lalou aptly typifies this religion with the words 'le sang et le poison'.²¹⁰ In this expression, poison may also be regarded as a very real symbol of the way kings, ministers and other aristocrats tried to make an effective end, in a time of revolution and disturbance, of mutual jealousy and rivalry, and blood as the sign of a religion of sacrifice, continually extending under the royal influence.

Already before the period of the Bon, funeral ceremonies and rituals for the dead must have counted for a great deal with the Tibetans. The early texts mentioned above show that there were differences of opinion in neighbouring regions regarding the manner of burial.²¹¹ There is no saying whether this concerned the clash of two cultures or the intruding of one particular cultural element, but it may be supposed that in this case too there were differences between conservatives keeping to the old tradition, and progressives who wanted to derive status from an innovation. The original manner of burial was probably to take the corpse – especially that of a person of rank – to a mountain-top or other elevation and simply leave it there. For the new style of burial a tomb or coffin was used. These two kinds of funeral were already in existence before the time of the kings, and it is worth noting that also in the Tibet of more recent times, these two forms were felt to express two different principles, as is shown by Thomas. This preoccupation with funerals and death has remained characteristic of Tibet, which with its deservedly famous Book of the Dead stands beside Egypt in comparative religion. Yet there is a great difference between Egypt and Tibet, where in those ancient times the whole object of the funeral ceremonies was to render the dead innocuous and to be rid of him, as it is with many primitive peoples of Asia and North America. Buddhism was never able quite to remove this fear of the dead. It appears very clearly in the contemporary book of a Tibetan, who idealises her country and religion in a most naive manner, but is quite of the old stamp in her shivering avoidance of the dead.²¹² This may be compared to the attitude of modern Navaho Indians, who are Western in every respect, but would not for the world come into contact with a dead body and the house where someone has died. Such feelings have deep roots.

The funeral rites, too, kept expanding and growing more complicated in the time of the kings, so that the various sacrificial specialists of the Bon included a separate group of funerary priests.²¹³ Some idea of the extent of these rites is conveyed by the pledge of a Tibetan king, who in gratitude for promised fealty undertook to build a tomb (!) at a vassal's death and sacrifice a hundred horses.²¹⁴ But not only animals, human beings too were sacrificed, a clear sign, in cultural anthropology, of a mounting level of civilisation.²¹⁵ The manner in which the sacrifice was carried out recalls the Aztecs in some respects.²¹⁶ In view of our main theme, it may be noted here that the third Dalai Lama still had to protest against human sacrifice in Tibet.²¹⁷ People were much preoccupied with the dead. A text of the Bon po – i.e. the followers of the Bon – is called 'The 360 ways of dying'.²¹⁸ In the funeral ceremonies the dead person was killed again by destroying his image.²¹⁹ The possibility is certainly not to be excluded that this fear, common to all men, may have increased when nomad herdsmen began to lead a settled life as conquerors in the agricultural regions. Comparative studies have shown that a positive valuation of the dead and the ancestors in a cult of the dead with naturally ambivalent, but in the main positive feelings, is a typical phenomenon of agrarian cultures,[220] while the fear of the Tibetan nomad herdsmen is connected with the same fear among hunting peoples, who hastily abandon their dead. Agriculturalists have their dead with them, lying in the same earth the crops sprout up from. When pastoralists, however,[221] who fear the dead, begin a settled existence, their fear will become much greater, and because they can no longer strike their tents and move on, it will manifest itself in more elaborate funeral ceremonies. In this way we have at least a reasonable and probable explanation of the Tibetans' preoccupation with death and funerals all through the centuries.

The centre of this religious complex of conceptions and practices was shamanism. 'Dans toute cette aire immense qui comprend le centre et le nord de l'Asie, la vie magico-religieuse de la société est centrée sur le chaman',[222] states Eliade in a work that is a masterpiece of learning and insight, commanding the respect of all students of shamanism. His words also apply to ancient Tibet, which was probably entirely shamanistic in the pre-Bon period, while the sacrificial specialists of the Bon were not seldom specialised shamans, so that the funerary priest *e.g.* continued the work of the shaman as conductor of souls in a more elaborate form. So fundamental was shamanism in Tibet, that Buddhism too was submitted to its by no means superficial influence. After everything which has been written about shamanism, Tibetan religion and Tibetan Buddhism, the argumentation may be considered complete.[223] Thus only a few subjects relevant to our theme will be discussed here. A shaman is someone who passes through a spiritual crisis, in which a vision determines his vocation, thereby acquiring the ability to control conditions of trance and ecstasy. He or she makes conscious use of this for the benefit of the community, travelling in trance to the upper or the under world, accompanied by spirit helpers, there to convey requests to gods or spirits or to force them, sometimes in a very aggressive manner, to adopt a milder attitude towards mankind. Thus the shaman is conductor of souls, healer,[224] miracle-worker and sometimes also priest, but he differs essentially from the priest and other religious functionaries through his technique of ecstasy.

It is important to note that among the primitive peoples, who have no mysticism in the true sense of the word, shamanism is 'the nearest approach to mysticism'[225] and, as Eliade has shown, not far from yoga, which rests on a more intensive and systematic introspection. Uncontrolled symptoms of trance with religious content, shamanism, yoga and mysticism may be set in a rising sequence. For the shaman too the world outside disappears in his trance, but he finds within himself a richly varied and lively world where he must maintain himself, if need be by fighting the spirits he meets. The yogin does not fight in his inner world, but he does try to gain power, which if necessary he may afterwards make magical use of in fighting demons. The pure mystic has no concern with power and aggressivity, knowing no other aim than loss of identity, un-becoming and fusing with the fundamental being of a positive Nothing.

Most characteristic is the vision in which shamans are called to their office. These marginal figures, often neurotic according to our ideas, and frequently lovers of solitude,[226] have the terrible experience in this vision of being cut into pieces by spirits, so that only their skeleton remains.[227] Not infrequently their flesh is eaten by the spirits of illness and death. These experiences and ideas are also found in other parts of the earth, even in Australia.[228] This suggests palaeolithic origins to Eliade. However that may be, one can at any rate conclude that this cutting into pieces – the 'Zerstückelung' or 'dépècement' – is extremely ancient and obviously common to mankind. Before discussing the latter aspect, it is worth remarking with regard to the problem of its origin in terms of culture history, that in the old hunting cultures the bones or the skeleton formed the essential imperishable element in animals and man.[229] To maintain the balance it was the custom, for instance, in Siberia to leave intact the skeleton of the animals that had been killed, giving this back as it were. In South America the fish-bones were in the same way given back in the river to the Lord of animals, and, in an interesting variant, the bladders of the seals they had killed were returned by the Eskimo through a hole in the ice at a special festival. In this way new animals could come into being. The idea of the skeleton as the lasting and essential part was applied to human descent in all Asia. Bone = essence = descent = family. In Tibet the expression 'of the same bone' meant of the same father, whereas 'of the same flesh' meant of the same mother.[230] Thus the shaman whose flesh was cut into pieces was renewed down to the bone – sometimes the marrow was even taken out and replaced –, so that he awoke from the frightful trance as a new man.

Although this cutting into pieces took place during a trance, one might say, paradoxically, that the shaman experienced it with clear, unimpaired consciousness, and that it was necessary for him to do so if he were to emerge from the process unscathed. He himself often looked on at the proceedings in such a vision, for the spirits who were going to cut him up, began by striking off his head and setting it on a plank in the yurt (tent). From there, it had to look on while the shaman was carved up.[231] A more evident symbol of human self-consciousness even in conditions of psychic crisis would be hard to imagine. The head on the plank, the maintaining of the Self is absolutely necessary for the shaman, who in this crisis in a long drawn-out situation of conflict wishes not to be disintegrated, but integrated. He will very likely remain a neurotic person, but in future he will be able to manage his neurosis and live with it. The experience of 'Zerstückelung' must not be regarded as a product of Asiatic culture in general, but as a universal human possibility of psychic experience and structure. Contemplation of one's own skeleton is not only found in Asia and with the Eskimo,[232] the Australian observations referred to also clearly postulate this consciousness of self. Furthermore, it is known to the author that a psychologist, unacquainted with these conceptions, when carrying out experiments with LSD distinctly and clearly experienced the 'Zerstückelung' of his mind while he remained conscious of it. The imagery of the flesh cut into pieces and the skeleton left over may rest upon an old cultural tradition, they express a fear which one might call a structural fear of the human psyche. Threatened by loss of consciousness (= loss of control) the mind feels the ego, body and soul, falling apart and flees to the only and ultimate point of refuge: the Self, the excentric centre. If this position cannot be maintained total disorganisation and insanity threaten.[233]

This subject was treated at some length, because it is not without importance in connection with the Terrifying Ones of Tibet. For these fundamental experiences form the basis of one of Tibet's most impressive creations, Chöd (gCod). The threat of falling apart into Nothing is a menace of death, and it is well-known that aggressive reactions may easily follow upon this fear. We shall meet with this aggression not only in Chöd, but even in the highest spheres of Tibetan mysticism. Characteristically enough, the sphere of shamanism is also marked by fear, even explicit fear of death and by aggressivity. At the birth of a shaman already 'the evil spirits multiply'.[234] If he really becomes a shaman, that will cost the life of several members of the tribe, not infrequently his relations, for 'elected shamans must have water from the river of death'.[235] At his vocation, the shaman in fact concludes a pact with the devil, in order to obtain power against the devil. The pieces of his body belong to the evil spirits and are their property.[236] It is typical that the infernal spirits who cut him up and devour him, are often the spirits of dead shamans![237] The shaman becomes a devil himself: 'The shaman's spirit interrupts and blocks the road by which he is threatened with evil, with dead people'.[238] In this way the connection between fear, identification and aggressivity is explicitly formulated. When the shaman must do his work for the community, it is not rare for him to become a bellowing, potentially death-dealing and destructive bull.[239] The greater part of his life is a battle. The shamans of the Eskimo, too, made for their great goddess to engage her in combat. There is one remarkable exception. In an obviously *sexual* rite the shaman goes to the female Spirit of Earth, to *ask* her for the sexual urge, the fertility of man and cattle. It is only permissible for shamans who have *no malignant or blood-thirsty spirit helpers* to carry out this rite.[240] The Yakut had a better understanding of the fact that sexuality (love) excludes aggressivity (hate) than many Tibetan magicians and yogins.[241]

The Tibetan shamans, who had a specific skeleton-soul, afforded clear evidence of the aggressive aspect of shamanism, for they were considered capable of cutting open their own bellies and taking out the entrails. The shaman's role as guide of the dead was afterwards taken up in Tibet by the Buddhist lamas, but the people insisted that priests of the Bon should be present, that is representatives of the ancient shamanism. The oracular function of the shaman – an essential part of his work, that he is found exercising as far as the Eskimo of East-Greenland[242] – proved so important that shamanistic oracles were given a recognised place in Tibetan Buddhism, and the great 5th Dalai Lama even instituted a state oracle. The séances of these oracles, carefully observed, described and photographed by De Nebesky-Wojkowitz, are very impressive. When 'possessed' by a Terrifying Deity, they not only identified themselves inwardly with these gods, but also outwardly.[243] They were then able to bend a hard iron sword in half with their bare hands, as that author himself has seen and checked, so that one might at last say a Tibetan mystery had been verified!

Finally, there is a Tibetan variation of the shaman showing how the marginal figures of shamanism and the 'mad monks' of Buddhism might easily be associated, in spite of the gulf that generally divided them. We mean the bard, the singer of the so martial and cruel epic of Gesar, who had to go into a trance before beginning his recital, and made use of the same technique as the shamans.[244] These bards were musicians, poets, dancers, acrobats, magicians, mediums and often *smyon pa* too, madmen, excentrics.[245] These poets and merry-andrews of the Tibetan people, like the oracles, preserved a part of the ancient Tibetan shamanism, which they also linked with the mad monk. In the figure of Mi-la re-pa, to whom we shall return, these two components found a classical synthesis, as fascinating as it was characteristic of Tibet's spirituality.

It should be noted, that in this chapter repeated mention was made of the national religion, as if this were a homogeneous whole. This was in so far correct as it referred to the religion of the petty kingdoms and afterwards of the kingdom, in which the religions of agriculturalists and nomads undoubtedly influenced each other and interpenetrated, with the royal cult as a kind of centre. Of the details, very little is yet known. It may be said in general, however, that there are many indications of a great influence of the dominant nomad herdsmen, a matter mentioned before and to which we shall return. The *sa-bdag*, the lords of the earth and especially of the mountains, generally considered typically Tibetan, are an example in point. Snellgrove discovered that in the central provinces these deities were only given their generic name in the ritual and not addressed by a personal name, from which he concludes that the *sa-bdag* were imported into Ù and Tsang.[246] One might go a step further and suppose that they were imported from the areas of the nomad herdsmen by the Tibetan kings. For in those regions the role of these gods is as central as it is vital. Not infrequently, too, they are associated with the ancestors. It is understandable that in their new country the Tibetan kings did not want to be without these gods, but that the farmers of the centre only regarded the new-comers as a group, never as individuals. Meanwhile, it does not seem likely that this amalgamation went smoothly, for in the religious sphere too the contrast between farmers and nomads must have made itself felt. There are clear indications of this in an old text. It is an expiatory hymn of the Bon po, but the content refers if not to the period before the Bon, at any rate to the time of transition. The hymn states that the sons of Skos make the land arable to cultivate it, break stones to build strongholds and cut down trees to burn wood fires, with the result that the spirits of the earth, springs, stones and trees are angered and send sickness. Another text describes how the divine beings are incensed by the breaking of stones, the mowing of grass, the digging up of the earth, the cutting of irrigation channels and the laying out of cemeteries. Among the things required for appeasing the irate deities are cattle-horns (!).[247] The first text may be supposed to cover the indignation of nomad herdsmen, who reproach some of their fellows with preferring the settled existence of rulers living in a stronghold in agrarian country to the mobility of a nomad principality. In the second text it rather looks as if the reproach were directed against farmers, or against herdsmen comporting themselves in a yet more anomalous manner, even mowing grass, cutting irrigation channels and laying out cemeteries – occupations that are all repugnant to a true nomad. The Indians of the North-American prairie may be cited here; they too laid their dead by themselves on a height (in their case an artificial elevation), and they also refused to till the land because they would not wound the earth. Apart from other diversity, the attitude of nomad pastoralists and farmers towards the earth is fundamentally different. For the herdsmen, there is in the first place the God of the heavens, and then there is the earth on which they wander from pasture to pasture, owned by the Lords of Earth – often ancestors – who are benevolent as long as their territory is not violated, for then they are as aggressive as nomad herders when attacked. Their dead, whom they fear, are left on a high place in the wide, open spaces while they go on their way. For the farmers, their settled existence begins and ends with the earth from which food comes forth, and in which they bury their dead, who form a community with the living. These are the differences one feels behind the texts referred to above, and they render it probable that religious conflicts and revolutions had already taken place before the coming of Buddhism, and that also in Ü and Tsang farmers and herdsmen reacted differently to the religion from India. There is still much to be done in this field of Tibetan culture and religion, but it already seems necessary to take account of these differences. There is a word in the Tibetan language, *ya-ma-zuṅ*, that means not-matching, and that is used of shoes, customs, languages and religions. The word is symptomatic of Tibet's dualist culture, and already before the coming of Buddhism it is applicable to the two contrasted groups composing the population. One may safely assume, though, that the two different religions would have managed to come to terms after a time, if Buddhism had not arrived on the scene. In history, such cases have always resulted in some form of syncretism. The contrast between nomad herdsmen and agriculturalists was considerably smaller than the gulf that separated the Tibetans from Buddhism.

Tibet then, as it was faced with tantric Buddhism in the beginning of the time of the kings, was a country of nomad herdsmen, agriculturalists, shamans and Bon priests. It was a country that had barely emerged from the stage we call primitive, and it was called barbarian by the inhabitants of its highly developed neighbours, such as China and India, just because its emergence was so recent. Barbarian may be said of the members of those societies which have worked themselves up to some extent by physical force and can neither be called primitive nor civilised. Their force and their numbers deprive them of the mental balance, social integration and religious profundity that may be attained by primitive peoples, as the North-American pueblo farmers and the Pawnee aggressors, the Australian food-gatherers and the Polynesian aristocrats can witness. Yet their force and their number do not make them civilised in the narrower sense of the word. Obviously the Tibetan king who sent for Buddhist missionaries was well aware of this. Through his decision the Tibet of nomad herdsmen with their mountain gods and Lords of the Tent, of farmers with anti-hail magic and water-sprites, of Bon po with their hecatombs and shamans with their trances, was set face to face with the Vajrayāna of yogins with their female assistants, the mudrās, of exorcists who also made magic, but in the name of Voidness, of monks for whom the killing even of animals was a capital sin, of artists with their images and paintings, of people with books and books full of endless reasoning to show the world did not really exist. Proud, barbarian conquerors opposite no less proud and haughty yogins. They had to clash.

THE CLASH OF CULTURES

Of course the matter was not, let it be repeated, simply the confrontation of a religion and a barbarous culture. Religions cannot just be detached from the cultures they are embedded in. If they are taken to another country, a large part of that culture is taken too, both material and immaterial. And indeed, the coming of Buddhism to Tibet was anything but an affair of high-toned sentiments and deep religious conversions. A later Buddhist historian certainly tried to portray it as such, when he let a king, whom we know from more realistic data to have been a powerful ruler and a great politician, say with almost a sigh to Padmasambhava and the abbot of Sam-ye (bSam-yas): 'Je pris le règne et la misère militaire'.[248] But another Buddhist historian with the same tendency to keep Tibetan history in higher spheres, unwittingly slipped up and betrayed something of the political reality. He wrote: 'As at that time the Tibetan subjects were disregarding the royal power, the king introduced laws harmonizing with the ten virtues and converted the Tibetans to Buddhism'.[249] Apparently the ruler could make good use of Buddhism with an eye to subjects who had too little respect for the royal power, and was himself the converting missionary. It is clear that this conversion did not come of its own accord, and was not entirely a matter of gentle persuasion. A characteristic example from a different period of the time of the kings conveys something of the prevailing mentality and atmosphere. In the time of Räl-pa-cen (Trshi-tsuk-de-sten), whose grandfather had been poisoned by his own mother, the anti-Buddhist nationalists spread the rumour that his wife, the queen, maintained illicit relations with a lama. Whether it were true or not, this scandalmongering had typical results. The lama was murdered, the queen committed suicide, and finally the king himself was murdered.[250] After these introductory remarks, it seems desirable to give a short chronological survey of the history of the kings.

It is in the Chinese chronicles of the Tang dynasty, that Tibet first appears in the searchlight of history,[251] and from then on Buddhist historians direct this light upon Tibet when Buddhist kings appear there. As to the events before that time, the argument is plainly stated: they did nothing for the Doctrine, so I will not write about them. This also applies, then, to king Nam-ri-song-tsen, who made Tibet a powerful state around the beginning of the 7th century of our era. The Tibetan word for king, rgyal po, does not like the Latin rex mean ruler, but conqueror. That is the right title for the king of a state by conquest, who had nomad blood in his veins. To the other members of the nobility he gave posts in the government, tax-free land and privileges, and dependents.[252] Apparently he himself was satisfied with his power, the prestige of the cult of royalty and the prospect of a grand, royal funeral with hecatombs of horses. His son Song-tsen-gam-po (620–650), however, sought prestige deriving its glamour from the exotic. A new religion would set him in a separate class from the nobility as an innovator, and would otherwise also have practical advantages. He married a Chinese and a Nepalese wife. From the stories it is clear that both countries regarded him as a barbarian, but as a powerful barbarian. In the history of acculturation women have always played a special part. The Navaho conquerors adopted half the Pueblo culture from their Pueblo wives, according to their own view. We see the same thing in Tibet, though the king's own struggle for high life was already great enough. He had a Tibetan alphabet made after the Indian example, had Buddhist texts sent from China and founded a few Buddhist temples (not monasteries). Culture was clearly his first concern, but in such cases culture and religion cannot be separated.[253] Other novelties came from China too, like textiles, metals, tea, the new technique of weaving, and courtly manners.

The ministers and nobility kept quiet, but were on the look-out, as appears from the fact that at the king's death it was the prime minister who assumed power. He was succeeded not by a king, but by his own son, another prime minister. It took the great-grandson of the first Buddhist king, Dü-song, who then came to power, a long time to get rid of this strong man of Tibet, who had made the name of the Land of Snows feared among nomads and foreigners. When Dü-song died, he had been able to do little on his own. His son, Me-ak-tsom (Trhi-de-tsuk-tsen: 704–755), again built Buddhist temples and had texts fetched from China. It is remarkable, that he made an abortive attempt to establish contact with India. Possibly he had learnt to distrust the policy of the Chinese through his wife, who was Chinese herself. Her influence was very great, for at her request Buddhist monks who had fled from Khotan were admitted to Tibet. Something now occurred which in numerous cases of acculturation has determined a fierce conservative reaction. An epidemic broke out, which entailed great loss of life and was regarded here too as a punishment for the apostasy of the progressive party, sent by the incensed national gods.[254] The nobility reacted at once. Apparently it required little discussion for them to realise the danger of an incursion of foreigners who would strengthen the king's power, even if only from gratitude. The influence of the nobility was strong enough to force the king to withdraw the permission he had granted to the fugitive monks, so that they had to leave the country again. After what was said in the second chapter about the problem of the monks in Buddhism, it is clear that outside India too the monks were not seldom hated. The fact that Me-ak-tsom had monks at his court who were also concerned with affairs of state, made this hatred still fiercer in Tibet. The king was accordingly murdered in the end. Murder by poison or the armed hand probably played an even greater part in the history of the Tibetan kings than we are aware of.[255]

As the heir to the throne was a minor, prime ministers again took the reins, forceful personalities who kept firmly to a nationalistic course. Probably it was at this time that the Bon was brought up to date, i.e. written down, enlarged and embellished, that it might meet with Buddhism on a par instead of being its barbaric opponent. In face of the new culture of the royal house and its following, the nobility required to set up some equivalent, while naturally engaged in the same struggle for high life as the kings. When the heir to the throne had outgrown his minority, however, the nobility at last found they had met their match. Trhi-song-deu-tsen managed to carry out what his predecessors had begun, but not completed: the establishment of a strong kingship with the help of Buddhism. He was a great general and statesman, who concluded an alliance with the Arabs to cover his flank, and then occupied Ch'ang-an, the then Chinese capital, in 763. Typical of raiding nomads, and particularly of the Tibetans, was that he returned with his warriors to their snowy home land after a fortnight, having taught the Chinese a lesson. Tibet had become a kingdom that counted, and the struggle for power in Asia lasted for forty years.[256] In this situation, Trhi-song-deu-tsen was too much of a statesman not to be aware, that it would be better to import culture of the immaterial kind from the innocuous India, than from his rival, China. He therefore invited a Buddhist theologian from India to propagate Buddhism, to counter-balance the strong Chinese Buddhist influences. In order to be able to go through with this invitation, the king first, by means of a trick, had one of his most dangerous, nationalist ministers walled up alive in a tomb. The other nationalists were willing to concede a reluctant agreement that Śāntarakṣita should be invited, if they could be assured that he would not preach obscene doctrines. After putting him through his catechism, they gave in.[257] This clearly indicates that the yogins with their sexualist ideas and practices had already gained a not inconsiderable influence in Tibet, to which the nationalists offered vehement opposition. Yet even the 'sexually' harmless Śāntarakṣita remained a Buddhist, and the nobility did everything they could to make his life intolerable. In the end he was compelled to fly the country, and he advised the king to invite Padmasambhava, as a sorcerer likely to make more of an impression on the Tibetans.

Padmasambhava did indeed prove himself able to deal with the problem of the Buddhist mission. He defeated the Tibetans with their own weapons. When he had worsted the demons of the Land of Snows by means of his higher magic, the nationalists and their Bon were also defeated – to all appearances, and for the present at least. The crown of his work was the founding of the first Tibetan monastery, Sam-ye (bSam-yas), in 787. The king also invited twelve monks of the Hinayāna, however, either as a counter-balance to the rather coarse practices of Padma and his colleagues, or to reassure the nobility, so that Tibet might see there was other Buddhism in India than that of the Vajrayāna. In this period Tibetans were also ordained as monks. The quarrel between progressives and conservatives flared up again, when one of the tantric warlocks had apparently made himself so obnoxious the nobility took the opportunity of protest and resistance. They demanded the death of the improper foreigner. The contest was bitter. Instead of the Vairocana complained of, the king executed a beggar, but he was betrayed by his own wife. Possibly from political motives, to cut the grass from under the feet of the nationalists, he had taken only Tibetan wives, but this now proved to have its drawbacks also. The queen, his principal wife, discovered the

8 Kye-ba rdo-rje (Skt. Hevajra) yab-yum. Bronze, early 19th cent. A.D. h.: 8 1/4 in. (21 cm)

8

fraud and pilloried Buddhism in a meeting of ministers and other nationalists. 'What they call a *kapāla*, is actually a human skull, *basuta* are nothing but intestines, their bone trumpet is made of human bones' – in this style she unmasked the Vajrayāna, to conclude: 'that is not the religion, but the evil India has taught Tibet'.[258] As a wise diplomat, the king chose to compromise. He had two tombs prepared for himself, one in the Buddhist manner – a *stūpa* – and one according to the rules of the Bon, a *bang-so*.

Then the moment came when the king, who had never interrupted the translation of the Buddhist writings into Tibetan, was powerful enough to draw off the velvet glove of compromise. He could then demand that the Bon po should either become Buddhists, or ordinary tax-paying civilians, or go into exile. Many departed, others gave lip-service to Buddhism. The conflicts of acculturation had reached a climax in Tibet. People who have to profess that the killing of animals is a heavy sin, while in their own religion animal sacrifice had a central place, come to harbour a deep-seated grudge. The struggle between Voidness and 'what the senses teach us' seemed to have been decided by the royal power, but culture contact is not concerned with form, but with value. In the marginal areas the Bon retained a good deal of influence, while in the centre Buddhism was lord and master, at any rate in outward matters. But the political problem was solved, and that was the main thing for Trhi-song-deu-tsen. Besides, he had other problems to work out. Now that he had silenced his enemies at home, it was necessary to check the foreign infiltration. The Chinese influences were stronger than he cared for, and so he convoked an ecclesiastical council, a method of solving political problems not unknown in the history of Western Europe.

At the famous Council of Lhasa the Chinese quietism was forbidden, and thus the Chinese infiltration and undermining tactics were countered in as subtle a fashion as they were carried out. The equally circumstantial and authoritative work of Demiéville renders this surprisingly acceptable. The Council was to decide who were right: the Chinese Buddhists who taught that salvation was best reached by abstaining from all activity, in so far as one could, or the Indian Buddhists, who made the active way of good works an indispensable condition of salvation. The Chinese lost, for there was a powerful ruler behind the council who, significantly enough, did not take the slightest interest in the differences between the magical sexualism of the followers of the Vajrayāna and the more orthodox representatives of the Hinayāna and the Mahāyāna, simply because it was a purely theological and internal difference of opinion. On the other hand he took a very great interest in the intentions of the Chinese, whose innocent-seeming quietism was undermining the military spirit and political resistance of Tibet.[259] The 'partie sinophobe à la Cour du Tibet' was not mistaken; the well-behaved, friendly gentlemen from China were preaching military non-violence together with their quietism – Demiéville's book gives rise to unpleasant sensations at the thought of our own times. The 'arrogance, mêlée d'une certaine crainte rusée' (Demiéville) of the Chinese, who were really prisoners of war allowed freedom of movement in Tibet, showed in peculiar habits. They would pray to the Buddha in full hearing of the Tibetan generals and other high-ranking officers, laying insinuating stress in their prayer on the way the great Teacher had forbidden to make war, 'humiliant devant le Buddha leurs maîtres tibétains'! Tibet's great king, under whose rule Tibetan power at home and abroad reached its height, gave proof of clear judgment when he convened the council and had the Chinese teaching condemned. It was not his fault that quietist notions had already penetrated and retained their influence, as Tucci says. The ideological offensive as such had been beaten off.

The tensions of acculturation, however, cannot be dissolved by military and political means. On the contrary, 'the military' and politics only intensify aggressivity, thus making the disintegrating tensions even worse. In people's consciousness and subconsciousness they continue to exist for a very, very long time. The successor of the great king had to pay the reckoning. He was no potent figure, so he was promptly murdered within the year, after he had three times attempted to introduce equal property (in land holding).[260] From a military and political point of view disaster came over Tibet. Kings came to the throne who took Buddhism seriously, and really wished to lead a devout life. It must be recognised that religion and matters of the spirit may be autonomous factors in history, even if one might hesitate with regard to the question, whether true piety and political leadership can go together. 'Wenn man die Bussübungen Ottos III als pathologisch bezeichnet, so qualifiziert man die Anschauungen einer ganzen Kulturperiode als pathologisch und gibt damit ein Werturteil zu Gunsten der eigenen Kriterien ab, wozu der Historiker nicht berechtigt ist', says Menno ter Braak of an altogether comparable instance in European history ('To call the penitential exercises of Otto the Third pathological, is to qualify the views of an entire cultural period as pathological, entailing a value judgement in favour of our own criteria which the historian has no right to give').[261] Only in Tibet there was a divided society, and the strong nationalist party had no use for all these novelties, but desired power for themselves and Tibet, not pious Buddhist practices. The next Tibetan king, Sä-na-lek (798–815), also did much good work on behalf of the religion from India. Like his predecessors, he promoted the work of translation, but he also had a learned committee normalise the terminology, so that in future there could be no doubt about the technical terms of Buddhism. This king abdicated the throne. A devout man? A tired man? A threatened man?

His son was completely unsuited to be a Tibetan king. He took Buddhism so seriously, that he not only slavishly adored the Doctrine, but also the monks. And we may be sure that these monks made the most of their chances, for many monks are politicians to whom power is sweet. Räl-pa-cen, as this bigoted monarch was called, must have been particularly orthodox, for there are indications that the texts translated under his rule were exclusively those of the Hīnayāna.[262] Perhaps, therefore, one should not call him bigoted, but a victim of the Buddha's wretched mistake in coupling his asocial, but grandiose Doctrine with the exceptional social position of monks. However this may be, such a king, preoccupied by religion instead of reign, presented no danger to his enemies. Furious at the fact that a monk was the king's prime minister, they first managed, through scandal, to get the king's more realistic brother exiled and then used the customary tale of adultery to get another of his supporters out of the way. Thus isolated, he was murdered. He was succeeded by Lang-dar-ma, who was not a Buddhist. Marcelle Lalou writes, that this king instituted a day of prayer for the prosperity of Tibet, in which both Bon po and Buddhists were to take part. Did he feel that in the miserable division of Tibet unity was a first requirement? In any case, his attempt failed. The nationalists had at last got their chance, and they paid back in the same coin. The Buddhists suffered under a religious persecution one can easily, if reluctantly, imagine. This made a Buddhist monk take pity on the heathen king, who was amassing more and more evil karma. To do him a service, the monk murdered him in 842.

Lang-dar-ma was the last Tibetan king. In every state centralisation is a main problem, and this was most especially so in Tibet, with its river valleys separated by mountain ridges. The bloody religious struggles, betraying both a political and a cultural discord, had hollowed out the state and greatly strengthened the decentralising tendencies. Tibet fell apart into little, warring states, each ruled by a family of rank, perhaps with attachments to a monastery. A dark era of some 150 years began for Central Tibet, in which tradition relates that sexual Tantrism came to excesses and debauchery, and political misrule and despotism were not lacking. Social rebellion and revolts of the slaves were already mentioned. The monasteries, of which there were then far fewer than in the 11th and 12th centuries,[263] were continually gaining influence in their immediate neighbourhood, also in the social and political sphere. In Guge in western Tibet Buddhism found a new royal almsgiver, who succeeded in making this region flourishing in religion and politics in the beginning of the 11th century. Not the Vajrayāna, but the Mahāyāna was regarded here as the way of salvation, and the tantric practices were put in serious doubt. When it was found that in Central Tibet some enthusiastic idealists were engaged in purifying the degenerated Buddhism of monks and laymen and preaching the Doctrine anew, they were supported by Guge. The ruler of this region not only again advanced the translation of Buddhist writings from India, he also invited Atīśa, a leading theologian and mystic from the Buddhist university centre Vikramaśīla, who purified the Doctrine. The best way of interpreting this is, that he stressed the Hīnayāna and particularly the Mahāyāna as the basis of practical religion and monastic discipline and that in texts[264] and ritual of the Vajrayāna he altered or deleted what might lead to abuse. He and others, who gave a mystical interpretation to the tantras, probably did not think of it that much of what remained, while having no sexual associations for them, might have them for others. Though one must indeed see the history of Tibetan Buddhism as a progressive purification of the tantric core, the tradition of the Tantric Path of sexual practices was preserved in Tibet, as will appear later. For people like Atīśa, however, the Vajrayāna with its sexual symbolism was a matter for meditation and contemplation.

After his sojourn in Guge, Atīśa went to Central Tibet where he gave strong support to the Tibetans already at work there, not without result. One might say that as Trhi-song-deu-tsen gave Buddhism a political basis, so Atīśa gave it a spiritual one, so that Tibet did not become a complete chaos of magical and sexualised superstition. This so-called second spreading of the Doctrine forms a curious episode in Tibetan history, proving that individual and spiritual factors may not be neglected in history when they are at work. Yet one would rather like to know the political and social background of this matter, which the Buddhist historians do not give us. It is known that Buddhism came to an end in India towards the end of the twelfth century, owing to the Mohammedan invasions. This meant that Tibet no longer had a teacher, a *guru*.

Typically enough, it was then that the orders or sects originated in Tibet. Apart from the Old School, the Nying-ma-pa (*rÑing-ma-pa*), who were, and to a great extent remained, the spiritual descendants of the exorcist Padmasambhava and his colleagues, a number of sects arose, that after the reformation of the Yellow Caps were called the semi-reformed orders. The Ka-dam-pa (*bKa'-gdams-pa*) maintained the high traditions of Atīśa, the Ka-gyü-pa (*bKa'-rgyud-pa*) practised yoga, at first in the magical, afterwards more and more in the mystic sense. To this order belonged the famous Mi-la re-pa. Nor must the Sa-kya-pa (*Sa-skya-pa*) be forgotten, whose order dated already from the time of Atīśa. Hevajra was their tutelar deity, and in view of what was said of the Hevajra tantra in a previous chapter, it will cause no surprise that magic had an important place in their order. All the same, numerous scholars were also found among them. Their main significance, however, was in the political field. Ever since the founding of Sam-ye the Tibetan monasteries had always been landowners and, especially in stirring times, this factor easily brought them into politics, while the aspirations of the monks themselves are not to be neglected either, as may be seen from the following. The abbots of the Sa-kya-pa were married. The son succeeded his father. When in the 13th century the Mongols were a formidable power, it was an abbot of this order who submitted to them, on the understanding that in future the Sa-kya abbots were to rule the whole of Tibet under the supervision of the Mongol emperors. It is clear that in a country where political power accrued more and more to monasteries, while the problem of decentralisation rendered it helpless against strong foreign powers, such a solution of the political problem was unavoidable as soon as a strong enemy approached. If one order had not done it, another would have offered its 'services'. They desired power, but their power in actual fact was only sufficient to decide the conflicts between monastery and monastery or statelet and statelet by force of arms.

From a Buddhist point of view, the situation was not exactly improved. A country ruled by the head of a church – the Sa-kya abbots may reasonably be considered the forerunners of the Dalai Lamas – is confronted with a queer medley of religion and politics. Obviously, the other orders were not always prepared simply to accept the sway of the Sa-kya-pa, and when the chance of Mongol reprisals seemed small, they did not restrict themselves to oral protests. In Tucci's monumental *Tibetan Painted Scrolls* there is fascinating information about this period. In principle, these troubled times ended in 1357, the year that Tsong-kha-pa was born. He is the great reformer from A-mdo, a region of nomad herdsmen and of farmers who admired the pastoral nomads. His great pertinacity enabled him to carry out his ideal: the return to as pure a form of Buddhism as possible. This did not mean the Vajrayāna was jettisoned. That was not possible, if only because then he might just as well have jettisoned Tibetan Buddhism altogether. Tsong-kha-pa really continued the purifying of Atīśa, the

effect of which had begun to pale, except perhaps in the order of the Ka-dam-pa. These he seems to have pretty well captivated, to serve as a point of vantage for the organisation of his purificatory undertakings. His followers were constrained to celibacy, and he let them wear – 'en fin psychologue' says Marcelle Lalou – a yellow cap, to distinguish them from the non-reformed and semi-reformed orders. These two, whose members were married, are indeed always bracketed together and referred to as the Red Caps. The number of Tsong-kha-pa's Yellow Caps was at first small, but he persevered. Besides being a great scholar, he seems also to have been rather a pedant. He cleansed the tantras and formulated strict conditions for their mystic use, he carefully ordered the daily routine of his monks, and prescribed them a way of salvation going from degree to degree according to the old Buddhist principles. He also took to heart the salvation of the common people, and wrote a separate catechism for the laity.

His interest in the people is a point worth studying more closely. It is questionable, whether Tsong-kha-pa's love for the common people was disinterested. The rise of his order is due to the favour of the people,[265] who must have been tired of the eating, fighting, marrying, tax-gathering and psalm-singing Red Caps, and probably thought that if monks were unavoidable, they would rather have monks who at any rate in one point proved themselves different from common men. If Tsong-kha-pa did not aim at worldly power, yet the foundation and extension of his order was not the work of a religious enthusiast, but of a tenacious organiser. Thoroughly acquainted as he was with old and new Buddhist writings, he knew how greatly the monks needed the people in general, and how dependent his attempt at reform in particular was upon the support of the Tibetan people. His pastoral interest in the people was coupled with the thesis, that the monks were the leaders of the people. He particularly appointed that before taking refuge with the Buddha, the Doctrine and the Community, according to the time-honoured Buddhist formula, laymen were to say: 'I go for refuge to the Lama'.[266] As the reformer did not break with the land-owning and tax-raising of the monasteries, it is a fair conclusion that he ultimately laid the foundation for the rule of his later successors, the Dalai Lamas. Under the earliest Dalai Lamas the order of the Yellow Caps continually increased, acquiring more monasteries, more property, more power. When the fifth in order, called the 'great Fifth' (1617–1682), obtained that power from the Mongols the Sa-kya abbot had once been entrusted with, the struggle with the Red Caps may be said to be decided in favour of the Yellow Caps. The ecclesiastical ruler was made the Tibetan representative of Gusjri Khan, a mongol conqueror, who in 1642 succeeded in establishing a Mongolian-Tibetan kingdom that included A-mdo, Kham and the regions around the Kuku nor, and of which Lhasa was the centre.[267] After the death of Gusjri Khan his kingdom fell apart, and the Dalai Lamas were able to rule their ecclesiastical state, sometimes more, sometimes less dependent on foreign countries.

The great Fifth was a considerable politician and diplomat. He deliberately dropped the purity of the Doctrine, which had been the pride of the Yellow Caps, and re-admitted all kinds of banned elements, to take the wind out of the sails of the Red Caps, and probably also to bind the people still more to his régime. As god-and-king – he was the incarnation of Avalokiteśvara – he had the same problems as the earlier kings, and the main one was centralisation. The kings had had to reckon with ministers and other members of the nobility, and with the possible defection of small potentates in the marginal areas; the Dalai Lamas had to reckon with the other orders and with the power of great monasteries that had their own soldiers. After a strict and intolerant persecution of the Red Caps, the great Fifth not only restrained his anger at the right moment, but also took measures of a conciliatory and politically centralising character. The New Year festival, already discussed in the present volume, is his creation, and it is patent that this stateman gave the festival a form in which the national feelings of the Tibetan people could find full expression. In other religious matters also he admitted ideas and customs of the Red Caps into the Yellow Church, as remarked above, thus coming closer to the people. For instance, he took a positive view of the shamanistic oracles, and even instituted an oracle of state, entitled defender of the faith. On the other hand he obliged the offended nobility by founding special, rich monasteries, where the leading positions were reserved for nobles. The ultimate end of all these measures was, of course, to strengthen the position of the Dalai Lama and to consolidate the theocracy. It was also the fifth Dalai Lama who instituted the game of dice played by the scapegoat, whose loss was a foregone conclusion! Not only did he consolidate, however; the builder of the Potala, the proud, fortified palace of the Dalai Lamas, also managed to extend the power of lamaist Lhasa. In this respect it was no fortuitous symbolism that he had the Potala built over the royal mountain, where formerly the strongholds of Tibet's great kings had stood, and which still bore the ruins of the last royal palace. The great Fifth was out to conquer, as Tibet's great king had been. Mention must be made here of the conquest of the eastern territories by the Yellow Church, by founding monasteries there. Bon po and Red Caps were not unknown here, especially after the former had been persecuted in the time of the kings and the latter by the great Fifth. But now the influence of the Yellow Church was considerably augmented in these regions and, though the matter requires closer investigation, the impression remains that this particularly concerned the nomad herdsmen. If this is really so, it would be an interesting correlation in view of the fact, that the Red Caps have taken almost exclusive possession of the more southern Himalayan states, such as Buthan, Sikkim and Nepal, which were agricultural.[268] The result of the other religious conquests of Lamaism under the fifth Dalai Lama was such, that Schulemann could write of his declining years: 'Vor wenigen Jahrzehnten noch flüchtig, bedrängt und den Untergang der Gründung des Reformators Tsong-khapa besorgend, erblickte er jetzt von seinem nahezu vollendeten Potala herab, wie mit dem äusseren Auge die Stadt Lhasa, ihre funkelnden Tempeldächer und den Kranz der strahlenden Klöster an den Berghängen ringsum, so in geistiger Schau, weite Gebiete Asiens der Gelben Kirche huldigend, Länderstrecken so ausgedehnt wie ganz Europa. Von den Ufern der Wolga und des Amur, aus den abflusslosen Steppen Innerasiens, von allen Nomadenfürsten, aus Peking der Kaiserstadt, aus den oberen Flusstälern der hinterindischen Ströme und den Himālaya-Ländern kamen Nachrichten vom

Blühen der Lama-Lehre, kamen Pilgerzüge, Gesandtschaften mit Geschenken oder wurde er als Schiedsrichter und Vermittler angerufen.' ('Only a few decades ago still oppressed and a fugitive, fearing the downfall of the Reformed Establishment left by Tsong-kha-pa, he now looked down from his almost finished Potala, beholding outwardly the town of Lhasa with its glittering temple roofs and the circle of shining monasteries on the mountain sides all around, and with the inner eye great tracts of Asia honouring the Yellow Church, stretches of country as extensive as all Europe. From the banks of the Wolga and the Amur, from the unwatered steppes of Inner Asia, from all the nomad princes, from Peking the imperial city, from the upper valleys of the rivers of Further India and the Himalayan countries came reports of the flourishing of the Lamaist Doctrine, came pilgrimages and embassies with gifts, or requests to act as arbitrator and intermediary.') Notwithstanding all this, it must not be forgotten that in one particular, but most important respect this dominion was a giant with feet of clay, for it had no army of any significance. Nevertheless the high regard in which the great Fifth was held even abroad as the god-king of Tibet, was of the greatest importance for his home policy. At first a cruel and pitiless ruler, then a calculating states-man, whose political insight was equally subtle and far-seeing, he spent the last years of his life in strict asceticism and meditation, completely indifferent to the world without, which had once roused his passions to such an extent that he not only occasioned the murder of political opponents, but also of his mother. What did *he* think of karma? This curious Tibetan, great in the context of his culture, died in perfect quiet. The soundness of his political views became apparent under the régime of his successor, a not unattractive libertine, fond of wine, women and poetry. According to Hoffmann he was to all probability a tool in the hands of the Red Caps, who in this way were trying to break the power of the Yellow Caps, as it were from within. When he listened to his religious teachers, their expositions of mental discipline faded from his mind, and his thoughts wandered to a beloved woman. He was a god in the unique royal stronghold of the Dalai Lamas, the Potala, but he lived alone there. And when he became painfully aware of his human loneliness, he sought the company at night of the wantons of the town. Between god and man, this Dalai Lama tried to find a solution in the religious sexual practices of the Red Caps, who made use of his compromise in their struggle against the Yellow Caps, on whom the Chinese had built their power in Tibet.[269] Tantric sexual rituals were again celebrated in Lhasa. The Chinese solved the difficulty of a renewed division in Tibet by having the 6th Dalai Lama murdered. They continued to pull the strings, with some interruptions, until a few years ago they definitely established their power by means of a so-called war of liberation, and annexed Tibet. In the twentieth century the same principle is still valid for the intercourse between peoples in which the first Tibetan kings believed implicitly: military power. This, then, is the history of Tibet: acculturation, war, conflict and aggressivity.

It was already remarked that by introducing Buddhism the kings initiated a process of acculturation. This may be very well compared to what happened on Hawaii in the Pacific when Christianity was brought there.[270] It is true that there the missionaries of the new religion were not invited by the ruler, but in Hawaii too the royal family soon became a factor of the same kind as in Tibet. Here again the king promoted the new religion to raise his status, while at first there was no foreign power in occupation. We find the same phenomena as in Tibet. The people at first clung to the old religion. The royal family and part of the nobility was christian, while the rest of the nobility remained true to the old religion. Yet both progressives and conservatives, feeling their own culture to be inferior, adopted many Western elements, so that the whole civilisation of Hawaii changed its character. This did not diminish the conflict between the two parties and, as in Tibet, it was determined by force of arms. The new culture and religion kept pushing forward. In Hawaii missionaries functioned as the king's prime minister, as they did in Tibet, and in both cases the spiritual leaders intended a kind of theocracy. The result in both cases was the undoing of the old culture. Other points of resemblance could be enumerated. The comparison is only intended, however, to point to the general laws governing the process of acculturation. The fact that in Tibet a religion of a fairly sexual trend was grafted upon a far more puritan culture, whereas in Hawaii a puritan religion was brought to a strongly erotic culture, in no way impairs the structural resemblance.

Acculturation is always characterised by reinterpretation. Objects and ideas are taken over from the strange culture, but derive their meaning from the context of the old culture in which they are now placed. Or again, indigenous elements of culture are given a new meaning in the context of the new, strange culture. Roman Catholic saints, for instance, are adopted but regarded as a new kind of ancestor (Madagascar) or as new gods (Haiti). And missionaries take over indigenous religious concepts or musical instruments and give them a place in their preaching and divine worship. In his magisterial work upon the epic of Gesar – a gold mine of information and discoveries for Tibetan acculturation, only small use of which could be made for the present work – Stein gives many fine examples of re-interpretation in Tibet. He particularly stresses the conscious reinterpretation and assimila-tion of Tibetan conceptions by the Indian and Tibetan buddhists. Especially Mi-la re-pa and other Ka-gyü-pa played a great part in this. Mi-la re-pa's detailed 'translation' of a Bon ritual is well-known. It is deserving of mention that particularly the Ka-gyü-pa sought close contact with the people, with whom they felt a sense of solidarity both in their social criticism of the nobility and clergy and in their religious dances and jokes. Inevitably, un-conscious reinterpretation of Buddhist concepts by the people – an unavoidable concomitant of culture contact – also played a great part in Tibet. As an example we may take the god of the dead, Yama, *gŚin-rje*, who will be discussed at length in the final chapter, and who in Tibet split up into numerous *gŚin-rje* such as the people had formerly known. Altogether it should be observed that conscious assimilation of old values by the missionaries is only possible because the people unconsciously hold to the old and cannot accept the new un-alloyed. Besides, as Stein very justly remarks, it was true of the Buddhists that 'ils étaient après tout eux-mêmes Tibétains'. Only through two-sided reinterpretation can a more or less integrated new culture originate, a composition of the old and the new together.

In Tibet the first king had already increased his prestige, after the example of his local predecessors, by means of the royal cult. This seems to have been kept alive by the people, and the Dalai Lamas continued the tradition.[271] But the Tibetan kings desired more. For their state and for themselves they wanted the lustre emitted by the great powers outside their borders. To that end were new materials, metals, tools, techniques, etiquette, writing and religion imported. As we have seen, other motives must also have carried some weight, but this desire for the raising of status is of primary importance, also because in the end, as history has proved, it was shared by a great part of the king's subjects, as soon as they came into contact with the superior culture and had an opportunity of adopting some part of it.[272] People who feel inferior always try to compensate this feeling, usually by becoming superior themselves also, either objectively or subjectively, actually or symbolically. If anything stands out clearly from the small number of Tibetan writings that have been translated, it is the Tibetan sense of inferiority. It is found again and again in different forms. Typical is the tale of the Tibetan children who keep making mistakes in the language lesson, pronouncing the words wrongly and giving the wrong translation, to the great hilarity of their teachers from India and to the despair of the first Buddhist king, who bewails 'ce Tibet barbare, terre obscure où la Loi manque'.[273] The hagiography of Padmasambhava, in which this story is related, contains other passages so vividly described, that they seem to be historical reminiscences. Yet even should this impression be quite mistaken, these passages remain typical of the Tibetan sense of inferiority in general. People in the underdeveloped Land of Snows were afraid of the far, strange world of India. When some youths were to be sent to India to learn culture there and bring it back home, their parents did not dare to let them go. They feared the terrors of the journey, 'il y avait la fièvre de l'Inde, le mal de l'eau, la grande jaunisse', and they bribed the king's messengers or fled.[274] One young Tibetan who did go to India afterwards, returned to Tibet, according to the story because he was pleasure-loving. It may, however, have been homesickness and misery that drove him, when one reads the experiences of his colleague who stayed and persevered. He, Vairocana, asked by his master whether he was content, replied in the negative and lay down with his face upon the ground. He proved to be ill, ill because he did not understand what was taught him.[275] The whole reaction is extremely characteristic of a boy from an underdeveloped country, who simply cannot understand things in a strange land. When five Tibetan monks travelled to India to learn wisdom from the guru Hūṃkāra, they were received by him with the words: 'Voici mauvais démons du Tibet'.[276] They promptly fell to earth, asseverating that they were not evil spirits. Altogether it is remarkable, that just in this biography of the first Buddhist missionary Indians and Tibetans continually show themselves to be deeply conscious of the inferiority of the barbaric Tibetans. Padma himself was insultingly contemptuous in speaking to the great king of his barbaric country with its monstrous men and ugly women.[277]

It is not only in the life of Padma that Tibet is aware of its insufficiency. In the harvest plays, for instance, the monks every year impressed upon the people what a barbarous country the Land of Snows had been before the coming of the Doctrine[278] (and of the monks, of course!). In the biography of Mar-pa, too, the Tibetans are spoken of in uncomplimentary fashion: 'They are just like oxen'.[279] Stein mentions a Buddhist chronicle, in which the foolish inhabitants of ancient Tibet are spoken of. One of the things adduced to show their foolishness is the fact, that they venerated the Sky, *i.e.* the Sky-god, who can in many respects be compared to the God of Genesis I.[280] Through the centuries, the Chinese have regarded them as barbarians, and made no secret of the matter.[281] The Japanese Kagawuchi was a Buddhist abbot who secretly travelled through Tibet, and in spite of his Japanese prejudice he managed to keep a detached mind. Yet he, too, repeatedly observes that Tibet was not exactly a refined country, that Lhasa was a 'metropolis of filth', and that even the most degenerate Japanese monk would be aghast at a figure like Padmasambhava, the very one to have been made something of Tibet's national religious hero![282] The Tibetans themselves felt the contempt of their neighbours. Their reactions were the same as those still seen among primitive peoples in their contact with the West. Sometimes they felt they were the most elect people on earth, and in their imagination let great Indian gurus bow respectfully in the direction of Tibet, as mentioned in the first chapter. Or they were industriously occupied in 'aping Buddhism' like primitives 'aping the white man'. This has remained a typical characteristic of Tibetan culture. Their exact, but quite slavish translations have been referred to. In their art, too, they were imitators. A connoisseur like Tucci leaves us in no doubt as to this, giving as an example that the Tibetan artists even put those Chinese land-scapes in their scroll paintings that had nothing in common with their own landscape.[283] But the foreign and superior was not only aped, it was also adored. Two things were extremely sacred in Tibet: *books* and *reading*. One cannot help thinking here of Hawaii, where two by no means stupid intellectuals blindly admired The Book.[284] In and outside the Tibetan monastery the mere carrying of a book was a sacred act, conferring religious merit. Books were far more sacred than images, for they came from India, *the* country of *the* religion.[285] For that reason long readings were regularly held – and irregularly in times of menace – from the sacred books, even if no one understood a word of them.[286] The Great Reading was a familiar rite.[287] One lama read the 108 volumes of the Kan-jur (bKa'-'gyor) the Tibetan canon, in about half a year for 50 ounces of silver.[288] These are only a few instances of slavish servitude to foreign books. The unconscious self-despisal resulting from this sense of inferiority, was curiously expressed by a dispute in which it was quite seriously debated whether it was permissible for Tibetans themselves to write commen-taries upon the holy scriptures from India.[289] It becomes comical, when a Tibetan with more self-respect and critical sense declares: 'Men born in Tibet have produced too many books on the Doctrine',[290] for the Tibetans had indeed started writing commentaries, and there was no end of them. The point is not, however, this remark which was based on sound judgment, but the continuation of the story, representing the remark as more or less blasphemous, and showing in the end how the man who made it came to a better insight. So Tibet did not write too many books in an attempt at 'aping India'.

92

It was upon the sense of inferiority of the unlicked and unlettered barbarians of Tibet, that the process of acculturation started by the introduction of Buddhism was in part founded. It is one of the universal elements in that process, as appears from comparative research, and is also found with ruling peoples. Therefore not only the Tibetan Buddhists were compelled to imitate Indian Buddhism, but also the Bon had to acquire cultured manners and link itself with the hateful, but superior religion. Their attitude towards books is not the only acculturative symptom here, but it is very typical. Just as the Hawaiian Kalakaua and numerous non-literate peoples, in their attempts either to adapt to or to resist the West, had an abysmal respect for books, so progressives and conservatives, Buddhists and Bon po, nobility and people of Tibet venerated the Book of India. This common trait should be kept in mind, because it is an indication that *all* members of a society which feels inferior, consciously or unconsciously try to adapt themselves to the superior culture with which they are confronted. They try to maintain their self-respect and their identity.

This by no means implies that all members of such a society react in the same way, although at first sight one might expect them to, because they all live according to the same culture pattern. In acculturation, however, a new element is brought in: the foreign culture. One might say that, strictly speaking, it is the separate concern of each individual whether he will accept or reject the foreign culture, or remain indifferent to it. Yet it is not possible to remain indifferent, because one's self-respect is at stake, so that one is forced to take action. Thus it becomes a choice of accepting or rejecting. Particularly in cases where the gap between the foreign culture and one's own is a wide one, both the positive and the negative reaction become charged with emotion. Obviously it is not a question of quietly weighing pros and cons, for tradition, faith and deep-lying values of life are at stake, those which consciously and unconsciously shape what we call identity: being one-self. A people who had lost their whole original culture and appeared, in prosperity, to have become entirely 'white', suddenly took up an old round game, to build up as it were a new-old culture with all its emotional associations around this core of identity.[291] Thus the question of acceptance and rejection leads to a deep conflict, and it is no wonder that acculturation almost without exception causes a social schism between progressives and conservatives. 'This social polarisation is understandable. Each individual attempts to solve the inner conflict aroused by the new situation by giving full stress to one of the two components, so that his life may again have a single sense instead of being divided in itself.'[292] A sober and calculating king or a simple man of the people are unavoidably touched by this inner conflict and forced to take sides. Naturally some individuals do so more keenly than others, but what matters from the social aspect is, that the conservatives and the progressives group themselves around two extremist centres. This contrast, that we consider normal in our own political life, is not taken for granted by cultural anthropology, but regarded as the result of new factors, of a change whose consequences continue to exert their influence for a long time, until the difference has become small enough to make it possible for the rules of democracy to come into play and be followed with true sportmanship.

This stage was never reached in Tibet. Even in recent times, relations between the Red Caps and Yellow Caps were acrimonious. All the same, the contrast changed its accent in the course of time. There are many examples of this with primitive peoples also. Seeing that history has only one-way traffic, as Nehru has said, no one can escape the influence of the new culture in its progress, yet the rift between conservatives and progressives remains. For instance, antagonism between pro-whites and anti-whites may change into the opposition between Roman Catholics and Protestants. In our day the father, who as a boy defended jazz against classical music towards *his* father, now rejects modern jazz, which is passionately defended by his son. Such a shift in values also took place in Tibet. One might suppose that at first the people remained outside this antithesis, but there is information showing that not even that was the case. The king was the intercessor for the people with the dangerous, demonic *bTsan*, so that the people, suddenly bereft of royal protection when the king turned Buddhist, became anti-buddhistic.[293] Yet, though we have no information on the point, it is extremely probable that also in Tibet he who paid the piper called the tune, so that the people in their way will have been divided as their masters were.

In the first phase a life-and-death struggle in the literal sense was carried on in Tibet between the Buddhists and the Bon po, in whose later writings the great national heroes of Tibet are still glorified.[294] But afterwards the acculturative contrast became that between the conservative Red Caps and the progressive Yellow Caps. At that time the latter no longer contested with the Bon po who, plus royalistes que le roi, had adopted just about everything of Buddhism with the negative sign, but with the detestable Red Caps, the archconservatives.[295] Later the once so anti-buddhist people adored the Buddhist Padmasambhava as a national hero,[296] while for the Buddhist Tsong-kha-pa he had been almost a personal enemy. Yet however the contrasts might change on the outside, the central point was and remained the conflict between old and new, between familiar and foreign. In the 17th century a little local ruler in an outlying district could still rebel, imprison all the monks and reinstate the Bon, so that the Dalai Lama had to call upon the help of the Chinese, who defeated the rebel for him.[297] Of this permanent resistance to foreign importation the Terrifying Gods became the living symbol, as will be discussed in full.

In culture contact there are naturally many strange things which for the sake of one's self-respect one may accept or reject. But as the gradation of individual acceptance and rejection culminates in a social schism, so the acculturative struggle not infrequently concentrates upon one particular element of culture, that becomes the symbol of the conflict. Although the historians of Tibet, more interested in theology than in history, do not give much information on this point either, it seems that in its first phase the acculturative quarrel centred upon the sexual practices of the tantric teachers. Naturally, one regularly finds sexual symbols and rites in agricultural societies, and so it would not be surprising if Tibet's protest against the dirty doings of the Buddhists contained a piece of nomad morality. However this may be, a large part of the Tibetan people did not see a religious value in the Tantric Path of sexual practices, but regarded it as an attack upon their own morals.

12 Magic dagger deity. Detail of a scroll painting with a Heruka mandala

12

13

Acculturation does not only mean a conflict of techniques and customs, but also of values. And there were fierce protests[298] against such moral de-valuation. The first time the Doctrine was spread, it was Padmasambhava and his colleagues who travelled around in the company of charming mudrās. Considering that around 800 the king had an adviser of this type,[299] one can imagine the indignation of the nationalist nobility. At the second spreading of the Doctrine, besides men like Atiśa, it was tantric masters like Mar-pa who made up the Buddhist mission. In his rituals he used various female assistants, and he was not ashamed to own that lust formed part of the mystic ecstasy.[300] In this way he obtained 'fame, happiness, clients and riches', as Bacot says.

From this it is evident that the modernists did not arouse opposition alone, but that they also found admirers and imitators among the Tibetans. On this essential point of culture too, opinions were polarised: either people turned away, revolted by these immoral practices, or they eagerly participated and, once the fences were down, even went a little further than the foreign teachers. In this connection the Japanese Buddhist Kagawuchi made a remarkable statement, which deserves consideration and verification. According to him the Tibetan tantras were not identical with the Indian ones, but surpassed them in obscenity.[301] This thesis conflicts with the painfully exact way the tantras were translated in Tibet, yet on the other hand it is hard to imagine this author making such a remark without any reason. In any case, there were commentaries in Tibet which took the tantras literally,[302] and the fact that later several texts in Lhasa were kept behind lock and key points in the same direction. The official Buddhist history of the church only admits, that in the dark ages after the time of the kings there were 'coarse practices of lay Tantrics'.[303] Even without prejudice and suspicion, one may take this with a grain of salt, if only because the layman is a convenient scapegoat in Buddhism. In the texts of the Old Style order there is a special term for tantric sexual activities,[304] and any person of common sense must see it is out of the question for the greater part of that order to have had full mastery of yoga, both in earlier and later times. As to the laymen – one can hardly assume that precisely in the dark ages a tantric laity originated. It is self-evident that before then there were also laymen who adhered to the Vajrayāna in theory and practice, possibly after industriously practising yoga for a fortnight. Though from obvious motives this part of history also has been covered with a heavy veil we can no longer raise, there is every reason to conclude from our scanty data that to the nationalists the Vajrayāna was a scandalous degeneration, to the progressives, monks and laymen, a new and not unpleasing religious exercise. This conclusion is based in part on the fact that the times were unsettled, that outward and inward conflicts had to be fought out, that many missionaries preached a doctrine which was not only extremely difficult for Tibetans, but also ambiguous, and that the Tibetans were of flesh and blood, in acceptance and in resistance. The main thing is, that the introduction of sexuality into the religion by strangers created a conflict of values.

An entirely different, but no less important contrast resulting from acculturation, was that between the centre and the marginal areas, more or less coinciding with the contrast between

13 *Charnel field with gods. Scroll painting. 37 × 23 5/8 in. (94 × 60 cm)*

town and country. When the first Tibetan king had succeeded in establishing his power, there can have been little difference between life at his court and in his realm, and life at the court and in the domain of his rivals, some of whom he had conquered, and some of whom he managed to keep outside his frontiers. There was, however, a contrast between the urban centre of this royal nomad herdsman in an agricultural area and the herdsmen outside it, mobile, individualistic and aggressive, who looked down with superior contempt upon settled existence, regarding it as just good enough to make unscrupulous raids on when there was a chance. Afterwards kings also succeeded in founding the state of Guge in the West of Tibet, but owing to various circumstances this realm was unable to maintain itself. Thus the main contrast in the Land of Snows remained that between the central agrarian provinces Ü (*dBus*) and Tsang (*gTsaṅ*) on the one hand and the regions of the nomad pastoralists, chiefly in the East and the North, on the other. It must not be forgotten that these barbarians had their own nomad principalities under strong leaders; in 1509 such a little nomad kingdom is still mentioned in the area of the Kuku nor, when it was conquered by the Mongol Ibula.[305] A contrast of this kind is to be found in every complex culture. 'Alle Hochkultur ist Stadtkultur' ('All highly developed civilisation is urban') says Rüstow, and once Lhasa had become a royal residence, it became the exponent of the centre in the face of what a Parisian calls the provincials, an inhabitant of Amsterdam 'the farmers', and a townsman of Lhasa the barbarians of the outlying provinces. In Tibet, however, this two-in-oneness had a special character. On the one hand it were the nomad herdsmen who had impressed their mark upon the agricultural area, and it is because of this one must call the Tibetan culture two-in-one. The time of the great kings, the time of war and conquest was never forgotten in Tibet, and when the Tibetans took delight in the heroic feats of the mythical Gesar, they were glorifying the royal nomads who had made Tibet great, intrepid and daring, hard and ruthless.

In the second place the contrast between the centre and the provinces was to a considerable extent determined by Buddhism. This was still expressed in recent times in the fact, already mentioned, that the monasteries outside the centre were called the monasteries in the barbarian regions. When the reformer Tsong-kha-pa preached his new and revolutionary ideas in Lhasa, the townsmen threw stones at him and contemptuously called him 'the long-nosed man from A-mdo'. And indeed, the Vajrayāna was propagated first, longest and most intensively in Ü and Tsang. In another connection we shall see, how at the consecration of a house in the pastoral area of A-mdo quite recently a national god was invoked, while on the same occasion in the centre a Buddhist deity was called upon. Altogether, a great deal of the old religion persisted, particularly in the region of the nomads, as Hermanns' study and the recently published work of Stein have shown us. Also in the field of social and moral values this contrast found expression. An example of this is the different appreciation of women. The ordinary word for woman in the central provinces is *skye-dman*, which means 'low-born', 'of contemptible descent'.[306] The nomad herdsmen's word for woman had a neutral, if not a more positive meaning, in accordance with the fact that various nomad

98

pastoralists, within the axiomatic patriarchal pattern, acknowledge and treat women as partners. An apparently trivial, but significant instance of this is the way a husband and wife in a nomad tent simply and unaffectedly kissed one another in the presence of a third person (Tafel, I, 273), showing a natural and realistic attitude towards sex. There can be little doubt that this contrast was to no small extent the work of the Yellow Caps, who with their celibacy also introduced in the centre the true Buddhist contempt for women. All the same it is a valuable indication how Buddhism increasingly determined the contrast between the centre and the provinces. In the list of contrasts already named – Bon and Buddhism, nobility and clergy, clergy and laity, rich and poor, etc. – which remain in need of a more differentiated sociological analysis, that between the centre and the provinces must not be forgotten; it was constitutive of the two-in-oneness of Tibet's population and culture pattern, and symptomatic of the influence of Buddhism. The reader who wishes to gain an impression of the gulf between 'agriculturalists' and 'nomad herdsmen' as it is expressed in almost every field from social organisation to character and outlook upon life, should read a book describing life in the centre – that of Das, for instance – immediately before one such as Ekvall has written about the life of the nomad herdsmen and robbers, lively, realistic, and informed with warm understanding.

The contrast between town and country had many other most interesting aspects. Of course there was a great difference between the luxury, refined manners and so on of the city and rural life. This comes to the fore very plainly in the autobiography of the brother of the present Dalai Lama, who not only finds Lhasa luxurious and sophisticated in comparison with the simple life in his native village in the mountains of the pastoral region, but also in comparison with life in the surely by no means uncivilised monastic town of Kumbum.[307] There is no objection to quoting from this contemporary book, for Norbu – like other Tibetans who have written about their country and themselves in a Western language – enlists the sympathy of all readers by the simple and matter-of-fact way in which he and his family obligingly comply with the demands of life in the city and at court, while treasuring in their heart the memory of A-mdo as the country of the simplest, and thereby greatest happiness.

This, too, is one of the many little things which make one curious what the result would be of a monograph treating the influence of the outlying districts upon the centre, not only in the political time of the kings, but also in the religious sphere in the following centuries. It might well be that nomad herdsmen and their descendants, whose disposition – as instanced by the kings of Guge and the Mongol Buddhists – is apparently not only aggressive and obstinate (Tsong-kha-pa!), but also spiritual, have had a purifying and stabilising influence in the Buddhist capital of the Land of Snows. In the nature of things, morals are looser in town. Even if one subtracts the factor of Kagawuchi's own Japanese attitude towards women from his information on this point, enough is left to make it worth while giving his opinion of the women of Lhasa, which deserves closer examination. In spite of their official status of 'low-born', they have their husbands under their thumb, this Japanese abbot tells us, and their general attitude is such, that he will not call them ladies, but would rather seek some word of a lighter kind.[308] What factual content there may be in such a remark may be explained first by the generally less strict morals of town, but chiefly by polyandry, which obviously gave women a certain power, which not a few will have made use of. Then one might also inquire, whether perhaps tantric traditions still played a part here. The Tantric Path of sexual practices was the first form of Buddhism to become known in Tibet, and it was in particular the centre, where this Path was preached and where afterwards 'coarse practices of lay tantrics' were found. The intrigues around the person of the 6th Dalai Lama also show, that at a much later time this path was still followed in Lhasa in a more or less spiritual form. If this supposition is correct, it points to a curious conflict of values which must have been active in Lhasa between tantric ideas and nomad morality, in which there was plenty of room for sexuality, but probably no place for the doublesided kind evinced by Buddhists who copulated, but not in an ordinary way, and who had mistresses of a superior kind called mudrā. However this may be, one can be rather more certain that the monks from the monasteries in the barbaric regions who were taken to Lhasa because they showed themselves possessed of a good understanding and a strong personality, must have looked with some surprise at the women of Lhasa whom Kagawuchi did not like to call ladies. Some may have come to rest in their arms, like the 6th Dalai Lama, who visited brothels and held orgies, and according to a tradition one would like to believe, found sublimation not in mysticism but in poetry. Others of the monks will undoubtedly have become better and firmer Buddhists in spite of and owing to the temptations. Here too the spirit was in opposition to what the sense taught. And in the intermediate region danced the Terrifying Ones, who – be it said in passing – after all this scientific objectivity make Tibet not mysterious, but very human and very appealing and admirable.

An element of culture directly related to the matters just discussed, that also resulted from acculturation and occasioned radical changes in Tibet, is begging and mendicancy. This too will have considerably increased under the rule of the Yellow Caps, but here again the principle lay in the foundation of Sam-ye. Buddhism introduced the mendicant monk, and the ultimate result was that a large part of the population of Tibet lived by begging. The beggars of Lhasa are notorious among travellers, but also outside Lhasa there was a swarm of begging monks and laymen. No doubt begging by the laity was much furthered by the heavy economic pressure exercised by the monasteries upon the laymen who did not belong to the nobility, to which we shall return in some detail. At the same time it is evident that one part of the population will the more readily take up such a means of livelihood if the other part has made an institution of it, and even invested it with religious value. In zoological gardens it is astonishing to see how those animals begin to beg, which one would not have expected to do so, once they understand they can get their living in this easy way. Many people think they lose a great deal of their animal dignity in this way, yet their behaviour is a sign of intelligence, for the typical, 'real' begging is only found with mammals.[309] One can indeed speak of a fundamental resemblance with human beggars, who have also been condemned by the upper levels of their society to a miserable existence like that in a zoo. Begging can also arise without a monastic state, but such a state is one of the socio-political forms of organisation particularly encouraging it, and Tibet is a striking example of this. In this context an observation of Rockhill is of great interest. He travelled for thousands of miles, chiefly through country of the nomad herdsmen, and he noticed that the further he came into parts under the direct rule of lamas, the more and the more impudent begging there was, both by high-placed and rich lamas and by the poor, while among the true nomad herdsmen there was no begging at all.[310] The remarks of this sober and clear-eyed observer are most pertinent and leave no room for doubt. On this point too more extensive research and more exact analysis is necessary, but in a general way one may speak of a correlation between monks and increasing mendicancy, while it is also clear there is a connection between nomad herdsmen and absence of mendicancy. The latter aspect is particularly interesting, because also the nomad pastoralist was only too human, and liked to get something for nothing. In that case, however, a nomad goes out to rob, not to beg, and it is fascinating to see how Tibet proves its duality in this point also, for the country is justly famed and almost notorious both for its beggars and its robbers. That rich monks beg and that whole tribes live almost entirely by brigandage, may be called characteristic of the Land of Snows, where the monks used the beggars to do good works, and where the robbers had their own gods, and not seldom used lamas to invoke a blessing upon their raids. In its meeting with Tibet Buddhism intensified old social contrasts here and gave them a negative aspect, and in the religious field it came to peculiar compromises, requiring as it did to make a virtue of necessity both with regard to beggars and robbers. In the same way, it made a virtue of necessity when it turned the national gods into devilish and dangerous defenders of the faith.

An important and equally general phenomenon in acculturation is the significant increase of black magic, of 'witchcraft'. It is difficult to find a single one of the primitive peoples who came into contact with the West, where black magic did not increase after the first contact.[311] The uncertainty resulting from the cleavage felt by the individuals and by society increases their fear, which is worked off in aggression upon scapegoats in their own society. Once solidarity is no longer taken for granted, people do not quite trust one another any more. One can, then, agree with Kluckhohn that asocial black magic provides the graduated scale by which the latent aggressivity of a society may be measured,[312] going up and down as the internal tensions swell or decrease. In the period of greatly increased tension in Tibet, when Das made his famous and notorious journey to Lhasa, black magic had greatly increased and witches were even officially punished.[313] In India the Vajrayāna of the outcasts was a hotbed of black magic for similar reasons. One may suppose it to have been no stranger to the turbulent Tibet of the time of the kings, before the coming of Buddhism, and when the two met witchcraft will surely have been greatly increased. There are no direct data, but plenty of indirect ones. The systematic scandal based on adultery and the no less systematic murders by poisoning border upon black magic from the psychological point of view. The fact that this magic became a national institution and was recognised as such, speaks volumes. From the biography of Mi-la re-pa, for instance, it appears that the Buddhists disapproved of black magic in theory, but that they made use of it all the same.[314] If asocial magic could not be a means of livelihood, it could at least be a lucrative side-line.

In concluding from the great importance of black magic that there was much latent aggressivity in Tibetan society, one is really only stating a truism. The whole cultural pattern of Tibet is taut and tense with open and latent aggressivity, as will be shown later by means of various instances. In general, we may begin by recalling Lalou's characteristic of 'le sang et le poison'. The naturally aggressive mentality of the nomad herdsmen was, of course, intensified in the state they had won, and the never ending dissensions and wars of Tibetan history, arising in part from ecological circumstances (problem of centralisation) and acculturative conflicts, were not conducive to lowering the level of aggressivity. First petty kings fought with one another, then Tibetan kings and their armies fought against foreign powers, while progressives and conservatives were at loggerheads at home, next local rulers fought against local rulers and monasteries against monasteries, then sects contended and finally the Yellow Caps oppressed and impoverished the Red Caps. Nor is this a complete list of the conflicts! In the religious field a form of Buddhism entered Tibet which was also loaded with aggressivity, as was set forth in a previous chapter. The aggressive results of the clash between this Buddhism and the Tibetan religion will be discussed in a following chapter. Finally, it must again be stressed that the existence of veiled or openly aggressive and anti-social magic as a social institution makes it only too plain that the comparative level of aggressivity in Tibet is not to be called normal, but definitely abnormally high. De Nebesky-Wojkowitz's book 'Where the gods are mountains' might also have been called 'Where monasteries are fortresses'.

A decisive and fundamental characteristic of Tibetan acculturation, not easily paralleled in ethnology, is the continual increase of the number of monasteries after the founding of Sam-ye and the almost unbridgeable gulf between monks and laymen which was its inherent concomitant in Tibet. In the Land of Snows the old Buddhist idea, that the monks formed an élite far above the people was not only maintained, but even expanded to such an extent, that the monks had a monopoly in nearly all spheres of life. Also in the time of the kings there was a feudal relationship between the nobility and the people. When a new order was created by the institution of monachism, there were two kinds of masters. Though the nobility never entirely lost its independence, it was pushed more and more into the background by the lords of the monasteries, who had the monopoly of reading and writing even while the nobles were still very powerful. The history of the mutual relationship of the nobility and the monks would require a separate sociological analysis, but in the main it is not unreasonable to say, considering that this development ended in the state of the Dalai Lamas, that the contrast between monks and laity was the most important structural aspect of Tibetan society, whose dominance increased in the course of time. In spite of the fact that the Tibetan people finally became Buddhists and even regarded Buddhism as the national religion, the contrast between the people and the monks was in many respects parallel to the contrast between the conservatives and the progressives. With the exception of the lay adherents of the Vajrayāna, of whom one hears no more in later times, the people kept alive their belief in the national gods and forced the monks to acknowledge these gods in one way or another. If the Red Caps had been the progressives in their heyday, afterwards replaced as such by the Yellow Caps, in both cases the conservative opponent was the people, who was gradually overcome in social, economic and religious respect, but never entirely conquered.

The socio-economic gap fixed between the monks and the people contributed not a little to the continuance of the cultural rift in Tibetan life. As the main stress will unavoidably fall upon this contrast, it should first of all be established that in one respect the monasteries formed a connecting link, unknown to the feudal organisation before Buddhism. The only possibility for a boy of the people to mount upon the social ladder lay in the monastery. There the mere fact of being a monk gave him prestige in ancient times, and there he could rise in the monastic hierarchy. Later he could even attain to such a position there, that a government function in Lhasa was conferred upon him.[315] Yet this social mobility was not so great as it seemed, for monks with money had more chances than monks without money. That is to say, a young monk with rich parents had considerably better prospects than a colleague with poor parents.[316] It is not, indeed, without significance that the non-Buddhist god *Pe har* or *Pe kar* was accounted the benefactor of deserving monks from poor families.[317]

Meanwhile, the poorest monk had a better economic position than most of his compatriots outside the monasteries. Only too often a boy of poor parents was sent to the monastery 'because no work, plenty to eat and without sin', as Combe's informant pithily expressed it.[318] In Tibet the monk was in theory and practice a being of a higher order. Just as in earliest Buddhism, it was quite certain here that it was totally impossible for a layman to attain enlightenment in this life.[319] Extra ecclesiam nulla salus meant in Tibet, that without the mediation of a lama no one could approach a deity, because laymen are merely 'owners of alms', 'benighted people', 'bound by fear'.[320] It was this that entitled the monks to lead a sinless life with little work and much food, and that was supposed to justify their other religious monopolies. Opposite the Potala, the enormous palace of the Dalai Lama in Lhasa, stood on another height the building of the lamaist medical faculty: the combination is symbolic of the fact, that the Tibetans depended body and soul upon the lamas. Although in their slavish imitation of India the Tibetan Buddhists showed little religious creativity with regard to sacred history, they found a most sophisticated way of sanctioning the monopolistic situation of the monks. They added to the holy places and events in the life of the Buddha one sacred place and event, often depicted in art: the Buddha taking the vows of a monk![321] These monopolising tendencies were in all probability much strengthened by the Yellow Caps in the state of the Dalai Lamas, but they find their origin in the time of the kings, when Sam-ye was founded and tax-free land was given to the first monastery with serfs to work it.[322]

Snellgrove gives a beautiful and useful description of life in the little monastery of Jiwong.[323]

It is almost an idyll, this monastery functioning as an organic part in the social body, its monks being inwardly contemplatives, outwardly priests and even protectors of the population against robbers. It is true that the rich receive more elaborate, thus more efficient ceremonies from the monks than the poor, but the general impression of his description is of harmonious integration, as is sometimes found in closed societies. This author certainly deserves implicit belief. Dorothy Sayers' fine description in 'The nine tailors' of the place and function of an Anglican clergyman may also be completely correct, without portraying the place and function of the Anglican church in English society as a whole. Place and function of the leading monasteries in Tibet is best conveyed by the proverb about the monastery sTag-lung-pa: 'One was unable to rival even a dog of sTag-lung-pa'.[324] The fact that a dog in a monastery is better off than a layman, and that people prove to be vividly aware of this, sets one thinking. It has been said that the easiest way to find the essential core of a culture is by noticing what the people of that culture regard as so perfectly natural that they never give a reason for it and never think about it. In this connection it is most interesting to read how Norbu, when he relates how he became abbot of Kum-bum, mentions in passing, altogether as a matter of course, that his predecessors had succesfully enriched the monastery.[325] When afterwards a Chinese communist reproaches him with the poverty of the Tibetans and the great number of beggars, he replies that a Buddhist must be able to exercise charity. It is unscientific to condemn this attitude, all the more as Norbu quite rightly remarks that the Chinaman only knew the happiness his faith dangled before his eyes. Happiness too is largely a convention. However, it is not unscientific to establish that for the people the wealth of the monasteries was not a matter of course, and that the Tibetan economy was extremely one-sided. The communist blames the old Tibet for wasting immense quantities of butter on the gods. We only regret that the laymen were not also in a position to sacrifice more butter than they did.

A real, free class of traders never grew up in Tibet, the merchants were more or less in the service of the government.[326] Trade was to a very great extent under the control of the monasteries, which were real wholesale dealers.[327] Das speaks of a monastery which received the takings of markets and shops.[328] Other sources of income were also possible, though, for instance a ferry service.[329] As money was extremely scarce in the Tibetan economy, assets were put by in the shape of butter, gold, grain, etc. Barley will keep for fifty years in the Tibetan climate, so the monasteries often possessed enormous granaries.[330] It must not be forgotten that this property belonged to the monastery. The monks were expected to provide their own livelihood, although they shared in the advantages of the monastic possessions. Meanwhile, those monasteries engaging in trade or keeping ferries and shops at least honoured the principle of service and counter-service. The same may be said with some truth of the foundry in the famous monastery near Shigatse, where thirty men were employed in making bronze images of the gods.[331] Other benefits accruing to monks or monasteries, however, were founded on the principle that monks are, and ought to be, special, privileged persons. Besides the regular taxes the people had to pay to the monasteries, themselves free from taxation, the begging of the monks formed an extra burden. In the harvest time of the year 1856 more than half the inhabitants of a certain monastery were away, having gone begging.[332]

Thus Waddell's already quoted characteristic 'the chief capitalists of the country' is far from erroneous. It is completely confirmed if we turn our attention to land tenure and the conditions of lease. In all non-industrial societies land and land tenure are of central and fundamental importance; in industrial societies their significance is still very great. Carrasco's analysis of these matters concerns the situation which had developed under the Dalai Lamas, but there is no doubt that this was but a systematisation and extension of earlier conditions. The monasteries of the Red Caps, too, were rich before the Yellow Caps despoiled them of most of their property. And as already stated – the very first monastery had tax-free land and serfs from whom to raise taxes.[333] Religion in Tibet cost a great deal, demanded a great deal and possessed a great deal. As five sixths of the Tibetans were agriculturalists under the Dalai Lamas, it speaks volumes that the Dalai Lama was officially styled 'the great Owner'.[334] He gave land to monasteries or also to clerics or civilians employed in administrative functions, to compensate them for their work on behalf of the state.[335] The tax-free possessions of the monasteries amounted to 42%, those of the government in Lhasa to 37% and those of the non-clerical nobility to 21% of all Tibetan land, so that the clergy possessed altogether 79% of the land in Tibet.[336] In the above, the property of the monasteries includes the land owned by so-called incarnate lamas, monks of high degree who are regarded as the reincarnation of a deceased predecessor of great sanctity. They are also called living Buddhas: 'the Living Buddhas are among the largest landholders of Tibet'.[337] Naturally they cede much of their income to the monastery for all kinds of ceremonies and for the cult in general, and to the 'church'; however, the benefit of these assets remains restricted to the clerical order. The central government in Lhasa also spent a great percentage of its income on religious life, for instance by subsidising monasteries. Now there was no division between economic and political power,[338] and Tibetan law did not allow a monk to be judged by a layman.[339] In view of the above, the few data given here are sufficient to make it more than plain that a very large unproductive part of the Tibetan people – about one third of the male population – consumed a considerable part of the national income,[340] that the members of the nobility, as landowners or government officials, lived in affluence, and that by far the greater part of the rest of the population, the economically really productive farmers, could not possibly live well.[341] The people either paid taxes to a landowning noble, thus supplying him with part of the taxes he had to pay himself, or paid taxes to a monastery or a clerical landowner. Regarded from the economic point of view, by far the greater part of what was produced disappeared behind the monastery walls.

The people were poor, and they knew it. 'An oral tradition claims that in order to express symbolically the real conditions of life in Tibet with their pronounced difference between rich and poor, the nine *dgra lha* should be painted in such a way that eight of them face the observer, while the ninth is shown from the back. Only in case all the Tibetans would become equally rich and fortunate, the artists would be allowed to depict all the nine *dgra lha* turned towards the observer.'[342] One can learn much from such information. It is an oral tradition, for the monks would not dream of setting down a tradition of this kind, that lives among the people. After all, there is the king who formerly attempted agrarian reform according to the rule of equal possessions, and had to give it up as impossible after three tries. So the impossibility had been proved and, in the view of the monks, this proved that the status quo was as it should be. *Dgra lha* means enemy-god(s), and these gods are pre-eminently capable of protecting their worshippers against enemies and of making them rich. They are national gods, and the people were very well aware, why one of the nine turned away his face. It requires little psychology to understand why these national gods had to be forced to keep their oath of fealty to Buddhism, and why they did not do so willingly.

There was a good deal of protest among the people, in songs that were extraordinarily popular and stated in so many words, that 'the gentry' by no means despised money:

> '*At first they speak of "Foes of our true Faith",*
> *And next they cry of "Foreign Devildom".*
> *But when they see the foreign money-bag,*
> *We hear of "Honourable Englishmen".*'[343]

In Gyantse there was a folksong giving a most plastic description of the good, or rather the fat living enjoyed by the monks of a great and famous monastery, for the smell mentioned in the last line is occasioned by frequent and lengthy visits to the kitchen:

> '*The young monks of Tashilunpo*
> *Walk shaking their hinder parts*
> *And making the large folds of their clothes to open wide*
> *They spread about smell of grease.*'[344]

Sometimes there is no good-nature in the criticism, only hard-hearted aggressivity: 'Shut the monks up in their monasteries with their lice, and they will soon find life unendurable'.[345] These are data of recent times, but the revolts of the 10th century are there to show, that the contrast between rich and poor was a standing evil in Tibet. More and more the monasteries took on the role of the propertied class, a role that had in principle already been sanctioned at the foundation of Sam-ye.

The monks, too, were aware of this contrast. This transpires chiefly from the way they describe in words how things really ought to be. In one word: paradisical. In the biography of Padmasambhava already referred to, this haughty, missionary warlock, who generally comports himself in a most self-assured manner towards the Tibetan king, as is fitting for a yogin towards a common mortal and an Indian towards a Tibetan barbarian, explicitly tells the ruler that his power and joyless existence is founded upon 'les serfs de la famine'.[346]

One wonders whether this is a reminiscence referring to the serfs of the feudal period before the coming of Buddhism, or the depiction of contemporary conditions by the hagiographer, whom one has no difficulty in believing when he speaks of the 'frustes Tibétains dans leur misère grossière'. Very different is the ideal of king Krhi-song-deu-tsen how Tibet was to be: all women and men are to be allowed to learn reading and arithmetic, all children to receive instruction, the sick to be nursed, the old men to have no more cares and to be respected, the debts of those without means to be halved, and so on. Needless to say, these pious wishes express exactly the opposite of the actual situation. The government in Lhasa followed the same tactics towards themselves and towards the people. The aim being the salvation of all mankind, it is natural that the regulations for collecting the taxes – translated by Das – are exceedingly humane. Of a more practical and crafty nature is the following piece of advice: One must gather taxes from the farmers as one takes the eggs from under a hen without disturbing the nest.[347] Quite cynical is another: 'The sheep that has wool, fleece it, the fish that has no hair, beat him'.[348] Every society has an ideal and an actual pattern of conduct, but in Tibet the cleft between the two was really rather deep.

The fact of the matter was, that the advice not to disturb the hen on the nest had a profound economic background of human tragedy. The pressure of taxation on the small farmers was so heavy, that it was not uncommon for them simply to desert their lands and become beggars. Measures had been prescribed to prevent this flight from the land. Here is objective proof, that Tibetan economy in its clerical-feudal structure was top-heavy.[349] Would not Central Tibet in the long run have done to itself what its governors had done to Western Tibet? For the tax policy of the Lhasa officials had made this part of the country into a dreary, depopulated waste, where houses and monasteries were left to decay.[350] At any rate, the result of this economy under clerical guidance was, that the gulf between monks and laymen was also a gulf between rich and poor. Although formally the new monastic élite only moved into the place of the former nobility, the economic contrast added a new element of tension to the contrasts Buddhism had already created in Tibet. The far from well-balanced economy following upon the founding of the monasteries, was another factor making the social and cultural life of Tibet unstable, and causing it to remain so.

If the signs of our scant information are to be relied on, Buddhism only accentuated the old social contrast. If any country might be said to exist under feudal conditions, it was Tibet, where there were two languages, two kinds of Tibetan, one to name whatever was owned or done by the nobility, another to indicate the belongings, actions, etc. of the people. In the Land of Snows a servant was required to address his master's cat as follows: 'Would honourable Puss Puss deign to come and drink this unworthy milk?'[351] For everything except sun and moon and heaven and hell, there were two words. Buddhism either promoted this development, or it took over this situation of extreme division and left it in being. In either case there was a dangerous discrimination of the people. However it might revere strength and power and bow before the divine power of a living Buddha, especially of the Dalai Lama, the examples given above indicate, that the people's attitude towards the monks was more realistic, and that their way of life stirred up ill blood. Where poverty is consciously felt, a sense of wrong remains. Just because such a culture has many factors hindering the resentment felt from finding easy relief in social disaffection and revolution, it must manifest itself in an indirect, symbolic way. A common, Buddhist and nationalist ideology of the entire people, as it gradually grew up, could enable society to function,[352] but it could not completely resolve such deep-lying tensions as the Buddhist-Tibetan acculturation had aroused in an atmosphere of extreme aggressivity. Religion might be the national product, to release these tensions in action a powerful army, such as the great king who punished the Chinese disposed of, would have been more effective. Instead, there was only the almost unimaginable monkish pride of the Dalai Lama, who coolly set forth that the relations between China and Tibet were those of almsgiver and monk.[353] Instead of an army, the aggressive Tibetans, whom the epic of Gesar inspired with enthusiasm because it was full of furious fighting, had to feed their national pride on their religion, which was monopolised by monks. In the next chapter it will be attempted to show that – to use a comparison which appears fitting – the Terrifying Ones took the place of the former army. They conquer all enemies outside Tibet, but also in Tibet. Because of the acculturative conflict this army can also turn against the Tibetans themselves, and therefore both monks and laymen fear it. If there was one thing linking all Tibetans, it was fear of their own ancient gods.

Before discussing this subject, the problem must first be considered, why in the process of acculturation Buddhism with its monasteries developed in the precise way it did. In China matters followed quite a different course, as appears from Zürcher's study. Even in its palmy days Buddhism could naturally never dream of a monopolising position in that complex culture as was the case in Tibet. Among the really primitive – not barbarian – Lepchas on the other hand Buddhism was watered down and the monastery became a purely formal institution, where the boys were ordained as monks for some ten days, after which they returned to ordinary life; real lamas are exceptional. In Ceylon, Buddhism – not indeed as Vajrayāna, and that again is an important factor in the comparison – became a definitely positive and integrating social factor. Nor can the development in Mongolia be equated with that in Tibet.[354] To pose this question then, is for the present better than to answer it, for it is obvious that an answer requires separate and extensive study. Yet an aspect of acculturation and cultural change has been raised which deserves the attention of cultural anthropologists and historians. The problem is complicated, but extremely fascinating.

In connection with our theme of the relation between aggressivity and sexuality, particularly in Tibet, a comparison with the Lepchas might be very illuminating. Gorer states with regard to this primitive people living in Sikkim and India, that an integrated culture repels foreign elements or changes them so that they become unrecognisable.[355] This fact is known from the study of acculturation, and a beautiful example is offered by the Pueblo Indians of North America, who cheerfully entertained a similar yielding yet resilient dualism of their own religion and Christianity as existed between Mun and Lamaism among the Lepchas,[356] not to be compared with Bon and Lamaism in Tibet. The mere fact of dualism implies that the foreign elements are not simply rejected. And even the most integrated culture, such as that of the *Pueblos* in North America, succumbs in the end to disintegrating influences.[357] In a certain sense it is quite a feat that the Lepchas, who were conquered and occupied by the aggressive Tibetans, did not succumb. One of the principal factors in this seems to have been their complete matter-of-factness and openness with regard to sex. Sexuality is the substratum of all psychological tendencies aiming at union and integration, and indeed this is evident from the culture of the Lepchas, in the absence of definite aggression, as Gorer particularly points out.[358] However, it is not simply the absence of aggressivity, as Gorer supposes (the culture of the Arapesh, for instance, contradicts this),[359] but the emphasis on sexuality which forms the bond, as is also seen with some autochthonous Australian peoples. The Lepchas, who in their dualism make no bones about giving a god two different names, elegantly express their desire for integration by letting their principal Mun deity and the principal deity of Lamaism marry one another.[360] As this is no systematic analysis, but merely a pointer to an interesting field of problems, there is no objection to simply calling this sexual intercourse between foreign and indigenous deities most revealing!

The dominance of sexuality with the Lepchas[361] and that of aggressivity with the Tibetans, to take this factor alone, entails a world of difference also in their attitude towards Buddhism in the process of acculturation. In Tibet Buddhism first regarded the Bon as a mortal enemy and later as a conquered enemy, to be dressed down by the Chinese in case of rebelliousness. Among the Lepchas there is good-natured indifference and tolerance. Only the priests on either side sometimes pass remarks. The Lamaists bring in aggressivity and accuse the Mun priests of sexual magic, whereupon the latter quietly point out that lamas are far more voluptuous and inclined to drink than common people! On a basis of fact Gorer was able to establish that at any rate the latter part of this remark is true.[362] While the aggressive Tibetans had so individualistic a pattern of life, that ultimately even each monk was supposed to look after himself, life with the Lepchas is entirely based on collectivity. Owing to its aggressive acculturation, Tibet had hardly any but demon gods, whose numbers were beyond calculation, whereas the Lepchas are pleased that they are less troubled with demons now that there are new exorcists among them. 'People say "there are fewer devils here now that we have lamas and their books" rather as they might say "there is less diphtheria here now that we have got the new drainage system".'[363] From psychologically easily understood motives, aggressive Tibet was haunted after the coming of Buddhism by fear of the dead and of death, but the Lepchas acknowledge death and the dead as dreadful enemies, and are silent. The Book of the Dead was common property in Tibet; among the Lepchas it is only used by lamas, and their cultural dualism unexpectedly finds expression in the carrying out of two death rituals – one of each religion – at the same time for ordinary people, it being left to the lamas to celebrate their own *bardo* rites.[364] While in aggressive Tibet the monastery was not only central, but had also taken over the functions of the former nobleman's castle, the monastery with the Lepchas stands alone at the margin of society, one of its uses being to store a few books that not even the lamas can read. The fact that a man is a lama, is only one aspect of his personality, a far less important aspect than his family relationships, his laziness or diligence, his friendships and his marriage.[365] This little reconnaissance might suggest the following working hypothesis: The Tibetans, who because of the aggressive pattern of life of their nomad herdsmen had already formed an individualistic society of several social layers, resting on the rule of a king, and were clearly on the way to a centralised state, did not succeed in permanently establishing such a state owing to the decentralised natural conditions of the country and the extremely individualistic and aggressive trend of acculturation. As a result, they stuck half-way in a situation in which the awe of the people enabled the monks to take the place of the aristocratic rulers, while centralisation could only be brought about with the aid of foreign military authority. One might also say that Tibet was no longer primitive enough to render the monastery harmless by integrating it in the indigenous culture, as the Lepchas had done. Yet, although it had progressed some way along the route of the conquerors, it was also not sufficiently differentiated always to be able to match the monastery from a central authority, as China could, thus preventing it from unchecked and rampant growth. In a socio-political development of this kind the monastery may be the transitional form combining civilisation with power. That the monastery in Tibet did this in accordance with the early Buddhist 'splendid isolation', was probably one of the principal factors causing the continuation of the break in the acculturative process in social, economic, political and religious respect. This was the cause that in the Buddhist Land of Snows Buddhism and Tibet remained enemies at bottom. And, as always in acculturation, the dividing line not only parted conservatives and progressives, people and monks, it also went right through the hearts of both parties. This universal phenomenon of acculturation, formulated by a Bantu as 'I am two', manifested itself in Tibet in the fact that the Bon tried to be more Buddhist than Buddhism and that Buddhism was Tibetanised,[366] without being able to reach a final and harmonious adjustment.

THE CLASH OF RELIGIONS

In a country where religion became a national product, owing to the decay of political power social, economic and political data are naturally scarce compared with those available for religion. The Buddhist historians took more interest in the life of an incarnate lama than in a battle or in social unrest. In addition, they were so full of their own religion, that also with regard to the development of Tibetan religion in general and popular religion in particular, we are still poorly informed. Yet how great the difference was between Buddhism and the Bon, can be seen from the fact that Śāntarakṣita, as representing a more differentiated Buddhism, had to give up his attempts and pass on his work to the exorcist Padmasambhava, who 'evidently succeeded better without celibacy or saintly calm'.[367] This man was obviously one of those touchy and aggressive yogins, who instead of by force of arms want to conquer the world by force of magic, and Hoffmann supposes that he wished to found a religion of his own.[368] The meditative preparation of his magic had little or nothing to do with mysticism, but everything with that inflation of the ego we saw with the god Hevajra as well as with Mi-la re-pa: I, I, I, the great yogin.[369] It is necessary to regard such a figure as objectively and realistically as possible, without falsifying his image by spiritualising it in the manner of Evans-Wentz or by leaving out details. Leaving aside the Terrifying Ones, there is an unmistakable tendency towards spiritual levelling in Tibetan art, also in the facial expression of buddhas, bodhisattvas and saints, yet even here it is plainly shown – as is too often forgotten – that Padma was urged on by strange, dark motives. It was Bacot who struck home here. 'Prophète, magicien, prédicateur du Bouddhisme au Tibet, fondateur de la secte des lamas rouges, il fut l'Epicure de la philosophie tibétaine, un homme étrange, peut-être un fou. Toutes ses représentations se ressemblent. Les yeux hagards ont une expression indéfinissable, que, je ne sais par quel secret, tous les artistes reproduisent, des yeux épouvantés, ouverts sur l'infini et en même temps arrondis par la concupiscence.'[370] It is very unlikely that cultural differences could here lead to a mistaken interpretation of the expression. Yet whether one sees the images of Padma as Bacot did, or discerns in his features and eyes the protruding fury of the imperious yogin, the fact that Padma was 'different' cannot be denied. He was a conqueror, obsessed by lust of power and concupiscence, only this conqueror did not choose the way of physical, but that of spiritual violence, in accordance with the Indian tradition that the yogin's concentration of energy subdues matter, the world and the gods. He was one of those figures whose disengagement from matter was a mere reculer pour mieux sauter, to treat kings brusquely and take kings' daughters to bed, his eyes fixed on the infinity of omnipotence. Tibet very rightly made him the Great Magician. With him, half sublimated aggressivity and sexuality were yoked in freakish ambivalence. Padmasambhava often carried out his spiritual exercises in charnel fields, and the ḍākinīs took a great part in them. Originally these were female spirits, distinguished by drastic sexuality and aggressivity, also in their external appearance. Sorcerers like Padma, however, can change them into charming fairies. The way this was done was very characteristic, though: according to our sources the transformation was either brought about by meditation or by visionary rape. One of these masters set out to meet the queen of the ḍākinīs, and on arrival in her palace he found a beautiful, regally dressed woman who smiled in welcome. But Tilopa knew what he had to do: he tore the clothes from her body and violated her.[371] Apparently, then, this method was also necessary when the fairy already was charming.

Padmasambhava himself 'fed on corpses and converted the ḍākinīs'.[372] According to a biography he sometimes preached the Doctrine, sometimes killed male demons and 'possessed' the female spirits, while sometimes too one of these monsters approached reverently, 'se tint agenouillée devant Padmasambhava et apprit à souhait l'union qui sauve'.[373] In another place too his different treatment of male and female beings from the supernatural sphere is described: 'Il tailla en pièces les mâles surgis, Mamo et Ḍākinī l'adorèrent, il posséda les femelles surgies et les rangea en son pouvoir'.[374] This atmosphere not only becomes vivid against the background of what was written about Tantrism in India in chapter II, but also confirms that what was said there was not exaggerated. Although Snellgrove regards it as a general linguistic phenomenon, we may therefore inquire whether there is not a more specific reason, why the word ḍākinī came to mean prostitute in Nepal.[375] Tilopa, indeed, lived for a considerable time as the servant of a whore, a fact of some significance both sociologically and psychologically – with regard to the Bad Mother and aggressivity. Of course Padma also had ḍākinīs of flesh and blood, and there is no doubt that for many Tibetans there was little difference between such a mudrā and a prostitute. For that matter, they were not the only ones to protest. It had already happened to Padma in India that his enemies raised the people against him when he was cohabiting with one of his women. The house containing the couple was set on fire, but when after some time the smoke cleared up, a great lake was seen where Padma and his partner, on a lotus flower, were still copulating.[376]

Perseverance was undoubtedly one of his qualities. He did not give up his battle against the Tibetan gods and demons either. His methods were more aggressive than those of the master who simply taxed a god who had destroyed a hundred camel-loads of grain by sending a hail-storm.[377] When Padmasambhava met the White Fairy of the Glaciers on his missionary travels, a demonic lady who wished to destroy the foreign intruder, he drove her into a lake which he brought to boiling-point through his magic power, boiled the flesh off her bones and plucked out one of her eyes, whereupon she finally sued for mercy and Padma assigned her the guardianship of some sacred books.[378] One may conclude from this mythology that it was war to the knife in Tibet. It is also clear that Padma – who converted the *earth of Tibet*[379] – defeated the Tibetans with their own weapon: magic. Obviously the struggle was not only carried on with poison and intrigues, but also on the battle-field, where magicians tried to over-awe the people with magical stunts and tricks. Padma shared the experience of missionaries in many countries: the national gods opposed him. Especially the Lords of Earth were his enemies.[380] It is of the highest importance that in this case also the national gods were not killed. Although Padma sometimes boiled them, he was not really allowed even to wound them, only to subdue them.[381] The position of the pro-Buddhist party of the king, who had to reckon with the conservatives and their power, so that they always had to be content with a compromise, is clearly seen in two statements about the opposition of the national gods. One text speaks of 'the *great* gods and demons of Tibet', the other of 'les Génies *malfaisants* du Tibet tous ensemble s'opposèrent'.[382] These words betray both Buddhist hate and contempt and Tibetan pride. The result of this ambivalence was, that the Tibetan gods became both great and malevolent: Terrifying Ones.

Even for the Buddhists it was true what an inhabitant of Sikkim once said of the national gods: 'We had better not to leave them out, they are very, very old'.[383] The Bon po, however, remained unconditionally faithful to the old gods and resisted the innovators. With some justice they regarded them as a threat to their old customs and values of life, as Tucci somewhere remarks. Supported by the nationalist nobility, they yet had one handicap. The modernists were learned, they possessed books, images and paintings and held profound discourses, in short they put the shamanist Bon po out of countenance, whose sacrificial ritual – the pride of Tibet – they indignantly and contemptuously dismissed as barbaric and sinful. Later developments and the inferiority complex of the Tibetans already referred to, suggest that we must not minimise this contrast. To us, someone like Padmasambhava may seem more like a charlatan than like a religious genius, to the Tibetans such people were eminent and superior masters of magic, to whom they looked up not only with hatred, but also with envy. They began 'aping Buddhism', as described above. Identification is a normal mechanism in acculturation.[384] Therefore, when it behoved the king to exercise the art of doing what was possible, a conference of Bon po and Buddhists (!) met with the purpose of putting the Bon in writing.[385] This was the beginning of a process by which in the end the Bon became externally quite identical with Buddhism, except that it had different names for the gods, drew the arms of the swastika in the 'wrong' direction, held that Padmasambhava was not born from a lotus, but of an ordinary woman,[386] etc. It is a pity it is not known whether, and if so how, old values were still hidden in this contrarious identification. Phenomena of religious acculturation elsewhere make such highly probable, but for lack of indications the matter must remain unsettled. There is a typical symptom though, which is widespread and manifests itself, for instance, among primitive peoples in the firm and reiterated conviction that the Bible is really their own book, which the whites have brought them after tearing out a few pages. The Bon po related that one of the pupils of their great *Gshen-rab* had taken bodily form in India in the family of the Śākya,[387] that is to say that the Buddha was only an incarnate adept of the Bon. It is also striking that both Tibetans and Westerners have observed that the monks of the Bon – for the monastery too had been adopted – were particularly chaste in their life and might be held up as an example to the Buddhists.[388] One may wonder whether this is only an identification 'plus royaliste que le roi', or perhaps a symptom of Tibetan opposition to the sexual practices of the Vajrayāna.

It is really a matter of course that emotionally the people always remained attached to the Bon, even when they had become Buddhists in name.[389] Such an observation by Ribbach, however reliable, has not half the force of a report by the keen observer Ekvall, who spent a considerable time among the nomads. He tells us how a man who got very angry began to swear. He began with a blasphemous appeal to the body of the Buddha and the holy Buddhist scriptures, but when this made him really furious, so that he sought for stronger language, he changed over to Holy Magic and the Heaven of the Bon.[390] Very important for inward cohesion with the past, is the fact that at marriages and deaths ancestor worship is still kept up.[391] And then, to take an example from the agricultural area, if in a disastrous year no rain fell, the wells dried up and the rain ceremonies of the lamas had no effect, the people would leave the monks in their monasteries and have recourse to the old rain magic they had inherited from their ancestors, which no lama knew.[392] Not only the monks, also the laymen of Tibet had their secrets, and it is to be regretted we do not know more about them. But it was not only in secret that the old religion continued. Buddhism was forced to acknowledge it, in one way or another. Characteristic is a myth which relates how the gods of India cannot achieve victory without the help of the Tibetan gods, venerated by Buddhists and Bon po.[393] The formidable mountain gods remained seated upon their majestic thrones, the water gods were honoured up to the present day,[394] and in the marginal areas the bandits and robbers had their own robber god, who lived in a little shrine on a mountain-top.[395] The Buddhists sometimes acknowledged the old religion in a paradoxical fashion. Thus the harvest plays, mystery plays displaying the life of very pious bodhisattvas in a didactic manner, were at the same time part of the harvest festival intended to conciliate the ancient mountain gods.[396] It should be mentioned that both mountain and water spirits were propitiated by means of a substitute sacrifice, a method already in existence before the time of the kings.[397]

On the other hand, the people adopted gods from the Vajrayāna. Van Gulik gives a beautiful Asiatic example of the general phenomenon of acculturative selection. The god with the horse's head, Hayagrīva, has everywhere absorbed the existing horse cult. Where there was no horse cult, as in China, the Buddhistic Hayagrīva remained a fairly theoretical and schematic figure, where the horse was of great importance and a horse cult existed, as in Tibet and Mongolia, this god came strongly to the fore.[398] The frequency and dissemination of Buddhist concepts and rites concerned with death, must rest upon the same principle of selection. Other factors must also have been active, such as the missionary methods of the Buddhists with their threats of death and hell, of which a man like Padmasambhava must certainly have been capable, and also the phenomenon of acculturative demonisation. Thus various circumstances contributed to bring the people of Tibet, preoccupied as they were with death and the dead, deeply under the impression of the doctrine of karma and the wheel of rebirth. The gruesome pains of hell foretold by Buddhism cannot have left their aggressive souls untouched, and were directly connected with the idea of rebirth. Everywhere in Tibet one saw the Wheel of Life depicted, and it is the grinning Yama, the god of death, who holds it in his claws. In this connection two Chinese have made an observation that has more than only literary significance: 'They – the Tibetans – visualize in all phenomena the significant *Khor* (= Wheel). The world rotates in a Khor around Mount Sumeru; the sun and the moon rotate around the earth; all living beings rotate around the wheel of transmigration. Life is a perpetual circumambulation around some holy object, be it a holy peak, a holy lake, a holy pagoda, a holy wall, or a holy man. Let everything whirl around – the beads around the fingers, the prayer wheel around the sacred formulas. There are table wheels turned by the fingers; portable wheels turned by the hand; tiny wheels turned by the winds; larger wheels propelled by human power; and the largest wheels of all, driven by hydraulic power. Wheels within wheels, whirling round and round. Imagine all the Tibetans muttering scriptures, counting beads and turning prayer wheels, and continually walking round their monasteries, their cities and their country, where hundreds of thousands of such wheels are perpetually in motion. So this is Tibet.'[399]

The above description is more than merely a happily formulated impression, based on Tibet's national symbol, the prayer wheel, and national occupation, the circumambulation. One might call it an x-ray photograph of the culture pattern of a people preoccupied with death, in the grip of the concept of the Wheel of Life and the Cycle of Rebirth, and who have not been able to free themselves from this idea, but have tied themselves more and more firmly to the wheel by aggressive and homoeopathic magic, deeply convinced of the truth of what the senses teach us. 'We whirl and whirl till into hell we fall' – thus Mi-la re-pa.[400] Only a small élite of individuals such as he could undertake the strict ascesis and the spiritualisation of meditation which liberated man from the senses and from rebirth. The others, equally afraid, sought for the short-cut which proved to be the vicious circle of similia similibus. Ribbach and Hermanns are agreed that the life of the Tibetans was ruled by fear of the darkly threatening karma and of the innumerable demons. The authors of the book, from which the previous quotation about the Wheel was taken, say: 'To the Tibetans the spiritual world is full of destructive forces and malicious elements'.[401] In the Tibetan Book of the Dead all demons are united in Yama, the god of death, who holds the Wheel of Life in his claws.[402] The conclusion is obvious. The fear of Yama is ancient and very great. The fact that he is practically the only god to have the same name with the Bon po and the Buddhists, is a clear indication that he was adopted and acknowledged by all Tibetans in the earliest times already. He played the central part in Tibet's greatest mystery drama, the 'Cham. According to Waddell, the lamas showed the laymen in this play how frightful are the horrors of hell, from which only the lamas could free them![403] In any case, many travellers have described the terror that overcame the Tibetans at the moment when Yama appeared in a 'cham. Deathly silence prevailed, and many flung themselves to the ground. He who is no mystic or master magician, seeks other means of protection from such an enemy. For instance, the people had a ceremony called 'cutting the noose of the Lord of Death', part of a ritual in which it was hoped to cut through the noose of the god of death by means of the age-old principle of substitution.[404] Or one might pray to Akṣobhya, the Buddha of the Terrifying Ones, to put an end to the wretched consequences of karma, so that one could enter into one of the heavens.

Of course, this does not mean that the Tibetans went about with frightened faces all day, any more than the good-natured and laughter-loving Eskimo. Yet in the soul of the Eskimo there yawns a gulf of demoniac fear, sometimes expressed in a devilish mask that does not look altogether out of place beside the Fearful Ones of Tibet.[405] The Tibetan people, too, laughingly enjoyed life, women and drink, but the word karma predominated in their vocabulary and was eloquent in their conduct, for prayers were continually on their lips and they turned the prayer wheels at every opportune moment.[406] For Tibet was only half converted. Tibet believed in the senses, revelled in musical plays glorifying the territorial and amorous conquests of the great king, and got drunk after religious ceremonies.[407] Tibet also believed in the punishment of sensuous life, the inexorable mirror of Yama, in which the accumulated evil karma becomes visible with cold objectivity. There might be some point in a comparison with the Christian Middle Ages, but in Tibet the contrasts were greater and harsher, and the ideal way of salvation was impossible for the people. Called upon to desist from laughing in a song, one verse of which is as follows:

'*Frönst du deinen Lüsten,*
Denkst du nicht ans Sterben,
Plötzlich jagt der Tod dich
Hinterrücks, er greift dich.
Wie der Wolf das Schaf schlägt,
Packt der Todesgott dich.
Darum sinne einsam,
Büsse in der Wüste.'[408]

('*Following your inclinations,*
never thinking of life's end,
hunting Death, in sudden seizure,
from behind will come upon you.
As the wolf may strike the sheep down,
so the god of death has gripped you.
Go and meditate alone, then,
doing penance in the wild waste.')

14 Acala. Scroll painting. 41³/₈ × 26³/₈ in. (105 × 67 cm)

15

they could only offer up a hasty prayer to the good Avalokiteśvara or Lha-mo, and put their hope in the power of the lamas. But fear remained, spoken or unspoken, visible or invisible. The Vajrayāna promised the quick way, salvation in this life. It is the question whether and when missionaries like Padmasambhava also offered that possibility to lay Tibetans. That Tantric laymen are spoken of in the Blue Annals leads us to suppose that this was indeed the case, and that it occurred between the first and the second dissemination of the Doctrine. As the missionaries needed clients and female assistants, it is self-evident that they must have acquired adherents among the people also, but it is impossible to determine how great this following was, for later times laid a strict taboo upon the sexual practices, and the great Fifth will not have been the only one to falsify historical sources.[409] The prohibition of king Räl-pa-cen can only have referred to aristocratic circles.[410] The very interesting information supplied by Prince Peter, that in Tibetan 'tantric' is sometimes to be equated with foreign and abnormal, with negative associations,[411] *could* be explained by the influence of the Yellow Caps during the last few centuries. Perhaps the most satisfactory supposition is, that the adherents of the sexual path were at first fairly numerous as followers of wandering yogins, that their number increased during the age of darkness and shortly afterwards, but could later be increasingly disregarded, remaining confined to small groups round a yogin. Considering the relations entertained by the sixth Dalai Lama, one is compelled to assume that the Vajrayāna rituals were kept in honour by the order of the Ancients, though it was no exception for the part of mudrā to be filled by a monk's own wife. Men and their wives could live in the same monastery and preach together,[412] so that the wife could take over the role of the mudrā of the yogins.[413]

Meanwhile, all this is but speculation, and it must be admitted that practically no details are known regarding the point where the clash of religions must have been greatest. We must keep to general outlines, then, and not regard this piece of the history of a people in the abstract, but view it as concretely as possible. With reference to the sexual tantric conceptions and practices and the moral conflicts occasioned thereby, it was already pointed out that there must have been considerable repercussion in Tibet, both of a positive and a negative kind. The Tibetologists, who surely do not as a rule believe the bare word of Buddhist historians, did believe that these sexual practices did not spread among the laity till the age of darkness. It is very much open to doubt, however, whether here too it is not a matter of idealisation, and consequently falsification of history. Naturally the age of darkness was a time of great social unrest, disintegration and laxity. Yet one may well ask whether the preceding time of the kings had been such a period of harmony and integration? A mere glance at the little we know of that time may serve to convince us that it was anything but quiet. The beginning was the usually not very peaceful establishment of royal power (*rgyal po* = conqueror), and the end the murder of a king by a monk, with in between continual conflict between progressives and conservatives, which socially, politically and spiritually must have had a disrupting influence. Remembering on the one hand that even the greatest of the kings had to take careful account of his nationalist and conservative enemies, and on the other that already around 800 A.D. a typical Vajrayāna figure appears as royal counsellor, one may well ask whether in such disquiet and confusion these practices were not easily taken up by a not inconsiderable proportion of monks and laity. Also the laity, for 'c'est faire allusion à tous ceux qui écoutaient l'enseignement de nombre d'individus isolés, hommes et femmes vivant de la religion – de leur religion à eux – suivant leur propre règle qu'aucune autorité religieuse n'a alors le droit de contrôler, plus ou moins instruits, plus ou moins édifiants'.[414] Marcelle Lalou is speaking here of the dark age, but her realistic description of the wandering yogins in the style of Padmasambhava is almost certainly also valid for a great part of the time of the kings, when not much centralised control can have been exercised either in political and religious matters.

In accordance with the contrast between the centre and 'the country', between agriculturalists and nomad herdsmen, the old tantric sects are of recent times found a good deal in the east, where the inhabitants greatly respect 'la vieille science bouddhique'.[415] Buddhism, that in the first centuries will have found little support among the nomads, afterwards also extended to these regions, where particularly the tantric Red Caps took and found refuge when they fell into disgrace with the Yellow Caps in the centre. Rockhill tells us that the Bon po were extremely popular among the agrarian population in the neighbourhood of the famous lake Koko nor, while the religious affiliation of practically *all* nomad herdsmen was to the monasteries of the Yellow Caps.[416] It is to be supposed that after the Bon the agriculturalists also accepted the Red Caps, whereas the nomad herdsmen accepted in their own way the purified Buddhism of Tsong-kha-pa. In their own way, for as appears from a prayer given below, these aggressive and self-willed people moulded both Buddhism and the lamas to their will. Yet once these herdsmen and warriors are gripped by the life of the spirit, they are completely serious, as the pious Tibetan kings were and the Mongolian mystics in their yurts, already referred to. Thus the true Buddhists among the nomads were to be found in the monasteries, and also in Lhasa. The social force of the monks was the same as that of the Buddhists in the distant time of the kings: magic, the spiritual side of war and conquest. In this way the country of the nomad herdsmen became a fascinating land of extremes, not only exemplified in the contrast between Yellow Caps and Red Caps, but also within the people themselves, regarding the tantric magicians they made use of with the deepest awe, and yet answering, when asked what the Wheel of Life is: 'une image peinte sur laquelle est representé quelque chose ressemblant à une roue'.[417] Various examples have been given in the present work, and others will follow, of the tenacity of the national religion in these parts, where the *sa-bdag*[418] were devoutly adored, where king Gesar is the national hero, and where Gesar's tutelar deity is venerated on the snowy top of Amñe-ma-čhen.[419] The historical conclusions are obvious. The same applies to a prayer composed in the 8th century by a lama of the Old Style order and addressed to the protective deities. The prayer was part of a ceremony dating from pre-Buddhist times, and still performed by lamas in the present century on the occasion of going to war or going out on a raid.[420] Gods, demons and protectors are fraternally united in this address, because every one's help is

16 rTa-mgrin (Skt. Hayagrīva). Scroll painting. 44 × 30¹/₄ in. (112 × 77 cm)

needed in the coming fray. It is clear, that here no problem whatsoever was constituted by sexuality and aggressivity, and it is equally evident that here the protectors did not protect the doctrine, but the life and possessions of the warriors. In this original habitat of the kings who impressed their stamp upon Tibet, the first and last concern was battle and victory. Anticipating a little upon the following chapters, it is worth quoting Roerich's translation of this Tibetan prayer here, to illustrate the historical background. In spite of being celebrated by lamas, the prayer has little to do with Buddhism, and very significantly requests the gods not to confuse enemies and friends:

'*Armée des dieux protecteurs bienfaiteurs!*
Ayant levé le drapeau blanc, sonnez dans la conque!
Armée de dieux, armée de démons, armée de protecteurs, vous trois!
Dieux et Esprits protecteurs, compagnons des Dieux protecteurs, – vous six!
Dieux de la richesse, de la nourriture et Divinités adjuvatrices, – vous neuf!
Divinités protectrices du commerce, des fêtes, des routes,
Divinités protectrices de la vie, – vous treize!
Revêtez vos corps de fortes cuirasses!
Prenez dans la main une arme aiguisée!
Montez un cheval rapide!
Ensemble avec vos compagnons, – vous
Goûtez les offrandes!
Esprits protecteurs de la doctrine, divinités protectrices, vous,
Ne vous trompez pas entre ennemis et amis!
Exterminez par le courage les armées de guerriers ennemis!
Pour que nous recevions la nourriture et la richesse des ennemis!
Nous les yogis avec les compagnons!
Si nous allons faire du commerce, soyez les plus grands marchands!
Si nous allons à la guerre, soyez les chefs!
Dans les razzias, si nous allons, soyez les maîtres!
Au départ, accompagnez-nous!
Au retour, recevez-nous!
Protégez les villageois!
Les gens, la richesse et la nourriture, ces trois, multipliez-les!
Soyez amis de la vertu pure!
La stérilité, le malheur, la pauvreté, détruisez-les!
Exterminez les voleurs, les mauvais esprits et les querelles!
Kï-Sō! Allons! Victoire aux dieux!'

Obviously faith in what the senses teach was as strong as aggressivity in the East, where one not only prayed for riches, but for the riches of the enemy. To return to the centre, aggressivity

17 Beg-tse. Meditation drawing in colour on a black ground. 16⁷/8 × 12⁵/8 in. (43 × 32 cm)

was also an important element in the part played in the clash of religions by the yogins and the monks, and is again stressed here because of its direct connection with the Terrifying Ones. The yogins, whose mental technique in itself heightened irritability and aggressivity, were outcasts or voluntary outcasts, as we have already seen. In their 'religion à eux' they voiced a protest against Indian society, for the shortcomings of which they found abundant compensation in barbarian Tibet. One is inclined to draw a parallel with the great number of ambitious men, greedy for power, from the lower and middle classes who have played such an important part outside their own country in the European colonies. However that may be, the aggressivity of the yogins has been sufficiently demonstrated. As to the monks, one need only imagine how some of them, barbarian yokels, agape and dumbfounded, were put through the mangle of acculturation in far away India, as described in a previous chapter. Nor were things easy for the boys who remained in Tibet and became monks there. They had to learn reading and writing and an entirely strange, complicated religion. For Buddhism is indeed a difficult religion, even for historians of religion. The matter-of-fact and certainly not stupid informant of Combe, who became a Christian, though his Christianity should not be regarded in too spiritual a light, to judge by his own statements, put it as follows: 'Buddhism was too difficult for me, Christianity was more easy to understand'.[421] The country lads in the time of the kings will have found it even more difficult than this Dorje Zödba did. Furthermore, one can well imagine conflict will not have been spared them. To become converted to the new religion in a country, where the majority regards such a thing as treason or apostasy, is always fraught with inward and outward conflict. Such was the case whether a boy got converted because he thought life in a monastery must be rather nice, or because he was in the grip of the message 'we whirl and whirl till into hell we fall'. In the situation of a boy becoming a monk in the time of the kings there were enough elements of conflict to strengthen his natural aggressivity in one form or another, and a sense of superiority towards the laity was not the least of these.

From the founding of Sam-ye till recent times yogins and monks have been the two focal points of Tibetan Buddhism. The historians expressed this in the two figures of Padmasambhava, who founded Sam-ye, and Śāntarakṣita, who was the first abbot of this monastery. The wandering yogins with 'leur religion à eux', are balanced by the organised monks, who may be controlled. The importance of the yogins must not be underestimated. They came into Tibet and defeated the evil spirits of that country, and in the twentieth century there were still yogins wandering around, still deeply venerated by the Tibetan people. The great popularity of figures so diverse as Padmasambhava[422] and Mi-la re-pa is only confirmed by such a little and apparently insignificant 'order' as the Z'i-jed-pa, the members of which were all yogins and were without exception regarded as saints.[423] Although other influences were also active, the main line of development could be negatively formulated: without Padmasambhava no Red Caps, without the Red Caps no Yellow Caps. The yogins have made an ineffaceable mark on the culture and religion of Tibet. In the biographies of the yogins of the 11th century and earlier their sexual activities may have been glossed over, and yogins who lived later may have given these pratices a lesser part in their life; in any case, this element did not prove decisive in aggressive Tibet. It was the magic power emanating from their secret knowledge and surely no less from their plebeian, but forceful personalities that captured the miracle-seeking Tibetans. Accustomed as they were to shamans, they understood after their own fashion the world of these strange and superior shamans. Though someone like Marpa might assert that religious ire is something quite different from ordinary anger,[424] the Tibetans also understood the aggressive bursts of fury against demons or men, and these must have made them regard the yogins as very human and very impressive.

In a by no means negligible number of cases, however, the religion of the yogins was also an authentic form of religion. True, one repeatedly feels the charlatanism even in the texts, yet a passionate cry such as 'Practise meditation till you feel hatred towards it'[425] has so characteristic and so authentic a sound one cannot but be convinced of the real passion with which the highest good was sought through ritual and mental training. In by far the majority of cases this highest good was spiritual power, not mystic release. By the short path, these men strove to attain salvation and supernatural power together in this life. Finally Tsong-kha-pa broke with this ideal, but by then it had penetrated so deeply, that even in the monasteries of the Yellow Caps the aim of the majority was to attain siddhi, magical power.[426] Yet the 'intellectual sportsmen', as the yogins have been called[427] formed the living conscience of the inmates of the monasteries who, if they did not sink into sloth, easily fell victims to the fallacy that learning is the same thing as mystic insight and that theology is also religion. One of the Tibetan theologians, who had received instruction in real religion, then remarked: on the bed of a great scholar the corpse of an ordinary man will be found.[428] And the historian Bu-ston explicitly declares that those who drink wine out of skull cups, wear ornaments of human bone and carry the trident, form part of Buddhism.[429] Apparently it was necessary to state this with some emphasis in the monastic milieu, but on the other hand this remark is nothing but a description of the actual situation which had come about owing to the deep respect in which the yogins were held by the people. There was a contrast between yogins and monks.[430] Even in the official biography of Mi-la re-pa the monks are repeatedly spoken of with contempt, and the life of an itinerant ascetic is glorified by contrast with their existence. Several passages are obviously directed against the monasteries, the monks and theology.[431] Yet the monks could do little but acknowledge these freelances. The people forced them to do so, and sometimes too the recognition that the ideal of the yogins was the true ideal.

The Old School distinguished a higher and a lower way in the monasteries. It is not improbable that this is the earliest monastic acknowledgement of the fact, that also in the monastery the yogin ideal remains the highest, but that not all are fitted to strive after it. Once the monastery becomes an institution not of the élite, but of society, such a religious contrast within its walls is unavoidable. Seeing the monasteries in Tibet have always increased, it is no wonder not a single reformer has been able to change this. There remained a great number who wore the garb of a monk, but otherwise differed little from the Tibetan laymen, also with regard to religion. Thus we find the result of the clash between the two religions to be, that Buddhism finally gained the day by bringing the enemy within the walls of the monastery. David-Neel formulates it pregnantly: 'L'éducation clericale tibétaine produit une petit élite de lettrés, un grand nombre de fainéants lourdauds, d'aimables et joviaux bon-vivants et de pittoresques rodomonts, plus quelques mystiques qui passent leur vie en de continuelles méditations dans les hermitages du désert.'[432] Naturally the setting of this study cannot include a summary of the many descriptions of Tibetan monastic life. Only a few significant particulars will be mentioned, directly connected with our subject.

The contrast between the monastery and the people was most clearly expressed in the mystery plays. The 'Cham, which was already mentioned, is the most important of these. All the mystery plays had a definite educative function in the sense that they afforded the people teaching by illustration on Buddhism and its perfections. In the 'Cham, moreover, they were reminded of the terrors of hell that awaited them. These interesting forms of primitive drama might also be termed home mission. The vanity and transience of life, the fugacity of sensual delight and the self-sacrificing love of the bodhisattvas, who can liberate man from that state, were set forth at length before an audience never entirely convinced at heart of the irreality of what the senses teach, but that could be moved by the miraculous love for man displayed by the saints, and that was fearful of karma and death. The mystery play was a dramatic bible of the poor, and in many respects it was also functionally to be compared to the middle English and other mediaeval mystery plays. As a form of home mission[433] the mystery play served to strengthen the not very orthodox Buddhism of the people and to display the power of the Buddhism of the monasteries. This power was not only apparent in that people could see before their eyes how enemies of Buddhism were defeated – aggressivity was openly expressed, and not infrequently Lang-dar-ma, the enemy of Buddhism, was represented as realistically as possible and then stabbed in an orgy of aggressivity[434] – but also from the circumstance that only lamas could perform the 'cham. Even as actors they had a monopoly.

Otherwise, people mainly had to do with lamas when they required some kind of protection against demons. Then they would send for monks, who celebrated their aggressive rituals for payment. The contradictoriness of human nature in general and Tibetan conditions in particular, is strikingly expressed in the way the Tibetans competed with one another – as in many aggressive and competitive societies – to call in more lamas than their neighbours had done on such occasions, though each additional lama might often mean greater poverty for them. This is a most interesting example of the way an integrating ideology, applied as a means of social competition, objectively increases the social contrast, while subjectively decreasing it. Lamas were needed against illness, the hereafter, drought, hail, and every other evil that threatened in this demonised country on the occasion of birth, marriage, death, building a new house, or setting out on a journey. The ever-present fear in the background

18 Beg-tse. Scroll painting. 18⅞ × 14⅛ in. (48 × 36 cm)

of Tibetan life is also apparent from the propensity at once to ask any lama one meets on the road to predict the future, as Mme David-Neel constantly observed on her well-known journey to Lhasa. The subjects, by the by, on which people sought information, were usually concerned with what the senses teach us.

That in the monastery itself the scholars regarded theology as the queen of all studies, is self-evident, nor is it surprising that the mystic faculty had the smallest number of pupils[435]. With regard to theology it should be mentioned, that the extremely critical Japanese Buddhist Kagawuchi particularly wished to state that the Tibetan theologians proved to be not only fully conversant with the dogmatics of their own order, but also with those of the whole of Buddhism, which in Japan was a rarity.[436] Here we again find, in the clash of religions, the receptivity of the inferior and conquered party, so convinced of their own worthlessness that they take refuge in the mere indiscriminate accumulation of knowledge. It is typical that the greatest Tibetan creativity in the ritual field was manifested in the yogic Chöd, while the epic of Gesar is also unmistakably related to those milieus (in correcting these pages it may be added that Stein very definitely attributes the creation of the epic of Gesar to two sects or orders which lived and worked in close contact with the people, as Mi-la re-pa did). The foundation of the popular life of Mi-la re-pa is the praise of the itinerant yogin, and the unique Book of the Dead is at any rate influenced by 'the short path'. It does not seem exaggerated to call commentary characteristic of the Tibetan monk and theologian.

Even with the more highly educated monks, however, aggressivity was a dominant and even indispensable factor in the pattern of their life. The only form of examination for every monk who wished to obtain a degree so that he might rise in the world, was the debate as taught in the department of logic. Various authors mention these debates, for they were struck by their spectacular and aggressive nature. According to the rules of the game, the debaters did not confine themselves to logical arguments when discussing, say, the definition of some concept, but reinforced their opinion by raising their voices, vociferously approaching the opponent in a threatening manner, confusing him with furious gesticulation, and so on.[437] He who confuted his enemy in this way was the victor, and such a keen debater was called 'someone possessed of a fierce doctrine'.[438] This was not an instance of the rabies theologorum familiar to us, but a generally accepted and approved manner of debating, no matter on what subject. Norbu, who often took part in these debates himself before he became abbot of Kumbum, describes them in a most amusing fashion, and says they sometimes ended in fisticuffs.[439] By preference, Tibetan thinking was couched in terms of battle. Culture and religion are full of them. In the time of the kings, and afterwards too, the Old School conducted a good deal of magic with the aid of gods whose body was a dagger, and magic itself not infrequently took the form of a fight. Tsong-kha-pa had tried to eliminate this to some extent at least, but it reappeared in logic as the debate by intimidation. Moreover, as it was the only form of examination by which one could move up a step, it is even of central importance for the culture pattern.

There was quite another way aggression was expressed in the monastery: in the person of the soldier-monk. It is not known how old this phenomenon is in Tibet, but it is in any case to be presumed that it arose after the dark era, when the monasteries must have been forced to fight not only for power, but also for self-preservation against invading nomad herdsmen or brigands. It may also be considered, with great probability, a symptom of the clash between the religions, for in a country such as Tibet the possibility must not be excluded a priori that in the earliest times, too, the monks may have had to fight to defend their lives. In later times, however, they fought for power, and in the monasteries the trophies of these battles were preserved until the present century. Those monks specialised in war, who also served to maintain order in the big monasteries, were the soldier-monks. The fact of their existence and their manner of life is very characteristic of Tibet. 'Stretch Ears... was the leader of the lamasery troops. Although a monk, he didn't know how to say his prayers and because he had killed several people was not allowed to have part in the chanting services. But he was considered a man of courage and audacity – greatly feared in the lamasery, a mighty friend and a terror to his enemies' – that is the portrait of a soldier-monk of Tak-tsang lha-mo in a region of pastoralists.[440] But also in the central agricultural area these gentry formed a regular part of the monastic population, and usually exercised quite a reign of terror. They were monks, but from a religious point of view they did nothing whatever. They trained for fighting, and at most sometimes helped in the big kitchens of the monasteries. Their training was intensive, and many travellers and explorers were impressed by the fighting qualities of these heavily built brutes.[441] Without doubt they were indispensable, for instance as an escort in areas terrorised by robbers, but it is very significant for Tibetan Buddhism that these colleagues of the brigands, organised as an institution, knew they were indispensable and accordingly behaved in a rude and churlish manner. These terrifying defenders of the faith, incarnate in flesh and blood, only believed in the evidence of their senses. In mysticism the Terrifying Ones could be allotted a place by identifying the phenomenal world with nirvāṇa, but it will have been more difficult to admit this social phenomenon, at least if anyone reflected upon it. No culture reflects upon that which is felt to be a matter of course. In a country where the clash of religions led the monks to concern themselves with politics already in the time of the kings,[442] and where afterwards the monasteries engaged in actual warfare,[443] the soldier-monk was a logical consequence. Even more typical of Tibetan Buddhism is the fact that it made even this piece of bad conscience into an esoteric secret. The soldier-monks, who only believed in force and violence, whose Tibetan name means 'scoundrels', had their own gods and their own secret cult![444] It would not be right to try and unmask all esoteric secrets as attempted deceit and self-deception. There may be both a positive and a negative meaning in the keeping of a secret.[445] But when something is hidden away as an esoteric secret, while it is nothing but a piece of bad conscience, there is no reason whatever why that should not be simply stated. The whole secret of the soldier-monks is, that they were evidently not to be reconciled with Buddhism, which also in Tibet forbade even the killing of animals, and that yet they were indispensable for Buddhist monks who wanted to maintain their position.

20 dDe-mchog (Skt. Śamvara) yab-yum. Scroll painting. 20¹/₂ × 30³/₈ in. (62 × 49 cm)

20

21

It may be useful, in treating of the Terrifying Ones, now and again to let one's thoughts go back to the soldier-monks.

Although there were certainly also irenic spirits in Tibet, who did not wish to make differences of opinion with regard to the doctrine into points of dissension, aggressivity came to the fore in this respect also. However, the phenomenon is not confined to Tibet, so this rabies theologorum is only mentioned in passing. To give some idea of the typically drastic manner in which others than the soldier-monks gave vent to their destructive tendencies, the following fragment may be quoted in translation:

> '*L'hérésie, où elle existe, est finalement humiliée:*
> *ses traités mêmes sont attachés a la queue des chiens,*
> *on y met le feu et on les distribue parmi les rangs du concile,*
> *et la fumée qui s'en échappe va droit aux enfers.*
> *"Sentez la rude main sur le nez", dit on.*
> *Et, en témoignage d'anéantissement, le roi temporel*
> *fait couper la main et la tête aux écrivains d'une telle doctrine.*'[446]

It is noteworthy that the king is used here as a kind of soldier-monk to protect the pure doctrine. The battle between schools and sects should of course be regarded as an acculturative displacement of the conflict between Buddhists and Bon po.

The above examples may perhaps suffice to show that we have to do here with a culture pattern originating from the clash of an aggressive missionary religion with a culture which owing to disposition (nomad herdsmen) and circumstances (establishment of central kingship) was by no means devoid of aggressive tendencies either. Accordingly, their clash resulted in extreme aggressivity which continued to dominate the culture pattern, and which can be demonstrated at vital points, also in monastic life, right into the twentieth century. Tibet managed to smooth away the sexual aspect of the Vajrayāna, at any rate in so far that it can no longer be called a primary factor. Aggressivity, dominant from the beginning, became central and remained so, in accordance with the phenomenon pointed out at the beginning of this book, that aggressivity usually has an inhibiting effect upon sexuality. On the one hand the aggressivity of nomad herdsmen and kings, after the disappearance of centralised royal authority and owing to acculturative conflicts, found open expression in Buddhism and its monasteries, on the other it was suppressed and rationalised. The same thing is seen in the principal liturgy of the Yellow Caps. The last, most important part of this is called 'the fourfold act' and consists in pacifying, gaining prosperity, gaining power and *destroying*. Originally these were four of the many common magic rites of the Mantrayāna and Vajrayāna, such as one finds *e.g.* in the Hevajra tantra. In the ritual of the monasteries this magic has now become an expression of 'Buddhist activity'. In itself this need cause no difficulty, for the authenticity of spiritual matters is not determined by their origin, but by their structure at the moment of their realisation. But the Buddhist activity includes the destroying of enemies as an essential part, and it is to be doubted whether Snellgrove's apologetic remark solves the problem even from a Buddhist point of view: 'Buddhahood cannot be just quiescent and nothing else, for it is active in overcoming evil...'[447] It seems to me that the serious student of religion cannot avoid drawing attention here to the psychological inconsistencies of this Buddhism. Logical inconsistencies are inherent in the nature of religion and mysticism, but psychological contradictions may often indicate inner conflicts and tensions. If by equating saṁsāra with nirvāṇa Tibetan Buddhism first professes an absolute monism, in which evil may be mystically tranformed into good, and then preaches the dualism of the battle of good against evil, enabling monks to murder kings and soldier-monks to live in monasteries, then this is not a matter of religious ambivalence, but a real cleavage, already implied in the term itself of soldier-monk.

Finally, the events of the third day of the New Year festival may be cited to prove that the aggressivity of the monastic population found expression not only in the soldier-monks and in the art of debate, but also in the public conduct of the monks themselves, which could fully equal the barbarous manners of the parts inhabited by nomad herdsmen and robbers. That day was the day of the attack upon Lhasa of the 20.000 monks of the big monasteries, who were given free play. Like gigantic packs of wolves the lamas in their red robes streamed towards the city from the West, North and East, on foot or on horseback(!). In avalanches of miles in length, their faces contorted with hate and smeared with soot, they poured into the sacred city and took possession of it, spurred on by greed and lust of power. Even persons of the highest rank they roughly pushed aside and hardly anything was safe from them, so that the citizens sedulously offered alms on all sides. The feelings of Schäfer, who saw and described these scenes,[448] are anyhting but negative with regard to Tibet, on the contrary, he fortunately admires the country and the people. Yet he found himself compelled to speak of the monks as fanatics, undisciplined and filled with greed, even to employ such terms in this context as parasites of the state, red hordes and beasts of prey. Quite evidently their reign of terror was an alarming explosion of sexuality and aggressivity, the first typical of the Yellow Caps, the second of the culture pattern of Tibetan monks in general, openly or in sublimation. Everything for the monk, nothing for the lay-man, is how Schäfer characterises the wild scenes of the New Year. He is certainly right, but there is more. The way of acting of the monks shows that their superiority was proved in the drastic Tibetan manner, in the way kings and nomads had proved theirs, though without robes. Did these hordes believe in Voidness? On the contrary, in them the Terrifying Ones took human form and raged through the streets as Yellow Caps. It was not really necessary for the scape-goat to tell the lamas at the New Year that he did not believe their doctrine. The lamas proved by their conduct, that they themselves could only believe in it with the aid of a New Year festival. The institution of monachal aggressivity at this festival is a striking symptom of the acculturative gulf that still lay between Tibet and Buddhism.

That the monk ought really to be a mystic was fully realised, as appears from the monastic liturgy. In the same ceremony that ends with the destruction of the enemies, a central place is taken by the union of monk and divinity through identification, ending in the state of pure Voidness.[449] Of course we only have to do here with mysticism which has become an ordinary communal cult, and which may be most impressive aesthetically, like the absolute silence that fell after the great communal ceremony in Kumbum. After the deep toned chanting, the liturgical formulas of the leader and the sound of the musical instruments, this perfect silence while all returned without speech to their own rooms in the lamasery, was the symbol of Voidness.[450] Here the symbol with its intended significance comes instead of actual realisation of the mystic intent. This displacement of intention and achievement goes a little further in the case of the administrative lamas, who in the great monasteries were so busy that they would engage poor monks to read and recite in their place, for payment in goods.[451]

Meanwhile nearly all monasteries disposed of ill-lit little structures, erected in quiet spots in the neighbourhood for the benefit of those who wished to go into retreat. The Red Caps even had monasteries whose inhabitants isolated themselves as a whole from the world for the sake of asceticism, contemplation and meditation. Above Ribo there was a monastery where the monks were only in contact with the world of men through a rope by means of which they drew up the necessary food to their high spur of rock. Another monastery was built on a little island in the middle of a great lake, so that it was isolated for six months in the year.[452] Many monasteries were built up against a mountain like aeries, symbols of life communing with itself. If their isolation was not so absolute, yet in practice it was isolation. The monasteries of the Yellow Caps too had their lodges for meditation. The capacity of the tea kitchen of Kumbum – 117 ten-gallon pails – compared with the modest number of 70 huts for meditation[453] illustrates the difference between this lamasery and the monastery of Ribo, yet it is very significant that hermits were held in high regard by the Yellow Caps also. They were men who actually practised religion, and though in this practice meditation and contemplation were often directed towards the acquiring of magical power, both monk and layman had always remained vividly aware that real practice was what mattered. Through the centuries the conviction remained alive in India and Tibet that it is possible for mind to rule over matter, and not by way of nuclear physics either. The solitary few who had gone some way upon this via magico-mystica were always looked up to. That ideal was never repudiated in the Tibetan monasteries. Implicitly the yogin was ranked above the monk. In a harvest festival play, which surely must have been written by monks, we find for instance: 'May there be a realization of victory like that of a hermit'.[454] The extremely popular, immoderately pious Nangsa, the heroine of the favourite one of these plays, does not in the end enter a convent, but goes into the mountains to live as a hermit, because 'religious belief is unstable, even in the practice of good lamas of Buddhism'.[455]

In this way we are back again with the men who brought Buddhism to Tibet and whose highest ideal has marked this country for good: the yogins. Naturally the name of Mi-la re-pa comes to mind again. His description is quite certainly an ideal, yet at the same time it is so human that also Westerners easily understand his popularity. The figure of this ideal yogin is a creation of Tibet that would well deserve detailed study by a specialist. In him many contradictions are reconciled in a way that is only possible in a living ideal; in the context of this study the most important aspect is perhaps that in Mi-la re-pa a consistent *siddhi* mysticism is linked both with the mysticism of pure detachment and also with a warm humanity, so that he forms a link between the Terrifying Ones and the Pacific Ones, between laity and monks. He stands out above both groups. He condemns the lazy life of the monks and is tolerant with regard to the differences between the orders. He preaches death and damnation, but drinks a pot of beer with his audience after the sermon. He himself is clearly already liberated in this life, for he knows no fear, he sings, dances and laughs, and in his poems he sees a swarm of bees like fluttering snowflakes in the light of the sun – the sun which is to him 'a canopy of happiness'.[456]

Mi-la re-pa was the dream of a people who did know fear. They had other dreams too, eschatological dreams. Cultural anthropology has become accustomed to look upon eschatology and messianism as closely connected with disintegrating acculturation. The end of the world and salvation by a messiah are not unfamiliar ideas over the whole of Asia – and may well be generally connected with social and cultural disintegration, though that would require further examination. Tibet, however, is so full of eschatological conceptions that a connection with the other symptoms of acculturation may be regarded as highly probable. Besides the messianic buddha Maitreya, Tibet already had messianic ideas in the time of the great king, that seem to have been concentrated around the Chinese buddhist Hva-shang.[457] Yet after Demiéville's masterly treatment of these matters one is easily inclined to suspect some form of ideological warfare here too. More free of suspicion is an old text prophesying the end of the world in a terrible flood, which still profoundly impressed the people around the turn of the century.[458] When Das made his incognito journey, if one does not like to call it a spying-trip, there were also prophecies in circulation of eschatological disaster.[459] There were also ideas of a coming 'welfare state', which it seems the Russians have tried to put to political use.[460] Characteristically, with a people who had once known better days under a mighty king, this welfare state was often associated with the return of a great ruler. As once in Germany the great Barbarossa, in Peru an Inca ruler, and in Russia a great czar were expected when times grew bad and tension rose in the country, so the Tibetans expected the great Gesar of the famous epic. Or Genghis Khan was expected or a great Mongol general with an army of giants. Mainly though, it was the return of their national hero Gesar that they awaited![461] Particular mention should be made of the promised land of the future, Ne-peme-keu (*knas padma bskor*), that was extremely ambivalent. On the one hand it is a future paradise, whither thousands of Tibetans departed in days of oppression and unrest to find a new, messianic kingdom there, as Russian farmers have left their villages for the far journey to a heaven upon earth, and as South American Indians have moved along for generations on the way to a paradisical Land without Evil. On the other hand this messianic dreamland was the kingdom of Yama, the god of the dead. Everyone who arrived there and saw him, died immediately.[462] This latter aspect is probably to be

22 dPal-ldan lha-mo. Statuette

ascribed to the horrible privations those who undertook the journey had to undergo. Yet it is typical that even in their messianism the Tibetans could not get away from the Terrifying Ones, for it is the same in other forms of messianism. A God could always become a demon, and a paradise a hell. But they kept on hoping. Their messianic longing was ineradicable, and thus also symptomatic of the nature of their culture. The mere variety of all these ideas indicates that there is a connection with the process of acculturation. Messianism is always or nearly always the result of social unrest: 'a messianic movement (or conception) may have an ideological starting-point in indigenous traditions, in Christian (or Buddhist) conceptions or in conceptions born from the distress of the moment, but such conceptions are always as many indications that a society is getting out of balance'.[463] Seeing the nature of Tibet's culture, fissured by acculturation as it is, it is most noteworthy that on the one hand the Buddhist messiah Maitreya was expected,[464] on the other the national hero Gesar. Even though a 'fierce' messiah is fairly general outside Tibet, it is still striking that in this tense, aggressive culture eschatological ideas almost without exception have negative associations: calamity, a terrible flood, Maitreya and Gesar who will play havoc. Magic and messianism are closely linked in primitive cultures with acculturation and the clash of cultures and religions; in Tibet they both bear an extremely aggressive character. It would be interesting to know whether the early Buddhist negative eschatology of the end of the Doctrine has exercised any influence here. Upon this matter also we may perhaps expect further information from the texts, only a very small part of which has been published and translated. In view of the travellers' reports quoted above, it would be strange if the one text found by Kagawuchi more or less by chance were the only one of its kind. On the contrary, the messianic facts already referred to point in a different direction, as does the fact that in his dictionary Jäschke makes use of another eschatological, apocalyptic text, the Ma-ong-lung-btsen. How deeply messianic and eschatological ideas were ensconced in Tibetan hearts – and how probable it is that there are more texts in this field – is conspicuous from the fact that the great Fifth, who did nothing without a reason and intention, made messianism the keynote of his New Year festival, *wherefore* it must have been cherished by the people and probably also by the Red Caps. The nineteenth day of the festival brought the culmination of the *popular* festivities. A tremendous camp of tents was erected in the old style, where the two New Year generals were expected, in whom the generals of the Mongol conqueror Gusjri Khan made a personal appearance, while there were also associations with the ancient kings of Tibet. The latter, however, were particularly activated on the twenty-third day, when another imposing military camp was set up in the field, so that one might imagine oneself back in the time of the kings. And indeed, the glorious old armies were expected, which were supposed to be engaged in battle somewhere, gaining a victory of course, after which they would make a triumphant appearance. And so they did, as troops of horse made available by the ministers and other nobility. They came with Tibetan banners sparkling in the sun, 'eine Vision aus asiatischer Heldenzeit' (Schäfer). When the troops had halted, they gave their report:

23 dPa'-bo dur-khrod bdag-po yab-yum. Fresco in the monastry of Dungkar

'*Mutig und erprobt sind die Krieger,*
Unwiderstehlich und scharf die Waffen,
Unzerbrechlich und hart die Schilde,
Ausdauernd und schnell die Pferde'. [465]

(Tried men and brave are the warriors, Irresistible and sharp the weapons, Unbreakable and hard the shields, Enduring and fleet the horses.)

The people feasted upon this military show, as at other times they delighted in the heroic feats and the battles of the epic of Gesar. The New Year generals were popular favourites. All this is set in its true perspective by the fact, that each year again the *commands* of the Great Fifth himself were read out at the beginning of the parades, and these commands also stated that the intention of the military festivities was to hasten the coming of the messiah Maitreya, whose reign was so ardently expected. The subtle policy of the great Fifth is not difficult to analyse. The Mongols had helped him to power when they founded a mongolian-tibetan state. So he arranged for a mongolian camp, and because of the nationalism and warlike feeling of the Tibetans, for a Tibetan one too with a parade of their own illustrious military past. The whole stood under the command of the fifth Dalai Lama, who made military preparedness subservient to the coming of the Buddhist messiah Maitreya. He would not have been able to do this without a strong messianic longing among the Tibetans (Gesar!), which for the sake of the political power of the great Fifth could be linked to their national warriors' pride, but because of his Buddhist divinity could not be linked with an indigenous messiah, but only with Maitreya. On one of the very last days of the festival Buddhism came altogether to the fore, when Maitreya and Maitreya alone was venerated, to hasten on the end of time when after smoke and fire and blood this messianic Saviour would renew the life of mankind, as other messiahs were to do for Indians, Melanesians, Israelites, Christians, Iranians and Aztecs. Yet even in this eschatological cult of Maitreya the main part was played by horses – horses, the status symbol of nomad herdsmen and kings, of ancient Tibet that for centuries had had to undergo the conflicts of continued, never terminated acculturation, and that passionately desired an ultimate reconciliation of Tibet and Buddhism in a new heaven and a new earth, even though it be (and how could it be otherwise in Tibet?) through a terrible phase of transition.

GCOD: SHAMANISM AND MYSTICISM

Not on the Tantric path of sexual practices, but by the way of aggressivity Tibet created a ritual, that from the point of view of religious history may be called a unique monument of the culture of that country. It is to be compared to the *Hako* of the Pawnee, the Mass of Roman Catholicism, the *Pesach* of the Jews, rituals that stand alone, and whose extant text should be known to every historian of religion, indeed to every civilised person, because they not only summarise a culture, but passing beyond that also concern people from other societies. Why Tibet follows the way of aggressivity requires no further explanation after the five foregoing chapters. It may be added that Chöd (*gCod*) also remains Tibetan, in that it is an exercise of solitary yogins, who after a long training finally manage to realise a higher state of consciousness.

The yogin was not altogether a stranger to the Tibetans. They were acquainted with the trance from their shamans, who also gave clear expression to their aggressivity, though not to any particular sexuality. If the yogins spoke in an orthodox Buddhistic way of the destruction of the ego, then again there was something in their own religion by which they could recognise it. For was not also the shaman cut into pieces in his vision, so that like the yogin he awoke as a new man after a terrible experience? The recognition of elements that are the same or partly so, or that may be compared, is of the greatest importance in every culture contact. As the studies of Eliade have shown that yoga and shamanism resemble each other in essential points, it is not surprising that in Tibet one day a single brain combined the two into an almost seamless whole, as grandiose as it is horrible. A good deal has been written about Chöd, but it has to be studied again and again, because it continually offers new perspectives. It proves that in spite of being so divided Tibet could bridge the gulf by being creative in an aggressive fashion, as also appears in the *mGon khang* paintings, to be discussed later. This ritual of solitary, mystic self-destruction has indeed meant a great deal to the Tibetans. David-Neel still saw it in recent times, and the author of the Blue Annals devoted a separate chapter to it, because the ritual was ancient and widely known: 'The practice of *gCod* was widely disseminated up to the present time'.[466]

That which the shaman is compelled to undergo, so that he tries to control it as actively as possible, is deliberately, defiantly sought by the adept of Chöd: self-destruction in the ancient Buddhist sense by shamanistic means. The fact that this destruction of the illusory ego is ritualised to a high degree, is a religio-historical indication that we have to do with a quite exceptional, intermediate form between primitive religion and mysticism. Primitive religion, like religion in general, lives in symbols and symbolic action, by which means man can as it were stretch forth his hands in the direction he would go, without ever being able quite to reach the goal. The ritual, whether a protestant church service or an initiation by rebirth in Arnhem Land, always gives no more than a foretaste of salvation – or an aftertaste, if it is identification with the primordial time that is striven for. The masks, sacred songs and passionate dancing of a primitive ritual may be more fiercely expressive of a will to identification than the collective ceremony of Tibetan monks, whose sudden silence is a far more uncommitted expression of the religious meaning which is their aim. In both cases only indirect contact is reached through a symbol. Mysticism, on the other hand, discards symbols as far as possible when trying to make salvation a reality. In Chöd a human being attempted mystically to realise salvation in himself by means of ritual symbols and symbolic actions. While each step of the dance had been carefully learnt, he let his head be cut off and his body devoured while remaining fully conscious, so that as a result he was free of his ego and had found a 'point of rest' in the Voidness of the virtual, eccentric Self. Thus these yogins not only linked shamanism and Buddhist yoga, but also shamanism and the ritualism of the lamas. Chöd has been characterised as a mystery play acted by one man.

One of the Indian elements of Chöd has not been considered so far; this is the terrifying goddess who plays the central part beside the human actor. Her name is Vajrayogini, a word that might be translated as the vajra-yoga-woman. A yogini really belongs to the same group of female figures as the ḍākinīs, and we have seen that various interpretations may apply there. They may be human women with whom men celebrate rites that may or may not be dubious, or they may also be goddesses, *i.e.* purely mental entities symbolising for the yogin some aspect of man and the cosmos. The Vajrayogini is one of the great Terrifying Ones. Already in India the goddess was sometimes shown carrying her own head in her hands, having cut it off. Bhattacharyya derives this representation from a similar one of the Hinduist Chinnamastā.[467] If the Hinduist goddess were indeed the original figure,[468] we should have a remarkable and unusual representation of the Great Mother, from an aspect of whom all such goddesses in India are derived. In this instance it would be one of the aspects of the so-called Bad Mother or 'fressende Mutter'. She is the destructive reverse of the mystery of life whereby life is conceived and brought forth, and with the same horrifying and grandiose indifference killed and taken back into the womb. She is nature devouring her own children. One need not be in agreement with Neumann's psychology to refer to his clarifying description and analysis of the Bad Mother.[469] In such a context one can hardly interpret the representation of Chinnamastā otherwise than as the ambivalence of life that, after having called itself into being, destroys itself.

This realistic and fearsome symbol of Mother Nature who creates, destroys, re-creates and again destroys in a wild dance, uniting sexuality and aggressivity at their deepest level where they are complementary to each other as two aspects of the same power, naturally evoked other associations in the Vajrayāna, in the framework of the ideas we are already familiar with. On a lower step this female combination of lasciviousness and lust of destruction could be raped by the yogin, *i.e.* conquered and made subservient to his will. This is a familiar mythological concept found in heroic myths, so that it has been named heroic incest. At a higher level she was the image of the dreadful sensory world, of nature, the body, sensuality and self-destroying lust, which cause man to believe in the illusion of an 'I'. By identifying himself with her according to the rules of Vajrayāna meditation and so perceiving her to be Voidness, man could attain his own salvation, because thus he liberated himself from the illusion of the ego. There is also an image of her compelling the yogin to 'meditate on the streams of blood issuing from the severed body as falling into the mouth of the severed head and into the mouths of the two yoginīs on either side of her'.[470] This form of meditation indicates, that also behind the Buddhist conceptions there lie hidden primordial thoughts of Hinduism regarding natural life, that bears and destroys itself, earth drinking the blood of her own children, that is of her own flesh, in an eternal cycle. A well-known representation of the Great Mother is a snake biting its own tail. In the Vajrayānā the representation of Vajrayoginī described above was perhaps understood as the evil of body and ego, destroying itself and achieving liberation according to the principle of *similia similibus*. The trinity of yoginīs might be connected with the three main sins.

The hagiography of Padmasambhava suggests the idea, that the representation of yoginīs or ḍākinīs holding their own head or heart in their hands, or who have cut their own body in half, is also linked with the sacrifice of one's own illusory being in the world of sense. This point of Tibetan esoterics was also associated with the struggle between body and mind and the dominion of the spirit over the body that was aspired to. Such ideas being found in his biography makes it not unlikely, too, that they were already made known in Tibet in the earliest period by this ḍākinī-specialist.[471] In the iconography of the Land of Snows, however, one also frequently sees Vajrayoginī with her head in the normal position.[472] Then too she remains a symbol of the cutting of the bonds tying man down to the world of illusion, as is expressed by the knife she has in her hand. Possibly the Vajrayoginī with her head in the natural place is the terrible goddess of the adepts of Chöd, who in their ritual so consistently applied the symbolic severing of the head to themselves, that the goddess could keep hers.

This Terrifying One was closely connected with meditation in charnel fields. The Buddha had already recommended this form of meditation as a practical way of convincing oneself the world is subject to decay.[473] Such meditation could prevent this conviction from becoming a purely theoretical matter without further consequences. It was a drastic means of turning the unmeaning and uncompelling 'everything will pass away' into a deep conviction, which for instance entirely suppressed sexual desire. Yet it remained an expedient on the road to nirvāṇa. Then came the Mahāyāna with its doctrine of the bodhisattva, called by Evans-Wentz – who sees nothing but exalted matters in Buddhism – 'perhaps the highest and most sublime aspect of the doctrine yet evolved by mankind'.[474] As we have already seen, one of the characteristics of a bodhisattva was that he gave himself away, not infrequently giving his own body and letting it be cut into pieces if this was required. It was also pointed out that this form of love and humility may also be lust of power in a subtle form. A combination of the early Buddhist practice with purely mystical Mahāyāna ideas is found in the account of an eye-witness already referred to, describing Buddhist mystics in Mongolia. Sitting in their tents as if turned into stone, they experience at the end of the via mystica the nothingness of those without an ego, with a kind of margin of what might be called generalised compassion (for humanity). These mystics, proving in deed that Buddhism may be something else than charlatanism, made practical and systematic use of the charnel field meditation, but they did it in imagination. If sexual desire proved not to be extinguished they practised the contemplation of skeletons or – to kill all desire and passion – they visualised their own body as one suppurating sore of which nothing remained but a skeleton, until finally from that skeleton, the core and essence of man, a flame shot out.[475] Their meditation – one can hardly imagine this being observed in the 20th century – ended in a completely imageless, abstract meditation which brought release.

Although a few shamanistic and Mahāyāna conceptions can be recognised here, this mystic meditation makes a classical impression. The great stress laid in the Mahāyāna on the body as enemy, however, also opened the way for a development which in some instances ended in actual self-aggression. In China cases of self-mutilation were not rare in certain periods, while in the 5th century the Buddhist 'sacrifice of the body' after the example of the bodhisattvas in the literal sense, led to an epidemic of self-conflagration called by Zürcher 'a macabre kind of fashion'.[476] It is hard to determine the boundary here between absolute demolition of the ego and absolute lust of power, not to mention mental derangement. These developments in Buddhism also penetrated into Tibet. With regard to religious suicide, we hear that missionaries in the Land of Snow have seen monks cut open their abdomen,[477] and one such case was observed by Tucci.[478] It is curious how even in religious suicide cultural patterns still persist – the reader will remember that a shaman was able to cut open his belly and take out the intestines. It does not seem, though, that such things often occurred in Tibet, although the instances described form an indication of the possibilities included in the Buddhist negation of life. The method of the short path easily leads to a mental short circuit.

The magical mysticism of the charnel field introduced by Padmasambhava, which in India had developed into a theoretical and practical system for destruction of the ego,[479] made more impression in aggressive Tibet, where preoccupation with death and the dead was so rife. There were no points of contact with Tibetan ideas for the sexual practices of our warlock, but there were for the concept of destroying the ego, symbolised by a goddess with severed head. Their own shaman had his head cut off when he was totally destroyed in the vision of his vocation, to be reborn as a fresh man. In the creative flash of a shaman's brain, or perhaps gradually, there was created a synthesis of the two conceptual complexes: the Buddhist destruction of the ego (carrying associations with the body as enemy and the bodhisattva ideal) and the 'Zerstückelung' (dismemberment) of the shamanist vision. The principal link was of course the severed head, but there were other points of resemblance besides, which gave this part of the new religion a familiar aspect.[480] The use of the human skeleton, particularly of the femur, was already known in Tibet in pre-Bon times.[481] The wild dancing of the shaman before and in his state of trance was recognised in the vajranṛtya, a tantric dance in which the adept invoked one of the Terrifying Ones and was possessed by the god, who threw him to and fro in a savage dance.[482] Thus in Chöd shamanism was raised to a conscious and introspective Buddhist level, where charnel fields are symbolic of the corruption of existence, but also of victory over that corruption.[483] For one may look upon the cemetery thinking 'that is all', yet if one's regard becomes insight one sees through all that, and then the macabre field of decay, conversely, becomes a sign of the highest, liberating insight. Chöd was the dramatic means of realising this insight. That the ritual is typically Tibetan and probably very ancient, is apparent from the fact that it was the common property of the Old Orders, the Yellow Caps and even the Bon po, who had a separate group of priests for the practice of Chöd.[484]

As many books have been written about Tibet, but there are few good eye-witness reports, like that of Pozdnejev about the mystics of Monogolia, regarding the really important phenomena outside the monasteries, it is a piece of good fortune that Alexandra David-Neel saw an adept celebrating Chöd. As she had practised the ritual herself, the meaning of what she saw in the moonlight on that funerary field in the mountains, was of course clear to her. In the following excerpt, however, her interpretation will be left out in order to give the reader a bald impression of what took place there. Subsequently the ritual will be followed step by step according to the translation of the liturgical text. From her encampment, David-Neel[485] every day saw a skinny and sickly looking young man in ragged ascetic garb pass near by. He was a pupil of Rabdjoms Gyatso, whom she knew to be residing in a cave higher up in the mountains for meditation. When one day she offered the pupil some medicine, he answered that he was not ill. She drew attention to his truly abnormal thinness, but did not insist when a look appeared in his eyes that seemed like that of a madman. Unlike most Tibetans who are usually rather talkative, he had already been reserved, and after this conversation he took a roundabout way so as not to pass the traveller's tent any more. A week or two later, when a herdsman in the neigbourhood had died and his body, according to Tibetan custom, had been carried up to a small tableland and cut into pieces there, Mme David-Neel was proceeding to that place to spend the night in meditation there. When she had gone part of the way in the bright moonlight, she heard a hoarse and piercing sound, followed by the rhythmic beating of the *damaru*, a drum made of two human skulls.

Approaching with caution, she was able from the cleft of a rock to watch the skeleton-like pupil of Rabdjoms Gyatso singing in the cemetery. After the song he remained sitting in meditation. Then he arose and took the trumpet made of a femur in his left hand, raising it on high, while he beat an aggressive staccato on the drum. His attitude became defiant, loudly and fiercely he called out to invisible beings, now and again uttering aggressive cries, as he engaged in a stamping dance. The effect on the onlooker was quite deafening. Now, chanting a liturgy, the adept began to set up a little tent. His manner became agitated and nervous. He kept looking at the pieces of the corpse, and then at the silhouette of the mountains nearby, clearly visible in the moonlight. He hesitated, and passed his hand twice or thrice over his forehead. Then he seized his trumpet. He sent its sounds in all directions, accelerating the rhythm. Then he disappeared into his tent, from which now and again singing could be heard and what seemed to be moaning. As the onlooker moved to depart, she heard a wolf growl and saw the animal pass just in front of her. Apparently it had been kept away by the noise made by the adept of Chöd. At that moment she again heard him cry out and blow furiously on his trumpet. Then she heard an awful cry and saw the tent rise, apparently because the young man stood up. He had jumped up, taking the little tent with him. When he had struggled out of the cloth, his eyes had an insane glare and he looked as if he were suffering intense physical pain. The wolf, that had gone to the top of the rock and looked down upon the scene, began to growl. According to the French traveller it was not aggression, but terror that made the animal growl. The celebrant made more and more vehement gestures at nothing, continually uttering howls of pain. Mme David-Neel no longer felt justified in looking on, and pity for the young man made her approach him. But he began to shout and she could not get near. When she tried anew to calm him, making use of her knowledge of what was going on in this wildly gesticulating young man, her efforts again went for nothing. The young man obviously took her for a supernatural being, so that it was impossible to make contact with him. The traveller then considered it her duty to go to his teacher and warn him of the deplorable state in which she had had to leave his disciple. The gist of her conversation with the master was as follows. Her warning that his disciple might easily become insane in this way was answered with unquestioning agreement. Of course he may go mad, was the style of Rabdjoms Gyatso's reply, but he has been explicitly warned of the possibility. Enlightenment is a precious gem and must be bought at a high price. May be that he will learn it later on.

This description, intended to show how little is left of religion if it is only described as behaviour, does not even give an impression of 'method in madness'. Yet Chöd is most methodical, and could only be learnt theoretically and practically under the guidance of a teacher. After the disciple had been seriously warned that illness, madness or death might ensue, he was subjected to severe tests. For instance, he was sent towards evening to the loneliest wilderness, haunted by a spirit or ghost, the home of beasts of prey. However terrified he might feel, he had to remain where he was. A pupil who too easily became accustomed to these tests, was unsuitable. Only if fear was heightened to the ultimate degree could success be expected. Obviously it was realised also in Tibet that individuals of too robust a psychic make-up are unsuited to the finer kind of work. In this case, however, there was more behind it. When his moment came, the pupil would meet Terrifying Ones and demons whom he knew to be nothing but his own projections. Yet – as already pointed out, and indeed it is of central importance – the strictly theoretical conviction of the irreality of the demons does not do justice to their comparative reality. Only by taking them com-

24 rDo-rje rnal-'byor-ma (Skt. Vajra-yoginī or Sarvadbuddhāḍakinī. Bronze. h.: 5⁷/8 in. (15 cm)
25 Ku-ru-kule (Skt. Kurukullā). Bronze. h.: 4³/8 in. (11 cm)

24

25

26

pletely seriously, can they be completely seen through. Only by going through the fear of one's own devils can one conquer that fear. That is why the psychically robust, who too soon grew accustomed so that they knew too little fear, were unsuitable. They could undoubtedly be without fear and even courageous in normal and even in abnormal circumstances, but for that very reason they would never attain to the ultimate fear of nothing, which could be tamed by Chöd.

When after these tests the pupil had learnt the liturgical text of the ritual by heart, he had to study the steps of the dance under his master's direction, who then seemed like an ordinary dancing-master. Such strict ritualisation, meanwhile, serves a most useful purpose, for it creates a fixed rule of behaviour for moments, when fear might lead to panic. The same applies to the lessons given in handling the bone trumpet and the drum and in the ritual raising of the tent. The pupil learned, indeed, that the trumpet served to command the demons, the drum to subdue the spirits that appeared, and the tent to remind him that his goal lay in an upward direction. When finally he had learnt the use and significance of the other paraphernalia,[486] the disciple could begin to practise Chöd. For it was more than plain from the seriously indifferent words of Rabdjoms Gyatso that the teacher could explain intent and meaning, could give advice and directions, but when matters came to the test the adept of Chöd stood alone and had to work his deliverance in this life on his own responsibility and his own risk.

He had to begin by visualising himself as the goddess of all-penetrating wisdom, in such fashion that in this identification he could fill the universe.[487] Thus the drama of Chöd had cosmic dimensions. Though the typical ego-inflation of the yogin is familiar by now, it is natural in this case that the adept should set himself up spiritually before beginning the battle with fear. After this meditative identification with wisdom turned goddess, the celebrant loudly blew his trumpet and danced the dance that destroys erroneous conceptions. But while he danced he continued to visualise, and in Tibet this did not mean forming vague ideas, but rendering visibly present whatever was visualised. The purpose of this dance also was that the yogin might challengingly prepare himself for the fight, for the first words he spoke in dancing were: 'I, the yogin who show intrepid courage.' It appears from the continuation that in this first dance he concentrated all his thoughts upon the identity of the phenomenal world and the world of absolute mind, of nirvāṇa and saṃsāra, and supported by this insight danced over human beings who personified the self. Actually the adept not infrequently danced upon corpses, or as in the case described by David-Neel, near a corpse. A corpse symbolised the 'I' the living body imagined itself to be before death. Having thus destroyed the illusion of the ego in his mind and with his body, the yogin in the second part of the dance called upon the spirits of teachers, 'heroes and heroines' and ḍākinīs to take part in the dance.[488]

When these had appeared, the adept danced with them the dance of the five directions. To the rhythmic staccato of the drum of human skulls, the demons were trampled down that cause the illusion of the ego to arise: the mighty spirits of hatred and wrath, the Lord of Death, the Ogress of Lust, the spirits of Jealousy and the Vampire of Stupidity. Two things should be stressed. Stupidity was conquered in the centre, the fifth point of the compass. It is characteristic of Buddhism, that from its very beginning to Tibetan Chöd it has regarded stupidity, ignorance as one of the principal causes that man remains bound to the imposture of the senses, falling a victim to the illusion of the ego. Significant is also, that in his dance the yogin trampled down pride and haughtiness in the shape of the god of death. Being the haughty, inexorable judge of the dead, he became the symbol of the sin of pride. Yet this god of death, Yama himself, was trampled underfoot by the dancing adept.

Tucci reproduces an interesting roll painting, though of small artistic value, showing the ḍākinī of the Chöd (= Vajrayoginī), remarking int.al.: 'on the right the god of death which gcod precisely defeats and annihilates'.[489] One begins to understand why the celebrant required the cosmic inflation of his ego, and what fear was to be conquered. Facing the absolute Nothing of the fear of death, the cosmic All of identification was set up. In contrast with other kinds of yoga though, which could also assume cosmic forms, this Tibetan ritual so directly envisaged death and its mortal fear in personal experience, that – as may appear from the sequel – the ego-inflation also has greater authenticity. Nor must it be forgotten that in this range of thought liberation from death equals liberation from rebirth, for it was Yama who with cool objectivity controlled the 'result' of karma, the punishment and the following rebirth.

After the dance of the five directions, the yogin visualised five ḍākinīs coming from the five directions to transfix with their spears of love, compassion, altruism, impartiality and knowledge the five sins that are the components of egoism, of being a self. It may be noted that in the liturgy the ḍākinīs transfix the components of the ego, but in the preceding instructions for the yogin it is stated that the celebrant will do so himself. In this meditation, then, he was to identify himself with all five goddesses successively, in order to liquidate his own principal failings. More significant is that a new element has come into the ritual. The theme is still the same as in the first two parts, in which the illusion of the ego and the causes of that self-deception were destroyed. Yet while in the second part, the dance of the five directions, the yogin in a cosmic extension of consciousness went himself to the utmost ends of the universe, there to dance down the fatal inclinations that lead to the illusion of the ego, now in the third part the ḍākinīs come from the East, the South, etc. to the centre, to transfix the sins there. The second part is centrifugal, the third centripetal. This is noteworthy, because in this aggressive mysticism centripetal tendencies mean self-aggression. In the next part such tendencies are fully expressed.

When the yogin had come to the fourth act of his lonely drama in the cemetery, he was to realise that his own body was the foundation supporting the illusion of personality, so that this body had to be destroyed if he wanted to become free of the ego. 'In the supreme blissfulness of the clear light of primordial consciousness' he called the Divine Teacher and the gods and goddesses, who came 'numerous as storm-clouds'. After praying that the white light of uncreated, absolute mind might dawn for those who are submerged in the ocean of sorrow constituted by the phenomenal world, the adept would take the explicit decision to free himself of hope and fear for the sake of conquering ignorance and comprehending the true nature of the real. It is characteristic of Tibet with its history of daring nomad herdsmen and conquering kings, that in religion stress was often laid upon the courage required for the exercitia spiritualia, the meditations and the bannings. In Chöd too the adept had consciously to free himself of hope and fear to attain the complete equanimity of the rope-dancer above the abyss of Nothingness, of the sportsman unconscious of hope or fear, because his mind is altogether concentrated upon the goal. Without hope and without fear he then offers his body:

> *'This illusory body, which I held to be so precious,*
> *I dedicate as a heaped-up offering,*
> *Without the least regard for it, to all the deities that constitute the visualized assembly;*
> *May the very root of self be cut asunder.'*[490]

The intention is now clear. The body, which is the origin of evil also in a spiritual sense, is not put out of action by self-mutilation or suicide, but sacrified, so that the yogin himself will have to undergo the pain and anguish. It must be cut off, so that the spirit, realising itself as Voidness, no longer receives from this disconnected body (gcod means to cut off) the deceitful messages of the senses that the world and the self are lasting. To be illusory not only in theory, but also in practice, the illusory body 'which I have held to be so precious' must be offered to the visualised assembly of the terrible gods – visualised, *i.e.* equally real and illusory as the body.

After this offering of his body, the yogin prayed to the congress of Terrifying Ones. He began the prayer by stating that externally they were his own thought-creations, who rose up against him as enemies in the shape of deities and demons, but that internally they were the sign of the concept of dualism, which gave rise to hope and fear. For it is through dualism, we may add, through splitting into subject and object, that the illusion of the ego arises, and of frustration, of separation. Next, the yogin in his prayer to the Terrifying Ones asked that all this – *including therefore the Terrifying Ones themselves* – might be cut off. Unity and un-becoming not by means of the unio mystica, but by cutting off! However, this cutting off is not a matter of suppressing and hiding away, but of enduring the destruction of one's own body and self. Let us here recall for a moment the behaviour of the Chöd adept whom David-Neel saw close to madness in the charnel field. The Tibetan text makes little ado about this side of the matter, so that there was no point in continually quoting the translation. Yet one need only call to mind the way the Terrifying Ones are depicted in art, and then if there is some private nightmare that is not entirely forgotten, one can form a faint and distant impression of the self-produced nightmare such a yogin lived in, with an intensity quite cutting him off from the external world. So completely absorbed was the young man described by David-Neel, that he took her for another demon. This visualised assembly of the gods, as it is so soberly called, was a hell.

Then came the culminating point. The adept was to visualise his body as fat and huge, and the radiant intellect within him as the most terrifying form of Vajrayoginī, who stood beside him and with her knife severed his head from the body – this too must be visualised realistically and in detail. Then she set this head, as a skull, on three skulls standing ready as a kind of tripod. These three skulls of the itinerant yogin are the three stones on which the nomad pastoralist sets his cooking-pot over the hearth-fire in the tent. Now she cut the body into pieces and threw these into the skull, which served as a great cauldron, as offerings to the deities. Here again all was the yogin's own mental activity, but at the same time an experience in which he had to remain simultaneously conscious of its objectivity and its subjectivity. The pieces in the 'cauldron' were transmuted into divine food. At the height of the Chöd, we see the shamanist Zerstückelung, but enacted with extreme lucidity of consciousness, letting the inner Self take action against the body and the ego. Here no random body or corpse was coolly analysed as means of advancing upon the mystic path, as in ancient Buddhism, but the yogin's own, formerly so precious body, was delivered up to destruction by his own spirit in the most drastic form imaginable. In the mysticism of Chöd the spirit made short work of the body and all it implies. It was the spirit which took its stand outside the yogin as radiant intellect in the shape of the Vajrayoginī, to destroy and transform him both. In this way the yogin made violent, but practical answer to the familiar exclamation of Archimedes: give me a spot to stand on. He placed himself in the excentric centre of human self-consciousness and cut off the ego with its physical illusions. There is Tibetan aggressivity and grandeur too in this mysticism, which may be called unique in the iron consistency with which it takes the Buddha at his word. Tibetans, so deeply convinced of the reality of 'what the senses teach us', took no half measures with this body 'which I have held to be so precious'. Even in the printed words of the liturgy there still vibrates something of the despair of 'now or never', but it is an authentic, grim hoping against hope, in sharp contrast with the mixture of sexuality and aggressivity of the tantrists, making a fortnight's trial of their yoga. Here too there is faith in the 'short path', but in this case it is by no means the way of least resistance. It is most characteristic in this hellish drama of a man alone with himself and against himself, that when Vajrayoginī has cut the head from the body, the body is spoken of as a corpse – 'she cutteth the corpse into bits and flingeth them inside the skull as offerings to the (terrifying) deities'.

After the almost superhuman exertion of this meditation – the word meditation usually suggests something rather different – the yogin called upon all the Terrifying Ones – externally the demons of his nightmare, in the inward mind his dualistic illusion – and invited them to partake of the meal formed by the pieces of his body 'this body which createth the distinction between the saṁsāra and nirvāṇa'. He invited them to come to this great feast like vultures flocking round a dead body. Proudly 'I, the yogin of dauntless courage' formulated the wish that all living beings might by this sacrifice be helped on their way towards liberation. In the liturgy of the text at present under consideration the adept of Chöd even spoke words of an unmistakable Mahāyāna tendency: 'Ungrateful would ye all

27 Tshoṅ-kha-pa. Scroll painting. 30³/4 × 21⁵/8 in. (78 × 55 cm)

28

be should ye not enjoy the offering most heartily'.[491] The principle of power through love is undeniable. It is to be hoped that more liturgical texts of the Chöd will come to light, so that it will be possible to compare them. In the summary of a Bon liturgy by Hermanns, already referred to, there is no sign of this bodhisattva compulsion, which quite cancels the sacrifice of self. For the present, it is to be presumed that various orders had different recensions of the ritual, as seems to have also been the case with the Tibetan Book of the dead.

Meanwhile it cannot be denied that in the very essence of Chöd there is a point of contact with this still self-confident and self-aware drive towards power of the boddhisattva. In the deepest sense, this mystic variation of the christian 'take, eat, this is my body' remains typically yogic. The cosmic expansion of consciousness with which the ritual begins, and which naturally also causes the ego to assume superhuman dimensions, apparently cannot be undone. Here lies an essential problem of the psychology of mysticism which is not easily answered, as lack of personal experience and lack of a differentiated theory regarding these states of consciousness leave us at a loss. One factor, however, seems to be of great importance. The grandeur of Chöd lies in the absolutely consistent way its meditation directs the mystical analysis, visualised in physical shape, against the yogin's own body ('the most essential thing is the practice of the mental imagery' states a Tibetan explanation). But in essence, the tendency is aggressive, and therefore destructive. Without denying that this form of mysticism has had a profound influence upon the personality structure of its practicians, one may question whether it will ever be possible for a man to attain the unity and un-becoming which are the ultimate goal of mysticism by the way of aggression. Such a query is justified in the first place because both at the end and beginning of this drama that perturbed the yogin in the foundation of his being, resounds 'I, the yogin', and secondly because another text betrays the fact, that in Tibet itself this danger was recognised. As to the former matter – if there is an aggressive reaction to this self-induced, spine-chilling fear of death, then something of a 'rebound effect' seems almost a psychological necessity, however much the subject may wish to liquidate the ego. Perhaps one might imagine the process, abstractly, in the following way: owing to the extreme heightening of sublimated aggressivity, the moving of the centre of gravity to the mind and the higher Self (the excentric centre of consciousness) occasions a 'rebound effect' in the direction of the ego, so that ego-inflation is produced after all. It may also be formulated in accordance with the 'loi de l'effort converti', in that the mystic attains what he wishes to evade, just as the inexperienced cyclist runs into the tree he is trying to avoid.[492] In this way a tentative approach may be made, in a slightly less vague manner than is customary, to the phenomenon of mysticism, and particularly to the incongruity of the liquidation of the ego and the ego-inflation which is characteristic of the yoga mysticism of India and Tibet. This incongruity was also realised in the Land of Snows, as already remarked. For in certain circles the yogins were so convinced of the undesirableness of ego-inflation that they considered a special meditation to be necessary to restore equilibrium. Without a sound and without any movement - a vivid contrast with the Chöd - they visualised themselves, in motionless meditation, as a tiny

28 *Tshon-kha-pa. Scroll painting. 56³|₄ × 30¹|₄ in. (144 × 77 cm); image 32¹|₈ × 217|₈ in. (82¹|₂ × 55¹|₂ cm)*

155

heap of charred human bones in the midst of a lake of black mud, the symbol of their own evil deeds. It was expressly stated that the aim of this meditation was to reduce the ego, which had grown proud, to nothing. The yogin who, amid horrors, had triumphantly offered his own body, must realise that he had nothing to offer, because he was nothing.[493] These counter-measures witness to an astounding honesty and an uncontrollable desire for self-knowledge, quite in accordance with the inner consistency characteristic of Chöd in general. The question remains, in how far these secondary measures, which from the psychological point of view are not entirely free of aggression either (burnt bone – lake of black mud), have been sufficient, whether they have led to the total detachment and unbecoming of pure mysticism. For the present we may do no more than pose the question.

Such concepts as ego-inflation should not arouse the impression, though, that these mystics were ordinary, puffed-up people whose spiritual exercises resulted only in pride and self-conceit, hidden under a spiritual coating. The outsider who absorbs the liturgical text as well as he can, will easily conclude that a man is indeed changed by such experiences. And if they were proudly conscious of their feat, it was nevertheless a considerable feat performed by these 'sportsmen of the intellect' who, if they succeeded after thus staking all their cards on one throw, attained to an enviable inward equilibrium and a 'Meeresstille der Seele' (becalming of the soul). They were freed from fear. That this was so, appeared also from the fact that the yogin who had once practised Chöd with complete success, no longer required any instruments, pacings or liturgy, but could celebrate the entire Chöd in his mind in silent meditation. Sometimes a number of them would feel the desire, like old soldiers, to repeat the battle they had once gained, in the ancient field. Then, to renew old memories, they went together in the dark night to the lonely wilds and danced the still remembered dances. David-Neel saw them once in the mountains 'dansant, sous le ciel étoilé, au sommet de notre globe.'[494] After the dance each sank into concentration. They remained sitting cross-legged and erect, in motionless meditation, till dawn. The critical inquirer will gladly agree with Bacot with regard to Chöd, when he writes: 'Il est regrettable ... que l'esprit de formation occidentale soit si prompt à déclarer absurde ce qu'il ne comprend pas et à rejeter comme fable tout ce qui ne s'accorde pas avec sa propre crédulité'.[495] This rationalistic stupidity proceeds from the same lack of moderation which leads to the other extreme of mawkish admiration for the Orient expressed by those who also do not wish to acknowledge that they do not belong to such an élite, wherefore they commence an imitation.

In somewhat simplified form one might summarise the above as follows. Tibetan mystics argued in this way: the Buddha has said the ego is an illusion, which is ultimately founded upon and nourished by the body; then we must settle accounts with the body in a radical way by the methods of meditation the Buddhists have taught us. They found a point of departure in the shamanist vision, and attacked the body with Tibetan (and shamanist) aggressivity. In doing so, they consistently maintained their stand in the virtual focus of the higher Self (the Vajrayoginī stood beside the body), but owing to the aggressive character

156

of this identification (the Vajrayoginī held a knife and a skull, not to speak of her terrifying appearance) their very absolutism caused a 'rebound effect'. Thus a revulsion indeed took place in the foundation of their being, and if this did not result in madness, a reorganisation, yet a heightened sense of personality was the involuntary result. As it is a hindrance to employ a varying terminology, it is best to adopt that of Rudolf Otto, who distinguished pure mysticism from the mysticism of *illuminati*, while establishing in the present instance that the Chöd was an exceptional, for typically Tibetan and aggressive, and also a highly developed form of the mysticism of illuminati.

The danger inherent in all mysticism, autism and ego-inflation of the type 'Was wirst du tun, Gott, wenn ich sterbe?' (What will you do, God, when I die?), has in that form become the avowed aim. For the usual goal of Chöd was siddhi, spiritual power over matter, even ultimate immortality. The ritual was often practised when some one was ill, having *e.g.* contracted tuberculosis while meditating in charnel fields. Yet it is again typical, that a man purposely got infected, to heal the disease by means of Chöd.[496] The individualist nature of these teachers who tried to cure the fear of death by forcing it up to an unendurable intensity, generally involves several variations upon the theme, as are to be found in the several parts of texts Evans-Wentz has published in translation. In one of them the yogin, like a regular exorcist, is to whirl the bag in which he has 'caught' the demons thrice round his head and then dash it forcibly to the ground.[497] The shamanist element comes to the fore here, and the bodhisattva ideal retires to the background. One wonders whether in the case described by David-Neel the disciple was not making an attempt of this kind, frustrated by his nervous disorder, to destroy the demons. In the 'red' version of the Chöd the celebrant has to identify himself with the wrathful Vajraḍākinī, and then strip the skin off his body.[498] Here we meet with the tendencies of the religious suicides of China and Tibet. In the 'black' version the yogin must as it were absorb into his own body all the black evil accumulated in all sentient beings since the beginning of time, then to let it be devoured by the demons and Terrifying Ones, who after this meal turn black themselves. Here we find the curious, mystical reinterpretation of the principle of substitution, which was already a familiar concept in Tibet before the time of the Bon. It is plain that further study of these texts will very probably produce results of great interest, not only with regard to the various possibilities of interpretation offered by the Chöd drama, but also with regard to the various mutual relations between the national religion of Tibet and Buddhism.

Chöd was an attempt to solve the human phenomenon, characterised by Plessner as follows: 'Gebunden im Körper, gebunden in der Seele und zugleich nirgends, ortlos ausser aller Bindung in Raum und Zeit und so ist es Mensch' (Bound in body, bound in soul and yet nowhere, having place nor tie in space or time, so he is Man).[499] This 'nowhere' outside space and time is what was called in Tibet uncreated mind, visualised therefore outside the body as Vajrayoginī. It now becomes clear why in Tibet this terrifying goddess had her head in the normal place instead of carrying it in her hands. In the first place the yogin himself did what she only expressed symbolically, so that he no longer required this symbol and in the second place she was the virtual point we call the Self, which had to undergo and 'survive' all horrors unshaken and unimpaired, if Chöd was not to end in madness. Consciousness in itself had to remain intact, in full integrity. The naked, red, wildly dancing Vajrayoginī, wearing only a string of fifty human heads, a tiara with five human skulls, a few armlets and anklets and the mirror which shows man to himself without distortion in his reality, according to the descriptions is in the full fair flower of her virginity. Although there may be some aesthetic dispute as to taste, this woman who seems unattractive to us is obviously an intermediate form between the repulsive ḍākinīs of the Himalayan regions and the beauteous goddess who is insight. She has the double aspect of that which is conquered and transformed by meditation and insight. Meanwhile her aggressive aspects predominate, as is only in agreement with the fundamental mood of Chöd. She is the mystic intellect as aggressivity. Besides her knife and her expression, her aggressive breasts with pointed nipples also indicate this.[500] But she remains a symbol, like the 'visualised assembly' of the Terrifying Ones who are present at the sacrifice of self.

By way of transition to the next chapter, it is perhaps not amiss to recall that the Terrifying Ones are externally the hostile, cannibal demons, ready to devour the yogin, but internally his erroneous concept of dualism, of the separation between saṁsāra and nirvāṇa, from which concept stems the delusion of the ego. Therefore the particular prayer referred to above really implies that the yogin is asking the Terrifying Ones that the Terrifying Ones may be cut off. The consistency of this reasoning is evident. If there is no longer an 'I', there is no more hungering and thirsting after life, requiring continual satisfaction and arousing a sense of frustration, which causes the projection of the Terrifying Ones. The combination of sexuality and aggressivity which forms their true essence, is merely a result of the thirst for life which brings separation between the ego and its unattainable aims. Actually, however, this separation is the break between the physical ego and the Self which is 'nirgends, ortlos ausser aller Bindung in Raum und Zeit' (nowhere, without any place or tie in space and time). Therefore the body must be eliminated. The discrepancy between the ego and the Self being thus done to naught, there are no Terrifying Ones left either. The formulas composed by the masters of Chöd offer theoretical and practical confirmation of the (mere) theory, that the gods are the projection of that human deficiency caused by the relative tension between the ego and the excentric centre.[501] They are 'my own (dualistic) thought-creations.'

THE TERRIFYING DEITIES IN RELIGION AND ART

'Lord of all who have taken the vow,
Slayer of all who refuse to submit,
Death to all perjurers,
Glory of all yogins,
Friend of us who now perform the ritual,
The command to action has now been given,
Subdue the raving fiends, cut down the hostile foe.

. . .

The time has come, so think well on your bond.
It is time for action, o King of obstructive foes.
Perform therefore your appointed task.

. . .

If you do not protect us living beings now in this last world-age,
Will you not perhaps be mindful of these happenings:
Firstly how Vajrapāṇi pressed the life from your heart on the way to the North,
Secondly how Padma-Heruka forced you into subjection on Mt. Hä-po by Sam-yä,
Thirdly how Vajra-Kumāra having collected together all the gods and demons on the
summit of the fair-formed king of mountains, forced them to take the vow.

. . .

O God of the Plain, we beg you to come.
You yourself and your following of nyen[502]
We shall honour with the most splendid of excellent offerings.'[503]

The prayer to the God of the plain, so beautifully translated by Snellgrove, from which the above passages are taken, is addressed to one of the national gods. Snellgrove draws attention to the way he is alternately threatened and implored. The god who is invoked as a terrible enemy of outsiders and as a friend of the faithful, must take action. He of all gods, himself the king of obstructive foes, must cut down other foes. Rather untactfully, he is reminded how Buddhist gods and saints once pressed the blood of life from his heart, subdued him, etc. If he will perhaps (!) remember this, he will know what he has to do. The next moment he is implored, and the most splendid offerings are promised him. It is curious one moment to give threatening orders, and to be on one's knees the next. In the psychology of human relations that would lead to the conclusion that the speaker, not the person addressed, was powerless, and helplessly dropping from one extreme to the other. Nor is a different conclusion to be drawn in the relationship between man and god. Obviously a god needing to be reminded in such fashion of an enforced oath of fealty, has the power and probably also the inclination to break that oath. It was Padmasambhava who had subdued the national gods and promised them that if they would protect the doctrine they could in future be certain of receiving due honour and proper nourishment. If this negotiation is not a business transaction, a compromise is the least one can call it! It is, besides, an unstable compromise, for the God of the Plain and his innumerable national colleagues were clearly much feared. Why then were they so feared, when they had officially been assigned to a subordinate position as protectors of the Doctrine?

Already the earliest Buddhism in India had to some extent acknowledged the gods of the people, who after all were the gods of those laymen upon whom the monks were dependent. They became protectors of the faith. Govinda remarks, that Buddhism everywhere honoured and acknowledged the gods of earth and sky and conciliated them as defenders of the faith.[504] Yet if one were to conclude from this that Buddhism was so tolerant, and amiable enough to admit the national gods into the lap of the mother church, one would be mistaken. That missionary religion had no other choice, and found a compromise in the concept of protectors that might be put to tactical use, even if it were not entirely consistent. The people could keep their own gods and the conquering Buddhist faith had saved its face. Meanwhile the native gods became the mercenary captains of a religion that did not itself approve fighting. If relations were not too strained between Buddhism and the indigenous society, a theological defence of this conception was easily possible, as the gods too were beings on their way to nirvāṇa who could indeed, in their relativity, be acknowledged. If the people were not unfriendly to the Buddhists, then their gods were not either, and in this amical atmosphere there was little chance of difficulties.

In Tibet, though, the doctrine of the Defenders of the Faith required to be systematised and rationalised, and this is indicative of a less easy relationship. Nowhere else was the concept of 'protector' so strongly emphasised or the idea so systematised, resulting *e.g.* in eight official, great Protectors, and nowhere else was their number so incalculable.[505] In view of the events of the time of the kings, this phenomenon is not strange. A great part of the Tibetans refused to accept the new religion, so that the Buddhists could not simply introduce their peaceful compromise of 'protectors'. The enmity of the national gods could not be gainsaid. Therefore they had to be first conquered and then *forced* to become protectors. This compulsion gave the Tibetan Buddhists a bad conscience, so that they always remained in fear of their protectors, reminding them daily of their oath of fealty. It is thereby implied that their terrible aspect was not only intended for the enemies of the faith, as theological theory maintained. This host of gods not only gazed out across the frontiers at the outside world, they turned the same ferocious look upon Tibetan monks and laymen alike. The fissure caused by acculturation in Tibet was already referred to as running mainly between the people (old) and the monks (new), but also extending through the very hearts of monks and laity both. It may be pointed out that it was in the first place the monks who as Buddhists demonised the ancient gods, and as Tibetans remained convinced of their power, so continuing the demonising work of Padmasambhava through the ages, in interaction with the people who had grown (and been made!) afraid of their own gods; thus all Tibet tried to pacify their own fear and aggression in the never ending conciliation of the Terrifying Ones. The present chapter intends to show that the Terrifying gods were one of the chief, if not the principal symptom of the fissure. The acculturatively dualist nature of Tibetan culture is impressively summarised by the Terrifying Ones in their double character of national gods and Buddhist protectors.

Generally speaking, it is only natural for a missionary religion to regard the indigenous gods if not as enemies, at any rate as inferior, and for these gods to protest through the mouth of their national worshippers. It may be maintained, however, that particularly in acculturation the native gods are easily demonised, or at any rate acquire a negative character. It has already been pointed out that acculturation is always accompanied by an increase of black magic, an indication of rising aggressivity. Particularly when the inferior party has no means of defence left and can only fight back ideologically in an aggressive situation of conflict, the gods will acquire demoniac traits and their number will increase. There must of course be an inward will to fight back, as otherwise the way of religious escapism will have more appeal, apart from those rare cases when a people turn their aggressivity upon themselves and, like aborigines of Northern Australia, live in an atmosphere of religious self-destruction, with gods who poison the people.[506] Such cases are exceptional, however. That there was a will to fight back in Tibet may be taken for granted. An example of the phenomenon we mean is found in the field-work of Deren, who studied the well-known *voodoo* cult of Haiti.[507] This religion has two branches; there is the ordinary cult and a magical one called the *petro* cult, of a very aggressive nature. It was found during field-work that this aggressive magic with its aggressive gods gained more and more ground as the process of acculturation advanced and social and individual disintegration became more serious.

A surprising circumstance is that the correlation between acculturation and demonisation in religion was acutely realised in ancient Tibet, without the help of objective religious studies. An old text of the 8th or 9th century, lamenting the decline of morality, clearly describes an acculturative and disintegrated situation. The ancient gods are despised, who are no longer so strict as formerly, and so obviously have less power. People do one another many injuries. Coarse people become rich and ride the high horse (elsewhere too war profiteering is often a result of acculturation!). Good people become poor. Central kingship is gone, and instead there are various kings, each with his own religion! Of this situation it is said in the beginning of the text: 'Thereafter, since religion and life had fallen upon evil days, all sorts of harm from demons and fiends arose in hundreds'.[508] This text and the comparative material make it extremely probable that the Terrifying Ones with their extreme aggressivity are also acculturative symptoms of a resisting culture. That does not mean, of course, that Tibet had no demoniac gods before the contact. On the contrary. Nor does it mean that Buddhism had not already introduced a number of diabolic figures like Hevajra (these, by the way, were also products of internal acculturation) through the intermediary of sorcerers like Padmasambhava. We have already seen that many factors contributed to a high degree of aggressivity. The *extremely* aggressive character, however, of by far the greater part of the national gods and their central position in the living religion are best explained as symptoms of acculturative demonisation. We have noted above that in one text the recalcitrant national gods were called the great gods of Tibet, and in another the evil gods. Both demonisation and its cause are comprehended in this.

The fact that many of them were both national and wrathful gods, renders it highly probably that in Tibet the theory of the defenders of the faith was also influenced by the Tibetan *dgra lha*, the enemy gods, who were in the first place spirits protecting the individual, and in the second place also general protective gods, who not only gave their worshippers protection, but also made them prosperous.[509] Meanwhile the *dgra lha* were only one group of the innumerable defensores fidei, and there were also benevolent gods among these familiar old protectors. Their typically schizoid character they too owe to the conflict with Buddhism, which made them also *dam can*, bound by an oath. It was not Buddhism, however, which originated the idea of specially binding them with an oath. Everything goes to show that the oath and this function of the oath belonged to the most ancient cultural pattern of the Tibetan nomad herdsmen. Already before the coming of Buddhism the Tibetan rulers used to meet once a year, according to the Chinese sources, to renew the oath of loyalty to the primus inter pares. Animals were sacrificed, and the future predicted from their entrails – a typical trait of pastoralist religion. Then the priests spoke to the assembly of rulers, great and small, saying: In case your hearts should change, know then that the gods observe it and that they will make you like these victims of sacrifice.[510] There was always the danger that one of the nobles might change his mind and attempt to seize control himself, so force of arms was supplemented by the force of an oath with religious sanction. There is every reason, therefore, to regard the Terrifying Ones as most dangerous vassals, whose power had to be fully reckoned with because, in spite of the oath they had taken, they might at any time change their mind. Nomad herdsmen are individualist and aggressive and let no one lay a finger on their honour. The gods of Tibet were no different.

The virulent character of these bound gods was characteristically expressed when an oracle went into a trance to identify himself with a Terrifying One, who was then reminded of the oath of fealty he had taken. This was by no means superfluous, for sometimes such a deity really became so aggressive that by means of his heavily armed medium he attacked and injured the onlookers, even causing fatalities.[511] In other cases also the oath proved too weak. A cruel demon who forced a monk to murder the future regent of the country, rewarded his accomplice with gold and silver. A year afterwards, however, the demon returned, killed the monk and took the gold and silver away again. After this really very demoniac conduct, he had to be bound overnew with a strong oath by a powerful and learned priest. Curiously enough this recidivist was held responsible for the sometimes very martial conduct of the monks of the Sera Monastery![512] One cannot help wondering how people could trust in such a deity as defender of the faith. But actually they were not trusted, otherwise they would not have been continually reminded of their oath. The theory was, however, that it was only after a demon had behaved meritoriously that he was promoted to be a protector of the faith.[513]

Although several of the Terrifying Ones were typically dressed in the rags also worn by the people,[514] and although the Book of the Dead also suggests a special relationship between the people and these deities,[515] the laymen feared them no less than did the monks. In the general atmosphere of aggressivity and the allied fear of the supernatural it will have made little difference to the laity that the demons were also protectors of the doctrine. Even if there is an understandable reaction against his work, one must in this respect still take account of the matter-of-fact realist Waddell, who wrote the first handbook of the religion of Tibet and whose opinion, based on experience, that every detail of religious life was dominated by fear, was indeed endorsed by others after long residence in the Land of Snow. According to Waddell even the popular Lha-mo, 'a great she-devil', was greatly feared and her name only spoken in whispers.[516] Ribbach's information, that beside Buddhism the people continued to profess the Bon, is thrown into even greater relief by the recent pronouncement, that the cult of the demonic protectors forms the link between Bon po and Buddhism, as both persuasions honour them assiduously.[517] Therefore the demonic aspect will have been more important to the laity than the protective aspect. For these were gods who threatened life. A good observer like Kagawuchi leaves no doubt as to the fear in which the protectors of religious law were held.[518] No doubt this fear was reinforced by knowledge transpired from the monasteries, that there were still more demons, who had not yet been bound by oath... Yet the dangerous power of the Terrifying Ones was exploited in magic, as may be seen from a curious representation of a yi-dam, a protector god. He is shown sitting down, with his hands, holding vajra and bell, on his raised knees. His head is bent backwards, and his mouth is open very wide. Such a figurine was used in cases of illness. It was held at the patient's mouth, and the medicine poured first into the wide open mouth of the Terrifying god, from where it ran into the mouth of the patient.[519] The idea is plain: the power of the medicine was greatly enhanced by the might of the god residing in his image. As far as we know, these quaint statuettes were not extant in the Indian Vajrayāna. Such magical use of the Terrifying Ones to battle with disease within the body is indeed in excellent agreement with the way of thinking of the Old Style Ones who are probably to be regarded as the creators of this medicinal yi-dam, with or without a Tibetan example.

Wedding ceremonies included a magical combat against Yama, not only as Lord of Death but also as lord of the demons,[520] a capacity in which he also appears in the Book of the Dead. Yet Yama was one of the principal protectors of the doctrine. Information supplied by a Tibetan also shows that the laity, in their general apprehension, hardly distinguished between the typically Buddhist and the more national defenders of the faith. The main thing was that they should be conciliated when incensed, whether the lama was to propitiate Lha-mo in the monastery or a *nag* at a fountain.[521] The laymen ought really to begin every morning by propitiating the protectors with offerings of tea and butter up on the roof.[522] They were afraid of them, and yet they called themselves Buddhists and Buddhism had become the national product. There lay the line of fissure for the people: to worship Tibetan gods in fear with shamanist rites and substitutional sacrifices, and on the foundation of that ancient cult to call themselves Buddhists. 'The priests must be constantly called in to appease the menacing devils, *whose ravenous appetite is only sharpened by the food given to stay it.*'[523] That is Waddell's clear and concise epitome of the situation. What a demonising effect the acculturative process had in Tibet is also apparent from the circumstance that even genuine Buddhist gods and saints could become Terrifying Ones, and that *e.g.* Tsong-kha-pa could be depicted as a Terrifying deity. One might, not without reason, call such a thangka Tibet's revenge upon Buddhism.

It is a pity no systematic study of popular religion was ever made on a basis of ethnological field-work in Tibet itself (not in neighbouring countries). Now we have hardly any other material than incidental observations like those quoted in the previous paragraphs and chapters. More data are available with regard to the religion of the monks. With them too the Terrifying Ones are the particular symptom of the clash between Tibet and India's Vajrayāna, whose consequences have always remained visible because the cleft was never completely bridged over and the disintegrating factors continued to have free play, a condition to which the stabilised schism of monks and laity (particularly the people) contributed not a little. In India a Buddhist theologian might say that the Hindu gods were always conspicuously armed and that this phenomenon could only be due to fear or to malignity(!),[524] yet the Buddhist theologians and monks had to admit the gods of Tibet who were armed to the teeth as defenders of the doctrine, while not infrequently they were open to suspicion as disguised enemies of that doctrine. They were signs both of fear and of malignity, as will be seen. In this connection it is interesting to read how the taming of the god *Pe har* by Padmasambhava was imagined.[525] *Pe har* seems to have been a mixture of Tibetan and foreign elements,[526] but even if the foreign elements were predominant, that in itself would be an indication that owing to the position of Buddhism, forced as it was to conquer and ban all national gods, the whole atmosphere in Tibet was filled with aggressivity and diabolic negativism. It cannot be sufficiently stressed that the lasting condition of acculturation – also expressed in the fact that in each generation Tibetan boys were taken from their homes to the more or less isolated monastery – left few things unaffected.

Pe har appeared to the missionary Padma in full power and splendour and with a large train. His appearance was so impressive that the sorcerer, though not easily shocked, fainted away. Presumably he would rather have tried conclusions with a female demon. However, he came to himself and began to meditate. A Layman (!) now appeared to him, looking very much like an Indian popular god. He proved to be the demon's son and began negotiations with the missionary, plainly setting forth his conditions. For if the protection of the sanctuaries was not entrusted to him, he would work malice. 'Et quand je voudrai nuire, le serment sera caduc et violé.' The answer to Padma's question, what would happen if the demon were to break his oath was truly horrific. In that case he would destroy houses, fields and property, making the wives of yogins insane and unfaithful, even turning them into enemies who would desert to the hostile foreign country. Then they would no longer speak of the gods, but call them demons! The sons too would suffer. For them starvation, madness and other disasters lay in wait. They too would flee. The fields would be barren, insects and hail would work destruction. The strong would die, so that only the weak were left. Wars would come. Even this was not the end. Pe har would also thoroughly disorganise meditation and render magic spells powerless. The clerics would feel impelled towards suicide, 'désirant le Vide et le Nul'. Brothers would kill their brothers-in-law and violate their sisters. To make a long story short: spiritually nor materially would anything be left whole in Tibet. Thus spoke a protector of the faith, who leaves his hearers in no doubt that he quite certainly believes in what is taught by the senses: 'I, the lord of the temples, stūpas and Scriptures, I shall possess the fair bodies of all virgins.' And this episode in the life of the great Buddhist missionary closes with the somewhat cryptic, yet in our context perhaps not unintelligible sentence: 'Adverse à la doctrine est la réalité, là où l'on partage les vivres'. This story with its revealing details speaks for itself. The Terrifying Ones were not so much defenders of the faith as of that which the senses teach us. We notice in this story, that with regard to the people Pe har is the potential destroyer of physical well-being and material possessions, and with regard to the clergy also aggressively defends sensory reality by making an end of their spiritual life and, most strikingly, leading them to seek Voidness bodily instead of spiritually, through suicide. The protesting scapegoat of the New Year festival did indeed belong to the camp of the Terrifying Ones.

In a religion in which, according to Tucci 'ontology... yields to psychology', a psychological comparison may perhaps be admitted whose main tenour was already voiced by Tucci, and which is possibly more than a comparison. There is reason to regard the Terrifying Ones as the lusty, earth-bound urges of the ancient, realistic Tibet, insufficiently suppressed by Buddhism.[527] No spiritual religion will succeed in really convincing the masses of the supremacy of the spirit. In Tibet, however, owing to the violent and sustained clash between Bon po and Buddhists, Red Caps and Yellow Caps, and also the cleft between monastery and people, the gods of the senses had not been absorbed by Buddhism as fairly innocuous satellites, but had penetrated into it as dangerous devils who could destroy life and property and desecrate religion. Their nature was concretely expressed in the *mGon khang*, the usually subterranean abode of the demons in the monasteries. The word means house of the Lord, of the tutelar deity of the monastery or the order. He lived in the mGon khang with a retinue of Tibetan gods, including the Lord of the soil where the monastery was built.[528] This abode of the demons – we follow the vivid description of Tucci – was a mysterious, secretly kept temple where no daylight could penetrate. A narrow and particularly low door gave entry to what on coming in seemed to be pitch-dark night. But once the eyes had become accommodated to the flickering light of a butter-lamp, the visitor was confronted with 'a chaotic, contradictory world like the images formed in a delirium'. In the country where to dream of a sword was a sign of luck and the arrow-of-life was a symbol of good fortune,[529] one need not be surprised that this inmost sanctuary of the demons was also hung everywhere with weapons which had served for battle and victory in war. Remains of conquered enemies were preserved here too.[530] Then there were stuffed animals, in all probability ancient Tibetan demons left over from the pre-Bon period.[531] Those few who have visited a mGon khang are agreed upon the ghastly character of this Tibetan underworld. Waddell speaks of 'a chamber of horrors'.[532] Most gruesome were the Terrifying Ones, who in the murky dusk loomed up as all-destroying cannibals, ferociously copulating with their *yum* in the obscure border region between animal and human, where men and animals lose their dignity. With a little imagination even reproductions can lead one to conclude that the word pandemonium is no exaggeration. Kept secret under the earth, the mGon khang was both that domain of the unconscious teeming with the untrammelled appetites and impulses of life, and Tibet's subconscious stored with the memories of ancient heathen times and of both old and recent wars. Here the profound truth applied which found a Tibetan formulation in the words of Mar-pa's son: 'Plus la montagne est haute, plus profonde la vallée. Plus grand est le profit, plus grand aussi le risque. Si la religion est profonde, le diable l'est aussi'.[533] That this was realised in Tibet, as testified by a similar remark 'Le Démon Noir se montrant profond en face de La Loi profonde',[534] is of no small significance for our subject. The relevant theories of depth psychology are too well-known to require a lengthy exposé here. For the rest, they are only rediscoveries of matters long known in the disintegrated religion of Tibet, in the integrated religion of the Pueblo Indians with their ceremonially blasphemous clowns, and in other religions too. In such pronouncements, it sounds almost as if Tibet were retaliating upon Buddhism with a gloating reminder of the 'loi de l'effort converti'.

When religion is deep, the devil is too – there we touch the essence of the Terrifying Ones, in name the protectors of Buddhist law, in reality the devils from the bottomless hell of Tibet's half subjugated and disintegrated culture, anxiously guarded in the mGon khang by special monks who spent their whole life there, attempting to mollify the Terrible Gods with sombre chanting and drumming. The texts of the dances in honour of these deities, who apparently could not be left alone for a moment, were kept a careful secret, like everything connected with them.[535] The Buddhist oath of these deities was actually the pact with the devil the Buddhists themselves had concluded. It is a general phenomenon that what is expressed in art is that with which the soul is most deeply concerned. The fundamental significance of the terrifying devils is underlined by art. One may even go further and state that the creativity of the Tibetan artist conclusively bears out the thesis of the present study. For it was these hideous demons who inspired the artists to their greatest and sublimest works. The mGon khang thangkas are the pinnacles of Tibet's pictural art,[536] which in other fields displays that trend towards slavish imitation we have referred to. But in the orgy of diabolised sensuousness these paintings show, the artists of the Land of Snow created a style of their own[537] giving, as do Chöd and the Book of the Dead, a unique place to Tibet in the history of human culture.

An art capable of adequately expressing the serene quiescence of a buddha or the suggestion of Voidness is sooner found outside the frontiers of Tibet, although 'the smiling artlessness of its heavens' (Tucci) has a peculiar charm. For an art of the diabolic, however, equalling that of Tibet one will have far to seek. Though all the very complicated iconographical precepts have been complied with, one notices nothing of that theological compulsion, which might easily have become a strait jacket for the artists. The thangkas have not only been painted with the perfect freedom of the true creative artist, but they are so charged with feeling that the demons still seem to be coming straight at us: they are 'sudden epiphanies'.[538] Pott very justly remarks that when one looks at these paintings, one feels that the unknown artists have really *seen* these creatures.[539] Everything has indeed, as we have seen, contributed to shape the conditions that made the Terrifying Ones develop in Tibet as they did nowhere else. No wonder then, that in a country where the demons are so much at the centre, they became the glory of the artists. These devils incarnate were enemies, but familiar if not cherished enemies. Red upon black or black upon red, sometimes indicated by very fine gold lines, the devastatingly real gods of the mGon khang were the infernal protest of ancient Tibet, of the old gods, of antique cannibalism, of the old aggressivity and the ancient faith in the sensory world. The artists gave them all they had – and what else was this but the legacy of a half-tamed nation of conquerors? Perhaps they were not conscious of their mastery. Perhaps while engaged upon their work, having performed the appropriate rituals, they thought only of the doctrine of the protectors of religion; or the more deeply initiated may have thought of the destruction of the sensory world and the ego. For the outsider, however, it is clear as day that the painters of Tibet nowhere felt so much at home as with their trusty old enemies of the mGon khang.

The blasphemy of the New Year scapegoat is the blasphemy of the Terrifying Ones, who were indeed honoured with most unorthodox rites.[540] One can state quite literally that under the Buddhist monasteries the old religion was alive. For while in the time of the kings the Buddhists still protested indignantly against the bloody sacrifices of the Bon po, the Terrifying Ones of the mGon khang – and they not alone – were nourished with flesh, bones and blood. In Kumbum the addition of pig's blood was specified, which was regarded as most effective.[541] It is true substitutes were often given, such as water coloured red, but the Bon po will have laughed at this pia fraus, as Chesterton would have laughed at non-alcoholic wine for Holy Communion. Surrogates for human sacrifice were offered also. Loud and harsh music sounded during the cult, in contrast with the melodious strains produced for the peaceful deities of the Buddhist pantheon. Not only in their appearance, therefore, but also in their cult is the repressed world of yesterday made manifest, now completely diabolised. One can only agree with Tucci, who sees the roots of human existence depicted in the gods of the mGon khang. Whoever takes the time and the trouble to let these paintings penetrate his mind unfiltered by aesthetic, moral or religious preoccupations which might keep out their impression, will find his own dreams often do not dare to tell him so much about himself as they do. In the context of Tibet's culture, however, they also stand for a primary symptom of incomplete acculturation, of a warrior nation that for the sake of Buddhism has had to give up a part of itself, of a Buddhism that for that warrior nation has also had to abandon an integral part, while the two have not found ultimate reconciliation.

An interpretation of the mGon khang in terms of cultural anthropology need not come into conflict with the mystic view in general, but it does with a mystical interpretation moving too easily from the earthy to the ideal. Tucci says that according to the Vajrayāna good proceeds from evil and that yoga, before entering into fields Western psychology knows little of, begins with the unconscious. It may be possible for a very small élite to put this into practice with regard to the Terrifying Ones themselves and in a general way – that is the subject of the following chapter – with regard to the mGon khang the idea that good may proceed from evil seems extremely apocryphal, regarded from the Buddhist point of view. Sexuality and aggressivity may be capable of transformation within the mystic himself, but nothing good can possibly come of the war trophies and the remains of enemies, if the doctrine of karma is to retain any meaning.[542] Besides, the fact that the Terrifying Ones daily required to be reminded of their oath, means the transformation had not yet taken place for all those monks who thought such a memento necessary. They saw these deities not only in the abode of their tutelar Lord, but also everywhere else in the monastery and in their own rooms, where a central position was assigned to them.[543] In Ji-wong too those who were bound by an oath hung on the walls in great numbers, and were reminded every day of their promise.[544]

Every day the monk began by identifying himself with his personal tutelar deity, nearly always a god of the wrathful type. In this connection it is noteworthy, remembering also the symptoms of aggressivity within the monastery walls pointed out in a previous chapter, that lamas could themselves become Terrifying Ones. Thus a very wise lama, who had been most unfairly treated by the authorities of Lhasa and even brought to death, became a terrible revengeful spirit, murdering until he was tamed and made into a protector of the faith.[545] A lama whose frozen corpse was treated with mockery and contempt by passing herdsmen, also changed into a terrifying deity. According to one of the myths, Yama the god of death was a frustrated ascetic, murdered by thieves one day before he would have entered into nirvāṇa, and so becoming a revenging spirit who spread death and destruction. This is by no means to deny that many lamas are amiable and wise men, but the existence of such tales, to which other examples might be added, is not entirely without significance in connection with the latent culture pattern. The theme at any rate deserves attention.

Extremely interesting is Snellgrove's description of an occasion when lightning struck in Ji-wong. This was blamed mainly upon the incensed, wrathful lord of the Soil, but also upon the Chinese communists and upon political trouble-makers in the village. One notices the threat comes from outside, and in this particular instance is also considered as an attack upon the status quo. Apart from this latter aspect – Bell recounts how fiercely the lamas were opposed to the formation of an army, which would curtail their power, and David-Neel states that in recent times most of the resistance to agrarian reform emanated from the lamas – the threat regarded as coming from outside the monastery would require more serious investigation. Suffice it to say that in the monastery of Kumbum the well-known Tibetan apparatus is to be seen with which one could catch demons not yet bound by an oath.[546] In the Sa-kya monastery chained witches were locked in the mGon khang, and the most sacred possession of the Sera monastery was a dagger,[547] the weapon used by the magicians in ancient times to combat the demons, while their own gods had a dagger for body, or were depicted altogether as daggers, the vajra-dagger.[548] These few facts are too meagre to serve as evidence, but they do suggest a particular line of research. The possibility should be taken into account that in a claustral community dominated by the Terrifying Ones, where duels in logic are fought out almost physically, and brusquely behaving soldier-monks have a secret cult, the inclination may easily arise to project at any rate part of the aggressivity upon the outer world. In the Asiatic part of the 'Mythology of all races' one finds the information that a phallus stood in front of a monastery, to keep a female demon at bay! In Tibet the women apparently did not need to be kept at bay. Somewhere I saw the remark of a Tibetan layman, who laughingly said: the children we take to the monastery were begotten by the lamas upon our wives. A joke of this kind naturally has little value as explanation, but it does confirm the general impression that sexuality was certainly not a primary problem in Tibet. There were times, however, in the Land of Snows when the monasteries had every reason to feel threatened, while in a later period the burden of their support weighed too heavily upon the surrounding populace. When the incensed Lord of the Soil was pacified in Ji-wong (with the collaboration of a Lord of the Soil who *had* remained true to Buddhism!), he was packed off with thundering curses by the monks, who were 'directing wrath and destruction upon all fiends and foes'. Instead of human fat, which was not obtainable, they made use of mutton-dripping for these cultic activities.[549] That the battle between protectors of the faith and enemies of the faith could be conceived in a most unequivocal way, appears from a photograph taken by Tafel of the frescoes in a monastery of the Ancient Order, to which were suspended the skins of conquered enemies of the faith.[550] This constitutes another reminder that it is best not at the outset to approach the intriguing Land of Snow with the theories of spirituality.

The fact that at the beginnig of every day a monk identified himself with his *yi-dam*, his personal, fierce tutelar deity, was undoubtedly characteristic of the great importance of these gods in the religious life of the monks. As by far the greater part of them, however, were no mystics, a problem cropped up that we have already approached in another context. What were these divine cannibals doing in a monastery? Very many of the monks will have given little thought to the matter, because they simply accepted their religion as it was taught them. Besides, against the background of their always more or less magical way of thinking

– and the importance of magic in Tibet can hardly be overestimated – it was not strange there should be demonic forces in life which one could only try to make use of, in this case under the auspices of the Buddhist doctrine. There were so many things one did not understand, and this secret was one of them. All over the world people acquiesce in their religion in this way, should a moment arrive when they turn their thoughts upon it. But in Tibet there have been many who went on thinking. To them, the Terrifying Ones were in the first place the protectors of the faith, subjugated enemies who had become friends, and who had to be kept friendly with the methods of religion. This line of thought was not essentially different from that of the Indian Tantrists who, full of social resentment, imagined their devilish gods dancing with delight at the thought of the flesh and blood of their enemies. 'Love is our business, and not dissension' – thus the Hevajra tantra. Love within and hate without, that is the very human, but also very simple solution of the emotional conflicts a human being is sensible of from birth. In this way one can understand that their believers could live with the Terrifying Ones, fearing them, but regarding them as a necessary evil, because they were simply there. And this fact of their simply being there, came to be regarded in the Tibetan emotional world and culture pattern as a matter of course, that did not need to be put into words.

Yet the thoughts of some went further, and the circumstance that there were various theories shows the Terrifying Ones were not just self-evident figures to the theologians. Thus there was a tenet describing these fierce protectors as the demonic forms of peaceful bodhisattvas, who manifested themselves in this way in order to be able to carry out their work of salvation in full. This theory was completely acceptable as long as one accepted that the devil had to be driven out with Beelzebub, so that a bodhisattva needed to be half a devil. That is not a popularized simplification. Fundamental emotional values and conflicts of feeling, that in themselves can be quite simply described, the theologians have in other religions also lodged in very subtle and very complicated systems, in a manner deserving of admiration. In Christianity the very human and simple conviction that God must simultaneously be infinitely good and exercise divine justice, has from Origenes to Calvin been the occasion of highly complicated rational concatenations. The history of Buddhist philosophy and theology, which are no less important in the history of human thought than the history of Western thinking, need not be glanced at here, for in religious history it is human feeling in relation to the divine which takes the foremost place. Philosophy was a closed book to most Tibetans, certainly to more than 90% of them, as all who know the subject will agree. The fact that the Terrifying Ones were regarded as transformed bodhisattvas was naturally reassuring in many ways. In an atmosphere of latent fear of the supernatural, however, such as various informants tell us prevailed even in the monasteries, this theory would almost automatically become associated with the assertion, already quoted from the epic of Gesar, that gods are demons too. The existence of many as yet untamed demons also constituted a difficulty. What religious feeling really boggled at might be abstractly and concisely formulated as the contrast between monism and dualism.

29 sPyan-ras-gzigs (Skt. Avalokiteśvara). Scroll painting. 36⁷/₈ × 23¹/₂ in. (95.5 × 59.5 cm)

29

30

The Vajrayāna, which had little philosophic foundation outside the circles of specialised philosophers,[551] was in essence a ritualistic gnosis, and therefore monistic. Yet already in India, and still more in Tibet with its many conflicts, it proved very difficult to see and experience man, earth and cosmos as a unity. Of the Mahāyāna it has been said that it preached a double truth. It may well be said that in Tibet theoretical monism was matched by practical dualism on an emotional basis.

The most deeply initiated theologians found the solution of the problem in the theory, that the Terrifying Ones were the divine powers of the visible world of phenomena and the symbol of material and physical activity, in contrast with the purely spiritual peace of liberating insight. This was the consistent working out of the principle saṃsāra = nirvāṇa, as was also expressed in the yogic practice of Chöd. Emotionally the danger of such a theory is, that one could not only argue: the essence is in the sensory world, which must therefore be transformed, but might also associate in the opposite way: the essence is in the sensory world, which is therefore divine in itself. That this danger is far from imaginary, is at once evident from the sexual pratices of the Vajrayāna in India and from the repeated attempts to isolate the tantras in Tibet. Only upon the very highest level of spiritual life, after strict physical and mental ascesis and continued meditative training can the via mystica be followed upon the razor's edge in this manner. It is clear that the sexual and aggressive symbolism of the copulating Terrible gods will more easily act upon the emotional life than the methods recommended by the Buddha. Not only sexual, also aggressive affects may arise. There is no misunderstanding the idea, found both in India and Tibet, that meditation upon the Terrifying Ones could be highly dangerous and have destructive effects on the spiritual exercise, and also upon the meditator himself.[552]

Symbols of material and physical activity in a country where the culture pattern and the general poverty forced material reality upon the attention of both laymen and monks, the Terrifying Ones were the sign of prepotent vital urges. Theoretically the theologians might regard these signs as mere pointers to visible reality, which is an illusion like the ego, emotionally a conflict remained. For as the negative symbols of Voidness they might in the monastic attitude towards life be clear and transparent with regard to man's own sexuality and aggressivity, as protectors of the doctrine and religious law the Terrifying Ones were active. They were an-nihil-ators, but not in the mystic sense. In Tibet too the story was known how, when the Buddha was preaching, the terrifying exorcist Vajrapāṇi made the demons disappear into the earth, but then the Buddha himself, moved by compassion, saved the demons and converted them.[553] Such a story is a vivid illustration of the conflict in feeling between mild, all-embracing compassion and the aggressive urge to destruction of the vice-general of the Terrifying Ones. In the earliest times the Old order and the other Red Caps probably did not worry over it, vitally aggressive Tibetans and sorcerers as they were. As more of the original and 'pure' Buddhist ideas became known, however, – for they too were brought to Tibet at an early date – the conflict became more serious. The Yellow Caps sought a compromise, which was anything but a synthesis. Certain forms of magic they did not tolerate in their monasteries, but they let them be carried out by magicians of the Red Caps, living outside the monasteries of the Yellow Caps. Revealing was that these persons, appointed to do the dirty work for Buddhist monks who did not want to soil their hands, bore the official name of protectors of the faith.[554] This too may be called in evidence for the thesis that in Tibet, which was dualistic in so many respects, ultimately even the Buddhist monks and theologians were unable to avoid an aggressive dualism, and were compelled to seek a compromise with other lines of thought from that standpoint. As a result, psychologically extremely improbable stories were produced, like that of the egregious monster Yamāntaka, who with his horrible violence drove Yama into his castle so that he was unable to escape and then, not even panting, proceeded in all peace and quiet to preach the doctrine to him.[555]

If the throttle of aggressivity is opened to blow off steam, a feeling of relief and relaxation will certainly result. It would be too much, however, to ask us to put this on a level with the peace of heart the bodhisattvas sought in the name of the doctrine. When the monks in their 'rites of destroying' had belched out hell and damnation over all their enemies, it must certainly have given them satisfaction, yet those who reflected must have had at least a vague sense that there was something out of joint. The fact that magic was set outside the monastery walls of the Yellow Caps and practised there for their benefit by onorthodox 'protectors', may certainly be considered evidential for the incompatibility of terrible protectors and Buddhism as it was professed also in Tibet. Yet the author was long in doubt whether as a Westerner and outsider he might not have missed some theological solution of the problem of the Terrifying Ones *within the monastery walls and in the religious life of the monks* (not as outward protectors), which might be perfectly satisfying to a Tibetan theologian or monk, also as a solution in life. The most foolish thing one can do is to judge others by oneself. Aggressivity, meanwhile, is a very universal and human phenomenon, that can be studied on behaviourist principles and introspectively in others and in oneself. It remained highly improbable that aggressivity in pure or sublimated form could ever change into that entire calm of the soul so impressively symbolised by the meditating Buddha. The definitive proof was finally afforded by a liturgical text which makes it perfectly clear, that also the monks and theologians were aware of that conflict in intellectual, but particularly in emotional life.

Communal worship of the Terrifying Ones differed as to details of the cult from the adoration of peaceable deities, as we have seen *e.g.* in the monastery of Kumbum. The movements and positions of the hands were different and in accordance with the appearance and nature of the protectors of the faith. The music was loud and harsh, and the paraphernalia were adapted to the objects of worship. The atmosphere was aggressive, not so much owing to the prescribed meditation which supposed identification with one of the aggressive Terrible Gods, as because of the decidedly aggressive clapping of hands that accompanied the entire liturgy. As usual, this liturgy contained devastating threats against all enemies. The following passage of the liturgy offers the proof referred to above: 'Obgleich auch die

Eigenschaften des geistlichen Wesens und die Sphäre der Ruhe unwandelbar ist, sind doch für die Abstellung und Wiedergutmachung des Unrechts die furchtbaren Götter erschienen, erfüllt von ausserordentlicher Macht. Sie sind die Hüter des Glaubens und der Lehre. Ich verneige mich vor den furchtbaren Gottheiten und den roten Henkern... Um Dschamssrang und seine Genossen zu erfreuen, verehre ich sie mit einem grossen Meere verschiedenen Blutes'.[556] ('Although the qualities of spiritual being and the sphere of rest are changeless, yet to do away with injustice and to repair it the terrible Gods have appeared, possessed of extraordinary power. They are the guardians of faith and the doctrine. I bow before the terrible Gods and the red executioners... To delight Dschams-srang and his companions, I honour them with the offering of a great sea of different kinds of blood'). In the word 'although' the conflict is implied. In the diamond sphere of complete rest there is no place for red executioners. This text does not attempt to solve the conflict by considering it with the mystic philosophy of monism. The monism of the vajra peace and the dualism of the red, terrible protectors are simply placed side by side and connected by a significant 'although'. The motivation of the activities of the red executioners lies entirely in the social, and therefore the dualistic, plane: they are there to repair injustice and protect religion and doctrine. What injustice was suffered by the monks of rich Kumbum? What wrong was done to the Doctrine, considering that the Doctrine and the vajra were above right and wrong? The only 'wrong' that had taken place, had been the resistance of the national gods of Tibet, who had wished to refuse entrance to the Buddhists and had then been accepted with the allowance of food and lodging, in the literal sense of both words, as protectors foreign to the essence of Buddhism. Their material activity was a continued resistance maintained in the monastery. Resistance to a wrong that *they* had suffered.

Thus a Yellow Cap could also make use of magic, for instance in the following words: 'It is the command of Tsong-kha-pa that you should obey. If you do not do so, I shall crush your skull with my words of power'.[557] The Terrifying Ones in the non-mystic cult must inevitably lead to an atmosphere preoccupied with matter and filled with aggression. The Yellow Cap employing these means inevitably became a Terrifying One himself, just as his great teacher Tsong-kha-pa was sometimes depicted as a Terrifying deity. In attempting to drive out the devil with Beelzebub, one cannot avoid the close correlation between aggressivity and identification, nor escape from the very bonds of the senses and of matter which one wishes to conquer. It should be added here, as Hummel points out, that animals have an important part in Tibetan religion and art, which does not always receive sufficient attention.[558] He even advances the thesis that the more the animal element is stressed in art, the more Tibetan it is. At any rate, it throws light upon the nature of the Terrifying Ones that in this respect too they represent sensory reality in the non-Buddhist sense, and in their half human, half animal shape betray a tendency to transformation in a direction opposite to that of the Vajrayāna. The circumstance that in olden times all the yi-dam were winged does not conflict with this, on the contrary it betrays the influence of the ancient shamanism, that made divine flight subservient to physical well-being. The old images of gods in the shape of daggers or animals, indicate as clearly that it is the nature of the Terrifying Ones to protest on behalf of the world of sense as do the lordly red executioners of the mGon khang.

The fact that they are very often represented *in coitu* with their yum comes second in connection with their sensory protest. In modern Western societies, where under American influence (originally puritans) the sexual element in written and pictorial form appears as a continual titillation in the ubiquitous advertisements, this may seem strange for a moment. In a country like Tibet, however, where aggressivity was dominant and sexual life was experienced realistically, it is a matter of course. We may recall here the amusing story told by David-Neel of an elderly husband quietly getting up with a few friends on the last night of a festival lasting several days in order to surprise his lively young wife in the act of adultery, with no other purpose than to impose a fine upon her lover so that they could keep up their carouse for a few more days. Except for yogins and monks, who lived in abstinence and for whom the yab-yum representations (*yab-yum* = father-mother, *i.e.* a sexually united pair) could be sensually exciting, this typical characteristic of Tibetan art will hardly have been an incitement to disgust or curiosity for most laymen. In the beginning these images will have met with the same fervent opposition as the sexual practices of the Tantrists, afterwards, they were images of gods who were feared. At most one could say the gods had licence not granted to men.[559] Besides, there was of course a meaning in this divine copulation. While our near-nakedness in advertisement hints at nothing but the physical, the yab-yum representations alluded to divine corporeality.

The official interpretation the monks gave to the union of a god with his yum, was that it signified the union of Means and Wisdom or Inner Vision. There was not always unanimity with regard to the meaning of the Means. They may be good works or compassion in general, or more particularly the preaching of the doctrine and mission, but in any case they imply a form of religious activity. He who succeeded in perfectly uniting these with the highest inner vision, was liberated. The lamas, however, seem often to have had a simpler conception of yab-yum. It was not infrequently said to symbolise the unity of matter and mind, even in the sense that matter was made living by mind.[560] These interpretations are by no means typically Buddhist and may even be styled unorthodox. Particularly fascinating in this context are the harvest plays, in which we become acquainted with the ideas of the lamas as they explained them to the people. In the play about king Song-tsen-gam-po there is an interesting prayer referring to the 'goddess of the power-receiving god'.[561] No unio mystica then, but a god who increases his strength by means of copulation. This recalls the ancient Chinese ideas regarding coitus reservatus, the intent of which was that the man should not lose, with the semen, his life force to the woman.[562] Curiously enough, the prayer containing this expression is spoken in China, where a bride is being fetched for the Tibetan king. However this may be, the play about the extremely pious heroine Nangsa uses two expressions that have more meaning for Tibet. The heroine sings a song in which happiness and charm of manner are constantly compared with religious persons or conditions, and

31 Tibetan prince of the church. Gilded bronze. h.: 7 1/8 in. (18 cm)

31

she speaks of 'to be pleasing as those who have the religious lap-sensual enthrallment. Like the maiden Nangsa, I, who have returned from death'.[563] By our standards this is the language of an overwrought virgin speaking of sensations to be expected in hysterical women. As according to the text these words are intended for the 'peaceful understanding of the common world', one can only conclude the Tibetans supposed saints to experience a religious orgasm, and their gods too, for Nangsa says that she wishes to be pleasing to the great and terrifying Akṣobhya. We find the same connection between humans and gods earlier in the story, when the saint explains that she has of course a physical father and mother, but that in the deeper sense these are two spiritual bodhisattvas. She ends her song as follows: 'To all fathers and mothers *outwardly and innately*, having wholly entered *joy and voidness*, reverent prostrations'.[564] Although the last word with regard to translation and interpretation must be left to the specialists, one may draw the general conclusion that the parts quoted above suggest that the ordinary conjugal relations of laymen were recognised as an adumbration of the mystic union, whilst the latter acquired sensory associations. There are evident 'vestiges' of tantrism in this folk play, so perhaps this was a way of paedagogically adapting yab-yum to the imaginative faculty of the people, so that the tantras still had a meaning even outside the monastery. That the gods copulate after a higher sensory fashion would in that case not be in conflict with the text of many tantras and the practices of the tantric teachers, and more in harmony with generally accepted ideas than a mysticism which was too ethereal for the realistic people of Tibet. One might even consider whether perhaps Nangsa's dedication to all fathers and mothers confers a kind of 'sanctity' upon the biological aspect of the lay marriage, making it an 'adumbration', but in that case this text cannot have been inspired by Yellow Caps.

The people and a great part of the monks also took a very realistic view of the representations of the gods in bronze or on scroll paintings. The thangkas were carried in processions as a 'poor man's bible', and itinerant lamas or yogins also had a few with them.[565] Mar-pa received as a legacy from his teacher two thangkas representing Hevajra.[566] In this way the illiterate populace, unable to read or write, could take cognisance of the horrors and the blessings following respectively upon an un-Buddhist and a Buddhist life, and also become acquainted with the gods and saints, upon whom everything depended.[567] Everywhere there were images of buddhas, bodhisattvas, gods and demons: in the monasteries, in the houses, on the rocks (in relief), in the books and on one day of the year in the butter-carvings, which delighted even the aesthetic Kagawuchi. Representations of the gods were regarded as their 'seat'. More, there were many stories of divine images which had made themselves or fallen from the sky, and images that spoke were to be found everywhere in Tibet.[568] So convinced were the Tibetans of what the senses teach, that when an image required to be repaired they invited the deity by means of a mirror to leave his abode for the time being. When the repairs were completed, they removed the cloth that had protected the mirror and requested the god to take up residence in his former quarters.[569] God and matter were intimately knit. In connection with the doctrine of the short path a thangka was sometimes called 'liberation through sight'.[570] The layman need only see, he need not visualise. But that was the way of salvation for the monk. The texts with exact instructions for the making of bronzes and thangkas and describing the many detailed characteristics[571] to which the appearance of the deity, his surroundings, his attributes and often also his attendants had to conform, were in the exclusive possession of the lamas. Although lay artists were not unknown, they always worked under the careful supervision of a monk.[572] The foundry of Shigatse was already mentioned in another connection, but a great many bronzes were also made by Nepalese, who had a considerable reputation in this field, though they too had of course to work according to precise indications. Differences in the social scale appeared here also: gilded copper was the most expensive, ordinary copper or bronze was the material for the images of the poor.

In principle the image was for the monk a temporary means in order to be able later on to visualise the deity without this help, or for those unable to engage in abstract and immediate meditation a permanent point of departure.[573] Yet also if the monk had no contemplative gifts, it became clear to him that the apparently so chaotic pantheon was ordered. Not only was an individual thangka built up in a systematic way, but a series of thangkas also had a mutual relation, and not infrequently the lay-out of a complete hall or an entire monastery rested upon a theological iconographic system. Such order also prevailed in the depiction of the Terrifying Ones, and for this reason alone a thangka cannot be compared to a Hieronymus Bosch. This desire for order has its origin in the meditation, which presupposes an exact and systematic mind. In passing, a warning may be given here against too loose a comparison with psychoanalysis. Although there are points of resemblance, a teacher either inside or outside the monastery did not dream of letting a pupil indulge in free association. He let him follow a path which had been exactly laid out, although in choosing the path the pupil's nature was taken into account.

The Terrifying Ones usually had a special place on the thangkas of the peaceful deities. In accordance with their function of protectors of the faith they were then shown on the borders around the central picture. This position was also interpreted as their marginal position between matter and the spiritual world, again showing that the line of cleavage went right through these gods. The same line of thought lay behind the many thangkas that showed the Terrifying Ones at the bottom, while buddhas or saints were seated above in the heavenly regions. How much the Terrifying Ones were feared and how important they were was plainly shown when a mGon khang thangka was made. Preparations, execution and dedication formed a religious ritual. Ideally, the painting of such a thangka is a meditation, in which the painter visualises the god and identifies himself with him. Considering the amazing evocative power of these masterpieces, in which the Terrifying Ones seem to lead an independent life, just as autonomous as the uncurbed primordial urges they symbolise, we may presume this ideal was not a dead letter. For the other thangkas too, however, it is valid that 'every painting is an invocation', as Tucci says, who is most expert in this field.[574] The art of painting and of bronze had no other function than the religious one, either in the magical or in the mystic sense. Both the preparation and the use of paintings and bronzes were sacred occupations. The insistence upon correct iconography even found expression in technique. Drawing and painting were two different employments, and usually carried out by two different persons. Not infrequently the drawing was copied, for instance by pricking it over, so that the artist need not concern himself with the correctness of the iconographical details. (Such astounding figures as the Nepalese citrākaras, who for payment were able in a few minutes to draw in exact detail any one of the roughly one thousand gods of the Lamaist pantheon, were never known in Tibet.[575]) Then the painter set to work. Although he had opportunity, for instance in treating the faces, to show presence or absence of talent, his first care had to be that the right colours were applied in the right places. The founder of the bronzes, who usually worked à cire perdue, also had to set correct iconography as his first aim, even though to us there are great differences between some masterpieces and the aesthetically worthless production. For the Tibetans it was more important that the bronze should be consecrated and that the space reserved inside contained the sacred text. Thus art too is completely subservient to religion, though the mGon kang thangkas are proof that this servitude need not lead to aesthetic impotence, if only a flash passed from the profound central truths represented by the Terrifying Ones to the artist and his craft.

No one can tell what would have happened if Buddhism had not, from a colonising religion, become the ruling power, so perpetuating the acculturative situation and 'congealing' it. Tucci shows there have been signs of emancipation in art.[576] Artistic freedom and growing aesthetic perception transpires in certain periods from the fact, that in Gyan-tse thangkas were signed, that the earth becomes visible in this art that was originally only dedicated to heaven, and landscape is timidly attempted, and that man appears in the picture, be it of course in his religious aspect. We have seen a similar development in the European history of art. In Tibet it was of essential significance that earth and mankind were brought into the picture. Before it had only been permissible to express these indirectly in the demonised forms of the Terrifying Ones. And afterwards too no more was allowed, for the foreign religion of Buddhism became more and more a 'colonialising' power in the hands of Tibet's own monks. These plainly betrayed their colonialistic tendencies by selling themselves and Tibet to a foreign power for the sake of their own rule. Perhaps, as short-sighted patriots, they thought they could run with the hare and hunt with the hounds, maintaining Tibet's independance by regarding themselves as the guardians of the Land of Snow and the Chinese only as alms-givers. Tibetan painting remained what it had been, nameless, timeless, flat without depth, rigid in composition and of frontal aspect. The last three traits only apply from the Western point of view. Never may we forget that the thangkas and bronzes were not made for us, so that Malraux' well-known attempt, as a 'conquérant' of the twentieth century, to appropriate the art of the whole world, is only permissible if in the 'musée imaginaire' one quite consciously re-creates the art of others according to one's own values. Owing to Malraux' undeniable force of mind his attempt may command our respect, yet one cannot help wondering what the values are the modern West could take as norm in re-creating the art of other cultures. In Tibet a work of art was an object of sacred use, excepting the reliefs modelled in butter, so highly praised by all travellers. Upon most of the Tibetans these had an aesthetic, fairy-tale effect, though many of simple faith knelt also before the gods in butter.[577] Though one cannot refrain from noting differences in craftsmanship, one can only arrive at a true appreciation of both form and content of this art by placing it in the context of religion and culture, which are both so evidently cleft in two that one is almost inclined to place the system of two matching colours with one clashing colour under the same head. Even the magnificent craftsmanship of the mGon khang thangkas should be seen in the first place as an expression of religious meditation, which could be so intensive and could so faultlessly be conveyed as a present reality in the painting, for the reason that the Terrifying Ones activated the deepest values and conflicts of the Tibetans: 'l'artiste Tibétain *sent*, il ne *sait* pas'.[578] Not from the Western, but from the Tibetan conception of life one can characterise them, who according to esoteric Buddhism ought to be symbols of the destruction of the ego, with Rosenzweig's words about the body, which roars I, I, I.[579] The contrast between these deities and the serene Buddhas can not be overlooked in Tibet. That it could become so unbridgeable was the result of a development whereby monks were able to lay hold of all monopolies. In the field of art this was not only expressed by their exclusive possession of the iconographical texts and their supervision of the making of works of art, but also in the fact that of all the deities depicted – yi-dam, buddhas, bodhisattvas, terrible gods etc. – the canonised monks, abbots and prelates stood upon the top rung of the heavenly ladder. To depict a sainted monk, *e.g.* Tsong-kha-pa, in the centre with one or more deities in a secondary position is perfectly normal in Tibetan art.

On the one hand art expressed the contrast between laity and monks, and on the other it was one of the elements composing the cement that kept Tibet's fascinating society and culture together. We have said that paintings and images were to be found everywhere, indoors and outdoors, with laymen, monks and mystics. The different way they were interpreted by the people and by the initiated can also be formulated in social terms that show how Tibet was two-in-one. The comparison with the feudal times of mediaeval christianity, which could have obtruded in another context, may be explicitly made here, for it enables us to see the shift in the social function of art, compared with primitive cultures. In the western middle ages, too, art was the means whereby the illiterate masses could assimilate the story of salvation. Then too, the plastic and literary arts were the medium. The mystery plays of the christian middle ages and those of Tibet, the cham, even have their drollery in common. Seeing how both Christian and Buddhist missionaries repeatedly chose to begin their work with the kings, one may hazard the guess, that when in an 'Überlagerungsherrschaft' the intrusive ruling groups wish also to introduce a new ideology, they are forced to make use of images, as their 'subjects' are illiterate. A conscious or unconscious use is then made of an inclination to regard the image as the seat or representative of a divine reality. This deep-seated inclination of the human mind is the most wide-spread tendency among primitive peoples. In Tibet it resulted in a plenitude of images that spoke.

182

In such cultures, however, it is no longer the attitude of *everyone*. There are many initiates among the ruling classes who know better. Thus the work of art is no longer just a means of expression and a symbol, it also becomes a means of power. In Western Europe the layman became emancipated, and as a result art developed from Giotto to Picasso. In Tibet the monks retained a monopoly both of mystery plays and of plastic arts, so that in the church-state a strictly ordered church-art could continue to exist. There is not the slightest need to pronounce value judgments here in an anti-clerical frame of mind. The parallel between Western Europe and Tibet causes us to suppose that in the feudal phases of development religion plays an exceptional part, and must necessarily do so. That then the urge to power becomes active among laity and clerics, goes without saying in a socio-political organisation explicitly based on power. In the twentieth century also ideology and art are used for the same purposes by rulers who like to quote Karl Marx on the correlation between feudal organisation and priests. Marx is right though, in so far that religion has a very special place in such societies, also as a means of power. The dropping out of the centralising political power in the isolated Land of Snow caused its culture, religion and art to become a classical illustration of the description given by the grand-master of American cultural anthropology, A. L. Kroeber, in a well-known, balanced passage: 'Organized religion has a way of being influential in the overturn and the reconstruction of major civilizations. It works first towards cultural change and then for conservation'. Be it repeated however, that in art also the Terrifying Ones are proof that the work of reconstruction was unable to fill in the gap between the old and the new.

THE TERRIFYING DEITIES IN MYSTICISM AND ART

In the eyes of the people the Terrifying Ones were the fearsome demons who were protectors of the faith, but who were not well-disposed towards people at home either. Unlike the pre-Buddhist enemy gods, the *dgra lha*, who were active tutelary spirits, these protectors were so charged with aggressivity and so dangerous, that their protection was as much to be feared as their enmity. The defenders of the doctrine may have seemed less ambiguous to the monks, because their activity was in the first place directed against everything outside the monastery walls. Yet their subterranean, volcanic presence in the mGon khang, and the necessity of reminding them every day of their oath, created an atmosphere of unreliability and threatened danger. The brutal impulse of unbridled sexuality and especially of all-destroying aggressivity, made their life a shrill contrast to the peace of the Buddha and the buddhas, in spite of systematic theology. Only a rather unconvincing 'although' could forge a liturgical link between the two. For great and small mystics, also, the Terrifying Ones constituted an almost insoluble problem, at least if they took the symbolism of these gods seriously. A copulating pair, that have fallen upon one another like two beasts of prey, seems a poor symbol for the supreme peace of insight and liberation. The partners will either devour one another so that nothing remains, or their hatred will melt away in the bliss of union.

Of course it was possible to regard these coupling devils as the essence of natural life: a senseless coupling of sexuality and aggressivity creating and destroying life, a view that will appear at the end of this chapter. But that was not the intention of the tantras like the Hevajra tantra, which glorified this diabolic coitus as the summum bonum, without realising the inward contradiction entailed. It appears to the present writer that Tibetologists did not realise this either, and always treated the two aspects of sexuality and aggressivity disjunctively. The faithful belonging to the circles of the Indian Vajrayāna are not to be blamed, for they were no mystics. Whatever the mystic theologians – quite rightly from their point of view – may have turned the tantras into in their commentaries, he who studies those writings should remain in regular contact with mystics like Eckhart, the mystics of the early Buddhist writings, William Law, Śaṅkara, Plotinus, Santa Teresa and others, that he may be continually conscious of the objective chasm separating their mysticism from tantric mysticism, even when the latter is authentic and practised by yogins who are able to actualise their theories wholly or in part.

A text like the Hevajra tantra is a valuable and interesting human document, but that does not imply mysticism nor even authentic yoga. It is a mixture of ritualism, coarse magic, and sexual practices, sanctioned by yogic and philosophic passages, the latter being intended to show that the body must be saved by the body. Such sects are also to be found in the history of christendom; there too profound truths from the Bible and from Christian philosophy are brought forward to render their social protest and their outburst of feeling acceptable, a typical trait of 'plebeian religions'. With reference to a meeting of a contemporary sect of this kind, the author once heard a professor make the refreshing remark: theologically speaking, they are largely right! In the Hevajra tantra sex and aggressivity are unconnected. 'Love is our business, not dissension.' Love is for internal, and aggressivity for external use. It is noticeable that the sexual passages contain little or no aggressivity, although one of the principal results of liberation is that one becomes possessed of magical power over women, enemies and so on. The aggressivity is directed against the enemies of this creed. When the god awakes from the rapturous intoxication of union with his partner, he springs to his feet as a fearsome demon, a deadly danger to his enemies. In the truly yogic passages, indeed, the aim is not mystic union and un-becoming, but the magic power of the yogin Hevajra with his megalomaniac cry of 'I, I, I!'. One might say, then, that in these circles an incoherent mixture of sexuality and aggressivity and yogic rationalisation offered a more or less religious outlet to those without yogic gifts, while those of some yogic talent desired to strengthen the magic powers of 'I, the great yogin' by means of coitus reservatus or strictly inward yoga. To observe that these ends differ considerably from the nirvāṇa of the early Buddhists and from the unio mystica of other mystics, is a matter of simple objectivity.

The way love and hate were distributed over friends and enemies in Tantrism might be the general human, practical solution of the problem how to ventilate both love and hatred without getting caught in conflicting situations, the god who was black with devilish ferocity while nevertheless peace ruled in his heart, did become a problem if and when mystics were to see in him and his yum the symbol of ultimate unity, of 'the extreme arrest'. For the complete and absolute concentration aimed only at losing the self in the ultimate reality which is nothing and everything, is ruinously disturbed if sexuality and aggressivity are carried to extremes, even if they are not physical urges but tendencies of the spirit. Aggressivity means destruction, analysis, maintaining and defending the self. Even in Chöd the adept proved unable to prevent the attempt at self-destruction through aggression from turning into self-glorification. Sexuality, on the other hand, stands on the mental level for construction, synthesis, union and loss of self. The will towards union can carry a certain degree of aggressivity, and even requires it, for instance when in the first stages of the mystic way detachment is to be arrived at through analysis. The closer one comes to the goal, however, the more the aggressive tendency will have to drop into the background. The coition of the Terrifying Ones shows aggressivity in altogether fiendish dimensions.

For proselytising sorcerers like Padmasambhava and their Tibetan pupils, however, this was no objection. They had no mystical intentions, they desired magic power by means of sexual practices or inward yoga. And indeed, most of what is rather carelessly labelled Tibetan mysticism was in reality magic on the basis of a certain amount of yoga, aiming not at loss of the self but at its maintenance. It should be kept in mind that the ego-inflatory tendencies of the Indian Vajrayāna and those of national Tibetan magic together occasioned a lasting yogic and magical undertone in the whole religious life of the Land of Snow. Even an ideal figure like Mi-la re-pa is extremely self-assured, banning demons and flying through the air; all the same, there is a great difference between him and a common charlatan with a minimum of yoga and a maximum of pretensions. In one of the four rituals of Yamāntaka, which in many books would be called mystic, the spoken or unspoken intention of the adept was: 'May I become governor', 'May that woman set her heart upon me', 'May that villain die'.[580] Other initiations though, David-Neel adds here, are aimed at increasing the possessions of the spirit. Yet these spiritual goods are in very many cases of a magical kind. It is not unusual for a man explicitly to pride himself on being able to achieve identification with the deity, while another 'was able by a mere order to invoke his Religious Protector'.[581] That is no un-becoming, no unio mystica. A superior attitude with regard to the gods was in itself in accordance with tradition, but the sublime indifference of the Buddha towards the gods was very different from this aggressive lust of power. One of the best-known methods to attain this yogic power by meditation consisted, with regard to the Terrifying Ones, in first visualising e.g. Yamāntaka and then his yum, after which one let the pair copulate. Then the adept could let the yum dissolve into the god, or let first her and subsequently the god melt away into nothingness. The essence of this and similar methods of meditation was, that the adept knew himself to be one with the Many and with the One, whereby he could realise Voidness. Although serious study of the texts concerned has hardly begun, all travellers' reports indicate, that in practice the result was not Voidness but inflation of the ego. Such is comprehensible to outsiders also. From beginning to end, this method of meditation is control, domination. It is the adept who produces the whole process and keeps it in check. His having part both in the One and nirvāṇa and in the Many and samsāra is indeed a variation of the Śaiva yoga, in which the yogin destroyed and recreated the world as he pleased. It is true that in this case Voidness was the beginning and the end, but autism, regarded as a danger in the mysticism that seeks to give up the self, was for very many a principle and an aim. Obviously the terrifying combination of sexuality and aggressivity could not become a fundamental problem in this yoga of self-maintenance, and meditative control over deities of this kind tended rather to increase self-assurance. We have already mentioned that Mi-la re-pa contemptuously called a god without a yum, his widower's aspect. These forms of meditation implied moving to and fro between static and dynamic, the one and the many, from which the ego had to free itself, to dominate them.

It should be repeated, however, that from this yogic point of departure it was possible to set out in various directions. Chöd too furthered inflation of the ego, but was yet a mental feat of the first rank. A different way was followed by men like Mi-la re-pa, a very great yogin who yet recommended meditation in charnel fields only as practically useful, warning

33 Za-byed rdo-rje mkha'-'gro. Bronze. h.: 6³/₈ in. (16 cm)

33

34

against excess.[582] A very great contrast was presented by the hermit who had retired to pass the rest of his life in a cave in the mountains, that he had closed with a wall of stones, leaving only a small opening. A Tibetan who had the opportunity one day of inspecting this meditation cell, found the cave hung with human hair, skins, skeletons and bones from hands, while a great number of dried female breasts were hanging on a line. The hermit had gradually collected these furnishings from a charnel field in the neighbourhood. His food bowl was the dried and prepared skin of a woman's breast.[583] The aggressive sexual collecting mania of such a person arouses some doubt as to the congruence of his conscious yogic intentions and his unconscious motivation. The surplus of symbols of mortality, particularly of female mortality, can with some probability be interpreted as an unconscious fixation on these mortal things, and as a protest against the mother breast, betraying the same fixation.

Mi-la re-pa belonged to the Ka-gyü-pa (bKa'-rgyud-pa), and the greater part of the yogins of this order were fully serious in their practice of meditation. It was an order of anchorites rather than of monks. There is a reliable account describing how after a course of theoretical and practical instruction by a teacher – the teacher was extremely important among the Ka-gyü-pa – the pupils retired for three months and three days to a little meditation hut of about one yard square, containing one or two divine images, a cup, a food bowl and a wooden frame to sit on. After this period of meditation, further studies and exercises followed, and then the pupil retired for three years, three months and three days. At the expiration of this time he completed his studies and training and so, fully prepared, withdrew into the meditation hut for the rest of his life, never to leave it again.[584] This is in entire agreement with the field-work of Pozdnejev in Mongolia, referred to above. It is clear one can no longer use the word magic here. Even if not nirvāṇa but yogic immortality were the aim of this life-long contemplation and meditation, its absolutism is no longer of a magic nature. Even if the yogic self-importance were to arise in such a life of spiritual concentration, its completely asocial and autarkic character would make it quite different, from the psychological point of view, from that of yogins who overawed kings and populace. Even if – for really reliable information is scarce, and even more in the mystic field than in all other departments of Tibetology we must for the present be content to make the best of what we have. Philologists tell us it will be a very long time before we have fuller material. We know very little indeed of Tibet, and even less of its mysticism. Therefore it must be emphasised again that this study of the culture, religion and mysticism of Tibet in their mutual relations is only intended as a preliminary exploration of fields that, when studied, are nearly always examined separately, while problems of mysticism are usually left to one side.

Recently a systematic exposé of the via mystica of the Ka-gyü-pa was given by a German who has joined this order. Such conversions are usually regarded with some suspicion, and rightly so, while serious scholars are inclined not to attach very much value to the information supplied by converts. There are exceptions to this rule, however. Every ethnologist knows the name of the Indian Nimuendajú, which hid the personality of a German who had identified himself completely with the South American Indians, having been accepted into one of their tribes, and who yet did extremely important work for the ethnology of South America. With regard to a European joining the Ka-gyü-pa it should be stressed that for purposes of study it is not of the slightest significance whether this European does or does not wear European dress, and has or has not practised the yoga he describes. The only question of any importance in such a case is *whether the information he supplies is correct.* In this instance the information is in any case systematic and precise. Until material can be published of a kind preferred by both philologists and cultural anthropologists, this information may at any rate be profitably compared with that already available. In this case of course the main emphasis will be on the role of the Terrifying Ones along the via mystica.

It is striking that in the mysticism aiming at loss of selfhood and at unbecoming which is expounded here, union and unification are of central importance. Although it is stressed, in accordance with Buddhist principles, that the mystic does not dissolve his being in the infinite or unite his soul with the deity, but without help from outside becomes conscious of his own completeness,[585] this realisation proves to be an inward unio mystica. In the mystic the two halves of his nature are united, and this ultimately leads to the unity of man and the world.[586] Light is certainly shed by the lines quoted from a poem by Rilke, certainly no stranger to mysticism, if a great aesthete.

> '*Denn der Geist, der uns vereinsamt, will*
> *völlig sicher sein, uns zu vereinen.*'
> (*For the mind that makes us lonely, wants*
> *To be sure that we shall be united.*)

The first phase of this mysticism consists of becoming conscious of the spaceless and timeless element present in the limited and temporal individual. One might also say with Plessner: on the one hand bound in the body, bound in the soul, on the other nowhere, outside all space and time. As such feelings are very vague and confusing, the next step is unification. This unity is found in the spirit which is clear, pure and imperishable like a diamond, that is capable of cutting anything else but can itself never be cut: vajra. When this insight has become not only a theory, but has caused a reversal of the very foundations of existence, 'the turning about in the deepest seat of consciousness', the mystic has made the change to a higher level of consciousness, so that he can see things and people in a bigger context, in a more objective way, *i.e.* unfettered by egotism, because upon this level of consciousness he is aware of the relativity of the ego-concept. In accordance with the alternating yogic process of analysis and synthesis, this unification is followed by the stage where the mystic allows the diamond-mind to unfold, wherein careful and exact visualisation is of supreme importance. 'Just as an artist must gain perfect control over his means of expression and makes use of a variety of technical aids in order to achieve the most perfect expression of his idea, in the same way the spiritually creative man must be able to master the functions of his mind and use certain technical aids in order to embue his vision with the power and value of reality'.[587] There is no place for vague emotions and confused ideas. One of the principal aims at this stage is the uniting of upāya and prajnā as yab and yum. Govinda gives the following psychological explanation: it is in essence the uniting of feeling and intellect. Intellect without feeling is sterile, rigid and destructive. Feeling without reason leads to vagueness and confusion, and crumbles away. The symbol of this union is the union of male and female. The active knower becomes one with his knowledge, and feeling, that is in communion with others, is consubstantiated with intellectual insight. Fundamentally, man and woman stand here as signs of the polarity to which life is subject, as modern science agrees, and in which it has its being.

A text also quoted by Tsong-kha-pa may show in the first place that the mystic theologians in Tibet were themselves also very matter-of-fact and realistic on this point, and secondly that a conformity between Govinda's exposé and Tibetan psychology cannot be denied. According to this text the highest state is attained by human beings for one infinitesimal instant without mystical exertions on the ocasion of 1) dying, 2) becoming unconscious, 3) falling asleep, 4) yawning, 5) coition.[588] It is evident that these mystics and mystic theologians had both feet on the ground, and in mysticism also took their point of departure in the body. The aim of the via mystica is the perpetuation, the eternisation of that one indivisible experience attached to these psycho-somatic phenomena. From the point of view of animal psychology it might be possible to pose, and perhaps to answer, the question whether this text might not refer to a number of 'displacement phenomena' of a very particular kind. In animal psychology a displacement activity is, generally speaking, a form of behaviour which results from two other behavioural tendencies that inhibit one another, so that displacement becomes possible and may also be regarded as a solution of the conflict.[589] The comparison of human and animal behaviour is certainly permissible in Buddhism, while it is also more and more regarded as legitimate by modern science.[590] We may therefore ask whether and which of the five human situations mentioned are moments of displacement, when an inward tension between two tendencies that has become too strong for consciousness to bear, finds a solution in loss of consciousness, which mysticism desires to transpose to another level. This very tentative question is posed on the basis of a hypothesis suggested in ethology that yawning may be a displacement activity in man also. Yet even if the answer were entirely in the negative, the question still has meaning in that it points to a direction which the study of mysticism should *also* take. If the Tibetan theorists may set such phenomena side by side, then they are giving a plain indication, by means of which it may in some way become possible to speak about mysticism in a slightly less vague manner. A remark like 'heaven and earth and hell become one'[591] is altogether too indefinite. We may here refer back to what was said in a previous chapter with reference to the fundamental tension between the ego and the Self, and the question whether this tension can be solved 'aggressively' or 'sexually.'

Govinda interprets the symbol of coitus as the cancellation of the polar tension between feeling and reason and between other polar contrasts. In the next phase, says this author, the mystic seeks to realise in his psychical and physical life the adamantine timelessness of the spirit which he has discovered in the union of intellect and feeling. The technique applied for this purpose is the Buddhist form of Kuṇḍalinī yoga, which is distinguished from the Hindu form, for one thing, by the absence of the sexual element. It is also interesting, that according to this system the Buddhist mystic is not interested in the slightest to know where the various 'lotus centres' are located, whether they do or do not correspond with certain parts of the nervous system (a problem which Avalon discusses at great length), but simply 'makes' these centres. For the object is to transform a man via certain states of consciousness, and the centres are merely the visualised symbols of those states. The logic of this train of thought can certainly not be denied. Along these rungs of the yoga-ladder the mystic wishes to liberate his self as it is bound to the body here and now. It is no longer a matter of finding the spaceless and timeless vajra-mind in which and in whose light there exists no ego, but of making the present soul and spirit lose the ego in this body. What is to be achieved is to render the ego-less vajra eternity a reality in man here and now. It is then that the Terrifying Ones loom up. When in the final phase the mystic becomes aware that he has reached this summit also, he suddenly, on the very top, finds an abyss before him and has no other choice – if he would lose all illusions of 'I' and 'mine' – but to jump, seemingly into nothingness. The ḍākinīs, who can be benevolent as well as terrifying[592], are symbols of the mighty impulses drawing the mystic on, the equally terri-fying Herukas, as symbols of activity, set him off. The terrifying copulation of these divinities in a fierce dance is the vision of the mystic, who does not jump into Nothing, but courageously springs across the chasm leaving as it were his ego behind him.[593] The violence **and** anguish of this last leap across the abyss of loss of selfhood shocks him who has the courage to carry it out to the inmost foundation of his being, so that he feels annihilated. One might also say that the furious dancing and the diabolic grins of the Terrifying Ones are the actual symbols of a human being who is torn from himself.

One might for a moment be inclined to think that this interpretation betrays the European and the German with his knowledge of Klages, Rilke and Jung (who are not by any means hidden away), but one soon sees that this intriguing view of the final phase of the via mystica of the Ka-gyü-pa not only agrees with Western opinions, but also with important data from Tibet and India. In the first place, it is no small thing that Evans-Wentz, whose informant Dawa Samdup also belonged to the Ka-gyü-pa, locates the Terrifying Ones in the brain centre,[594] an association which is repeatedly stressed by Govinda. The 'place' of the Terrifying Ones is the brain centre, while the Peaceful deities are visualised as dwelling in the heart lotus.[595] This indicates that the intellect is an aggressive and destructive function in man, which can destroy life. There is agreement on this point between a European and a Tibetan member of the Ka-gyü-pa, and many intellectuals will not wish to gainsay this thesis. We can also establish a direct connection between the aggressive character of these 'brain gods' and that which was said above on the subject of aggressivity and self-preservation. For the first time it is acknowledged here on the basis of Tibetan data that aggressivity

35 Dus-'khor (Skt. Kālacakra) yab-yum. Scroll painting. 14⁷/₈ × 10⁵/₈ in. (38 × 27 cm)

35

cannot lead to the unio mystica, and it is to be hoped that the relevant texts will soon be translated. Not only is aggressivity psychologically directed towards self-preservation or increase of power, but it was also found that a clear correlation could be shown in the practice of yoga between aggresssivity and self-preservation and ego-inflation. Thus it is most consistent that at the moment when the mystic forces his way through the barrier of the ego – Govinda speaks of 'breaking through' in this context – the Terrifying Ones appear to him as a symbol of the final fear of losing the ego. This fear is in essence related to the fear of death. 'Whosoever will lose his life, shall save it.' Only very few, though, find the courage of wishing to lose their life and self. The genius of Freud discovered that the ego is the true seat of fear. Thus only he can be without fear, who has lost the illusion of his ego. He who dares undertake this loss, will have to find the courage to pass through a fear that borders upon mortal terror. To what Govinda tells us one might add the interpretation, that the copulating Terrifying Ones signify the ego's desperate attempt, in the instant of that leap through fear lasting for moments of Eternity, to clutch in terrified sexual aggressivity at the world of sense, to which it owes its illusory existence.

Comparing this via mystica with Chöd, we may well suppose that there is less danger of the 'rebound effect' of Chöd in the mysticism of the Ka-gyü-pa, because the sexual element of loss of selfhood at a sublimated level plays a far greater part in Chöd. Probably it is the very force of the aggressive attack upon the ego which causes this effect in Chöd. On the other hand the mysticism of the Ka-gyü-pa too retains a typical yogic atmosphere. Govinda several times mentions the violence of this decisive experience. Only in a mysticism in which the ego receives such emphasis can its loss be so vehement, in contrast with mysticism in which the drop dissolves into the ocean or the salt into the water. This is surprisingly confirmed in the experiences of the uncouth and violent Śaivite yogins, who probably contributed to the formation of Tibet's yogic and mystical traditions. However this may be, their experiences confirm Govinda's information in an altogether trustworthy manner. For when these yogins, who sought salvation in an atmosphere of vehement self-assertion and no small inflation of the ego, saw their great god Śiva appear before their spiritual vision, they called this 'the breaking in of the vision' and 'bhairava', a word that refers to Śiva in his terrifying aspect.[596] Also for these self-assured and protesting figures the barrier of consciousness and the ego could only be broken through the violence of fear, although to them this did not mean loss of selfhood, but a new identification with their terrifying god. In this context it is not without significance that the Prairie Indians, whose pride, strong self-confidence and great, if controlled, aggressivity cannot be doubted, had to struggle for a vision and only saw salvation after breaking down the barrier of the ego, which was not infrequently also a matter of physical violence.[597] In Tibet also at the highest mystic level the ego resisted in extreme terror, before breaking up as an empty illusion and disappearing into nothing.

Everything in the Vajrayāna as it was introduced by Padma and everything in Tibet itself which was only intensified by the culture contact, contributed to strengthen aggressivity

36 sRid-pa'i 'khor-lo (Skt Bhavacakra). Scroll painting

and thereby the urge of self-preservation. It is now clear that also in purer forms of mysticism it grew into a barrier of fear. We can now understand, why preoccupation with the ego, the seat of fear, made the yogins of the school of self-preservation afraid of the Terrifying Ones, who could completely destroy rituals and meditation, and who could be unimaginably demanding, incalculable and dangerous in the life of a serious yogin.[598] A most fascinating interdictory ceremony of Mi-la re-pa not only brings us into the marginal area between mysticism and the yoga of exorcism, but also plainly shows the ḍākinī as a marginal experience of the ego. When the female demon had appeared to him, he realised on the one hand that she was the projection of his own doubt and desire, but on the other hand he also saw her as the phantom of a wicked woman. He managed, however, to maintain against this 'wilde Gift des Weibes' (fierce poison of woman) that one thing is much worse than any demon: ego-ism and perception, scepticism and passion, which all originate from belief in the ego. Though the story – translated by Laufer – does not explicitly say so, this authentic realism enables us to sense that it was with difficulty Mi-la re-pa recognised her as the malevolent materialisation of his own sexual desire and fear of losing his selfhood. He remained at last in the yogic magical sphere, when through this insight he succeeded in changing her from an enemy to a protector of the doctrine. In mysticism this change, which is 'only' the result of the change taking place in the mystic, means that the ḍākinī becomes a positive, inspiring and driving force.

In the dance of the Terrifying Ones when the barrier of the ego is forced at last, these goddesses are in sexual union with their male partners. That is the element, which is entirely lacking in Chöd. In that ritual all aggressivity was loosed upon the ego at once, and the adept had to withstand the fury and violence of the demons by maintaining his consciousness in the Self. In the mysticism of the Ka-gyü-pa, however, we have to do with a path comprising several stages. Before the mystic arrives at the point of the decisive leap across the abyss[599] – the Self leaps, the ego falls – he has already traversed some of these, and it is of the greatest importance here that not only analysis and aggressivity, but also and especially synthesis and sexuality characterised the via mystica. In fact, it may really be said that 'yab-yum… emphasizes in visible form, what is present in *every* process of enlightenment and in each symbol of Buddhahood, even though it may be put into the form of the male aspect only'[600] Therefore the breaking-through to unification can be expressed by a Terrifying One as the highest symbol of this mysticism of selflessness: it is an 'experience of inner unification'.[601] Socially too this finds expression: the mystic is freed from the deadly isolation in which his ego and ego-ism had placed him, appearances to the contrary notwithstanding. It is signified by Avolokiteśvara's descent to earth. We have returned to the bodhisattva ideal, but now as a mystic experience. It is only possible as such in a mysticism proceeding through unification and loss of selfhood.

Although this subject has more aspects than can be discussed here, there seems to be justification for regarding the union of yab and yum as the decisive factor. Their horrific quality expresses the terror of losing the ego, which must unavoidably play a great part in this mysticism also. Yet their sexual union supplies the courage required to venture the leap into loss of selfhood; here there is no aggressive attack upon the ego, but a breaking-through towards oneness. It was said above: the Self leaps, the ego falls. Perhaps it would be more correct to say that the ego breaks through its limitations, dares to spring across to the Self, and loses itself in union with the Self. Far too little is known to speak with any certainty here. For the present, however, there seem to be several arguments in favour of the formulation suggested here. In union with the self the ego loses its power and a complete deflation of the ego takes place, for it can no longer refer everything to its centre, as it is now centred upon the Self and has become subservient to it. As a result, the Self can regard the ego with the same impartiality as the ego of anyone else.[602] The probability of this supposition is increased, when one realises that as inspiring muses the ḍākinīs attracted the mystic to a very different level of sublimation than the yums of Hevajra attracted that divine yogin... before they woke him again. They are the representatives of wisdom and the faces, distorted with wild terror, of the Terrifying Ones uniting with them, reflect the fear of the mystic, who also enters in unto the wisdom of the Self. The terror is communicated to the ḍākinīs, but it is a fear that lasts no longer than the leap, and once arrived at the 'other side' – to use an often employed Buddhist metaphor – the mystic finds the unity of tranquil buddhas with their yums as symbol of his own union with wisdom and insight, with prajñā. It is perseverance in union which makes possible the leap, 'an experience of unification', first causing anguish and alarm because the ego feels itself breaking up into nothing, then blissful as the ego is absorbed into union with the Self. The greatest of these is charity...

The great and decisive part played at the fateful moment by the ḍākinīs as symbols of the urge towards unity, and the fact that at each stage of the mystic way each new insight, and consequently each new state of consciousness, is expressed as the union of yab and yum, sufficiently indicate the dominant significance of sexuality as a sublimated urge towards unity. The difference between this via mystica and Chöd can also be interpreted psychoanalytically. Then Chöd is the ritual in which the adept, obsessed by the aggressive Bad Mother, directs this mother symbol against his own ego that he may be destroyed by her and so reborn. He can stand up to all the terrors of this hell, except union with the terrible Great Mother, so that in spite of the radical nature of Chöd a distance inevitably remains and the ultimate union and loss of selfhood are impossible, as is evident from the inflation of the ego. In the via mystica of the Ka-gyü-pa on the other hand the mystic decides to go in unto the Bad Mother. By reason of the historical tradition and the cultural context, in this instance of Tibetan mysticism also the Great Mother is negative and aggressive, so that the mystic has to transform her (there was no suggestion of this in Chöd!). Here the process is succesful, because he is not afraid of contact with her. Thus his mysticism can become a mysticism of discarding the private self, of union with the opposite pole which is insight and wisdom. This psychoanalytical interpretation is certainly not without significance, also in connection with the negativisation of woman in these circles. Preference must be given here, however, to an interpretation in the more general terms of the two vital powers of sexuality and aggressivity, which in the present study have been regularly referred to Tibet's culture and religion, and proved to have validity without carrying a reference to mother symbols. Such an interpretation is also to be preferred because these terms are not only more general, but will also prove to be more fundamental.

That there is a connection in human life between sexuality and aggressivity can be taken for a fact, although there is one school of psychology that only wishes to regard aggressivity as a result following upon frustration. In view of the history of mankind it is a little difficult to maintain this. The never ending story of human aggressivity, which seems to be reaching a new peak in our days, can hardly be explained by means of a theory of frustration.[603] To keep to this theory, it is necessary to regard human existence in itself as essentially and fundamentally frustrated. But it is one of the principal characteristics of all animal life, that it can bear down upon its objectives, *aggrediri*. The necessity of self-preservation and the intensity with which this *aggrediri* is carried out, determine the more or less destructive character of aggressivity. Besides, the fact that life lives on life, and that much animal life lives on other animal life is difficult to put into a modish concept like frustration. Primitive peoples have clearly perceived the relation between the two vital powers of sexuality and aggressivity. Examples are plentiful. Among the Maori *toa* meant both a brave warrior and a virile man, while 'the peculiar state of the virile organ of a warrior when engaged in mortal combat is a matter well recognised in Maori superstitions'.[604] On the one hand sexuality is expressed in aggressive terms, as when, for instance, the men say to the women: we will spear you, on the other hand aggressivity is expressed in terms of sexuality, when for instance a Keraki head-hunter says to his dying victim, that the spirit of the bull-roarer is copulating with him (the victim).[605] There is a remarkable correlation, then, between wanting to control the world and maintain one's self, and the desire for union and loss of selfhood.

Animals, too, demonstrate this striking connection. Outside the reproductive period, we find that many social kinds of animal also display a remarkable correlation between an obvious need of social contact and the need for aggressive self-assertion, so that a certain 'critical distance' is observed between the individuals, the limit of which is not transgressed.[606] Leiden research workers have been able to observe, for instance, that the distance between the nests of terns breeding in colonies is greater with a more aggressive kind of tern than with a less aggressive species. The problem whether this social behaviour is in any way connected with the relation between sexuality and aggressivity must remain undiscussed. It is quite certain, however, that this relation is of the greatest importance in that form of social behaviour which is decisive for the continued existence of the species, in mating. There are clear indications that the critical factor for successful mating is the mutual relation of sexuality and aggressivity or that of sexuality and flight reaction.[607] As flight reaction is difficult to measure, little or nothing is known of the latter combination. The relationship between sexuality and aggressivity has been studied particularly in the ethological laboratory of the National University of Leiden. All problems were not, of course, solved, but a great deal of information was obtained, only a small part of which has been published. One of the results of this research among various kinds of animals, comprising innumerable observations in the field and in the laboratory, concerns us here.

When the three-spined stickleback, a very small fish, comes into a reproductive phase and begins to build a nest, his aggressivity rapidly increases. He defends his territory, of which the nest is the most aggressively defended centre, even when not in the middle, against all intruders. It can be shown experimentally that meanwhile sexuality also increases, and must continue to increase until it finally becomes stronger than aggressivity, if the animal is to exhibit mating behaviour.[608] Put into human terminology: the urge towards self-preservation must become subordinate to the urge towards contact and towards loss of selfhood in the form of loss of semen. Setting aside a few other problems, this is a clearly defined result, which the author found confirmed in a series of experiments in which a choice had to be made. If during the entire reproductive phase a stickleback is several times a day offered a 'choice' between a male and a female model – on the well-founded supposition that the choice of the male means preponderant aggressivity and the choice of the female preponderant sexuality – then his responses, graphically expressed, show at first a strongly increasing aggressivity and subsequently also an increasing sexuality. The two tendencies may sometimes vie with one another for a short period, but normally sexuality becomes stronger than aggressivity. Then the male can lead a female to the nest, stimulate her to laying eggs by what in human psychology would be called sublimated aggressivity coupled with sexuality – which supposes physical contact – and then fertilise the eggs. Once mating has taken place, the aggressivity of the male rapidly increases again, which may be regarded as an indication that it is only for reproduction that sexuality need be dominant.

The normal course of events seems so much a matter of course, that comparatively little attention is paid to it until a concrete incident illustrates its significance. One of the subjects in these experiments was in a condition of extreme sexual excitement according to all the experts. When the observer was seated in front of the aquarium, the slightest movement of a shoe was sufficient to make the subject shoot towards it in a zig-zag movement, like an orange flash. The zig-zag movement is a characteristic form of sexual behaviour. Most surprisingly, however, in the experiments the animal always 'chose' the male. To eliminate faults of observation in the lightning reaction of this three-spined stickleback, the assistance of other observers was requested, who in many experiments confirmed the continual choice of the male model. The female model was practically ignored, in spite of the condition of sexual excitement the animal seemed to be in. That the observations had been correct was made evident, when the animal was given the company of a real female, who had to be removed from the aquarium not once but three times, because the male attacked and bit her in a highly aggressive manner. In natural circumstances the female would of course have been able to swim away. Only then did the author fully realise that if sexuality does not become stronger than aggressivity, life cannot continue. Such a male is not capable of reproduction. Be it mentioned in passing that Dr. J. J. A. van Iersel of this university, whose assistance made it possible for these experiments to be carried on for several years, states that also in a normal social context extreme aggressivity can apparently not be tolerated, as such individuals are expelled by the others. Evidently aggressivity must in general remain subordinate both to the social and the sexual tendency.

The following hypothesis is suggested by the above. Just as reproduction and the birth of new life is not possible on the biological level unless sexuality is stronger than aggressivity, so upon that level of the human spirit we call mysticism, rebirth to a new life is not possible if the urge towards union is not stronger than the urge towards distance and self-preservation. Let it be stressed that this is not meant as a simile, but to express the surmise that the same law applies to various levels of life. Only when the Terrifying Ones unite with their yum and when this union counts for more than their frightfulness (in the mating of animals too there remains an aggressive element), is rebirth made possible, so that man is no longer centred in his ego but can lead a new life in the Self. The purely aggressive Chöd holds considerable danger of madness, besides the inflation of the ego. The above conjectures require further elaboration, particular attention being paid to the mysticism of the early Buddhist texts, as the mysticism represented there is of an exceptional kind.[609]

One might ask whether these *exercitia spiritualia* will evoke the same forms, the same symbols and the same experiences in every adept. Mysticism is the affair of individuals, and particularly Buddhism with its strong streak of individualism since the earliest times might raise the expectation that such individual experiences would have a decidedly personal character, differing from one individual to another. In the first place, however, mysticism of all times and countries displays such striking conformity of structure that coincidence may be excluded and mysticism may be regarded as affording *proof* that the human mind has the same structure everywhere. It is simply astounding, and only to be explained by the anti-spiritual attitude of our time, that psychology, so much in vogue, has paid no attention to this matter, but just goes on developing new tests. Rudolf Otto's comparing of the work of Eckhart and Śaṅkara alone would afford work for many psychologists. Via theoretical understanding, the accepted way of the West, such work would also open up the possibility of authentic understanding and interest in these terra incognita, so that interaction would be possible. Uniform as the general structure may be, there are nevertheless individual, but especially cultural variations upon the theme which are no less worth while. In this respect Buddhism in general and particularly Tibetan Buddhism are of very great importance. It is therefore worth pointing out once more that ultimately mysticism, too, is culturally determined, and that individual variations only move within a small margin. In Tibet the relationship between teacher and pupil was of central importance, and it should be mentioned in this context that the most important directions were often given by word of mouth, great value being attached to the oral tradition. Of free mental association, as already remarked, there could be no question.[610] The pupil was shown a way, this way was exactly indicated, and if the pupil did not wish to follow it, he could leave, like poor Mi-la re-pa, who deserted in despair when his master Mar-pa made him carry stones and do building till his whole back was one great sore. It has been noticed in the West that the patients of Jungian psychiatrists have Jungian dreams, whereas the patients of Freudian analists dream in a Freudian dialect. Neither is it surprising that in the visions of the Tibetan adepts and mystics the same images appeared in the same order, especially since they had already been trained consciously to visualise most of them. Yet this again does not mean that their yoga or mysticism was a matter of auto-suggestion or a 'Wiederbelebung der Dichtungsformen' (reliving of poetical constructions), as sceptical Yakuts called the trances of their shamans![611] This was one of the reasons why in these circles in Tibet the written word was regarded with distrust. They were afraid of 'words, words', because they were aware that once something has been written down, people think they know it and have realised it, when they have read it. Indeed, as one reads one thinks one is sharing in the experience oneself and taking part in the action. The yogic and mystic teachings were too important for that. They were concerned with ultimate salvation, 'the extreme arrest', but this required not to be read, but to be made into living reality in man. Thus there is on the one hand an institutionalisation of mysticism, so that mysticism too becomes part of a culture, on the other hand resistance against too great an institutionalisation through the written word, because then the acultural part of mysticism would be lost and a man would come to think he could read his own salvation instead of 'working it out with fear and trembling' in the words of Paul.

In this way the Terrifying Ones, who found their prototypes in the Vajrayāna of India and in the demons of Tibet itself, became one of the most typical charateristics of the Land of Snow after the coming of Buddhism, as the result of a process of acculturation that confronted the Tibetans with bizarre shamans like Padmasambhava, and that ultimately demonised practically all the national gods. As the acculturative tensions continued through the centuries, the Terrifying Ones also continued to be the most important gods of Tibet. That Tibetan yoga and mysticism developed in such a unique fashion, is readily explained from the circumstances of this cultural heritage found by the yogins and mystics, with which they had to compromise. That is the cultural tie of mysticism. Yoga and mysticism could not escape acculturation either. The fervent aggressivity of Chöd is striking evidence of that, but also proves that Tibet was capable of a creativity which has assured it of a unique place in the history of human culture. As long as there are specimens of homo sapiens who do not only think in terms of physics and technical undertakings, there will be a deep-felt admiration for this country with its grim contrasts, which has enriched our image of man with a few essential facets. Chöd, Mi-la re-pa, Book of the Dead and mGon khang paintings – there are cultures that have less to offer, in quantity but above all in quality. Yet the Terrifying Ones most of all incorporate in art and religion the specific individuality of Tibet, Tibet that was forced to explore the hell of the soul and had the courage to do so. The purpose was, of course, to conquer the devils. The religion of the Land of Snow may be largely characterised as a fight with the devil. They fought him with his own weapons. They certainly obtained results, but it often seemed that the demons had only been domesticated, that power and aggressivity had the last word, in spite of the Buddha and Voidness. It seemed as if the Wheel must eternally revolve in this atmosphere. But there were Tibetans who discovered that the Terrifying Ones did not have the very last word. In spite of the soldier-monks, lamas also found in the monasteries – and this deserves some emphasis amidst the negative criticism of the present study – a tranquil humanism and a mild tolerance in and through the doctrine of the Buddha, a tolerance that even the cynical Waddell was impelled to acknowledge in the Tibetan people. Mystics such as the Ka-gyü-pa explicitly found that the Terrifying Ones were not the final stage, but the last but one, the horror that a man must withstand on his way to happiness and peace, for in Tibet a man could get away from his ego even less than elsewhere.

Outside the order of the Ka-gyü-pa too, the aggressivity of the Terrifying Ones was known to screen an entirely different perspective. David-Neel tells an impressive story of this, the truth of which she cannot guarantee, but which she herself is inclined to regard as historical because of the reliability of her informants. It is fortunate she tells us this, as we are now at liberty not to believe it. No matter whether it actually happened or not. Even if it is only a story, even more so in that case, it shows an ideal, a trend of thought of the Tibetan mind. The merchant Dadul, who was young and happily married, one day saw the signs of leprosy upon his body. When the doctors of a mission hospital far away could not help him, he went to an anchorite and asked him for a method of meditation to prepare himself for death. He was given the method or cycle of Yamāntaka, and the hermit instructed him. After having put his affairs in order, set his wife free from the obligations of marriage and entrusted his little son to the care of his parents, the young merchant built in the lonely mountains the meditation hut that was to be his tomb. He shut himself away from the world in it and was alone with Yamāntaka painted on a thangka, dimly lit through the little opening high up in the shelter. He meditated, and the days and the months and the years went by. In the village they began to forget him. The thangka had gradually become unnecessary for Dadul. Without it, the demonic Yamāntaka now appeared with his yum, a monstrous and frightening pair in which lust of power and sexual lust indulged their all-destroying orgy. Dadul saw the pair before him, but more and more he looked through them. He saw the essence of their being. He understood how man is driven on by desire, how action follows upon desire and after action everything falls away and desire rises up anew, creating new images and new bonds with the world of illusion. He saw in the pair before him the fever of life that believes in the ego, and the endless chain of rebirths resulting therefrom. He saw and he understood. One day a loosened stone fell down from a wall of the meditation hut; these shelters were always lightly built. Then a few more. Finally a large part of the wall fell to the ground. The sun which he had not seen for years, shone in. Once more he saw the sky, light, the valley, the mountains – and he saw that all this was the form of Yamāntaka the Terrible. He saw not a beautiful world, but a terrifying illusion. Only it no longer troubled him. He realised he did not need to mend the wall, because he no longer needed a meditation hut. He went to drink at a stream nearby, and then he saw in a pool of still water that he was leprous no longer. He examined his entire body, but everywhere his flesh was sound and whole once more. He bowed in the direction of the dwelling of the anchorite who had initiated him into the 'service' of Yamāntaka. Then he set forth, not to his village, not to his home, but in search of a master who might teach him the last stages of the path to ultimate salvation, the part of the road beyond the Terrifying Ones.[612]

This is one of those stories that speak for themselves across all cultural frontiers. It is a miraculous tale, yet curiously enough even the miracle in it is not irritating. The reader will have understood from it, why this chapter – in spite of its title – did not discuss art. In this sphere of life art and the gods are used as long as they are needed, and then simply left behind. That is not to say they were unimportant. Without the thangka, without the great Terrifying One, Dadul would not have been able to set out for that which lies beyond aggression and lust. But the thangka was an object of mystic use, not a work of art.

YAMA AND YAMI: A TERRIFYING DEITY AND HIS SISTER

The Indo-Iranians must already have known the god Yama and his sister in prehistoric times, before they split up, for these two afterwards belonged to the common heritage of Iran and India. In Iran the god and his sister were called Yima and Yimak. Yima was the first man, who was driven out of his paradise because of a sin he had committed. It is not impossible that this sin was marriage with his sister, a matter that the aristocrats regarded as legitimation for their own incestuous marriages.[613] Yimak was Yima's twin sister, just as in India Yamī was Yama's twin.[614] Evidently the pair must also in ancient India have entered upon an incestuous union and so become the parents of mankind. But the Aryan conquerors who had invaded India and settled there apparently refused to accept this incestuous legacy. The earliest of their compositions, the Rigveda, contains a dialogue in which Yamī tries to seduce her twin brother, but is rejected by him. The arguments of the brother and sister are highly interesting. Yamī, who is very impassioned, defends nature and says the Creator already made them man and wife in the womb. One of her brother's objections is, that no one has seen anything of that day. He also gives warning that if they commit incest their posterity will follow their example, and points out that the 'spies' would see them. In his objections he particularly refers to Varuṇa and Mitra, the gods of cosmic and social order. Yama, then, holds to social order and morality.[615]

That social order is one of the main, if not the principal reason for the prohibition of incest, may be taken as established after Lévi-Strauss' magisterial work.[616] To summarise: marriage is the principal form of exchange between the various families in a particular society, whereby the society is kept together; if brothers did not exchange their sisters with one another, society would fall apart into a number of little family societies that regarded and treated one another with hatred and envy; thus marriage is the result of the principle of reciprocity, without which a society cannot exist. In the incest taboo man forbids himself his incestuous tendencies, because he realises and acknowledges his dependence upon society. So if a class of aristocrats does conclude incestuous marriages, this class places itself beyond the pale of society. The deep-lying incestuous tendencies find remarkable expression in one of the other vedas. There it is said that Yamī cannot forget her twin brother after his death and continues to long for him. Only when night has been created does her beloved Yama at last disappear from her thoughts.[617] That is to say, the sister would have continued to yearn for her beloved brother, if through the rift between eternity and time – the alternation of day and night makes time – historical reality had not made itself felt, in which the social order demands and also makes possible that the incestuous desire is repressed and forgotten. In religious history incest is sometimes one of the traits distinguishing eternal primordial time – the dream time, Australian tribes call it – from historical reality.

Man has always been able to project his dreams upon primordial time, including the dream of immortality. It is no wonder, then, that Yama the first man, who marks the transition from incest to ordered marriage, also had to pass from immortality to mortal life. For the Aryan Indians of those ancient times Yama was the first mortal, the first sacrificer, who found the way for many. At first this way led to a paradisian hereafter, although the optimism was not quite unmixed.[618] Soon, however, pessimism got the upper hand and Yama became the lord of dark death. As such, he was 'tantôt dieu, tantôt homme'.[619] A still deeper ambivalence is concealed here. Yama was a symbol of the mystery, that death and life belong together, that life carries the seed of death and that death again gives rise to life. On the one side he was King of the Dead (Lord of the Fathers), on the other also 'the husband of women and the lover of maidens',[620] while his virility was expressed in other ways also. The idea of death as virile and fecund is found in ancient Egypt (Osiris) as well as in modern Haiti, where Ghede the god of the dead is a phallic corpse, 'both tomb and womb'.[621] Such concepts relating to Yama were probably also inherent in his names, which had reference to the fertility of the earth. Above all, however, he was a stern monarch resident in the south, symbol of ineluctable death.

The mystics of the Upaniṣads, who also felt this inevitability and no longer believed in the ritualism of sacrifice, sought a solution by the way of 'thou art that'. In later times one of them conceived Yama the lord of death as the great instructor, who teaches the mystical secret of the essence of all that is: he who communes with himself, recognising the Eternal in himself and as his Self, may surmount grief and joy and soar above life and death.[622] This mystical initiation into life by the lord of death completes the image of Yama for the coming centuries. In the course of his long history he will be acknowledged to a lesser or a greater degree, aspects of this image will be eliminated to be readmitted later, but nothing essential will be added to it. Much, much later only will Tibetans try to veil the mystery of Yama in yet another manner. That is why the history of this god has been chosen to conclude the present study. The development sketched from the second to the eighth chapter may be briefly recounted in conjunction with an epitome of the disturbed history of Yama and Yamī. The mere fact that a god who originated on the Indo-Iranian plateau passed through the Vedas, Hinduism and Indian Buddhism, finally to be made tutelar deity of the first monastery of the Yellow Caps by the Tibetan reformer Tsong-kha-pa claims the attention of any one interested in the history of man and his ideas.

Yama then was the sombre Lord of Death, resident in the South, sometimes acknowledged as ruler with fatalistic acquiescence, sometimes addressed in supplication or with attempted coercion, while some sought to conquer him by unravelling his secret in the mystical transformation of the spirit. During the time when the Vedic religion had to retreat before Hinduism, his twin sister was relegated to the background. She no longer had any real function, because her only significance lay in the fact that as Yama's sister she was the mother of human kind. When he became more and more the god of death, her figure became indistinct, though she was never entirely forgotten. Countries like India with its various cultures and its written traditions besides never forget completely.

One of the reasons why Yama had become a gloomy god of Death was the concept of *karman*, which more and more took hold of the souls of the Indians: the weight of men's deeds that with the objectivity of a natural law determines his lot in a following life, so that he is imprisoned in an endless chain of rebirths. The idea already appeared in the Upaniṣads. It would seem as if a sovereign Lord of Death could have no more meaning or function, scarcely any place at all, in the face of such a neutral, all-powerful might. But only the unhappy few were capable of thinking out and consistently living in this icily objective view of life. For nearly all people, who in India like everywhere else were fortunately not only irrational in their fears, but also in their hopes, [623] karma took on a visage, the visage of Yama. And naturally people tried, in spite of everything, to influence him and so undo the iron law of karma or to mitigate it. 'L'instinct de vie a suscité partout des compromis'. [624] Sometimes the conviction could even subsist that Yama was a just judge. In any case, he did not become an allegory, as Varenne suggests. The difference between an allegory and a symbol may be clearly stated, and one may then draw the conclusion that *e.g.* in the West Goodman Bones is a harmless allegory. Yet few will care to have him in the living-room next to an allegory of Youth, Agriculture or Technology.

It does not seem to be coincidence that beside the concept of this iron law, eternally ruling out all hopeful prospects in life, the warm conception of *bhakti* came to the fore: surrender to a god conceived as a personal god, in childlike confidence and burning love, which was sometimes of a most passionate kind. The purest spirituality, the urge of divine passion and icy karman – India was certainly the subcontinent of religious extremes. Meanwhile the gods to whom the people gave their love and confidence were not those of the Vedas. In the second chapter it was related how they were dethroned and had to make place for gods like Viṣṇu and Śiva. One of those reduced in rank to be gods of the points of the compass was Yama, who retained his old place in the South. But his position was not 'of a mere accessory character' like that of his colleagues. In the South he continued to guard the dead, and thus in Hinduism too he remained the God of Death, powerful, sinister, and feared. The new and lively young Śiva might give him a beating, as he did the rest of the gods, Yama did not leave the scene and in Śaiva circles too received the honour due to him from mortal men. [625] Oderint, dum metuant might have been his motto in this period. He even retained very human aspects, though. His great importance for the people and also the tenacity of Vedic tradition is seen in the festival, when every man must let himself be invited and regaled by his sister. He who neglects this is carried off by the death spirits who have been let loose by Yama to seize anyone who is not in his sister Yami's good books. The Vedic religion of the conquering rulers had become the religion of the people! The people knew of the dialogue that had passed between the twins, and as here too the relation-

206

ship between brother and sister was of a special kind, the brahmans had maintained the incest taboo with a tactful sublimation: they related that Yamī, instead of trying to seduce her brother, had asked him to dinner and that he had gladly accepted the invitation.[626] In this respect too the descendants of the Aryan conquerors had had to compromise. That this story of Yama and his twin sister and the festival based upon it must have been extremely popular, appears from an identical festival among the primitive Bhil, who have taken it over from the Indians. There too the sister gives the brother a special present on a certain day, and vice versa.[627] The connection becomes clear if one observes that the Bhil either call the god of death by their own name for him, Zom, or by the Indian name of *Yām Rāj*, King Yama. At death the soul is carried off on Yama's orders and by a typical example of acculturative syncretism, is brought before the judgment seat of the Highest God of the Bhil. At this last judgment the question is always repeated, whether the brother has been good to his sister![628] Finally, it is interesting to see that with the Bhil also Yama is not simply a dreaded demon, but that he is a just god besides.[629]

Even Yamī was not forgotten, let alone her powerful brother.[630] Generally speaking, however, the figure of the sister had lost colour, while the relations between the two had become a good deal less close, as we saw in the folk customs just referred to. Incest was not tolerated. Yama as god of death had completely replaced the primordial father, so that Yamī's significance automatically diminished, while the link with her brother's lot became looser. In Śaktism, the cult of the feminine with a pronounced sexual bias, which so strongly influenced the religion of Śiva, we find Yamī once as one of the seven Mothers, a group of goddesses of a very ambivalent character who via Śaivism afterwards also became known in Tibet. Yama's official sister, however, had now become Yamunā through a verbal association. She was the unimportant goddess of a river bearing the same name, and now served officially to eliminate all incestuous association.[631] Yama also had other female partners. One of them attained to considerable importance in Śaiva circles. This was Cāmuṇḍā, a goddess of pre-Aryan India, who resided near cemeteries and to whom human sacrifice was once offered.[632] This sinister personage was a fitting partner for the god of death, certainly in those circles that in later Hinduism busied themselves by preference with necromantic and similar practices in cemeteries.

This gruesome partner, who was depicted sitting on a corpse, had a regular place among the Mothers referred to above, who in the religion of Śiva were also represented as the eight partners of the eight terrible manifestations of Śiva, the Bhairavas.[633] Pott has explained this combination in the context of the systematic theology of tantric concepts concerning cemeteries and charnel fields.[634] The eight demoniac Bhairavas correspond to the eight cemeteries which were of great importance in tantric yoga as the eight points of the leaves of the heart lotus, where the Śaiva yogin conquered his ego-ism. Sometimes, Pott tells us, the eight Bhairavas were replaced by eight Hindu gods, of whom Yama made one. We may presume that this was regarded as evidence by the Śaiva believers that their god comprehended the ancient gods and terribly transcended them. When thus presented, the eight

Hindu gods had the eight Mothers as partners, and according to Pott this was how Cāmuṇḍā came into the company of Yama. Their combination might have been strengthened by another theological manipulation. For the same author points out a peculiar triad also found on Tibetan paintings: Śiva and his consort in their destructive aspect as Kāla and Kālī, with Yama making a third. As the first two were often to be found in cemeteries, this trinity is not surprising. Now if it was combined with the group of eight Bhairavas and their partners, then, according to Pott, the rules of systematic theology would again assign Cāmuṇḍā to Yama as his partner. Constructions like this are indeed by no means improbable among these devotees, who certainly had need of 'method in their madness', and whose yogic leaders will not have failed to build up a system. If it was the case in India, however, as has been observed elsewhere, that systematic theology followed popular religion, then the connection between Yama and Cāmuṇḍā in these Śaiva circles, which originally belonged to the lower social milieu in India, may simply have been due to the fact that in the cemeteries they frequented Yama was already present as lord of death and Camuṇḍā as a monstrous funereal folk goddess. The former had come to the people, the latter had always belonged to them. Pott's ingenious construction at any rate makes it abundantly clear how important Śaivism was for the further development of Buddhism. As to Cāmuṇḍā, it should be stressed that in the eyes of Śiva's worshippers she was the partner and śakti of Yama, even his principal śakti, but that there was not the slightest evidence to be found that she played the part of sister. In the Śaiva tantra already cited, translated by Avalon, in which Yama is explicitly acknowledged and honoured, incest is spoken of with abhorrence, so that we may be certain Cāmuṇḍā's role was restricted to that of an ordinary śakti.

Yama was depicted in human shape, a man riding on a male buffalo and holding a club or staff to signify his judicial and punitive function.[635] Yet it was not unusual either for him to be depicted as a male buffalo, *i.e.* entirely theriomorphous.[636] In Vedic times he had been mounted on a brown horse, so this change is rather peculiar. Can this change of mount be connected with social changes or with the increasing influence of popular religion and the way his character had become more and more sinister? In any case his bull was not one of the sacred species which has become so famous. It was a water buffalo, *ma-he*, an animal of decidedly negative associations.[637]

For the earliest Buddhists the gods were really quantités négligeables. Indeed, Varenne thinks that in this Buddhism Yama was little more than a schematic allegorical figure.[638] Yet such an opinion fails to take account of the significant gulf between monks and laymen, to whom the worship of their own gods was permitted. Even more important, though, is the fact that for the Buddhist missionaries Yama was anything but an allegory. 'The end of your life is approaching, and there Yama awaits you', that is how one might summarise countless exhortations of these missionaries. Yama was not an allegory, but a divine ally for these men who preached hell and damnation. There is some psychological difference between the two concepts. After the Buddha's decisive meditation, in which death was of central importance, death-with-a-face, that is Yama, always played the part described above in Buddhist missionising, as the terrible combination of death and karma. This means that when laymen were converted to Buddhism, in very many cases fear of Yama was the determinant factor in their conversion. There is every reason, then, to say that in Buddhism Yama was one of the few gods with a sharply defined personality.[639] He had a real part in it, as appears from his honorific title 'King of the Law', an old name that took on a special significance in Buddhism. Wayman has shown that although Yama was sometimes equated with Māra, he did not bear the latter's negative character of enemy and seducer. 'Māra has built up an evil reputation in Buddhist literature, while Yama is 'King of the Law', a model of justice.'[640] The judge who pronounced an absolutely objective sentence after death was certainly more than only god of death and king of evil spirits. In contrast with the merely fiendish seducer Māra he was an aristocrat, a god of fearsome majesty. He did not tempt, he observed and carried out the law.

This position, which he retained in the whole course of development of the Mahāyāna also, Yama suddenly lost in the Vajrayāna. The god who from the earliest Vedas till in Hinduism and Mahāyāna Buddhism had resided in the South as undisputed ruler, disappeared almost without trace in this last phase of Buddhism.[641] Very rarely he was still tolerated as a subordinate Hindu god of the South, but he had absolutely nothing to do any more with the sinister majesty of death and karma. While all religions and sects continued to acknowledge him in this capacity, the adherents of Tantric Buddhism broke with that tradition. Apparently they were not only anti-Veda and anti-Mahāyāna, but also anti-Hindu. That anti- was an important characteristic of these groups we have already seen. Perhaps opposition to the caste system was strongest in Buddhist Tantrism. However this may be, to prove their superiority the adherents of the Vajrayāna created a new god of their own: Yamāntaka, he who conquered and made an end of Yama. In their fervent hate they seem to have regarded Yama as a personal enemy, for their god Hevajra too, for instance, holds him in one of his hands as a victim. Yamāntaka became one of the very greatest gods of the Vajrayāna, which completely ignored Yama. A connection between the unending praise of Yamāntaka[642] and the also by no means rare social protests does indeed seem probable.

This new god, victor at once over death and Hinduism, presents us with a fascinating but difficult iconographical problem. Although he was also shown with a human head,[643] he often bore the head of a bull.[644] This is generally regarded as a matter of course, and is always explained by referring to a Tibetan myth which supplies first Yama and then Yamāntaka with a bull's head, the latter deriving that theriomorphous trait from the former.[645] A myth is not an explanation, though, and certainly not a Tibetan myth when an Indian phenomenon is concerned, for Yamāntaka already had his bull's head in India, while Yama did not have one there. Snellgrove suggests Iranian influence,[646] but this seems unlikely, for then there would have to be other links also between Iran and Yamāntaka, who is certainly not out of place in India, where animal-headed deities were quite familiar. It seems far more reasonable to seek for a link where the Vajrayāna itself placed the connection: between Yama and Yamāntaka. The name of the latter and the complete ignoring of Yama in the diamond vehicle are eloquent of contempt, protest and victory. What is more likely than that the Buddhists let their god gain the victory over the Hindu god in that form in which he was most contemptible in Buddhist eyes, as a bull? Their own conqueror acquired the bull's head as a trophy, and naturally there was nothing shameful about this, as it had an esoteric meaning. Also, to conquer through identification was one of the most common forms of meditation in the Vajrayāna for various purposes.

It seemed, at any rate in Buddhism, that Yama's career had come to an end. In Tibet, however, he got his own back. Official church history and literature do not immediately show this. Bu-ston tells us that Yamāntaka and his manifestation Yamāri were very important. Their liturgies or cycles are repeatedly mentioned, and once reference is even made to a Raktayamāri tantra of 300000 lines.[647] The Blue Annals, a history of the church composed in the 15th century, speak of the cycles of Yamāntaka and Yamāri again and again, so that at first one thinks that in Tibet, too, the conqueror of Yama is an autocrat commanding life and death. In this great work Yama is only mentioned three times: 1) as god of black magic, 2) as a kind of bogey whose sinister assistants are to frighten too studious monks so badly that they begin to meditate again, 3) probably again as god of magic, this time in company with the Mothers.[648] For important magic, however, such as ensuring success to a Buddhist monk in murdering a non-Buddhist king, recourse was had to the services of Yamāri.[649] Here we are obviously in the sphere of kings and monks. It was the latter who hoped to gain the victory in the name of Yamāntaka, and who did so. And Yama would certainly have disappeared in Tibet also, if the people had not reinstated him. A familiar contrast once more appears in this instance.

The available data enable us to reconstruct the course of events with a good deal of probability. The Tibetan people were preoccupied of old with the dead and with death, and in the time of the kings this interest was reinforced. Then Buddhism brought its message, no doubt backing it up by emphasising Yama and his empire. The followers of the Vajrayāna might no longer require this god for their own use and even ignore him completely, when there was missionising to be done and a barbarous country to be won for the doctrine, the Buddhist missionaries will certainly have taken Yama 'off the shelf' and used him as an argument in mission work according to the old tradition. That this is not an idle supposition appears not only from the tradition of proselytisers always holding up Yama as a threat, so contemptuously spoken of in China, but also even more plainly from the fact that the monks continued to use him in the home mission field. In the harvest plays the familiar pronouncement that everything is transient and subject to decay was underscored by a reference to Yama,[650] who was also held up before the sinful hunters as a warning of what awaited them.[651] The monks went further, however. In the very popular play about the saint Nangsa there is a scene that will not have failed to make a deep impression on all onlookers. After her first death this saint appears before the judgment seat of Yama and begs and prays for mercy. In her speech she says that she did not indeed become a nun,

37 gŚin-rje (Skt. Yama). So-called meditation drawing. 16⁷/8 × 12⁵/8 (43 in. × 32 cm)

38

but that yet she did everything for religion in her life that she possibly could.[652] So the audience saw before their eyes what awaited them, and if a saint had to beg in such a manner, then where would they be!

The Tibetan people must have understood that they must reckon with this god. The yogins and the monks might have complicated rituals with accompanying liturgies by means of which they could get the many-headed, many-armed and many-legged Yamāntaka ts solve such problems, but Yama was less complicated, and after all he was the real enemy whom everything turned upon. One did not need to be initiated into the cult of Yama. Thus the people chose the part of the enemy of the monks' god, be it in fear and trembling. Perhaps even, as one might think from the hagiography of Padmasambhava,[653] the yogins who brought Buddhism were at first so strongly under Śaiva influence that they paid more attention to Yama, with whom their charnel field practices brought them into direct relation. The biography even speaks of a Yama tantra, while Yamāntaka's near-absence is quite noticeable. It is even related that in the oldest monastery, Sam-ye, the '300 reflections on Yamāntaka' with other tantras were not translated, but laid aside. All this is entirely consonant with the nearly always magical role of Yama whenever he appears. That Yama had become the great folk god of the dead at an early date is evident from the unusual circumstance that he bore the same name with Buddhists and Bon po: gŚin rje, lord of the dead.

There were in Tibet many spirits and demons of illness, of death and of earth. In this respect Hoffman's discovery is very important, that before the coming of Buddhism the Tibetans had spirits of the dead who pursued the living. They were called gśin-'dre, and a connection between this word and Yama's Tibetan name, gŚin rje, is highly probable.[654] One gains the impression that Yama had a centralising effect in this matter also. We have already seen that the national religion had a preference for groups of gods or goddesses, and in this context it is typical that unlike India, Tibet could accept many Yamas, so that Yama could be surrounded by a group of eight Yamas. He himself, however, became the central figure in that gloomy borderland where the Tibetans felt peculiarly threatened. He became the epitome and the king of all demons.[655] If Buddhism was a strange and incomprehensible religion to the people, this god they certainly understood in his inmost being. Then Yama had other qualities which made it easy to accept him as one of their own gods and to treat him so. The fact that he could also appear as a bull removed all strangeness. The Tibetans themselves recognised black bulls of the earth, and very typically the monks called Yama's bull by his Indian name, while the people called it by the name of their own familiar yak.[656] The black bulls – one of which Padma had to conquer – were not infrequently lords of earth, and this again evoked associations with Yama who guarded the dead in the South. That a god who could appear as a man or as a bull could also become a man with a bull's head to the people of Tibet cannot be called a great effort of thought, especially as the people will certainly have shaped their god after the image of the Yamāntaka of the monks, who never acquired a firm hold outside the monasteries.[657] Hermanns, who gives this latter piece of information, adds that Yamāntaka was the exclusive possession of the Yellow Caps,

38 gŚin-rje (Skt. Yama or Yamarāja). Bronze. h.: 6⁵/₈ in. (17 cm)

but this is a historical extension of the contemporary situation during his field-work. The order of the Old Style Ones, who were the progressives in their day, had also taken over Yamāntaka together with the other gods of the Vajrayāna, as appears from the Blue Annals and e.g. from an old magical thangka of the Nying-ma-pa showing Yamāntaka treading Yama underfoot.[658] In connection with the bull's head acquired by the folk god Yama in Tibet, one may finally also think of the conscious or unconscious motive that the people considered their own death god just as powerful as the one of the monks, and would not have him less.

He was treated like one of their own gods. Thus he was conquered and subdued in a trance according to all the rules of shamanism.[659] In fighting enemies, Yama was called on and vows made to him.[660] When in cases of illness nothing availed, the people tried to buy off Yama with a sacrifice and a substitute,[661] a method dating from pre-Bon times and already referred to. The aim was to make Yama rest content with a picture of the patient. In this context it is most interesting to juxtapose the following two reports. When in A-mdo, an area of nomad pastoralists, a newly built house was inaugurated, the earth lord was propitiated.[662] In Central Tibet, that in the nature of things was more intensely Buddhist, Yama was honoured at the consecration of a newly built house, and his mask and arms were hung upon a stake by the new hearth.[663] In A-mdo the national Lords of earth managed to maintain themselves for a very long time. Yet Hermanns could say that there too at the time of his sojourn Yama was the great god of death among the people. There are many other indications of the popular character of this god, such as his position in the Book of the Dead and his taking the place of Māra as the one to hold the Wheel of Life in his grasp.

Although his position there was subordinate compared with Yamāntaka, Yama was not unknown in the monasteries. We mentioned that he was known as god of magic. The Indian yogins as well as the Bon po and the Old Style order were very much inclined to magic in early times, and this too might have been a reason why Yama had the same name in Buddhism and Bon. A pact with the devil is dangerous, but to the real magician it is also tempting, for he who has death as his ally can do whatever he will. This pattern of coercing death was retained, though later it could be of a somewhat more spiritual nature, as with that incarnation who 'bound to his allegiance... the blessing of gŚin rje'.[664] More typical of earlier periods, if we follow e.g. the Blue Annals, is the fresco found by Tucci in Tsaparang, showing the four Yamas of magic with the characteristic arrows signifying magic and luck.[665] The other way of getting Yama into one's power was by meditation; the monk first visualised Yamāntaka and Yama and then let the latter be worsted by the former in a drastic manner.[666] Yamāntaka, indeed, was given the names of executioner and tamer.[667] As an enemy who when conquered could serve as a magical helper Yama was acknowledged in the monasteries, being a folk god they could not ignore, not to mention his importance for the home mission. Therefore he was reinstated in his dignity and given the ancient name of King of the Law. But Yamāntaka was mightier in the monastery. The people believed in the hard fact of death as the senses teach it. The monks believed in Yama's conqueror, who yet ultimately again became a kind of super-Yama, as Lessing puts it. It is curious to see how the contrast between a Hindu god and a Buddhist god, constructed by the Indian Vajrayāna, in Tibet turned into the contrast between laity and monks. Thus Yama took on the peculiar double aspect of a national Tibetan and also a Buddhist god. This was officially recognised, when both Yamāntaka and Yama were included in the eight official, great protectors of the doctrine, even though in meditation one was radically destroyed by the other.

Yama was represented as a naked Terrifying One with a bull's head crowned with skulls, a fierce aspect, penis erectus (the glans often noticeably red), a string of death's-heads round his body, the noose in his left and his characteristic club topped with a death's-head in his right.[668] On his chest he wears the wheel of the doctrine – typifying the folk god who had to be specifically 'marked' as a Buddhist god. Yama stands on a bull, and in very many cases the animal is lying on top of a woman. This motive, a typical Tibetan renovation, most investigators passed by in discreet silence, apparently unacquainted with similar representations elsewhere and unable to feel in their soul the deep sense of kinship between man and his brother mammals, as both the ancient Tibetans and the Buddhists could, though each side appreciated it differently. De Nebesky-Wojkowitz tersely stated what any one could have seen before, viz. that most commonly the bull is copulating with the woman, and in the same year Hermanns independently made the same observation.[669] Apparently most of their predecessors imagined one can make cuts in a culture and a religion as one can in a film. Various representations show the woman wrapping both her arms and her legs around the bull, while other considerations also place the fact of cohabitation beyond doubt.[670]

Sexual commerce between man and the animal world in myth or ritual is not exceptional in comparative religion. Excavations in India unearthed a prehistoric representation of a bull impregnating a woman[671], while ritual sexual contact with animals is known among the Celts and in India.[672] The marriage of a Bengali princess who weds a lion and gives birth to twins[673], belongs to a type of which many examples may be adduced. Hermanns shows that especially in Tibetan myths of descent the yak appears as divine fecundator, and makes out a very good case for regarding the bull and the woman under Yama's feet as the primordial parents of humankind.[674] This interpretation gains in likelihood in view of the Chinese spring festival, in which the chief part is taken by a clay image of a bull, that is accompanied by a young woman. The popular account is that the bull was once a Chinese emperor who married his sister, the girl, and because of this infraction of the incest taboo was changed into a bull that must be led about by his sister till the end of time. According to the well-known sinologue De Groot, the girl is the goddess of the earth and the bull is 'le boeuf du printemps au champs', i.e. the principle of male fertility. Whether the idea of the primordial parents was an underlying concept here, or whether the nomad herdsmen interpreted the Chinese custom according to their own ideas, or whether an original pair of primordial parents of the pastoralists was changed by agriculturalists – those questions must be left to specialists. In any case, the information connecting the festival described by Tafel, that he saw quite close to Tibet,[675] with the Tibetan conception is valuable. The hypothesis of Hermanns is all the more convincing because such a conception is by no means rare. Primitive peoples of Asia and North America described a primaeval pair formed by a dog and a woman.[676] That in Tibet the animal partner is a yak bull is a matter of course. Thus interpreted, the design has meaning: the god of death, perhaps too in his role of first man (as once in India!),[677] treading down the primordial parents who started the wheel of life, and are as it were responsible for the endless chain of rebirth since then. Here Yama is death who is already present in life at the instant of its inception. Taken in this way, this part of Yama's iconography can only have originated in the monasteries. The Buddhist outlook degrades the primordial parents and thereby Tibet, and also degrades Yama as a symbol of the decay inherent in life. Quite in agreement is the Buddhist story, that Yama's servants counteract the depopulation of earth in the guise of fair women, hindering the merciful work of the bodhisattvas, while those same servants at a man's death drag his soul to Yama to have him sentenced for his sins, which include intercourse with the fair women![678] This vile tale, that smears and utilises Yama, is highly characteristic of the Tibetan folk god, who professes the world of sense, and as judge of the dead defends Buddhism.

Yama does not always stand alone on the primordial pair, he often has a female partner with him, standing to his left. In contrast, however, with what one would expect of the evil demon in the story just quoted, and also in contrast with nearly all Terrifying Ones, Yama was never shown in yab-yum with his partner. The question who his partner is, is difficult to answer. The iconographical texts allow of the possibility of placing his sister Yamī on the god's left. Grünwedel took this possibility as his point of departure, and the iconographical handbooks have followed his example.[679] Getty and Gordon do not even mention Tsamundi or Tsamunti – the Cāmuṇḍā of the Śaivas – yet she is explicitly named in the texts and is Yama's principal, if not his only partner in art. If one compares the translated texts that are available, there proves to be only one characteristic by which one can distinguish Yamī and Tsamundi: the former holds only a skull-bowl filled with blood, the latter also has a trident in the other hand.[680] It is not much, on the other hand Śiva's trident is very characteristic in the case of Tsamundi, a typical Śaiva goddess. She was the regular partner of Yama in these circles, and the religion of Śiva had a great influence upon Buddhism and particularly upon yogins of the type who brought Buddhism to Tibet. As the texts do not equate the two females, we must keep to the trident for the definite identification of Yama's partner, and it then appears that, in so far as could be checked, Yamī is never depicted as partner, as the woman in Yama's company always holds a trident in one hand. On the thangkas, too, she often has an oxhide on her back, which makes it still more certain she is Tsamundi.

As Tsamundi is an ordinary śakti, the question arises why she is not shown with Yama in coitu, as nearly all the Terrifying Ones are. Why is precisely Yama, repeatedly depicted with penis erectus, never shown in yab-yum with Tsamundi? Why is precisely Tsamundi kept at a distance from her god, whereas she is a goddess 'with the heat of karma', whose 'thought is agitated with the water of lust'?[681] That she is indeed in a condition of excitement can be plainly seen on several thangkas. On those she does not stand beside Yama, but is 'riding' on his leg; it is noteworthy, though, that none of the thangkas seen by the author show a position such that her vagina is in contact with Yama's thigh. This 'riding' position is a more archaic way of representing yab-yum[682], while still earlier the Śaiva śakti was shown in India as sitting on the knee of the god in a more or less idyllic fashion. There is a similar picture of Yama and his partner.[683] But the riding position of the yum can no longer be taken to express sacred cohabitation, when all other gods are quite definitely copulating with their partners. On the contrary, the great difference only accentuates the obviously exceptional situation of Yama.

When Yama entered Tibet his partner, we can be pretty certain, was Tsamundi.[684] She was his śakti, not his sister, and unless there are found to have been objections in India already against too close a contact of these two, there was no reason why the pair should not be shown in yab-yum. Now before the coming of Buddhism the Tibetans had a god brother-and-sister, i.e. gods who were thought of as brother-and-sister two-in-one, meaning they could not be separated.[685] Such a conception is the projection of incestuous desires, and it is very doubtful whether the Tibetans ever thought of, let alone depicted, real sexual union between brother and sister in this context. It should be remembered that what is kept at a religious distance by words, comes all too tangibly into our presence when it is depicted. An example of such a pair is 'le frère et la soeur le Roi-Dragon Génie du Sol et la Tortue'.[686] These brother-and-sister pairs will not have influenced the Vajrayāna; yet may it not have been the other way round? May not Tantric Buddhism with its deities in yab-yum have attached itself to these national brother-sister concepts, to the indignation of the Tibetans? The Indian Buddhists may either not have understood that the pair were brother and sister, or they may have had in mind that in several tantras the sister opens the way to the highest perfection. With regard to this question, a form of Yama that was mainly adored by the Old Style order, the rNing ma pa, is particularly intriguing. For he has two names. One is 'The master of the cemetery, brother and sister', the other 'The hero, the master of the cemetery, śakta and śakti (in sexual union)'.[687] It would seem that in this case the new idea of yab-yum really has been superimposed as it were upon the old concept of brother and sister. The fact that the śakti is *not* described in the iconographical text is a clear indication of the protest aroused by sexual Buddhism from the beginning, and which continually increased within Buddhism itself also, leading to the progressive purification that finally ended in the comparative isolation in which Tsong-kha-pa placed the tantras. Some books were kept under lock and key in Lhasa, and the fact that in a much greater country like China it was also practicable to carry out a wholesale anti-sexual purge, compels us to allow for the possibility that in Tibet practically nothing may be left of ancient concepts in this field. That original sexual union with a yum is not to be excluded in the case of Yama, appears also from a list of players for the 'Cham' noted by Hermanns in a Bon (!) monastery. One of the actors is Yama yab-yum, that is in coition with his partner.[688]

The appearance of a female figure in the New Year mystery play of Tashilunpo points in the same direction. Sven Hedin, who saw this festival there, calls her *Chöjal Yum* and says she carried a trident.[689] There are really some grounds for supposing that Yama and Tsamundi, once in normal tantric union, have been parted.

Eager to learn, the Tibetans began to fetch texts from India and to study them. They could not possibly find much about Yama there, as he had disappeared in the Indian Vajrayāna, having had to make room for Yamāntaka. The single Yama tantra already mentioned must, indeed, have come from a Śaiva milieu.[690] In any case, Tsamundi was his regular partner. Only the studious Tibetans saw more than only tantras. They are known to have also translated and studied texts of the Hīnayāna and Mahāyāna, and even to have paid attention to the Vedas of India the sacred country. There they might read that Yamī, whom as *gŚin-rje-ma* they only knew among the Mothers or as the yum of other gods than Yama in a very subordinate position – as appears from Tucci's investigations in Tsaparang[691] – was actually the sister of Yama, who had roundly turned down her advances. It is to be supposed that a conflict arose between what they *read* and what they *saw*. That which was written about a Partner of Yama patently referred to his Vedic twin sister. What they saw depicted was Yama with his yum Tsamundi. Moreover, Indian informants well acquainted with the religion of Śiva could confirm that Yamī was the sister of the god of death whom he had rejected because of her incestuous intentions, and that Cāmuṇḍā was his legal śakti. That at some time confusion arose upon this point is apparent from a myth which is an obvious reinterpretation, and also a symptom of the fairly great importance Śiva still had in Tibet. An existing myth of Śiva[692] in which Tsamundi was Śiva's sister, was altered so that she became the sister of Yama, and Tsamundi and Yama were the children of Śiva.[693] This confusion and attempted reinterpretation will have been facilitated by the fact that there was a great affinity between Śiva and Yama, and that both were called Mahākāla, the Great Black One. That is no wonder, as both were concerned with the practices in cemeteries and on charnel fields, both were reckoned among the great protectors of religion, and they had iconographical resemblances with one another.[694]

Tsamundi was the link between the two Great Black Ones, and in so far as the Tibetan Yama was concerned, Yamī was a new-comer. Therefore she does appear in iconographical texts, but – on the above grounds – we may assume that she was put down more or less as a memorandum by conscientious theologians who could not prevent Tsamundi having made herself at home with her trident and ox-hide. It seems very unlikely that in the bronzes and paintings we possess Yamī is even once depicted. A parallel confirming this line of thought is found in China, where under the appellation of 'twin', 'double' and 'the great double monarch' – names sometimes also given, quite mistakenly, to the Tibetan Yama by some iconographers – Yama is of recent date. Yet he himself, without a sister, was already known in China in the third century, and played a great part from the fifth century onwards, as Prof. Dr. E. Zürcher very obligingly informed the author. *Shuang*, the double one, does not appear till a late compilation around the twelfth century.[695]

Meanwhile, all data go to suggest that the Tantric Path of sexual practices found more and more opposition, certainly after the eleventh century. The practices were also rejected by Buddhists; however, these retained the yab-yum conceptions because of their esoteric meaning. But Yama and Tsamundi formed a problem, because they were brother and sister. Apparently a compromise was arrived at by depicting them in the archaic form of yab-yum, which made any idea of actual incest impossible and at first left any initiate free to think whatever he wanted to. The exceptional situation of this couple in the midst of the other copulating deities and the eliminating of Yama's śakti (and sister) in the text referred to above may thus be explained. The Vedas, indeed, were not Buddhistic, but they were ancient and they came from India, and for these reasons the Tibetans with their great respect for India may perhaps have attached some importance to Yama's indignant rejection of incest. More important was very probably the fact that in Tibet itself incest was a tender point, heavily charged with associations. As among all strictly patriarchal nomad pastoralists, there was a strong prohibition against incest among the nomad herdsmen, reaching much further than only mother and sister.[696] On the other side, there are reports that this taboo was not very strictly observed, and real marriages even took place between brother and sister.[697] These reports, however, refer to Central Tibet, where the polyandrous form of marriage had become not uncommon. Prince Peter of Greece and Denmark has shown in a profound and extensive study, that the much disputed Tibetan polyandry is in the first place a fact, and in the second place must be explained mainly as the result of economic conditions. The Tibetans themselves thought it sensible for a few brothers to marry a single wife, because in that way there was no need to divide the available land between them, in which case their livelihood would have been less assured than by taking care of the land in common. It may be added that the economic pressure of the monasteries may well have promoted the increase of polyandrous marriages.

Prince Peter makes it very clear, though, that polyandry evokes incestuous associations.[698] Especially in this field the psychological argument is very important. If a father and a son have the same wife, as sometimes happened, the association of 'being married to one's mother' and 'being married to one's daughter' is only a small step, and the probability of its being subconsciously taken borders upon certainty. Brothers, too, who share the same wife may subconsciously connect their common wife with the sister they used to have in common. Also from the idiom this author concludes that in Tibet there has been 'preoccupation with incest even in the most ancient days'. It would be of interest to know just when polyandry originated and when incest became a problem. However this may be, there was a certain atmosphere around these relationships that was obviously much more intense than in other cultures. As a result of this atmosphere, some people put the associations into practice, so that here and there marriages really were concluded between brother and sister, exceptional though it was. Although individualistic Vajrayāna yogins and their followers might attach the highest value to the sister in an esoteric light, it is extremely unlikely that the organised monkhood of Tibet will have encouraged incest. On the contrary, they will have combated it, firstly in their action against Tantric debauch, secondly in their attempt to maintain the social order, which is hardly stabilised by incest. Near Chöten Nyingma there was a lake that washed off the sin of incest. To those who had bathed in it, the abbot handed out a certificate of purity.[699] If not an indication that incest was fairly frequent, this is at any rate an indication that some thought was given to the subject. We may also deduce that religion was a stabilising factor, condemning incest as sinful and with a monopoly of cleansing people of these sins.

It is not improbable, then, that in this atmosphere the lamas vehemently opposed the depiction of an incestuous coitus, especially as Yama already aroused all kinds of incestuous associations (in connection with Lha-mo). Once lamas came to the centre from the nomadic herding tribes, whom incest disgusted, these lamas will no doubt have been fiercest in opposition. The tangibility of art, making all too actually present that which in ideas and emotions may still be rendered abstract and vague, therefore led them to break with Yama yab-yum. And even if one might argue to oneself that Tsamundi was not a sister but a yum, the atmosphere of incest surrounding Yama was sufficient reason not to take any risks and to prefer the compromise of the archaic mode of representation. The heavy pressure of the incest taboo is seen from the fact, that also the other yums of Yama, as described by De Nebesky-Wojkowitz, all stand to Yama's left and are not thought of as united with him. Tibet's decentralisation, however, permitted of the continued existence of the Bon po and the Old Style order and other non-Yellow Cap orders outside the official religion. Ancient traditions lived on. In recent times, as we have seen, the lama Yongden could tell Tibetan laymen that Mme David-Neel was the tantric assistant and religious wife of his father. With the Red Caps the mudrā was apparently a recognised institution regarded with a certain respect, even if tantric matters were exotic and strange to the greater part of the people. Other old traditions, too, certainly lived on among these and other orders. Thus one gains a strong impression, on reading the Blue Annals, that a religious tradition founded by a brother and sister did not remain without influence in Tibet, and that it is quite possible this famous tradition has been preserved until recent times somewhere in the Land of Snow, if not as a practice, then as a yogic teaching.[700] They were Za ma.

Za ma brother and sister formed a most remarkable and intriguing pair in the history of Tibet. The sister felt a repugnance for marriage, which afterwards proved a repugnance for ordinary marriage. She left her husband and devoted herself to religion. This meant that she became the tantric assistant or mudrā of the master rMa, and in this religious marriage she learned many tantras from her husband and instructor. It is particularly recounted that she had a vision in which she saw her teacher as the god Heruka and herself as his yum in love's union. Her 'semen' was however transmuted into energy on a higher plane. After some time, all the same, she was troubled by carnal desires, so that she suffered from 'a daily discharge of semen' as Roerich translates. It was the master Dam-pa who cured her of this disease and also explained its causes to her. Some of these causes were that she had also rendered tantric assistance to other masters than rMa and that she had

39 gŚin-rje (Skt. Yama) and Tsamundi. Detail of a scroll painting
40 gŚin-rje (Skt. Yama) and Tsamundi or Yamī. Bronze. h. 9⁷/₈ in. (25 cm)
41 gŚin-rje (Skt. Yama) yab-yum. Gilded bronze. h.: 5⁵/₈ in. (14.5 cm)
42 gŚin-rje gśed dmar (Skt. Raktayamāri)? h.: 5⁵/₈ in. (14.5 cm)

40

41

42

43

been jealous of rMa's other mudrās. So mystic adultery and mystic feminine jealousy had been her failings, and one can only conclude that the tantric masters, too, upheld the well-known double standard: the man may, the woman may not be unfaithful. After her recovery she was completely initiated together with her brother. This brother was also a great tantric master. The relations between brother and sister do not become quite clear. One gets the impression that in some periods of his life the brother led an independent existence, while in other periods he lived with his sister, who is called 'the only eye of the followers of the Tantric Path of sexual practices'. There are two reasons why we should like some closer information about the nature of the relationship between brother and sister. The first is the lapidary name 'Za ma brother sister,' suggesting a special unity. The second is intriguing in the context of this chapter. It is stated in the Blue Annals that the real name of the brother was *Chos kyi rgyal po*, King of the (religious) Law. *Chos kyi rgyal po* is the great honorific name of Yama! In itself this name is not conclusive, because there are a few other instances of it as a man's name. In connection with the 'brother and sister' one cannot escape the thought that it would be very much of a coincidence if this real name were written down without intent.

As the secret tradition of Za ma brother and sister, and thereby of *Chos kyi rgyal po* brother and sister has a place of its own in the religious history of Tibet, it may at any rate be regarded as the best background for a bronze the author found in the reserves of the Museum voor Land- en Volkenkunde in Rotterdam. In so far as can be checked this bronze is unique and defies all iconographical rules.[701] Yama and a female partner are standing on a bull engaged in most realistic copulation with a woman lying beneath it, who is embracing her animal husband. Yama has his usual characteristics, but three extremely important marks of the exoteric Yama[702] are lacking. In his hands the club with the death's-head and the noose are missing, and there is no Buddhist wheel on his breast. The latter point might indicate heterodoxy, but may also be one of the numerous iconographical slips that are not supposed to occur, but that are found all the same. This does not apply to the absence of the club and noose, for the god very clearly has both hands in the karaṇa-mudrā, a position of the hand whereby thumb and middle finger meet in the palm of the hand and the ring-finger is also folded against the palm, while the index and little finger are stretched out. The female partner is standing opposite him. She is quite naked except for anklets and bracelets. Her expression is fierce, her mouth wide open. Her left hand holds the skull-bowl filled with blood, the right is in karaṇa-mudrā. The peculiar thing about this Terrifying pair is, that the erected penis of the god almost touches the vagina of the yum, while the dancing position of the god and the yum's right leg lifted on high also express excitement. Whereas normal adults can easily accept the representations of yab-yum as a familiar situation symbolically intended, this image is not without inward contradiction. As the situation is not described in the texts, an interpretation is not easy. Prof. Dr. F. D. Lessing was so kind as to submit a photograph of this bronze to a few learned lamas. That the partner might be Yamī they deemed quite impossible. Some were inclined to answer the question, whether this might be a precursor of representation in yab-yum, in the affirmative.

In an earlier study this bronze was regarded as representing Yama and Yamī and as precursory to yab-yum, the difficulty of breaking through the incest barrier being too great to allow yab-yum to be straight away represented in full.[703] As regards Yamī, the mere fact that this would be the only Yamī appearing as Yama's partner is a warning to be prudent. It is true she is not holding a trident, but her right hand has that peculiar posture which also typifies the god, suggesting a certain cooperation. Therefore she is best identified as Tsamundi, who, for that matter, is also the god's sister. In interpreting the group as a first step towards yab-yum, thus towards incest, these gestures were left out of account, but they are of great importance, the more so as both partners have this mudrā as their sign. A sign of what? There is not sufficient information to be found about this gesture in the usual literature dealing with mudrās.[704] Yet it is often seen in Tibet. In those museums that could be visited the author found this mudrā formed only by Terrifying Ones, but by them very frequently. Then it is not unusual for the vajra to be held by a hand in this position. Both data are combined in a gold on black drawing – which must be very fine, to judge by the reproduction – of Dam-tschan Rdo-rje-legs, a local national god conquered by Padmasambhava at the first spreading of the doctrine, and 'converted'. One sees the powerful sorcerer up above in the middle, while the centre of the picture is filled by the Tibetan god riding on a billy-goat. He looks like a magician and has the vajra in his raised right hand in karaṇa mudrā.[705] Thus we have the link Terrifying One-vajra-magic, a combination particularly appropriate to Padmasambhava, his pupils and his converts. Finally, this mudrā is found in the Tibetan Book of the Dead with the gods who form the transition between the Peaceful and the Wrathful Deities, but have most in common with the latter, in keeping with the fact that these gods open the way to the brute world of sense. Evans-Wentz notes, probably upon the authority of Dawa Samdup, that this gesture is yogic, and controls and alters the forces of the body.[706] We can, then, completely agree with Pott's statement that in his opinion the name of this gesture refers to the method (of coercion) and that it may be described as 'krodha-fist', i.e. Terrifying One's fist.[707] As usual, Evans-Wentz does not concern himself with manual spells, but his accentuation of the yogic character of this mudrā is certainly most illuminating here.

So this typical Tibetan gesture, serving to coerce Terrifying Ones by means of control over one's own bodily powers, and also seen in the gods to signify their power as a result of this control, is the characteristic trait of the Yama and Tsamundi of our bronze. They coerce one another and also, divine yogins, they coerce themselves. The pronounced sexual character of the group suggests that particular emphasis will fall on controlling the sexual forces, as was also the case in Kuṇḍalinī yoga. In view of the above it is to be assumed that the two deities, under great sexual tension, prove to themselves and others by means of karaṇa mudrā that they have the force of sexuality under control. The gods coerce themselves. Now we may assume that this is all, that we have here a representation in bronze of a Tibetan form of that yoga which confers control and transformation of the forces of the body, especially of sexual power. One might take the stand that the two deities prove their perfect yogic

226

self-control by going to a physical extreme without letting it slip. From a yogic point of view this in itself may well be so, but yoga is not usually practised à deux, certainly not in the form represented here. And to name the final argument, which some readers may find indelicate, but that is a fact Kinsey would also have mentioned: the member of the god is decidedly too close to the genitals of the goddess, and the latter has brought her right leg into such a position that one expects her to take up the position of a yum with her legs wrapped round the god. One cannot but regard this group as an introduction, a prelude. Very probably the transformation of forces was imagined here in the way Za ma brother and sister imagined it. For let us not forget that this bronze too represents a brother and sister.[708] The yogic path that runs from India to the mountains of Tibet is set before us here in symbols of the utmost consistency. Not a man and a woman, but a brother and sister are attempting here to make good the tantric hypothesis that it is not by suppressing, but by strengthening and purifying the passions that man is liberated. By passion the world is bound, by passion is it freed, states the Hevajra tantra, where also the sister is named as partner for the highest liberation. So this extremely ambiguous brother and sister, their faces contorted with hate and in the highest sexual excitement, keep themselves and each other under control and after these preparatory exercitia carnalia et spiritualia will take the last step upon the Tantric Path of sexual practices.

The continuation and crowning of these yogic and tantric practices is seen in a small bronze that at first also seemed to be unique or very rare, though four of its kind are now known. Yet this subject, complete yab-yum of Yama and his sister, is not mentioned in the iconographical texts we know of, so that it is to be supposed they belong to the same undercurrent as the bronze discussed above.[709] These statuettes show Yama and his partner in coitu. Anatomical reasons put this beyond doubt. The female partner has her left leg wrapped round Yama's waist. Yama has the usual attributes. Unfortunately the pair are pressed together so that one cannot see if he is wearing the Buddhist wheel or not. In his hands the god has the usual club topped with a death's-head and the noose. He is girded with an animal skin that allows the penis to pass through an opening. His partner holds the skull-bowl with blood and the trident, so there can be no doubt that she is Tsamundi. Her hair is rather untidy – another of her traits – and crowned with a half vajra. She is naked except for some ornaments. Two points are very striking. Although in coition, the partners do not embrace. On the contrary, it looks as though they wish to avoid any suggestion of doing so. Then they are holding their attributes in such a way as to make one think all four hands are forming a particular gesture. It is true there is no question of karaṇa mudrā in this case, as the ring-finger is also stretched out, but the way both deities have grasped their attributes between thumb and middle finger, with the index, ring-finger and little finger extended, certainly suggests a ritual gesture.

Yet even if this hypothesis with regard to the position of the hands were mistaken, the completely atypical attitude of coition remains eloquent. If the word be not overcharged, one might even call the attitude unnatural, particularly compared to the way Tibetan yab-yum is otherwise shown. Whereas then the god always enfolds the goddess in his arms, the contact in this case is exclusively genital, while both deities keep their arms entirely free. Here then we have pure union, in which no posture of the arms could be held to convey the slightest hint that one partner takes possession of or envelops the other with any semblance of will towards possession, power or aggression.[710] This brings us into the sphere of yoga or yogic mysticism, where sexual union has no sexual aims, at least does not intend or allow of such aims, and where the object of uniting the bodies is only to transform their humours into a kind of higher energy in both partners. In this respect alone, these bronzes are unique. Although by no means of the first rank, they yet constitute a revolution in Tibetan art, for it is a revolution in the religious background. This change manifests itself in the altered position of the arms, as a change in the spiritual atmosphere manifested itself in European painting when Giotto introduced the spirit of Francis of Assisi into the form and content of art. In Tibet it is 'merely' an alteration in the position of the arms that indicates a different attitude towards the inner world. An old tradition has dared to make plastic utterance and, on the razor's edge, to set a sign of that highest union whereby the body transforms itself. This sign carries all the more weight because it is the god of death who gives the divine example, and because he unites himself with his sister. In these circles the incest taboo, so inexorable elsewhere in Tibet, was broken in bronze also. The highest unity is, as the tantras had conceived it, unity with one's bloodrelation, the unity of brother and sister. Both born from the same womb, they find again their original unity on a transformed plane. A long, long time ago in Vedic India another sister had said to Yama that they had been created as a couple in the womb. She used the argument with natural intentions. Many centuries later in the Land of Snow the same argument was the starting-point for yogic unity on the plane of the spirit which refused to resign itself to being the body's serf. However dubious and sometimes faintly ridiculous the tantric path may seem to us, that refusal is expressed not without conviction in such a statuette. *Grandeur* and *misère* lie close together.

There is every reason, then, to regard these bronzes as the culmination of the Tantric Path of sexual practices, of which the Rotterdam bronze shows the penultimate stage. That these circles were preoccupied with the control and transformation of the physical powers is evident from a statuette showing Yama in his widower's aspect, without a yum, but with both hands in karaṇa mudrā.[711] Precisely this bronze, however, demonstrates that the circles concerned deemed the lonely yoga of a self-sufficient individual inadequate. Beneath this Yama just as beneath all others, the woman and the bull are copulating. *Only* when Yama unites with his sister without embrace, only when this 'extreme arrest' is attained does one see the bull and the woman separated and lying as far apart as possible. The bull lies with all four legs drawn up against the belly, so that virile activities are impossible. At the other side the woman lies on her back, equally impotent. Both are lying under the feet of the united couple, whose legs are set far apart. Better evidence that an utter extreme is represented here could hardly be imagined. Upon this point the original interpretation can be completely maintained. When in the union of Yama and Tsamundi salvation has been attained, the ruthlessly turning wheel of life and rebirth is brought to a standstill and the primeval parents who once set it in motion are separated for ever. This is indeed 'the extreme arrest'. This interpretation, purposely avoiding a psychological explanation and remaining within the context of Tibet's culture and religion,[712] found surprising confirmation in the Tibetan language, in which the begetting of children may be called 'to sow the seed of the wheel of life'.[713] The argumentation is thus completed. Even if one were not to regard the bull and the woman as the primordial parents, they yet so clearly remain symbols of sexuality and procreation, that their separation through the union of god and goddess means the ending of the senseless procreation of sensory illusions. *Yab* and *yum* mean respectively father and mother. Physical parenthood, which can only produce new births in the chain of misery, is eliminated and abolished in the union of the divine father and mother, who moreover are brother and sister and so symbolise perfect unity, and with whom the yogin can identify himself with or without a mudrā.

Such violation of the incest taboo and of the iconographical rules[714] was advocated – as it was attempted to show above – in circles that to some extent united yoga and magic. It is almost impossible to lay down frontiers here. The essentially ambivalent character of the tantric path left open *all* possibilities. Besides for general magical purposes, yoga was not infrequently applied to the specific end of gaining immortality, which in Buddhist terms might be formulated as Voidness, but not seldom took a literal meaning in Tibet. In the present instance of Yama brother-sister yab-yum one's thoughts naturally take that direction. The phallic god of death of the Vedas, who in the Katha Upaniṣad taught mystic initiation into the mystery of Life from death, became a symbol of the same secret in Tibet, though in a Buddhist Tibetan context, in which curiously enough the ancient motif of incest played a central part. The incest refused by Yama hundreds, almost thousands of years ago, now became the symbol of ultimate salvation. Although no texts have (yet) been found referring to this situation, it is not improbable in a country like Tibet that Yama yab-yum was also interpreted in the strictly mystical sense. In any case it is worth while to make a comparison with other mystic texts, because in this instance also aggressivity makes place for sexuality and unio mystica. In contemplation and meditation Yama was usually overcome through visualising how Yamāntaka defeated him. On the real esoteric plane Yama was no longer death, but the 'corruption dwelling in the mental substance'.[715] The translations of Wayman are of great value in this field. Yama as spiritual death in life, as corruption in the mental substance which had to be purified, was set at naught not by Yamāntaka, but by his form Yamāri according to the same texts. It is most intriguing to see how this was symbolically represented in art. This victory again prevented the bull and the woman from continuing their sensory activity, but in this case the woman lay trampled and helpless on top of the bull, so that there could be no question of any contact. In connection with the Yama bronzes just discussed any other interpretation seems very improbable.[716] The ultimate aim of these exercitia spiritualia was also the highest unity, expressed as the unity of 'what is to be tamed and the taming agent'. This was an intellectual mystic illumination, only to be attained after acquiring the insight that aggressive elimination of mental corruption was an inward process. Although this meditation differs from Chöd in very many respects, there is an essential similarity with respect to aggressivity. At least, it hardly seems possible for the present to regard the Yamāri meditation otherwise than as a form of highly sublimated self-aggression. In this respect too the very real difficulty subsisted that in an aggressive mysticism unity must either be attained through the destruction of the ego by the Self with the 'rebound effect' of ego-inflation, or in the unity of aggressive identification, and regarding the latter it must be queried whether it is a real unity, because aggressivity separates or actively incorporates in identification. In how far these disadvantages could be checked through insight in the voidness of one's own thought products, must be left undecided for the present. Certainly this form of meditation has not Chöd's disadvantages of extreme aggressivity with physical manifestations and the staking everything on one throw. It is also certain that the atmosphere of these contemplations, however subtle and spiritual, was aggressive.

Therefore it cannot be denied that the mystic interpretation of Yama brother and sister yab-yum is more harmonious. Losing oneself in each other is an evident losing of the ego in unio mystica. The mystic who identifies himself with Yama and in conformity with the rules experiences his yum as highest insight, does indeed lose himself in Voidness which is liberation. There is another aspect, of significance because of its inward consequences. In this mysticism of union Yama is no longer 'tamed' – as the usual term is – by a terrifying protector of the doctrine, as he is in the Yamāntaka-Yamāri conceptions, where mysticism too is still in the key of the exorcising Terrifying Ones. In the present symbol it is also expressed that *Yama tames himself*. He has brought himself under yogic control – the Rotterdam bronze – to be able to lose ego-hood and duality in a sublimated unio mystica, the aim of mysticism in all times. Death eliminates death because in death there is life, as in life death lies hidden from the very beginning. So we come to the final 'paradoxical expression' characteristic of all mysticism. Even if this were but an equally fascinating dream-illusion as the phenomenal world is according to this mysticism, even then it is an impressive token of man refusing to be content with himself and ever and again trying to transcend himself. And we must not forget that even if these mystics did not succeed in conquering death, the élite among them did succeed in finding peace in life. In the objective analysis and examination of a culture its élite must not be forgotten. The above discussion is based on the idea that these bronzes served as 'support' for adepts without assistants who realised unity in themselves. If this was not so, it yet cannot be denied the symbolism has inner consistency. Chöd is at once Buddhist and Tibetan, yet Tibet also shows its creativity in these bronzes. In contrast with the Indian Vajrayāna, it reinstated Yama and again took up the tie, be it indirectly, with Vedic traditions. Thus it could create the possibility and the idea of Yama-sister yab-yum, the Lord of Death, *gŚin rje*, taming himself in yab-yum. One seeks in vain for an idea of such originality in the Indian Vajrayāna.

Yama the folk god was, we have seen, more respected by the laity and the yogins than by

230

the monks. The reformer Tsong-kha-pa, who particularly claimed attention for the religious interests of the people and wrote a special 'catechism' for laymen, acknowledged the importance of the people and of Yama by giving him an official place. Yama as yi-dam of the monastery of Gan-den meant that he was the chief of the Terrifying Ones in the mGon khang.[717] Nevertheless, Yamāntaka was and remained the great god of the monks and the tutelar deity of the order of the Yellow Caps, who were finally to rule over theocratic Tibet in the person of the Dalai Lama and those around him. Was not perhaps Tsong-kha-pa already a religious politician, binding the people to the Yellow Caps by acknowledging Yama, yet on the other hand making it clear that he was subordinate to Yamāntaka, the protector of the monks? In this way the relationship between Yamāntaka and Yama would reflect that between the monks and laymen. And indeed the yoga-magic-mysticism of Yama yab-yum in the bronzes we have discussed may be justly called popular yoga-magic-mysticism. Tsong-kha-pa might wish to promote the interests of the people, but he did not leave it in doubt that the monks were the leaders. That the laymen were almsgivers was simply a matter of course. The ancient social structure of Buddhism was completely maintained even in the last phase of Tibet's cultural and religious development. We need not even think of Yama's function as bogeyman to be convinced that his acknowledgement by the Yellow Caps had a double advantage, and that Marcelle Lalou is quite right in calling Tsong-kha-pa a 'fin psychologue'.

It would seem that his successors and followers laid still more stress upon Yamāntaka and that once the people had recognised the power of the Yellow Caps for good, they made attempts to drive Yama from the field. This would explain how it is that Yama's place in the 'Cham' sometimes seems to be taken by Yamāntaka, and that modern scholars sometimes do not seem to know whether they have to do with Yama or with Yamāntaka.[718] Actually Yama and Yamāntaka may both appear in the play, but if there is only one of them it is always Yama. The Great Fifth on the other hand, as we know, was forced to compromise in order to make his political position as strong as he could, and to take the wind out of the Red Caps' sails. One of the theories he made use of was that the dreaded Yama, who held each man's fate in life and death, was only the negative aspect, only the reverse of the great, all-good Avalokiteśvara, who was incarnate in the Dalai Lama.[719] In this way the Dalai Lama ultimately wielded power over his subjects in life and in death. Few rulers have ever dared assert as much. Avalokiteśvara had power to descend to hell and there as Yama to change evil into its counterpart. The people simply prayed to Avalokiteśvara to intercede with Yama that the god of death and judge of the dead might forgive their sins.[720]

The momentous changes the Yellow Caps brought about in Tibet, which we can probably not yet fully evaluate, are in all likelihood also expressed in the iconography connected with Yama. One of the heads of the eleven-headed Avalokiteśvara, who is very general in Tibet, has the face of a Terrifying One. Pott interpreted this face as that of Vajrapāṇi.[721] As this bodhisattva, however, belongs to a different 'family' – that of the vajra, while Avalokiteśvara belongs to the lotus family – it is preferable to identify this Terrifying One as Yama, as

Govinda does.[722] It is particularly the theory of the Great Fifth which hardly admits of a different interpretation. We must, after all, continually bear in mind that by Yellow Caps and Dalai Lamas Tibet was greatly changed, and that nearly all travellers' reports and nearly all art objects in our museums stem from this altered Tibet.

There is a second, far more important point in Yama's iconography that raises questions as to the influence of the Yellow Caps. It is noticeable that the theme of the bull and the woman comprises so many variations as is quite surprising in this strict country. There is a significance here merely from the formal aspect, for it proves the Tibetan artists could be inventive and go their own way, when they were not tied down by iconographical texts. For the motif of the bull and the woman was a Tibetan innovation, so that there was no need to comply with Indian instructions! Their inventiveness around this motif, however, is of a very special kind. The stately archaic conception of the bull and the woman, austerely and objectively shown in older bronzes, acquires in these variations certain emotional qualities of a negative kind. Although they objected to Yama in coitu, they had no objection to the most repulsive representations of sexual intercourse between a bull and a woman, if one can still call it intercourse here. Apart from an occasional definitely sensual treatment of the theme, expressed by a rather too warm embrace on the part of the woman, or her stretching out a concupiscent hand towards the animal's member, there are also extremely aggressive variations. One gouache shows two women lying beneath the animal, which has torn open the abdomen of one of them with its horns. With Tibetan accuracy (and Tibetan faith in the sensory phenomena) the intestines are displayed.[723] On a scroll-painting – with Tsong-kha-pa in the centre of attention and adoration – the bull has kicked a rear foot into the vagina, from which a good deal of blood is flowing.[724] Here the Yellow Caps are very far from mysticism. The sensuousness of these pictures makes one wonder whether there are not sadistic factors at work here. It is again typical of Tibetan art that when it is free to let itself go, as in the mGon khang thangkas, aggressivity is the driving force. Yet a comparison with those masterpieces at once makes it clear that in the bull and woman depictions aggressivity has become moralistic and so has a false note. In the mGon khang there is pure demonism, here there is moralistic corruption of demonism, to vary a Tibetan mystic expression.

It is clearly the intention to depict the sexual act as altogether abhorrent, but the circumstantiality with which it is done betrays a secret enjoyment hiding under the criticism. Owing to polyandry it was the woman who 'kept the purse' in Tibet, but otherwise she was a being of a lower order according to the official theory, particularly in the central provinces, as we have seen. A projection of this idea is seen in the concept that the entire world lies enclosed in the belly of a monstrous witch.[725] A like projection is the theme of the bull and the woman. Sometimes only the bull, sometimes both he and the woman are painted green, which is the colour of the animal kingdom, of 'the spiritual darkness of the animal kingdom'.[726] This means that in the first case the woman has commerce with an animal, and in the second that she simply *is* an animal. The celibate monks (only for the Yellow Caps was celibacy obligatory) who saw things depicted in such a way, could only say, with Mi-la re-pa 'I am proud that I have obtained the truth through being a man'[727]. This object lesson taught that the sexual act was to be absolutely rejected, that repulsive combination of sexuality and aggressivity having finally been demonised by the Yellow Caps just as the Terrifying Ones had been diabolised. The effect upon the monks will have been both a strengthening of their self-confidence and a preventive weight upon their conscience. The fact that in some variations upon the theme[728] aggressivity has even altogether taken the place of sexuality, suggests for a moment that the ancient Buddhist analysis of corpses and skeletons and the later cemetery practices may be returning here. One of the representations referred to above does indeed recall charnel field pictures. This would imply that it is requisite to analyse woman to pieces. However this may be, it would seem that this moralising demonism was one of the last acculturative short circuits between Tibet and Buddhism: the primordial parents of an archaic past degraded to be an example of bestiality. Harrer states in so many words that homosexuality was very prevalent in the Yellow Cap monasteries, and was even regarded as a virtue, because this form of sexual connection proved women no longer played any part in the life of those concerned.[729] Woman as *origo mali* driven out by homosexuality is a familiar theme. Schäfer is a little less explicit, but quite plain when he calls the poultry yard by the Gesar temple in Lhasa where there were only cocks, which not only crowed but also courted one another in pairs, one of the most characteristic symbols of the topsyturvy ('verkehrte') state of the lamas.[730] Without going into the psycho-analytical details of this contempt for women, it may suffice to observe that owing to enforced abstinence many monks sought refuge in homosexuality and so felt compelled to justify both their pure Buddhism and their sexual compensation for it by despising women. The motif of the bull and the woman offered a suitable occasion of branding woman and natural cohabitation as brutish – just as many homosexuals outside Tibet do. This contempt for the other sex became almost comical in Kumbum, where both women and men who had been in contact with women were scrupulously kept well away from the mGon khang, because the Terrifying Ones who lived there could smell women and sexuality at a distance and in blind fury would bring the most terrible calamities over mankind if they approached.[731] Again the Terrifying Ones play a peculiar part and again we see how difficult it was for Tibet to come to a compromise with the cultural heritage of Padmasambhava. These gods who were continuously and vigorously copulating, objected to mortals who did the same thing occasionally. It was a curious reinterpretation of the ancient tantric ideas, not to speak of the self-deception involved in the homosexual attitude. But the drastic variations upon the theme of bull and woman become quite eloquent against this background.

When a primitive culture was devaluated by acculturation, it was almost inevitable that also the members of the non-white society became incapable of regarding as natural that which in the context of the old culture had been a matter of course to them. Religions like Buddhism and Christianity finally succeed in transferring their sense of sin. Thus when Hermanns tells us that Tibetans who had an image of Yama with the bull and woman in a dark corner of their house, spoke of it not only with great reserve but also shyly and ashamed, it is by no means impossible the above phenomenon was involved. In that case Yama would not only have become the dreaded lord of death, but also the bad conscience of laymen who could no longer think even of their conjugal relations without being reminded of 'the spiritual darkness of the animal kingdom'. The central position taken by the great and deeply dreaded King of the Law in the Tibetans' conscious life, clearly appears from the childhood memories of a contemporary Tibetan, who tells us about his country in a charming and intelligent way. Obviously he has become a Westerner, this son of the Land of Snow, who reads Aldous Huxley's Antic Hay in a mountain pass at a height of thousands of feet and quotes Omar Khayyam with effortless ease. But he has struck a balance between irony and love which enables him to write of his country with affection, and with deep love and respect of his admirable grandmother, who diligently heats the still, does not drink a drop of alcohol herself, and is extremely pious. Gods he does not speak of. Plainly they are done with. Yet one god he names repeatedly, often not without irony, as in our world we sometimes refer to Davy Jones' locker. In spite of all irony, he has no English word for this god, only his Tibetan name: Shenji.[732]

From his youth in the Indo-Iranian highlands to the decay of old age in the heart of an Anglicised Tibetan – that is the long life of Yama. In Tibet he became the great, dreaded god of the people, who with magic and sacrifices tried to conciliate, to coerce or to deceive him. For he was more than the god of death, he was also the great King of the Law, who weighs good and evil at the end of each life. He became one of the great protectors of the faith and the dark aspect of Avalokiteśvara. The followers of an ancient tradition associated him with mystic ideas, so that in conjunction with his sister he became the symbol of the 'ultimate arrest' of the human spirit. In all this, he retained the profound ambivalence characteristic of every great god. For the mystics, the phallic death god became an ambivalent figure, a god who on the one side was the 'corruption dwelling in the mental substance', and so the representative of the sensory world proclaimed by the scapegoat, and on the other symbolised that condition of the mind in which it was not bound to the senses. So it was that one could attempt to let Yama tame himself, to let death conquer death when the human spirit relinquished itself. Yet he who is not attuned to mysticism will have no difficulty in sympathising with the sixth Dalai Lama, who sighed to Yama:

> 'Righteous Lord of Death, whose mirror
> Shows all deeds, both good and evil,
> Justice is not found on this side.
> Grant it there, when I pass over'.[733]

This poem has become depressingly topical now that in the past years Tibet has had the bitter experience that also in the twentieth century might is still right. The country of a never fully tamed people of conquerors now seems to have become occupied territory for ever. Even the Terrifying Ones can no longer protest, for if the rumours are true, there may soon be none left to have faith in them.

NOTES AND COMMENTARIES ON THE PLATES

NOTES

1   L. A. Waddell, *The Buddhism of Tibet or Lamaism.* London 1895, p. 478, 481, 505f.

2   ibid., p. 512.
    W. W. Rockhill, *Tibet ... according to Chinese sources.* s.a., p. 211f.

3   E. Schäfer, *Fest der weissen Schleier*[3]. Braunschweig 1952, p. 136, 145. This book gives a lively and detailed description of the New Year Festival in recent times (p. 108-199).

4   Thubten Dschigme Norbu, *Tibet, verlorene Heimat.* Erzählt von H. Harrer. Wien usw. 1960. p. 38 ff.

5   M. Hermanns, *Die Familie der A-mdo Tibeter.* Freiburg 1959, p. 336, where a German translation is given.

6   Ch. Bell, *The Religion of Tibet.* Oxford 1931, p. 139.
    H. Harrer, *Sieben Jahre in Tibet.* Wien 1952, S. 222, relates that these poems were still for sale in Lhasa around 1946, and that the poems and their author were very popular with the Tibetans.

7   R. Benedict, 'Religion'. In: *General Anthropology*, ed. F. Boas. Boston etc. 1938, p. 633.

8   Sarat Chandra Das, *Journey to Lhasa and Central Tibet.* London 1904, p. 145.

9   M. Hermanns, *Mythen und Mysterien, Magie und Religion der Tibeter.* Köln 1956, p. 16.

10 G. Tucci, *Tibetan painted scrolls.* Roma 1949, vol. I, p. 54.

11 P. Demiéville, *Le concile de Lhasa. Une controverse sur le quiétisme entre Bouddhistes de l'Inde et de la Chine au VIIIe siècle de l'ère chrétienne.* Vol. I. Paris 1952.

12 M. Weber, *The religion of India: the sociology of Hinduism and Buddhism.* 1958. (Original German ed.: Tübingen 1921).

13 Cf. S. N. Eisenstadt, 'Anthropological studies of complex societies'. *Current Anthropology*, vol. 2 (1961), pp. 201-222.

14 E. Zürcher, *The Buddhist conquest of China.* 2 vols. Leiden 1959.

15 W. Y. Evans-Wentz, *Tibet's great yogī Milarepa.* 2nd ed. London 1958, p. 148. Cf. *The Blue Annals*, transl. by G. Roerich. Calcutta 1949, vol. I, p. 44, 254; vol. II (1953), p. 435 *int. al.*

16 M. Lalou, *Les religions du Tibet.* Paris 1957, p. 12.

17 F. Sierksma, *Een nieuwe hemel en een nieuwe aarde.* 's-Gravenhage 1961, ch. 2-4.

18 This seems to be the best explanation of the ambivalent behaviour (both extreme aggression and self-aggression) of king Moctezuma after the landing of Cortés, excellently described in M. Collins, *Cortés and Montezuma.* London 1954.

19 F. Sierksma, l.c., passim.

20 W. Goldschmidt, *Understanding human society*, London 1959, is a new and interesting attempt in this field after many abortive endeavours.

21 H. R. H. Prince Peter of Greece and Denmark, *A Study of Polyandry.* 's-Gravenhage 1963, p. 570, in connection with the Tibetan forms of polyandry stresses the factor of isolation.

22 F. Sierksma, 'Religie en politiek leiderschap in primitieve culturen'. *Ned. Theol. Tijdschr.*, vol. 10 (1956), pp. 209-236.

23 G. Tucci, *Minor Buddhist texts*. Part II. Roma 1958, p. 142 f. Cf. p. 149.

24 Ch. Bell ,l.c., p. 6 f.

25 L. A. Waddell, l.c., p. 194.

26 S. H. Ribbach, *Dragpo Namgyal*. München 1940, p. 257.

27 G. Tucci, *Tibetan Painted Scrolls*. Roma 1949, vol. II, p. 721.

28 L. A. Waddell, l.c., p. 152 ff.

29 G. Tucci, l.c., vol. I, p. 320 ff.

30 R. de Nebesky-Wojkowitz, *Oracles and Demons of Tibet*. 's-Gravenhage 1956, p. 136 f., where the complete translation is given.

31 H. Hoffmann, *Die Religionen Tibets*. Freiburg 1956, p. 151.

32 G. Tucci, *To Lhasa and beyond*. Roma 1956, p. 31, 56, 124.

33 E. Kagawuchi, *Three Years in Tibet*. Benares 1909, p. 286, 163.

34 Cf. D. Snellgrove, *The Hevajra tantra*. London 1959, vol. I. (II, 5: 'Black I am and terrible ... But my inner nature is tranquil').

35 *The Blue Annals*, transl. by G. N. Roerich. Calcutta 1953, vol. II, p. 434.

36 E. Lamotte, *Histoire du bouddhisme indien des origines à l'ère Śaka*. Louvain 1958, p. 687.

37 J. N. Banerjea, *The development of Hindu iconography*². Calcutta 1956, p. 489 f.

38 ibid., p. 83, 166 f.

39 ibid., p. 177.

40 L. Renou et J. Filliozat, *L'Inde classique*. Vol. I. Paris 1947, p. 277.

41 J. N. Banerjea, l.c., p. 71.

42 F. B. J. Kuiper, *De goddelijke moeder in de Voor-Indische religie*. Groningen 1939, p. 5 ff.

43 L. Renou et J. Filliozat, l.c., p. 320

44 P. Radin, *Primitive religion*². New York 1957, p. 15

45 F. B. J. Kuiper, l.c., p. 10.

46 S. Dasgupta, *Obscure religious cults as background of Bengali literature*. Calcutta 1946, p. 73.

47 M. Eliade, *Yoga*. Paris 1936.

48 W. E. Mühlmann, *Chiliasmus und Nativismus*. Berlin 1961, p. 358 ff.

49 H. von Glasenapp, *Brahma und Buddha*. Berlin 1926, p. 83.

50 J. N. Banerjea, l.c., p. 337 f.

51 The term civic is taken from M. P. Nilsson.

52 H. von Glasenapp, *Buddhistische Mysterien*. Stuttgart 1940, p. 159.

53 J. N. Banerjea, l.c., p. 76.

54 R. G. Bhandarkar, *Vaiṣṇavism, Śaivism, and minor religious systems*. Strassburg 1913, p. 112 ff.

55 E. Lamotte, l.c., p. 7, 434.

56 H. von Glasenapp, l.c., p. 200.
S. Dasgupta, l.c., p. 83.

57 J. Evola, *The doctrine of awakening*. London 1951, passim.

58 ibid., p. 20.

59 F. Heiler, *Die buddhistische Versenkung*². München 1922, p. 7.

60 F. Sierksma, *De religieuze projectie*². Delft 1957, pp. 159-190.

61 E. Lamotte, l.c., p. 17.

62 ibid., p. 44.

63 N. Wiener, *The human use of human beings*². New York 1954, p. 122.

64 F. Heiler, l.c., p. 30.

65 L. de la Vallée Poussin, *Mélanges chinois et bouddhiques*. Vol 5. Bruxelles 1937, p. 210, 227.

66 F. Heiler, l.c., p. 39.

67   J. Evola, l.c., p. 48.

68   L. de la Vallée Poussin, l.c., p. 192.

69   ibid., p. 189 ff.

70   E. Lamotte, l.c., p. 67.

71   G. van der Leeuw, *Phänomenologie der Religion*. Tübingen 1933, p. 474, where also an excellent exposé of mysticism in general.

72   F. Sierksma, *De religieuze projectie*². Delft 1957, pp. 159-190.

73   Lamotte quite rightly speaks of 'nirvaniser'.

74   E. Conze, *Der Buddhismus. Wesen und Entwicklung*. Stuttgart 1953, p. 59.
        E. Lamotte, l.c., p. 85.

75   E. Zürcher, *The Buddhist conquest of China*. Leiden 1959, Vol. I, p. 265.

76   W. Somerset Maugham, *The complete short stories*. London 1957, pp. 1-38.

77   F. Heiler, l.c., p. 38 f.

78   ibid., p. 55.

79   E. Lamotte, l.c., p. 66.

80   Bu-ston, *History of Buddhism*. Translated by E. Obermiller. Heidelberg 1932. Vol. II, p. 80.

81   E. Lamotte, l.c., p. 68.

82   ibid., p. 59, 71 ff., 88 ff., 317 ff., 686 ff.

83   ibid., p. 74 f. Cf. p. 386, 394, 431 ff.

84   ibid., p. 55, 83.

85   ibid., p. 612, 689.

86   ibid. p. 210 ff., 220, 550 ff., 775 ff.

87   ibid., p. 300.

88   D. L. Snellgrove, *Buddhist Himālaya*. Oxford 1957, p. 108 ('essentially anti-social').

89   E. Conze, l.c., p. 128.

90   G. Mensching, *Vergleichende Religionswissenschaft*. Leipzig 1938, p. 26, 28 ff.

91   W. Somerset Maugham, *Complete Short Stories*, Vol. III. London 1959, p. 1297.

92   J. Bacot, *Trois mystères tibétains*. Paris 1921.
        M. H. Duncan, *Harvest festival dramas of Tibet*. Hongkong 1955.

93   A. David-Neel, *Textes tibétains inédits*. Paris 1952, p. 52.

94   E. Bryner, *Thirteen Tibetan tankas*. Indian Hills 1956, p. 29, 30, 31, 33, 34, 35, 36, 58, 59, 64.
        G. Tucci, *Tibetan painted scrolls*. Roma 1949. Vol. II, p. 442 f.

95   E. Bryner, l.c., p. 96.

96   ibid., p. 32.

97   R. Benedict, *Patterns of culture*². 7th pr. New York 1950, pp. 160-205.

98   B. Bhattacharyya, *The Indian Buddhist iconography*². Calcutta 1958, p. 1.

99   E. Lamotte, l.c., p. 447 f., 455.

100   J. N. Banerjea, l.c., p. 122 f.
          E. Lamotte, l.c., p. 697, 753, 762.

101   E. Zürcher, l.c., p. 189.

102   H. von Glasenapp, *Buddhistische Mysterien*. Stuttgart 1940, is still to be regarded as the most concise and lucid introduction to the Mantrayāna and Vajrayāna, and also facilitates the reading of the more comprehensive, excellent surveys by Dasgupta, Tucci, Snellgrove. It continually appears, in passing, from v. G.'s summary that Tibet's Vajrayāna is a thing apart.
          G. Schulemann, *Geschichte der Dalai Lamas*. Leipzig 1958, p. 129-178 gives an excellent summary of the Vajrayāna of Tsong-kha-pa and the lamaism of the Yellow caps, quite rightly

beginning with the 'common man' and his beliefs, as they were according to Tsong-kha-pa, but not according to our studies.

103 L. Renou et J. Filliozat, l.c., p. 451, 453, 628.
      D. L. Snellgrove, l.c., p. 63 (Śiva the greatest defender of the Buddhist faith).

104 J. N. Banerjea, l.c., p. 449.

105 R. G. Bhandarkar, l.c., p. 122f., 127.
      J. N. Banerjea, l.c., p. 451 footnote 2.
      L. Renou et J. Filliozat, l.c., p. 629f.

106 J. Woodroffe, *Shakti and Shaktā*. London 1918, p. 67ff.
      H. von Glasenapp, l.c., p. 160.
      R. G. Bhandarkar, l.c., p. 146f.

107 J. N. Banerjea, l.c., p. 172, 488f., 491ff. (on activation of ancient mother goddess.)

108 H. W. Schomerus, *Der Çaiva-Siddhanta. Eine Mystik Indiens*. Leipzig 1912, p. 63ff., 331ff., 380ff.

109 A. Avalon, *The serpent power*. London 1917, p. 272.

110 The fakir with his snake is indeed an externalised remainder of Kundalini yoga.

111 A. Avalon, l.c., gives a complete description.
      P. H. Pott, *Yoga en yantra*. Leiden 1946, p. 7ff. gives an extensive summary.

112 Striking is the coiled snake as symbol of the Uroboros, which also symbolises the beginning of a development and is also bisexual. Cf.:
      E. Neumann, *Ursprungsgeschichte des Bewusstseins*. Zürich 1949, p. 19-52.

113 A. Avalon, l.c., p. 15, 30. Cf. p. 158 footnote 2.

114 F. Sierksma, *The gods as we shape them*. London 1960, p. 39f.

115 A. Avalon, l.c., p. 213, 235.

116 A. Avalon, l.c., p. 75. Cf. p. 49, 134, 151, 236, 251.

117 ibid., p. 72, 107f., 208, 269.

118 ibid., p. 219

119 G. Tucci, l.c., Vol. I, p. 226ff; Vol. II, p. 333ff.

120 A. Avalon, *The great liberation*[2]. Madras 1927, p. 89, 123, 193ff.

121 ibid., p. 139, 354.

122 ibid., p. 208.

123 ibid., p. 82.

124 ibid., p. 329.

125 ibid., p. 52f., 62, 188, 224f., 233, 238, 240, 304.

126 ibid., p. 256ff.

127 ibid., p. 323.

128 F. Sierksma, *De roof van het vrouwengeheim*. 's-Gravenhage 1962. Chapter 11.

129 W. E. Mühlmann, *Chiliasmus und Nativismus*. Berlin 1961, p. 335ff., 284ff.

130 J. W. de Jong in: *Indo-Iranian Journal*, vol. 2 (1960), p. 198ff., draws attention to the fact that there is little philosophy in the tantras.

131 H. von Glasenapp, *Buddhistische Mysterien*. Stuttgart 1940, p. 154.

132 S. B. Dasgupta, *An introduction to Tantric Buddhism*. Calcutta 1950, p. 61.
      According to some authors the terms Mantrayāna and Vajrayāna are interchangeable, according to others Mantrayāna is the vehicle of higher and lower forms of magic and Vajrayāna the vehicle which added sexual conceptions and rites to the Mantrayāna.

133 R. G. Bhandarkar, l.c., p. 156: Śaivism in 2nd cent. A. D.

134 Forms of sexuality, intermediate between the natural act of sex, recognised as natural, but regarded as sacred in a religious context, and its complete spiritualisation and transformation

in mysticism, naturally have a double sense in the literal meaning of the word, so that in such circles one may find serious searchers and simulators, and conscious or unconscious cheats. While in so-called nature religions man may say phallus and mean God, in the circles of half-sublimated sexuality the danger is great of saying God and meaning phallus (c.q. vagina).

135   Cf. S. B. Dasgupta, *Obscure religious cults as background of Bengali literature*. Calcutta 1946, p. 20f.
      D. L. Snellgrove, l.c., p. 85 ff., 104, 113 ff. Cf. p. 103.
136   S. B. Dasgupta, l.c., p. 62, 78.
137   E. Zürcher, l.c., p. 78f., 117.
138   M. Hoffmann, *Die Religionen Tibets*. München 1956, p. 23.
139   Compare, for instance, the Bantus of South Africa, who only have liberty in the religious field, and who have hundreds of different churches and chapels.
140   G. Tucci, *Tibetan painted scrolls*. Roma 1949. Vol. I, p. 248.
      D. L. Snellgrove, *The Hevajra tantra*. London 1959. Vol. I, p. 8.
      These two authoritative scholars inform us, the first that some tantric rites are too drastic to be fully described, the second that some passages of a translation have been toned down or left out. This is not as it should be. In serious learning no facts may be kept back. Latin is the generally accepted medium for avoiding conflict with the canons of good taste or the taboos of one's own culture.
141   D. L. Snellgrove, l.c., II 2, 8.
142   S. B. Dasgupta, l.c., p. 60.
143   D. L. Snellgrove, l.c., II, 3, 55-60.
144   S. B. Dasgupta, *An introduction to Tantric Buddhism*. Calcutta 1950, p. 79 f.
      Cf. G. Tucci, l.c., p. 232.
145   R. Otto, *West-östliche Mystik*[2]. Gotha 1929, p. 95f.
146   S. B. Dasgupta, *Obscure religious cults* etc., p. 42
147   Cf. G. Tucci, l.c., Vol. I, p. 219f.
148   G. G. Scholem, *Major trends in Jewish mysticism*. London 1955.
      R. J. Werblowsky, *Mystical and magical contemplation*. History of Religions, vol. I (1961), pp. 9-36.
      D. Bakan, *Sigmund Freud and the Jewish mystical tradition*. Princeton 1958.
      The fact that even in Judaism, so pronouncedly patriarchal and monotheistic, social pressure could engender a mysticism of the same kind, in which female figures have so important a place, is most significant in this connection.
149   J. N. Banerjea, l.c., p. 301.
150   B. Bhattacharyya, l.c., p. 11: 'Śūnyatā is designated as vajra' (translated text).
151   It is interesting, that in a Śaivite yoga upaniṣad both the idea of Voidness and the symbol of the bell appear, while not Kuṇḍalinī but prajñā is led upwards:
      F. Nowotny, *Eine durch Miniaturen erläuterte Doctrina Mystica aus Srinigar*. 's-Gravenhage 1958, p. 36, 50f.
152   H. Zimmer, *Kunstform und Yoga im indischen Kultbild*. Berlin 1926, p. 75f., 81, 179.
153   D. L. Snellgrove, *Buddhist Himālaya*. Oxford 1957, p. 81 ff.
      A. Govinda, *Foundations of Tibetan mysticism*. London 1959, p. 96f.
154   J. N. Banerjea, *The development of Hindu iconography*[2]. Calcutta 1956, p. 23f.
155   D. L. Snellgrove, *The Hevajra tantra*. London 1959, I, 1, 11; I, 3, 11; I, 10, 2.
156   B. Bhattacharyya, *The Indian Buddhist iconography*[2]. Calcutta 1958, p. 166.
157   A. Govinda, *The psychological attitude of early buddhist philosophy*. London 1961.
158   D. L. Snellgrove l.c., II, 2, 35-51.

In one or two places Snellgrove's translation has been altered according to suggestions by prof. dr. J. W. de Jong, or in agreement with the translation of Dasgupta, Introduction, 157f.

159   ibid., II, 8, 5.

160   ibid., II, 5.

161   ibid., I, 8, 49.

162   A. Govinda, *Foundations of Tibetan mysticism*. London 1959, p. 96f.

163   R. Bleichsteiner, 'Tibet'. In: H. A. Bernatzik, *Die neue grosse Völkerkunde*. Bd. 2. Frankfurt a.M. 1954, p. 90.

164   J. E. Lips, 'Government'. In: *General anthropology*, ed. F. Boas. New York 1938, p. 519.
K. Birket-Smith, *Geschichte der Kultur²*. Zürich 1948, p. 167ff., 210.

165   M. Eliade, *Le chamanisme et les techniques archaïques de l'extase*. Paris 1951, passim.

166   F. Flor, *Haustiere und Hirtenkulturen*. Wiener Beiträge zur Kulturgeschichte und Linguistik, Bd. 1. Wien 1930, p. 22.
H. A. Bernatzik, *Die neue grosse Völkerkunde*. Bd. 1. Frankfurt a.M. 1954, photo opposite p. 348 (Abb. 129).

167   G. A. Combe, *A Tibetan on Tibet*. London 1926, p. 105.
F. Sierksma, 'Two pastoral customs in Tibet'. *Man*, vol. LXII (1962), no. 111.
M. Hermanns, *Die Nomaden von Tibet*. Wien 1949, does not mention this custom. In *Die Familie der A-mdo Tibeter*, Freiburg 1959, p. 180, however, he says: 'oder sie blasen in die Vagina der Kuh'. This should have been included in the aforementioned article in *Man*.

168   K. Dittmer, *Allgemeine Völkerkunde. Formen und Entwicklung der Kultur*. Braunschweig 1954, p. 228ff.
What is said here with regard to the Viennese School also applies to the books of M. Hermanns, especially that of 1949, though these are otherwise of value.

169   W. Goldschmidt, *Understanding human society*. London 1959, p. 215.
K. Dittmer, l.c., p. 229, 259ff.

170   F. W. Thomas, 'Ancient folk-literature from north-eastern Tibet'. *Abh. d. Deutsch. Ak. v. Wiss.* Berlin 1952, 3. Berlin 1957, p. 92. Cf. 54.

171   J. E. Lips, l.c., p. 520.

172   W. Goldschmidt, l.c., p. 211.

173   E. A. Bacon, *Obok. A study of social structure*. New York 1958.

174   E. E. Evans-Pritchard, *The Nuer*. Oxford 1940, p. 16: 'Cherchez la vache is the best advice that can be given to those who desire to understand Nuer behaviour'.

175   O. Postma, *Samle fersen*. Snits 1949. Dl 1, p. 121f. It is very significant that childhood memories led this great poet, who also published as a physicist, to write a poem about cattle in which the cows are explicitly called 'acquaintances' and 'friends of our people', and which gives the insider a shock of recognition, because of the memories of sense perception called up by its simple, but evocative word power.

176   K. Dittmer, l.c., p. 225, 248.

177   W. Goldschmidt, l.c., p. 215.
M. Hermanns, l.c., p. 227ff.
R. E. Ekvall, *Tibetan sky-lines*. New York 1952, gives a very lively, realistic description of life and mentality of the nomadic herdsmen of Tibet.

178   K. Dittmer, l.c., p. 223, 241f.

179   H. Consten, *Weideplätze der Mongolen*. Berlin 1920, Bd. 2, p. 108.

180   J. van Baal, *Godsdienst en samenleving in Nederlandsch-Zuid-Nieuw-Guinea*. Amsterdam 1934, p. 244.

181 A. David-Neel, *Le vieux Tibet face à la nouvelle Chine*. Paris 1953, p. 11, and passim.

182 R. Bleichsteiner, l.c., p. 90.

183 F. Sierksma, *Religie en politiek leiderschap in primitieve culturen*. Nederlands Theologisch Tijdschrift, dl. 10 (1956), p. 222.

184 A. Rüstow, *Ortsbestimmung der Gegenwart*. Bd. I: Ursprung der Herrschaft. 1950, p. 40.

185 M. Hermanns, *Die Nomaden von Tibet*. Wien 1949, p. 277f.

186 Information received from prof. dr. J. W. de Jong.
R. A. Stein, *Les tribus anciennes des marches sino-tibétaines*. Paris, 1959, *passim*. This work came to the attention of the author too late; he found several of his suppositions exactly confirmed by Stein's vast knowledge, and hopes to return to the place in culture and history of the Tibetan nomad herdsmen in a following publication.

187 H. Harrer, *Sieben Jahre in Tibet*. Wien 1952, p. 217f., relates that the Tibetan soldier has always retained a recognised right to booty, so that plundering was not rare. This too may well be considered a culture element of the nomad pastoralists or robbers. The same applies to the Tibetan passion for picnics and the pleasure they took in living out of doors in tents, as described e.g. in E. Schäfer, *Fest der weissen Schleier*[3]. Braunschweig 1952, p. 177.

188 F. Sierksma, l.c., p. 225.

189 E. Siao und H. Hauser, Tibet. Leipzig o. J., p. 18.

190 G. Ch. Toussaint, *Le dict de Padma*. Paris 1933, p. 154.

191 P. Carrasco, *Land and polity in Tibet*. Seattle 1959, p. 10 ff.

192 *The Blue Annals*, transl. G. N. Roerich. Calcutta 1949, vol. I, p. 35.
D. L. Snellgrove, *Buddhist Himālaya*. Oxford 1957, p. 129.

193 P. Carrasco, l.c., p. 222 ff.

194 D. L. Snellgrove, l.c., p. 174 ff., only devotes three pages to the pre-Buddhist religion of Tibet. Here this author's work requires balancing with the writings of Hoffmann, De Nebesky-Wojkowitz, Lalou and others, who treat the religion(s) of Tibet less one-sidedly from the Buddhist outlook.
H. Hoffmann, *Quellen zur Geschichte der tibetischen Bon-religion*. Wiesbaden 1950, gives the most important and extensive discussion of the Bon.

195 F. W. Thomas, l.c., p. 56 ff.

196 The Blue Annals, l.c., vol. I, p. 38.
M. Eliade, l.c., p. 172f., 175 ff., 182 ff., 433, 438.
Apparently the learned dispute concerning the so-called High Gods is still dominated, with respect to Tibet also, by controversies regarding the Viennese School, whose 'Kulturkreise' are more deserving of criticism than the facts brought to light about the High God.
H. Hoffmann, *Quellen zur Geschichte der tibetischen Bon-Religion*. Wiesbaden 1950, p. 156 is very explicit about the sky-god, who 'in der ursprünglichen Bon-Religion in zwei Aspekten verehrt wurde, als unpersönliche, namenlose Macht und als persönliche Gottheit' (who in the original Bon religion was venerated under two aspects, as an impersonal nameless power and as a personal Deity).

197 Term employed by G. van der Leeuw.

198 E. E. Evans-Pritchard, *Nuer religion*. Oxford 1956, pp. 1-27 and passim.

199 G. van der Leeuw, *Phänomenologie der Religion*. Tübingen 1933, § 9.
Th. P. van Baaren, *Wij mensen*. Utrecht 1960, p. 63 ff.

200 H. Hoffmann, *Quellen* usw. p. 138, seems to forget that the good, propitious spirits were demonised by Buddhism and later on by the monks, and that this did not fail to leave its mark on the Bon. The attitude described by Tafel towards a *sa bdag* or ancestor, who is thanked

for his protection and asked to continue it, after a 'Hail thee and all thy brothers', has a very different religious sound than the adoration of demons:

A. Tafel, *Meine Tibetreise.* Stuttgart 1914, Bd. I, p. 202.

For the *original* religion of Tibet it would be useful to look through not only old texts of the Bon po and rÑin-ma-pa, but also the descriptions given by travellers, especially those traversing the regions of nomad pastoralists and robbers, with this end in mind.

201 H. Hoffmann, *Die Religionen Tibets.* Freiburg 1956, p. 7.

202 R. de Nebesky-Wojkowitz, *Oracles and demons of Tibet.* 's-Gravenhage 1956, p. 291 ff.

203 Thubten Dschigme Norbu, *Tibet, verlorene Heimat.* Wien 1960, p. 48, 50.
R. de Nebesky-Wojkowitz, l.c., p. 332 f.
F. Sierksma, *The gods as we shape them.* London 1960, p. 45 f.

204 R. de Nebesky-Wojkowitz, l.c., p. 344: 'God of the hunt and owner of all mountain game.' id., *Where the gods are mountains.* London 1956, p. 155 f., 158, 160: 'lord of all mountain creatures' with the Lepchas. De Nebesky-Wojkowitz was obviously not acquainted with the universal hunters' god, the potnios or potnia thèroon, who was sometimes imagined in anthropomorphous, sometimes in theriomorphous shape. The terms 'lord', 'owner' and 'game' are particularly characteristic. That the original character of this god was better preserved among the Lepchas, is to be explained by their never having become so Buddhistic as the Tibetans.

205 M. Hermanns, *Die Nomaden von Tibet.* Wien 1949, p. 50.

206 F. W. Thomas, l.c., passim.

207 R. de Nebesky-Wojkowitz, *Oracles and demons of Tibet.* 's-Gravenhage 1956, p. 129.

208 F. Sierksma, l.c., p. 166 f., pl. 45, reproducing a Lord of the Tent of the Gilyak, who were excellent carvers in wood, but thought a mere indication sufficient for the inexpressible gods.

209 F. W. Thomas, l.c., p. 58 f.

210 M. Lalou, *Les religions du Tibet.* Paris 1957, p. 12.

211 F. W. Thomas, l.c., p. 4 f. H. Hoffmann, *Quellen* usw., p. 188 f.
Comparison of the data suggests, that in the pre-Bon period the bodies of nomadic rulers were laid on a high mountain-top, that later under the influence of the farmers the body was buried, at first under a tent-shaped hillock (!! l.c., p. 188), and that finally the building up of the Bon and the cult of royalty led to the introduction of burial in great tombs.

212 Rin-chen Lha-mo, *We Tibetans.* London 1926, p. 179 ff.

213 M. Lalou, l.c., p. 11.

214 ibid., p. 12.

215 E. Volhard, *Kannibalismus.* 1939, p. 388. At a still higher level of civilisation human beings are eaten, as also occurred in Tibet.

216 H. Hoffmann, *Die Religionen* usw., p. 10 f.
M. Hermanns, *Mythen und Mysterien der Tibeter.* Köln 1956, p. 145.

217 M. Hermanns, *Die Familie der A-mdo Tibeter.* Freiburg 1959, p. 254.

218 H. Hoffmann, l.c., p. 11.
A. David-Neel, *Mystiques et magiciens du Tibet.* Paris 1929, p. 29 ff.

219 S. H. Ribbach, *Dragpo Namgyal. Ein Tibeterleben.* München 1940, p. 209-235, 260.
W. W. Rockhill, *The land of the lamas.* New York 1891, p. 81.
D. L. Snellgrove, l.c., p. 274.
Cf. R. de Nebesky-Wojkowitz, l.c., p. 540
I. A. Lopatin, *The cult of the dead among the natives of the Amur Basin.* 's-Gravenhage 1960, p. 35, 40, 57 ff., 94 f., 125 f.

220 Ad. E. Jensen, *Mythos und Kult bei Naturvölkern*. Wiesbaden 1951, p. 357.

221 Or hunters and raiders of a nomadic habit, like the Navaho, who after they had changed to a settled existence, also developed an almost pathological fear of the dead:
Cl. Kluckhohn and D. Leighton, The Navaho. Cambridge 1959, p. 125 ff.

222 M. Eliade, *Le chamanisme et les techniques archaïques de l'extase*. Paris 1951, p. 18.

223 R. Bleichsteiner, *Die Gelbe Kirche*. Wien 1937, p. 180 ff.
R. de Nebesky-Wojkowitz, l.c., p. 538 ff.
M. Eliade, l.c., p. 381 ff.
H. Hoffmann, l.c., p. 13 ff.
M. Hermanns, *Mythen und Mysterien der Tibeter*. Köln 1956, p. 255 ff.
H. Hoffmann, *Quellen zur Geschichte der tibetischen Bon-Religion*. Wiesbaden 1950, p. 197-210, who mistakenly agrees with Ohlmarks' designation of shamanism as a surrogate for religion. *Schamanengeschichten aus Siberien*. Aus dem Russischen übersetzt und eingeleitet von A. Friedrich und G. Buddruss. München 1955 (quoted henceforth as Friedrich-Buddruss) is a yet little known, extremely valuable fund of oral information and texts.

224 M. Bouteiller, *Chamanisme et guérison magique*. Paris 1950.

225 F. Sierksma, *De religieuze projectie*[2]. Delft 1957, p. 163 ff.

226 Friedrich-Buddruss, p. 133 ff., 136 ff., 138 f.

227 M. Eliade, l.c., p. 47 ff.

228 ibid., p. 55 f.

229 M. Lot-Falck, *Les rites de chasse chez les peuples sibériens*. Paris 1953, p. 205 ff.
O. Zerries, *Wild- und Buschgeister in Süd-Amerika*. Wiesbaden 1954, p. 165 ff., 362 f.

230 Cl. Lévi-Strauss, *Les structures élémentaires de la parenté*. Paris 1949, p. 461 ff., 486.
Friedrich-Buddruss, p. 37 ff.

231 Friedrich-Buddruss, p. 139 f., 151, 157 and passim.

232 K. Rasmussen, *The intellectual culture of the Iglulik Eskimos*. Report of the 5th Thule Expedition, vol. VII, 1. 1929, p. 114.

233 At this point we approach the field of psychiatry, where one would be glad to hear the opinion of specialists. The problem also has other aspects deserving of closer examination. The excentric structure as a fundamental characteristic of human existence will be discussed in the chapter devoted to mysticism. See:
H. Plessner, *Die Stufen des Organischen und der Mensch*. Berlin 1928, p. 288 ff.
F. Sierksma, l.c., passim.

234 Friedrich-Buddruss, p. 150.

235 ibid., p. 151.

236 ibid., p. 138.

237 ibid., p. 140.

238 ibid., p. 147.

239 ibid., p. 324 *sub voce* Stier.

240 ibid., p. 201 f.

241 The examples given in this paragraph are all from the Yakut. Comparisons with this and other (North and Central) Asiatic peoples have also been made by others and are recognised as legitimate within the context of shamanism.

242 W. Thalbitzer, *Die kultischen Gottheiten der Eskimos*. Archiv für Religionswissenschaft, Bd. 26 (1928), p. 375.

243 R. de Nebesky-Wojkowitz, *Oracles and demons*, 409-454 (441!).
id., *Where the gods*, 204-226 and the photos opp. p. 160, 161, 176, 177.

244 R. A. Stein, *Recherches sur l'épopée et le barde au Tibet*. Paris 1959, p. 321 f., 326 ff., 335 f., 339.

245 ibid., p. 327, 490.

246 D. L. Snellgrove, *Buddhist Himālaya*, Oxford 1947, p. 176.

247 H. Hoffmann, *Quellen* usw., p. 179.

248 G. Ch. Toussaint, *Le dict de Padma*. Paris 1933, p. 268.

249 Bu-Ston, *The history of Buddhism*. Transl. from the Tibetan by E. Obermiller. Heidelberg 1932, vol. II, p. 184.

250 ibid., p. 197.

251 Tsung-lien Shen and Shen-chi Liu, *Tibet and the Tibetans*. Stanford 1953, p. 20.

252 P. Carrasco, *Land and polity in Tibet*. Seattle 1959, p. 14 ff.

253 According to Hoffmann, Buddhism was mainly a matter of culture to this first Buddhist king, according to Lalou the tantras were already preached at that time. In such circumstances it is difficult to draw the line between culture and religion.

254 H. Hoffmann, *Quellen* usw., p. 216.

255 D. L. Snellgrove, *Buddhist Himālaya*. Oxford 1957, p. 138.

256 Tsung-lien Shen and Shen-chi Liu, l.c., p. 25.

257 H. Hoffmann, *Die Religionen Tibets*. München 1956, p. 34.

258 ibid., p. 60 f.

259 P. Demiéville, *Le concile de Lhasa. Une controverse sur le quiétisme entre Bouddhistes de l'Inde et de la Chine au VIIIᵉ siècle de l'ère chrétienne*. Vol. I. Paris 1952, p. 174, 180, 182, 237 ff., 249 f., 302 f., 315. G. Tucci, *Minor Buddhist texts*. Part II. Roma 1958.

260 Bu-ston, l.c., vol. II, p. 196.

261 M. ter Braak, *Kaiser Otto III. Ideal und Praxis im frühen Mittelalter*. In: Verzameld werk, dl. 1. Amsterdam 1950, p. 560.

262 Ch. Bell, *The religion of Tibet*. Oxford 1931, p. 43.

263 G. Tucci, *Tibetan painted scrolls*. Roma 1949. Vol. I, p. 5.

264 M. Lalou, *Les religions du Tibet*. Paris 1957, p. 51: an old, unbowdlerised, and a new, expurgated Mahāmudrā.

265 G. Tucci, l.c., p. 42.

266 A. Tafel, *Meine Tibetreise*. Stuttgart 1914, Bd. I, p. 188 f.
G. Schulemann, *Geschichte der Dalai Lamas*. Leipzig 1958, S. 231 f.
Also in A-mdo and Kham little agricultural states persisted. The great difference was, however, that in the centre nomads and herdsmen were despised, while in the northeast they were regarded as superior, as shown by Ekvall and by Hermanns too.

267 G. Schulemann, l.c., p. 108.

268 ibid., p. 252 ff.

269 H. Hoffmann, *Die Religionen* usw., p. 178 f. G. Schulemann, l.c., p. 277 ff.

270 F. Sierksma, *Een nieuwe hemel en een nieuwe aarde. Messianistische en eschatologische bewegingen en voorstellingen bij primitieve volken*. 's-Gravenhage 1961, pp. 13-37.

271 D. L. Snellgrove, l.c., p. 237.
The battle for power among the nobility was also continued in the ecclesiastical state. In Lhasa in 1947 an ex-regent attempted the life of the regent with a time-bomb, which led to a miniature civil war and the shelling of the monastery of Sera with howitzers:
H. Harrer, *Sieben Jahre in Tibet*. Wien 1952, p. 187 ff.
Compare the remark of another regent: 'Wir vermeiden Krieg, von dem wir nicht sprechen, um ihn nicht zu beschwören' (We avoid war, and do not speak of it, not to call it up). This very Tibetan remark in:

E. Schäfer, *Fest der weissen Schleier*³. Braunschweig 1952, p. 28.

272 As in many cases we have insufficient information, it is not always clear whether a particular symptom of acculturation should be placed in the first or the second phase of the introduction of Buddhism, or even in the period of Tsong-kha-pa's reformation. Mistakes in this will have to be corrected, but the fact of acculturation itself is not, of course affected by these problems in chronology.

273 G. Ch. Toussaint, l.c., p. 274.
H. Harrer, l.c., p. 242 f., gives an eloquent example of this sense of inferiority on the part of a most intelligent, most likable and most exemplary Tibetan. Compare also:
E. Schäfer, l.c., p. 164, where an oracle in favour of the German expedition says, that these people do not treat the Tibetans like children, and:
A. Tafel, *Meine Tibetreise*. Stuttgart 1914, Bd. II, p. 155.
J. Bacot, *Le Tibet révolté*. Paris 1912, pp. 345-364, gives the autobiographical impressions of a Tibetan taken to France by Bacot. This document requires a separate analysis. It is clear that even in the most favourable circumstances imaginable – Bacot is his 'father and mother' – this Tibetan is constantly in danger of losing his sense of personal dignity and identity, because he is not himself a subject, but an object, looked at, laughed at, etc. Most revealing is the remark in connection with Bacot's receiving guests, the Tibetan being present in national costume: 'Il me montra ainsi que les choses rapportées'. In this favourable climate, stability is found in the estimable decision, not to give up Tibetan habits, and in the desire to return to Tibet.

274 G. Ch. Toussaint, l.c., p. 280.
275 ibid., p. 285.
276 ibid., p. 305.
277 ibid., p. 255
278 M. H. Duncan, *Harvest festival dramas of Tibet*. Hongkong 1955, p. 114f.
279 J. Bacot, *La vie de Marpa, le 'Traducteur'*. Paris 1937, p. 9.
280 R. A. Stein, *Les tribus anciennes des marches sino-tibétaines*. Paris 1959, p. 62.
281 D. MacDonald, *Twenty years in Tibet*. London 1932, p. 28.
282 E. Kagawuchi, *Three years in Tibet*. Benares 1909, p. 264ff.
283 G. Tucci, l.c., vol. II, p. 277, 283.
284 F. Sierksma, l.c., p.p. 13-37.
285 Ch. Bell, *Tibet, past and present*. Oxford 1924, p. 244.
286 G. Tucci, *Shrines of a thousand Buddhas*, p. 53
287 S. H. Ribbach, *Dragpo Namgyal. Ein Tibeterleben*. München 1940, p. 192 and passim.
288 W. W. Rockhill, *The land of the lamas*. New York 1891, p. 104.
289 The Blue Annals, vol. I, p. 165.
290 ibid., vol. I, p. 262.
291 A. Lesser, *The Pawnee Ghost Dance Hand Game*. 1933. F. Sierksma, l.c., p. 158ff..
292 ibid., p. 86.
293 G. Tucci, *Tibetan painted scrolls*. Roma 1949. Vol. II, p. 728.
294 M. Lalou, l.c., p. 8ff.
295 G. Tucci, *To Lhasa and beyond*. Roma 1956, p. 31 (still discord between Yellow Caps and Red Caps in 1948).
S. Ch. Das, *Journey to Lhasa and Central Tibet*. London 1904, p. 308, 275.
296 G. Tucci, *Tibetan painted scrolls*, p. 374ff.
297 H. Hoffmann, l.c., p. 93.

298 Bu-ston, l.c., vol. II, p. 188, 212.
Ch. Bell, *The religion of Tibet*. Oxford 1931, p. 49, 50, 54.

299 D. L. Snellgrove, l.c., p. 161 ff.

300 J. Bacot, l.c., p. 23, 29f., 32, 43.

301 E. Kagawuchi, l.c., p. 410 ff.

302 The Blue Annals, vol. II, p. 416.

303 ibid., vol. I, p. 204.

304 ibid., p. 110 (explanation of Roerich).

305 A. Tafel, l.c., Bd. I, p. 188f.

306 H. A. Jäschke, *Tibetan-English dictionary*[4]. London 1958, p. 28 (*skye-dman*).
S. E. Giraudeau et F. Goré, *Dictionnaire Français-Tibétain, Tibet oriental*. Paris 1956, p. 114, 125. This difference was confirmed by two Tibetan informants, who when asked the expression for 'Tibetan woman', gave the term bod-pa'i skye-dman, not bod-mo. Prof. dr. J. W. de Jong kindly returned to this subject afterwards, and found *int. al.* that for wife na-mo was mentioned as a word from the East, which one cannot use in Lhasa.

307 T. D. Norbu, *Tibet, verlorene Heimat*. Wien 1960, p. 185.

308 H. Harrer, l.c., p. 108f., 180, 193 etc. leaves the penetrating reader in no doubt, that the women of Lhasa are anything but shy and puritanical.
E. Schäfer, l.c., p. 43.
This description also seems to be valid for the central region outside Lhasa. In that case there is all the more reason to wonder whether in the end the culture pattern of agriculturalists, offering an easier religious starting-point for sexual tantrism, and economically forced to the solution of polyandry, was not a decisive factor in the origin of this conduct on the part of the women of Ü and Tsang, who by preference used equivocal language.
E. Kagawuchi, l.c., p. 474.

309 H. Hediger, *Skizzen zu einer Tierpsychologie im Zoo und im Zirkus*. Zürich 1954, p. 145f.

310 W. W. Rockhill, *Diary of a journey through Mongolia and Tibet in 1891 and 1892*. Washington 1894, p. 278f., 286, 309.

311 F. Sierksma, l.c., p. 87.

312 C. Kluckhohn, 'Navaho witchcraft'. *Papers Peabody Museum*, 22. Cambridge (M.) 1944.

313 S. Ch. Das, l.c., p. 281.

314 W. Y. Evans-Wentz, *Tibet's great yogi Milarepa. A biography from the Tibetan*[2]. London 1958, p. 67f., 117.

315 Ch. Bell, *The religion of Tibet*. Oxford 1931, p. 169, 184.

316 A. David-Neel, *Mystiques et magiciens du Tibet*. Paris 1929, p. 11, 29, 97 ff.
T. Y. Pemba, *Young days in Tibet*. London 1957, p. 54.

317 R. de Nebesky-Wojkowitz, *Oracles and demons of Tibet*. 's-Gravenhage 1956, p. 129

318 G. A. Combe, *A Tibetan on Tibet*. London 1926, p. 22.
E. Kagawuchi, l.c., p. 492f.

319 E. de Schlagintweit, *Le bouddhisme au Tibet*. Lyon 1881, p. 67.

320 L. A. Waddell, *The Buddhism of Tibet or Lamaism*. London 1895, p. 170.
S. H. Ribbach, l.c., p. 213.

321 G. Roerich, *Tibetan paintings*. Paris 1925, p. 4.

322 G. Tucci, *Minor Buddhist texts*. Part II. Roma 1958, p. 59.

323 D. L. Snellgrove, l.c., pp. 217-274.

324 The Blue Annals, vol. II, p. 695.

325 T. D. Norbu, l.c., p. 88.

326 P. Carrasco, l.c., p. 214.
Cf. A. David-Neel, *Le vieux Tibet* etc. Paris 1953, pp. 139-173. In connection with another remark we must assume that the merchants described here by David-Neel are also accredited members of the administration.

327 A. David-Neel, *Mystiques et magiciens*, p. 104. E. Kagawuchi, l.c., p. 325.

328 S. Ch. Das, l.c., p. 115.

329 ibid., p. 192.

330 Ch. Bell, *Tibet, past and present*. Oxford 1924, p. 43.

331 ibid., p. 86.

332 E. de Schlagintweit, l.c., p. 101.

333 Before the eleventh century there were far fewer monasteries, but most probably economic pressure was equally heavy, owing to the nobility.

334 P. Carrasco, *Land and polity in Tibet*. Seattle 1959, passim.

335 ibid., p. 26.

336 ibid, p. 116 ff., also giving a list of the lands belonging to the church.

337 ibid., p. 126.

338 ibid., p. 79, 120 ff., 216.

339 ibid., p. 81.

340 ibid., p. 218 ff.

341 For further particulars, also as to the origin and induration of Tibetan bureaucracy, see the afore-said work of Carrasco.

342 R. de Nebesky-Wojkowitz, *Oracles and demons of Tibet*. 's-Gravenhage 1956, p. 335.
H. Harrer, *Meine Tibet-Bilder*. Text H. Woltereck. Seebruck 1953, p. 18, gives an incorrect, romantic picture of social conditions in Tibet. That the Tibetans are not much attached to worldly goods is really a height of romanticism in a book appearing under the name of one who has lived in Tibet for seven years.

343 Ch. Bell, *Tibet, past and present*. Oxford 1924, p. 70. Cf. p. 158, 160.
H. Harrer, *Sieben Jahre in Tibet*. Wien 1952, p. 131, takes too innocent a view, in my opinion, of these derisive songs, that were forbidden, whereupon they went underground (!). Besides, the author himself mentions them in connection with the Tibetan inclination towards laughter, especially at someone else's misfortune and pain. It seems extremely probable that a good deal of aggressivity finds its expression in this malicious amusement. A closer analysis of this phenomenon, of the scruples with regard to killing worms, insects, or anything living and of the open aggressivity in other spheres of life is most desirable. Cf. l.c., p. 134, 153 f., 169, 182 (football forbidden because of fighting, a reason for Harrer to propagate tennis).

344 G. Tucci, *Tibetan folk-songs from the district of Gyantse*. Ascona 1949, p. 55.

345 Ch. Bell, *The religion of Tibet*. Oxford 1931, p. 173.

346 G. Ch. Toussaint, *Le dict de Padma*. Paris 1933, p. 255. Cf. p. 256 for another instance of Tibetan self-contempt.

347 S. Ch. Das, *Journey to Lhasa and Central Tibet*. London 1904, p. 243.

348 D. Macdonald, *Twenty years in Tibet*. London 1932, p. 191 f.

349 P. Carrasco, l.c., p. 212.
G. Tucci, *To Lhasa and beyond*. Roma 1956, p. 38.

350 G. Tucci and E. Ghersi, *Secrets of Tibet*. London 1935, p. 131 f.

351 T. Lobsang Rampa, *The third eye*. London 1956, p. 10, 18.

352 W. J. Goode, *Religion among the primitives*. Glencoe 1951, p. 223: 'Religion *expresses* the unity of society, but it also helps to *create* that unity'.

353 Ch. Bell, *Tibet, past and present*. Oxford 1924, p. 111.

354 R. J. Miller, 'Monasteries and culture change in Inner Mongolia'. *Asiatische Forschungen*, Bd. 2. Wiesbaden 1959.
L. M. J. Schram, *The Mongours of the Kansu Tibetan frontier*. Part II: the religious life. Transactions of the American Philosophical Society, vol. 47, 1. 1957. These give interesting material for a comparison with Lamaism in Mongolia, showing many resemblances to the Tibetan form, but also important differences, at any rate from the cultural aspect.

355 G. Gorer, *Himalayan village. The Lepchas of Sikkim*. London 1938, p. 195.
It would be a simplification to say that Lepchas and Pueblos had an integrated culture *because* they lived in primitive, closed societies. Primitive cultures also may be disintegrated to a greater or lesser extent.

356 F. Sierksma, *Een nieuwe hemel en een nieuwe aarde*. 's-Gravenhage 1961, p. 77, 106f. (cultural and religious dualism attending acculturation).

357 Ch. H. Lange, *Cochiti. A New Mexico pueblo, past and present*. Austin 1959, gives perhaps the best documented description of this. It is of great importance for comparison with the Lepchas, because here too a high degree of social integration, frankness with regard to sex (the famous clowns !) and a very little developed aggressivity have enabled a culture to make a dualistic response to one of the great religions – in this case Christianity – and to integrate it, as the Lepchas have done with Buddhism.

358 G. Gorer, l.c., p. 439ff.

359 M. Mead, *Sex and temperament in three primitive societies*. New York 1950, pp. 15-118.
F. Sierksma, *De roof van het vrouwengeheim*. 's-Gravenhage 1962, pp. 43-48.

360 G. Gorer, l.c., p. 188.

361 ibid., p. 444f.

362 ibid., p. 187f.

363 ibid., p. 207.

364 ibid., p. 345ff.

365 ibid., p. 194

366 F. Sierksma, *Een nieuwe hemel en een nieuwe aarde*. 's-Gravenhage 1961, p. 111: 'Identification means that one does not wish to be oneself, but another. As one cannot get away from oneself, this results in two incomplete individualities in one individual, that detract from each other and prevent one another from fully expanding. It is to be released from this painful situation that conservatives and progressives lay extreme emphasis on one of these two "personalities".'

367 Ch. Bell, *The religion of Tibet*. Oxford 1931, p. 38.

368 H. Hoffman, *Die Religionen Tibets*. Freiburg 1956, S. 39-56.

369 H. Silberer, *Probleme der Mystik und ihrer Symbolik*. Wien 1914, p. 168, 182, already pointed out in his still interesting study the connection between siddhi and auto-eroticism, thus choosing an important starting-point, deserving of further elaboration.

370 J. Bacot, *Le Tibet révolté*. Paris 1912, p. 236.

371 A. David-Neel, *Mystiques et magiciens du Tibet*. Paris 1929, p. 174ff.
H. Hoffmann, l.c., p. 136ff.

372 G. Tucci, *Tibetan painted scrolls*. Roma 1949. Vol. II, p. 542.

373 G. Ch. Toussaint, *Le dict de Padma*. Paris 1933, p. 146.

374 ibid., p.112.

375 D. L. Snellgrove, *Buddhist Himālaya*. Oxford 1957, p. 175 footnote.

376 G. Ch. Toussaint, l.c., p. 208: 'le couple enlacé dansait'.

377 *The Blue Annals*, transl. G. N. Roerich. Calcutta 1949, vol. I, p. 192.

378 G. Ch. Toussaint, l.c., p. 244f.
379 ibid., p. 328.
380 Bu-ston, *The history of Buddhism.* Transl. by E. Obermiller. Heidelberg 1932, vol. II, p. 184 etc.
381 M. Lalou, *Les religions du Tibet.* Paris 1957, p. 26f.
382 *The Blue Annals*, vol. I, p. 43.
     G. Ch. Toussaint, l.c., p. 235.
383 Ch. Bell, l.c., p. 20.
384 F. Sierksma, *Een nieuwe hemel en een nieuwe aarde.* 's-Gravenhage 1961, p. 79ff., 91f.
385 G. Ch. Toussaint, l.c., p. 311f., 317ff., 330.
     M. Lalou, l.c., p. 29f.
386 Ch. Bell, l.c., p. 17.
387 H. Hoffmann, l.c., p. 76ff.
388 S. Ch. Das, *Journey to Lhasa and Central Tibet.* London 1904, p. 275.
389 S. H. Ribbach, *Dragpo Namgyal. Ein Tibeterleben.* München 1940, S. 209.
390 R. B. Ekvall, *Tibetan sky-lines.* New York 1952, p. 102.
391 M. Hermanns, *Die Familie der A-mdo Tibeter.* Freiburg 1959, p. 24f., 283ff.
392 S. H. Ribbach, l.c., p. 193.
393 R. de Nebesky-Wojkowitz, *Oracles and demons of Tibet.* 's-Gravenhage 1956, p. 337.
394 T. Y. Pemba, *Young days in Tibet.* London 1957, p. 14, 149.
395 R. B. Ekvall, l.c., p. 106, 170.
     R. de Nebesky-Wojkowitz, l.c., p. 332f.
     R. A. Stein, in: *Journal asiatique*, vol. 1956, p. 230 (*mGon-po jag-lha* = dieu des brigands, and *jag-la 'gro-ba'i jag-dpon* = chef de brigands allant au brigandage).
396 M. H. Duncan, *Harvest festival dramas of Tibet.* Hongkong 1955, p. 10ff.
397 L. A. Waddell, *The Buddhism of Tibet or Lamaism.* London 1895, p. 484f.
398 R. H. van Gulik, *Hayagrīva. The mantrayānic aspect of the horse-cult in China and Tibet.* Leiden 1933, p. 95.
399 Tsung-lien Shen and Shen-chi Liu, *Tibet and the Tibetans.* Stanford 1953, p. 141f.
     It is remarkable that the land of the Wheel of the Doctrine obstinately refused to take the wheel into use as a means of transport:
     H. Harrer, *Sieben Jahre in Tibet.* Wien 1952, p. 135.
400 W. Y. Evans-Wentz, *Tibet's great yogi Milarepa*[2]. London 1958, p. 179.
401 Tsung-lien Shen and Shen-chi Liu, l.c., p. 132.
402 For the Tibetan people it is not māra, but *gŚin-rje*.
403 R. de Nebesky-Wojkowitz, l.c., p. 515.
404 G. Tucci, l.c., vol. II, p. 348.
405 F. Sierksma, *The gods as we shape them.* London 1960, p. 55, 62, 186.
406 L. A. Waddell, l.c., p. 567, 572.
407 T. Y. Pemba, l.c., p. 110.
408 S. H. Ribbach, l.c., p. 199.
409 L. A. Waddell, l.c., p. 40.
410 Ch. Bell, l.c., p. 43. Cf. p. 49f., 54.
     M. Lalou, l.c., p. 38.
411 Prince Peter of Greece and Denmark, *A study of polyandry.* The Hague 1963 (cohabitation with the woman superincumbent is regarded as tantric, strange and abnormal).
412 S. Ch. Das, l.c., p. 33, 305.
     The Blue Annals, vol. I, p. 153: 'With the help of the Explanatory Notes of Chos-rje bla-ma

I obtained an exceptional faith in the class of religious texts known as the Old Tantras, and was not affected by the defilement of abandoning religious vows.'

413 A. David-Neel, *My journey to Lhasa*. New York 1927, p. 175, provides a reliable indication that also in recent times the wife as secret assistant in tantric groups was known to the people, who regarded such a woman with respect, although the tantric ways were not considered indigenous (see note 411).

414 M. Lalou, l.c., p. 38.

415 G. de Roerich, *Le parler de l'Amdo. Etude d'un dialecte archaïque du Tibet*. Roma 1958, p. 5.

416 W. W. Rockhill, *Diary of a journey through Mongolia and Tibet in 1891 and 1892*. Washington 1894, p. 91. There is no reason whatever to suppose matters to be otherwise in the East than in the North-east, described here by Rockhill. With practically all nomad herdsmen sexuality has little or no place in public and religious life, while they also set the sky-god above all else (cf. l.c., p. 105).

417 G. de Roerich, l.c., p. 95.

418 If Snellgrove is right in supposing (Buddhist Himālaya, p. 176) the *sa-bdag* to be strangers afterwards imported into Central Tibet, it would mean that also in this important point of the living national religion the nomad herdsmen had a decisive influence. They must then have imported the *sa-bdag*.

419 G. de Roerich, l.c. p. 102f.

420 ibid., p. 84f.

421 G. A. Combe, *A Tibetan on Tibet*. London 1926, p. 29.

422 G. Tucci, Tibetan painted scrolls. Roma 1949. Vol. II, p. 374f.
T. D. Norbu, *Tibet, verlorene Heimat*. Wien 1960, p. 114.
E. Kagawuchi, *Three years in Tibet*. Benares 1909, p. 163 (K. regards it as 'a blasphemy against the Buddha' that an image of Padma, sometimes venerated in Tibet above the Buddha himself, was placed beside an image of the latter).

423 L. A. Waddell, l.c., p. 74.

424 W. Y. Evans-Wentz, l.c., p. 130.

425 *The Blue Annals*, vol. II, p. 921.

426 L. A. Waddell, l.c., p. 152.

427 A. David-Neel, *Initiations lamaïques*. Paris 1957, p. 15.
G. Tucci, *To Lhasa and beyond*. Roma 1956, p. 127.

428 *The Blue Annals*, vol. II, p. 874.

429 Bu-ston, l.c., vol. II, p. 121.
D. L. Snellgrove, l.c., p. 87, already pointed out that yogin and scholarly monk formed the two-fold aspect of religion.

430 *The Blue Annals*, vol. I, p. 205ff.; vol. II, p. 442.

431 W.Y. Evans-Wentz, l.c., p. 220ff. e.g.

432 A. David-Neel, *Mystiques et magiciens du Tibet*. Paris 1929, p. 96.
id., *Le vieux Tibet* etc., Paris 1953, p. 175, where she says the same, rather differently formulated and in a different tone, evoking negative associations. Indeed the whole book is not entirely free from resentment against countries that place restrictions upon travellers, as England and Tibet have done.

433 J. Bacot, *Trois mystères tibétains*. Paris 1921, p. 23f., 297f.
A. Tafel, *Meine Tibetreise*. Stuttgart 1914, Bd. I, S. 234.

434 L. A. Waddell, l.c., p. 518f., 527.

435 W. Filchner, *Kumbum Dschamba Ling*. Leipzig 1933, p. 124ff., 140.

436 E. Kagawuchi, l.c., p. 544.
437 ibid., p. 305 ff., 543.
   E. Schäfer, *Fest der weissen Schleier*[3]. Braunschweig 1952, p. 134.
   H. Harrer, *Sieben Jahre in Tibet*. Wien 1952, p. 206 f.
438 *The Blue Annals*, vol. I, p. 295.
439 T. D. Norbu, l.c., p. 109, 124 f.
440 R. B. Ekvall, l.c., p. 96.
441 E. Kagawuchi, l.c., p. 291 f.
   W. Filchner, l.c., p. 213 ff.
   T. D. Norbu, l.c., p. 97.
   H. Harrer, l.c., p. 204 f.
   E. Schäfer, l.c., p. 129 and passim.
   They even attack ministers and lay their cudgels to foreign envoys. The dictatorship of the
   monks that Harrer speaks of, p. 66, 125, is expressed in the dictatorship of the soldier-monks.
442 P. Demiéville, *Le concile de Lhasa*. Paris 1952, p. 226 ff.
443 W. W. Rockhill, *The land of the lamas*. New York 1891, p. 69, 216, 270 and passim.
   L. A. Waddell, l.c., p. 254.
   Ch. Bell, l.c., p. 171 f., 183, 187.
444 Tsung-lien Shen and Shen--chi Liu, l.c., p. 78.
445 F. Sierksma, *De roof van het vrouwengeheim*. 's-Gravenhage 1962, pp. 175-192.
446 G. Ch. Toussaint, l.c., p. 66. Cf. p. 63: 'Douceur et ampleur restent sans effet, il sera dompté
   par force et contrainte.'
447 D. L. Snellgrove, l.c., p. 258.
448 E. Schäfer, l.c., p. 142 ff.
449 D. L. Snellgrove, l.c., p. 251.
450 W. Filchner, l.c., p. 252 ff.
451 W. W. Rockhill, l.c., p. 100.
452 ibid., p. 123, 237.
453 W. Filchner, l.c., p. 223.
   T. D. Norbu, l.c., p. 217.
454 M. H. Duncan, l.c., p. 101.
455 ibid., p. 245 f.
456 B. Laufer, 'Aus den Geschichten und Liedern des Milaraspa'. *Denkschr. d. K. Ak. d. Wiss. Wien*,
   phil. hist. Kl., Bd. XLVIII, 2. Wien 1902, p. 12 f., 51 f.
457 F. D. Lessing, *Yung Ho Kung*. Stockholm 1942, p. 21 ff., 25.
458 E. Kagawuchi, l.c., p. 496 ff.
459 S. Ch. Das, l.c., p. 281.
460 E. Kagawuchi, l.c., p. 496 ff.
   Ch. Bell l.c., p. 77 f.
461 A. David-Neel, *Le vieux Tibet* etc., Paris 1953, p. 22 ff.
462 J. Bacot, *Le Tibet révolté*. Paris 1912, p. 10 ff., 331 ff., 353, 361.
463 F. Sierksma, *Een nieuwe hemel en een nieuwe aarde*. 's-Gravenhage 1961, pp. 250, 252.
464 E. Abegg, *Der Messiasglaube in Indien und Iran*. Berlin 1928, p. 58 f.
465 E. Schäfer, l.c., p. 183 ff.
466 *The Blue Annals*, transl. G. N. Roerich. Calcutta 1949-1953, vol. I, p. 97; vol. II, p. 980 ff.
467 B. Bhattacharyya, *The Indian Buddhist Iconography*[2]. Calcutta 1958, p. 247.
468 J. N. Banerjea, *The development of Hindu iconography*[2]. Calcutta 1956, p. 560 f. (footnote) explains

matters in the contrary direction, and supposes Vajrayoginī to have influenced Chinnamastā.

469 E. Neumann, *Ursprungsgeschichte des Bewusstseins.* Zürich 1949, pp. 53-115.

470 Translated text. Relevant note mislaid.

471 G. Ch. Toussaint, *Le dict de Padma.* Paris 1933, pp. 58, 111 etc.

472 W. Y. Evans-Wentz, *Tibetan yoga and secret doctrines*[2]. London 1960, p. 173 ff.; reproduction opposite p. 155.

473 E. Lamotte, *Histoire du bouddhisme indien.* Louvain 1958, p. 699.

474 W. Y. Evans-Wentz, l.c., p. 297.

475 A. M. Pozdnejev, 'Dhyāna und Samādhi im mongolischen Lamaismus'. *Zeitschr. f. Buddhismus und verwandte Gebiete*, Bd. 7 (1926) p. 396, 398.

476 E. Zürcher, *The buddhist conquest of China.* Leiden 1959, vol. I, p. 282.

477 R. Bleichsteiner, *Die gelbe Kirche.* Wien 1937, pp. 30, 32.

478 G. Tucci, *To Lhasa and beyond.* Roma 1952, p. 160.

479 P. H. Pott, *Yoga en yantra.* Leiden 1946, pp. 83-110.

480 Of course it is quite possible that ultimately both sets of ideas are of shamanistic origin.

481 F. W. Thomas, 'Ancient folk-literature from North-eastern Tibet'. *Abh. d. Ak. d. Wiss.* Berlin, Kl f. S.L.K., Bd. 1952, 2. Berlin 1957, p. 60.

482 G. Tucci, *Tibetan painted scrolls.* Roma 1949. Vol. I, p. 249.

483 ibid., vol. II, p. 542, 615.

484 M. Hermanns, *Mythen und Mysterien der Tibeter.* Köln 1956, p. 256 f., where also a summary of a Bon text of *gCod* which is almost completely shamanistic.

485 A. David-Neel, *Mystiques et magiciens du Tibet.* Paris 1929, p. 136 ff.

486 W. Y. Evans-Wentz, l.c., p. 320.

487 ibid., p. 301.

488 S. Hummel, *Elemente der tibetischen Kunst.* Leipzig 1949, p. 28 ff., would accept parapsychological views here. There can be no objection to doing so, except perhaps that Western parapsychology has little explanation to offer as yet. Also, at such a distance one cannot tell whether materialisation or intense psychic experience is responsible for certain phenomena.

489 G. Tucci, l.c., vol. II, p. 368; vol. III, pl. 45. Here the ḍākinī or yoginī is shown holding the drum and trumpet, which may be regarded as a sign of the identification of the yogin with the Vajrayoginī.

490 W. Y. Evans-Wentz, l.c., p. 309.

491 ibid., p. 310.

492 F. Sierksma, *De religieuze projectie*[2]. Delft 1957, p. 163 ff., where the theory of mysticism is to be found, as elaborations of which the hypotheses in the text are intended. The rebound-phenomenon is derived from the physiology of reflexes (W. H. Thorpe, Learning and instinct in animals[2]. London 1958, p. 26) and was adopted by animal psychology, where it is also called post-inhibitory facilitation. The concept thus has the advantage of uniting high and low, which is not the same as putting high and low on the same level, though uncharitable critics obstinately maintain that it is. The 'loi de l'effort converti' of Ch. Baudoin states that conscious volition simultaneously evokes allied and contrary tendencies in the unconscious, and thus may have quite a reverse effect. It should be investigated which of these terms may best serve to describe the yogic and mystic phenomena, taking the relation between the ego and the Self to be fundamental, and S and A (rather than sexuality and aggressivity) to be two contrary tendencies in biological, psychical and spiritual life.

493 A. David-Neel, l.c., p. 134.

494 ibid., p. 148.

495 M. Lalou, *Les religions du Tibet*. Paris 1957, p. 4, where Bacot is quoted.

496 E. de Schlagintweit, *Le bouddhisme au Tibet*. Lyon 1881. *The Blue Annals*, vol. II, p. 992, 994.

497 W. Y. Evans-Wentz, l.c., p. 321 f.

498 ibid., p. 326.

499 H. Plessner, *Die Stufen des Organischen und der Mensch*. Berlin 1928, p. 291.

500 F. Sierksma, *The gods as we shape them*. London 1960, p. 180, 190, pl. 83.
E. Neumann, l.c., p. 45 f., 76, 172 f.

501 F. Sierksma, *De religieuze projectie*[2]. Delft 1957, passim.

502 *nyen* are a group of autochthonous gods.

503 D. L. Snellgrove, *Buddhist Himālaya*. Oxford 1957, p. 239 ff., gives the complete translation.

504 W. Y. Evans-Wentz, *The Tibetan book of the dead*[3]. London 1960, p. LV.

505 H. von Glasenapp, *Buddhistische Mysterien*. Stuttgart 1940, p. 80.

506 F. Sierksma, *Een nieuwe hemel en een nieuwe aarde*. 's-Gravenhage 1961, pp. 186-210. The developments with the Unambal described and analysed here are extremely illuminating with regard to 1) the relation between the increase of black magic and demonisation of the gods; 2) demonisation of the gods in itself. With regard to the latter, there is in this instance a historical development, observed and written down (Berndt, Lommel, Petri), showing us how as a result of acculturation benevolent and propitious deities, quite devoid of demonic aspects, change into devilish powers that are explicitly compared to deadly poison: l.c., p. 197.

507 M. Deren, *Divine horsemen. The living gods of Haiti*. London 1953.
Ch. H. Lange, *Cochiti. A New Mexico pueblo, past and present*. Austin 1959, offers documented evidence that in a closed, primitive society, completely directed towards social integration and the common good, acculturation does indeed produce the rift between progressives and regressives and cause an increase of witchcraft (p. 93, 194, 201, 252 ff.), but does not result in demonisation of the gods. The *Ka'tsinas* remain good and benevolent, even when kept secret (p. 288). This is rare, however, just as the social integration of the pueblos is a rare thing. See note 357. One of the two parties has been known to leave the pueblo, as e.g. in Oraibi, rather than make war.

508 F. W. Thomas, 'Ancient folk-literature from North-eastern Tibet'. *Abh. d. Ak. d. Wiss.* Berlin, Kl. f. S.L.K., Bd. 1952, 2. Berlin 1957, p. 48.
G. Tucci, *The tombs of the Tibetan Kings*. Roma 1950, p. 48, gives a translation of an edict of king K'ri sroñ lde btsan, who reintroduces Buddhism because 'There the Tibetan law is not good. By various prayers to gods and rituals, everybody is addicted to (actions) not good, ... some put red colour on their body, some are addicted to causing damage to the government, some are addicted to causing disease to man and cattle, some others to producing famine.' This conveys an excellent impression, how in the time of the kings opposition to the king's rule was seen in a religious context by the king and the Buddhists, at any rate officially. Thus the negative character of Tibet's national religion was automatically stressed, as supposed – and no doubt also real – black magic, pride of nomadic descent setting magic against men and cattle before magic against the crops. Cattle was then not yet connected exclusively with the inhabitants of the barbarian regions, as in later times, but with the royal house itself!

509 H. Hoffmann, *Quellen zur Geschichte der Bon-Religion*. Mainz 1950, p. 161, 171.
R. de Nebesky-Wojkowitz, *Oracles and demons of Tibet*. 's-Gravenhage 1956, p. 318 ff.

510 B. C. Olschak, *Tibet, Erde der Götter*. Zürich 1960, S. 7.

511 R. de Nebesky-Wojkowitz, l.c., p. 335, 376, 429, 441.

512 ibid., p. 131.

513 G. A. Combe, *A Tibetan on Tibet*. London 1926, p. 81.

514 R. de Nebesky-Wojkowitz, l.c., p. 7.

515 W. Y. Evans-Wentz, *The Tibetan book of the dead*³. London 1960, p. 132-135.

516 L. A. Waddell, *The Buddhism of Tibet or Lamaism*. London 1895, p. 364.
Is the popularity she enjoyed according to Hermanns perhaps characteristic of A-mdo?

517 Tsung-lien Shen and Shen-chi Liu, *Tibet and the Tibetans*. Stanford 1953, p. 86.

518 E. Kagawuchi, *Three years in Tibet*. Benares 1909, p. 561.
S. H. Ribbach, *Dragpo Namgyal*. München 1940, p. 164.

519 A. Tafel, *Meine Tibetreise*. Stuttgart 1914, Bd. I, S. 182, shows such a bronze. There is an identical one in the Museum voor Land- en Volkenkunde, Rotterdam, inv. 29166. According to two Tibetan informants the name of this god is *Za byed mka' 'gro'*, or *Za byed rdo rje mk'a'*. The custom described by Tafel was not known to them. One of them stated that to the best of his knowledge seeds were burned in the open mouth of the god before a certain form of meditation by contemplatives of advanced degree. In the meditation all the sins of man are 'eaten up' by the god. I gained the impression that the ritual action was a sensory symbol of what is actualised spiritually in the meditation. Unfortunately the informant, though a geshe, could tell me no more. To let sins be devoured by a god in meditation is also known in another connection, cf. Evans-Wentz, Tibetan yoga etc., 1960, p. 326, 327 footnote.

520 M. Hermanns, *Die Familie der A-mdo Tibeter*. Freiburg 1959, p. 154.

521 G. A. Combe *A Tibetan on Tibet*. London 1926, p. p. 76f.

522 ibid., p. 46f.

523 L. A. Waddell, l.c., p. 570.

524 E. Lamotte, *Histoire du bouddhisme indien*. Louvain 1958, p. 436.

525 G. Ch. Toussaint, *Le dict de Padma*. Paris 1933, p. 437ff.

526 R. de Nebesky-Wojkowitz, l.c., p. 94ff.

527 T. Y. Pemba, *Young days in Tibet*. London 1957, p. 141, relates that he studied with pleasure at a Western school, only did not like singing and poetry; 'Both were too cherubic for me'.

528 G. Tucci, *Tibetan painted scrolls*. Roma 1949, vol. I, p. 321 ff.
Tsung-lien Shen and Shen-chi Liu, l.c., p. 86f. saw far less of a *mGon khang* than Tucci. Comparison of the two reports offers interesting aspects.
A. Tafel, l.c., Bd. I, p. 222 ff., gives a most exact description of the *mGon khang* of Kumbum. His matter-of-fact enumeration and commentary and his criticism of Filchner prove once again how excellently well-informed this intrepid traveller was. Deep respect is due to the vanished generation of explorers who observed the conditions of the soil and the temperature, the stars and the birds, ways of building and the sewing outfit as well as dialects and rituals. Of interest in the passage referred to is the sentence: 'Die zornigen Tschüs dyong sind vielfach auch die Kriegsgötter der Tibeter geworden.' (The angry Tschüs dyong (*i.e. the defenders of the doctrine*) have often also become the war-gods of the Tibetans). Cf. the prayer translated by Roerich in his study of the dialect of A-mdo.
L. A. Waddell, *Lhasa and its mysteries*³. London 1906, p. 228f., says of the 'Devils' Chamber of Horrors'' of the monastery of Gyantse, which he visited, that its purpose was to frighten the superstitious laity. The gods have human form, but the heads of monsters and animals, and all are devouring human corpses. According to him they belong largely to the Bon pantheon.

529 G. A. Combe, l.c., p. 61, 68.

530 R. de Nebesky-Wojkowitz, l.c., p. 402.

531 F. W. Thomas, l.c., p. 59f.

532 L. A. Waddell, l.c., p. 292.

533 J. Bacot, *La vie de Marpa, le 'traducteur'*. Paris 1937, p. 47.

534 G. Ch. Toussaint, l.c., p. 390.

535 A. David-Neel, *My journey to Lhasa*. New York 1927, p. 260, on the same thing in Lhasa, where 'dark recesses' hold the Terrifying Ones, 'which Tibetans have never been able to forsake'. In this context she also speaks of 'even worse creatures', whom she does not specify.

536 G. Tucci, l.c., p. 284, 286, 320 ff.

537 S. Hummel, *Geschichte der tibetischen Kunst*. Leipzig 1953, S. 19.

538 G. Tucci, l.c., p. 323.

539 P. H. Pott, *An introduction to the Tibetan collection of the National Museum of Ethnology, Leiden.* Leiden 1956, p. 59.

540 L. A. Waddell, l.c., p. 292.

541 R. de Nebesky-Wojkowitz, l.c., p. 343 f.
 A. Tafel, *Meine Tibetreise*. Stuttgart 1914, Bd. I, p. 224.

542 P. H. Pott, l.c., p. 59, regards the mGon khang as 'the symbolically developed representation of the cemetery where the "I" undergoes its dissolution'. This interpretation cannot be accepted in cultural anthropology. Although the author is quite right in emphasising esoteric interpretations in a culture like the Tibetan, they should not be made absolute. Yoga and mysticism form the superstructure of a culture which is 'menschlich, allzu menschlich' like any other. It is so evident that history and drive-impelled action have penetrated into the mGon khang in the shape of arms and trophies of war, that an interpretation on the timeless and spiritual level is inadequate, even in the context of the Vajrayāna.

543 R. Bleichsteiner, *Die gelbe Kirche*. Wien 1931, S. 193 f.

544 D. L. Snellgrove, l.c., p. 243.

545 G. A. Combe, l.c., p. 82. R. de Nebesky-Wojkowitz, l.c., p. 131 f.
 F. Maraini, *Geheim Tibet*. Amsterdam s.a., p. 138, gives a fine example showing that the belief that dead lamas might 'return' as Terrifying Ones was still alive in recent times. Around 1920 a lama was robbed and killed in South Tibet. He revenged himself as the terrible Namka-bazin, whose cult spread over the whole adjacent area. In the district concerned he even became one of the most important figures of the 'cham!

546 W. Filchner, *Kumbum Dschamba Ling*. Leipzig 1933, p. 145.

547 D. MacDonald, *Twenty years in Tibet*. London 1932, p. 129, 250.

548 S. Hummel, *Geheimnisse tibetischer Malereien*. Leipzig 1949, p. 39 ff., 60 ff.

549 D. L. Snellgrove, l.c., p. 260.

550 A. Tafel, *Meine Tibetreise*. Stuttgart 1914, Bd. II, facing p. 176 (Tafel XXXVII).

551 J. W. de Jong in *Indo-Iranian Journal*, vol. 2 (1960), p. 198 ff.

552 P. H. Pott, l.c., p. 60.

553 G. Tucci, l.c., vol. II, p. 458.

554 L. A. Waddell, l.c., p. 477.
 H. Hoffmann, *Die Religionen Tibets*. Freiburg 1956, p. 166.

555 E. Pander, *Das Pantheon des Tschangtscha Hutuku*. Berlin 1890, p. 61.

556 W. Filchner, l.c., p. 265 f.

557 S. H. Ribbach, l.c., p. 147.

558 S. Hummel, l.c., p. 33 f., 51. It is a pity this author's remarks on what he has observed are so vague and generalised in the Jungian direction, as thereby they lose much of their value.

559 Cf. E. Pander, l.c., p. 59.

560 S. B. Dasgupta, *An introduction to Tantric Buddhism*. Calcutta 1950, p. 110.
 S. H. Ribbach. l.c., p. 251.

561 M. H. Duncan, *Harvest festival dramas of Tibet*. Hongkong 1955, p. 147.

562 R. H. van Gulik, *Sexual life in ancient China*. Leiden 1961.

563 M. H. Duncan, l.c., p. 236. In this part of the drama the saint has only just arisen from the dead.

564 ibid., p. 180.

565 G. Roerich, *Tibetan paintings*, Paris 1925, p. 17.

566 J. Bacot, *La vie de Marpa, le 'traducteur'*. Paris 1937, p. 35.
S. Hedin, *Trans-Himalaya*. London 1909. Vol. I, opposite p. 394 (pl. 165) has a photograph of a nun singing the explanation of a thangka that is hung up.

567 E. de Schlagintweit, *Le bouddhisme au Tibet*. Lyon 1881, p. 130
L. A. Waddell, l.c., p. 328.

568 Tsung-lien Shen and Shen-chi Liu, l.c., p. 86.

569 P. H. Pott, l.c., p. 51.

570 G. Tucci, l.c., vol. I, p. 287.

571 F. Sierksma, *The gods as we shape them*. London 1960, discusses the image of a god as one or a small number of 'releasers' or shorthand symbols. He should have added that just as primary religious experiences can be built up and expanded into a theological system, the image of a deity can also become a systematised piece of theological doctrine, which may be very complicated, as in India and Tibet, or with the Aztecs.

572 G. Tucci, l.c., p. 281.

573 H. Zimmer, *Kunstform und Yoga im indischen Kultbild*. Wien 1926, p. 36 and passim.

574 For an exhaustive discussion of the technical, historical and other aspects of art the reader is referred to the books of Zimmer, Tucci, Roerich, Hummel, Pott, Getty, Gordon and others, already quoted from. Zimmer is still very important and most illuminating. Tucci's Tibetan Painted Scrolls is the unparalleled standard work on the subject of painting. Roerich gives complete information about technique. Pott gives a succinct and expert exposition, touching on pretty well all aspects of the subject, and also including the industrial arts. Naturally it is not the intention in the present monograph to repeat what has already been said by these and other authors.

575 B. Bhattacharyya, *The Indian Buddhist iconography*[2]. Calcutta 1958, p. 7. The book includes several reproductions of such drawings.

576 G. van der Leeuw, *Wegen en grenzen*[2]. Amsterdam 1948, is a first and interesting attempt to sketch the comparative evolution of art from being tied to a fixed cultural and religious scheme to full liberty. Although there is far more free art among primitive peoples than supposed by this author, his work remains a valuable starting-point. It is a pity that, many-sided as he was, he was apparently not acquainted with Tibetan art. Herein we have a classical example of an art almost completely tied down to prescribed forms, and one wonders whether precisely in such cultures *conscious* control of art has not also social and political aspects. Van der Leeuw related art to religion, but omitted to relate them both to the cultural context.

577 A. Tafel, l.c., p. 240.

578 J. Bacot, *Le Tibet révolté*. Paris 1912, p. 122.

579 G. van der Leeuw, *De primitieve mens en de religie*. Groningen 1937, p. 148.

580 A. David-Neel, *Initiations lamaïques*. Paris 1930, p. 107.

581 *The Blue Annals*, vol. I, p. 77; vol. II, p. 652.

582 B. Laufer, *Aus den Geschichten und Liedern des Milaraspa*. Wien 1902, p. 22.

583 G. A. Combe, *A Tibetan on Tibet*. London 1926, p. 171.

584 D. MacDonald, *Twenty Years in Tibet*. London 1932, p. 141ff.
E. Schäfer, *Fest der weissen Schleier*[3]. Braunschweig 1952, p. 77f., gives an account of this

mysticism with charnel field meditation. In how far this belongs to the practice of the Ka-gyü-pa, could not be checked. The studies of Li An-chi were not available.

585 A. Govinda, *Foundations of Tibetan mysticism.* London 1959, p. 80f.

586 ibid., p. 103f., 162, 198, Cf. p. 93, 208.

587 ibid., p. 92.

588 A. Wayman, 'Studies in Yama and Māra'. *Indo-Iranian Journal*, vol. 3 (1959), p. 57.

589 Cf. P. Sevenster, *A causal analysis of a displacement activity. Fanning in Gasterosteus Aculeatus L.* Leiden 1961.

590 W. H. Thorpe and O. L. Zangwill (ed.), *Current problems in animal behaviour.* Cambridge 1961, p. 167: 'We are now coming to realise that there is hardly any aspect of the behaviour of animals which may not have some reference to problems in human behaviour' (Thorpe).

591 S. B. Dasgupta, *An introduction to Tantric Buddhism.* Calcutta 1950, p. 139.

592 W. Y. Evans-Wentz, *Tibetan yoga and secret doctrines*[2]. London 1960, p. 172ff.

593 ibid., p. 190ff., 198ff., 206.

594 W. Y. Evans-Wentz, *The Tibetan book of the dead*[3]. London 1960, p. 31, 85.

595 A. Govinda, l.c., p. 165, 176, 201f.
P. H. Pott, *Yoga en yantra.* Leiden 1946, discusses, mainly with regard to the heart lotus, a different tradition of yoga of a more Hindu (Śaiva) character that is much bound up with practices in cemeteries. Though this yoga was also not unknown in Tibet, the real Tibetan school differs from it in several respects: there are fewer centres, the heart lotus is the seat of the Peaceful Ones, prajñā instead of Kuṇḍalinī, etc. Such diverse pronouncements as those of Govinda and Mi-la re-pa show, that the Ka-gyü-pa only assigned minor importance to cemeteries and charnel fields as means of attaining fearlessness.

596 R. G. Bhandarkar, *Vaiṣṇavism, Śaivism and minor religious systems.* Strassburg 1913, p. 130f. Cf. B. Bhattacharyya, *The Indian Buddhist iconography*[2]. Calcutta 1958, p. 25: the appearance of the god in meditation is an 'explosion of śunya'. Very probably this may be regarded as an echo of the violent 'breaking in of the vision' of the Śaivas. It confirms the typical character of this form of Indian yoga, the implications of which deserve further study.

597 F. Sierksma, *Een nieuwe hemel en een nieuwe aarde.* 's-Gravenhage 1961, p. 149.

598 F. D. Lessing, *Yung Ho Kung.* Stockholm 1942. Vol. I., p. 134.
P. H. Pott, 'A remarkable piece of Tibetan ritual-painting and its meaning.' *Intern. Arch. f. Ethnographie*, vol. 43 (1943), p. 230ff.
B. Laufer, l.c., p. 68.
R. Bleichsteiner, l.c., p. 176.

599 The last two phases of this via mystica are of course also discussed by Govinda. The 'breaking-through' analysed here is not only of central importance for the subject of the present study, but also in the mysticism of the Ka-gyü-pa.

600 A. Govinda, l.c., p. 198.

601 ibid., p. 207f.

602 F. Sierksma, *Phaenomenologie der religie en complexe psychologie.* Assen 1950, p. 220ff., traces a connection between 'der hinter sich liegende Fluchtpunkt der eigenen Innerlichkeit' (that element in the background of one's inner being, away from which one takes one's direction) in Plessner's analysis of our structure of living and Jung's 'Selbst' which cannot be objectified, one of the valuable empirical elements of Jung's unequal psychology. In *De religieuze projectie* the author tried to approach Western and Buddhist mysticism from the relation between the ego and the Self. Here and on other pages an attempt is made to develop these ideas.

603 Cf. J. Dollard, W. E. Miller, L. W. Doob and others, *Frustration and aggression*. 2nd. ed. New Haven 1961.

604 E. S. Craighill Handy, 'Polynesian religion'. *Bulletin Bernice P. Bishop Museum*, no. 34, 1937, p. 144.

605 F. Sierksma, *De roof van het vrouwengeheim*. 's-Gravenhage 1962, pp. 98, 100.

606 H. Hediger, *Skizzen zur Tierpsychologie im Zoo und im Zirkus*. Zürich 1954, p. 110 ff.
J. H. Crook, 'The basis of flock organisation in birds'. In : W. H. Thorpe and O. L. Zangwill, l.c., p. 125 ff., 130, 138 ff.
'Contact species' have been left out of account.

607 This information was kindly given by Mrs. A. C. A. Sevenster-Bol and Dr. J. J. A. van Iersel.

608 J. J. A. van Iersel, *Ambivalent gedrag*. Leiden 1959, blz. 17v. Cf. W. H. Thorpe and O. L. Zangwill, l.c., p. 114 (quotation from D. Morris).

609 The fact that Buddhist mysticism was split up almost at once (E. Lamotte, l.c., p. 67), might suggest that it is problematical whether the original ideal (that we would describe as completely sublimated a-mysticism of intellectual analysis coinciding with *direct* mystic experience of this insight in a contemplative trance) can be mystically realised.

610 E. Conze, *Buddhist meditation*. London 1956, p. 37 ff., also points out the great differences between Buddhist meditation and modern psychotherapy; in the former man wishes to leave the world, in the latter he wishes to adapt himself to it. Conze also, quite rightly, draws attention to the modern European repugnance to mental discipline in a wider sense.

611 A. Friedrich und G. Buddruss, *Schamanengeschichten aus Siberien*. München 1955, p. 79.

612 A. David-Neel, *Initiations lamaïques*. Paris 1930, pp. 187-194.

613 J. Darmesteter, 'Zend Avesta', vol. I. *Annales du Musée Guimet*, vol. XXI. Paris 1892, pp. 126-134.
Cf. West in *The sacred books of the East*, vol. XVIII, p. 204, 418.
J. Darmesteter, *Ormuzd et Ahriman, leur origine et leur histoire*. Paris 1897, p. 106 note 2.

614 Prof. Dr. F. B. J. Kuiper, who most kindly assisted the author with literature regarding Iran and India and with valuable advice, states that *yĕmā* (Yasna 30, 3) means twin.

615 K. F. Geldner, *Der Rigveda*. Bd. III. Cambridge 1951, X, 10.

616 Cl. Lévi-Strauss, *Les structures élémentaires de la parenté*. Paris 1949.
J. P. B. de Josselin de Jong, *Lévi-Strauss's theory on kinship and marriage*. Leiden 1952, p. 33, supposes, rightly I think, that a psychological factor must also be taken into account. Data from animal psychology, particularly with regard to family life and the 'incest taboo' among geese, go to strengthen this conjecture. It is highly desirable, therefore, that this fundamental characteristic in social life and religion, which is also of central importance in the symbolism of Yama, should be examined more closely. A beginning was made by:
K. Kortmulder, *Enkele opmerkingen over het incest-taboe*. Doctorale scriptie biologie, afd. ethologie en culturele anthropologie, Rijksuniversiteit te Leiden 1959. Typescript incorporating valuable information sent by prof. dr. K. Lorenz, and also discussing the data referring to geese in O. Heinroth, 'Beiträge zur Biologie, namentlich Ethologie und Psychologie der Anatiden' / *Verhandlungen des V. Intern. Ornithologen-Kongress*. Berlin 1910.

617 L. von Schröder, *Mysterium und Mimus im Rigveda*. Leipzig 1908, p. 277.

618 K. F. Geldner, l.c., p. 157.
A. Wayman, 'Studies in Yama and Māra'. *Indo-Iranian Journal*, vol. 3 (1959), p. 50, 55 (Yama = mṛtyu in Rigveda).
L. Renou et J. Filliozat, *L'Inde classique*. Paris 1947, p. 335.

619 A. Wayman, l.c., p. 50, who quotes Bergaigne.

R. N. Dandekar, *Yama in the Veda*. B. C. Law Volume. Calcutta 1945, pp. 194-209, regards the god-man Yama as stemming from a bisexual primordial being. If this hypothesis is correct, the notion of a primordial hermaphrodite must be very ancient, in view of the Iranian twin Yima and Yimak. Dandekar's article gives many particulars regarding Yama in the Veda and the development of his various aspects, rightly stressing his ambivalence. As a marginal figure between god and man, life and death, and perhaps too between man and woman, such a god must necessarily be ambivalent, so that all kinds of speculations can be linked up with him, which may lead to real or seeming contradictions.

620   A. Wayman, l.c., p. 62.

621   M. Deren, *Divine horsemen. The living gods of Haiti*. London 1953, p. 37 ff., 102 ff.

622   H. von Glasenapp, *Brahma und Buddha*. Berlin 1926, p. 107f.

623   J. Varenne, *Le jugement des morts dans l'Inde*. Paris 1960, p. 215f., is mistaken in disregarding this irrational element.

624   L. Renou et J. Filliozat, l.c., p. 556. Cf. p. 484, 495.
Prof. Dr. F. B. J. Kuiper drew attention to:
L. Scherman, 'Eine Art visionärer Höllenschilderung aus dem indischen Mittelalter'. *Romanische Forchungen*, Bd. V (1889), p. 539-582, who also gives a number of instances when Yama was induced to relent. Altogether Scherman gives important information about Yama.

625   A. Avalon, *The great liberation*. Madras 1927, p. 382, 387, 391.

626   W. Koppers, *Die Bhil in Zentral-Indien*. Wien 1948, p. 170.

627   ibid., p. 168f.

628   ibid., p. 263 ff.

629   ibid., p. 298.

630   H. von Glasenapp, l.c., p. 129, says that in Hinduism Yama and Yamī are married, which is in conflict with other statements, and also with the information given by Koppers.

631   J. N. Banerjea, *The development of Hindu iconography*[2]. Calcutta 1956, p. 504.

632   ibid., p. 187, 274, 504f.
E. T. Atkinson, *Notes on the history of religion in the Himālaya of the N-W P. of India*. Calcutta, 1883 (?), p. 96f. mentions a text in which Durga is called the sister of Yama. Cf. note 692 and 693. As already remarked in connection with popular religion in India and ideas of the primitive Bhil, the fact that Yama has a sister has remained a living part of religion, in contrast with what is usually assumed by Indologists. That is why incestuous associations kept cropping up. Perhaps even more account should be taken of this with regard to Tibet than was done in the present chapter, which indeed is only a first, tentative attempt.

633   Originally their number was 7.

634   P. H. Pott, 'A remarkable piece of Tibetan ritual-painting.' *Int. Arch. f. Ethnographie*, Bd. 43 (1943), p. 234 ff.
id., *Yoga en yantra*. Leiden 1946, p. 90 ff.
id., *Introduction to the Tibetan collection of the National Museum of Ethnology, Leiden*. Leiden 1951 p. 96.

635   J. N. Banerjea, l.c., p. 525 ff.

636   L. Renou et J. Filliozat, l.c., p. 485, 495.

637   M. Hermanns, *Mythen und Mysterien der Tibeter*. Köln 1956, p. 130 ff.

638   J. Varenne, l.c., p. 220 ff.

639   H. von Glasenapp, l.c., p. 216, 242.

640   A. Wayman, l.c., p. 55.

641   B. Bhattacharyya, *The Indian Buddhist iconography*[2]. Calcutta 1958, p. 251f., 352, 361.

642 G. Tucci, *Tibetan painted scrolls*. Roma 1949, vol. II, p. 583.
id., *Indo-Tibetica*. Vol. III, 2. Roma 1936, pp. 78-84.
B. Bhattacharyya, l.c., p. 166f.

643 A. Foucher, *Etude sur l'iconographie bouddhique de l'Inde*. vol. 2. Paris 1905, p. 56f.

644 B. Bhattacharyya, l.c., p. 166.

645 E. Pander, *Das Pantheon des Tschangtscha Hutuktu*. Berlin 1890, p. 61, seems to have been the first to mention this myth. Iconographically it has hardly any value, but it is very typical of the interconnection of yoga, frustration, aggression and identification:
F. Sierksma, *The gods as we shape them*. London 1960, p. 162.

646 D. L. Snellgrove, *Buddhist Himālaya*. Oxford 1957, p. 204f.

647 Bu-ston, *The history of Buddhism*. Transl. E. Obermiller. Heidelberg 1932. Vol. II, p. 170f., 220, 221, 222, 224.

648 *The Blue Annals*. Transl. G. N. Roerich. Calcutta 1953. Vol. II, p. 523, 732, 930.
G. Tucci, *Indo-Tibetica*, III, 2. Roma 1936, p. 56, 76f., 82f., 92f., 95f., 98, from which it is evident that also in Tsaparang both Yama and Yamī held a very subordinate position in official theology, while Yamāntaka is the judge of the dead and the king of the law.

649 Bu-ston, l.c., p. 198.

650 M. H. Duncan, *Harvest festival dramas of Tibet*. Hongkong 1955, p. 194.

651 ibid., p. 106.

652 ibid., p. 211ff.

653 G. Ch. Toussaint, *Le dict de Padma*. Paris 1933, p. 293, 333, 335, 343f., 356.

654 H. Hoffmann, *Quellen zur Geschichte der tibetischen Bon-Religion*. Wiesbaden 1950, p. 162.

655 M. Hermanns, *Die Familie der A-mdo Tibeter*. Freiburg 1959, p. 154.
W. Y. Evans-Wentz, *The Tibetan book of the dead*[3]. London 1960, p. 147.

656 M. Hermanns, *Mythen und Mysterien der Tibeter*. Köln 1956, p. 132.

657 ibid., p. 130.

658 G. Tucci, *Tibetan painted scrolls*, vol. II, p. 588; vol. III, pl. 199.

659 R. A. Stein, *Recherches sur l'épopée et le barde au Tibet*. Paris 1959, p. 323.
E. Schäfer, *Fest der weissen Schleier*[3]. Braunschweig 1952, p. 84, describes yogic-shamanist rituals that include fighting with Yama for years of life.
H. Harrer, *Meine Tibet-Bilder*. Text H. Woltereck. Seebruck 1953, 132ff., gives an interesting example of the banning of Yama, witnessed by the American H. Forman. Whether or not this banning exercised a parapsychological influence on Forman (his book was not available), the banning of Yama is in itself of considerable interest and importance, as it was carried out by Red Caps and was obviously based on very ancient ideas.

660 G. Tucci, l.c., vol. II, p. 655.

661 S. Ch. Das, *Journey to Lhasa and Central Tibet*. London 1904, p. 180.

662 M. Hermanns, l.c., p. 53.

663 S. Ch. Das, l.c., p. 268.

664 G. Tucci, l.c., vol. II, p. 414.

665 id., *Indo-Tibetica*, III, 2 (Tsaparang), pl. 58-59.

666 A. Wayman, l.c., p. 125ff.

667 G. Tucci, *Tibetan painted scrolls*, vol. II, p. 589; vol. III, pl. 199, where Yama and yum are trampled underfoot by Yamāntaka and yum.

668 R. de Nebesky-Wojkowitz, *Oracles and demons of Tibet*. 's-Gravenhage 1956, p. 82ff.
A. Grünwedel, *Mythologie des Buddhismus in Tibet und der Mongolei*. Leipzig 1900, p. 168f.
A. Getty, *The gods of Northern Buddhism*[2]. Oxford 1928, p. 152f.

A. K. Gordon, *The iconography of Tibetan Lamaism*. New York 1939, p. 91.

S. Hummel, *Geschichte der tibetischen Kunst*. Leipzig 1953, p. 38.

669 R. de Nebesky-Wojkowitz, l.c., p. 82.

M. Hermanns, l.c., p. 128

670 P. H. Pott, 1943, p. 217, where a representation of this kind is reproduced.

671 H. Mode, *Das frühe Indien*. Stuttgart 1959, p. 69f., also discusses the same representation in Asia and Hither Asia.

672 M. Draak, 'Some aspects of kingship in pagan Ireland'. In: *The sacral kingship*. Leiden 1959, p. 656f.

P. E. Dumont, *L'açvamedha*. Paris 1927.

673 E. Lamotte, *Histoire du bouddisme indien* etc. Louvain 1958, p. 133.

674 M. Hermanns, l.c., p. 128f., 133, 172. Hermanns and his informants seem to identify Yama and the bull. That different interpretations are given of a single symbol within the same religion is not strange, but in this case the interpretation given in the text is to be preferred, in connection with the Buddhist view of the popular god Yama and the use to which he was put.

675 A. Tafel, *Meine Tibetreise*. Stuttgart 1914, Bd. I, p. 208f.

676 W. Koppers, *Der Hund in der Mythologie der zirkumpazifischen Völker*. Wien 1930.

677 L. Scherman, l.c., p. 573, note 78, mentions an interesting report of the year 1774 regarding the primitive Kamchadals, in whose religion the Lord of the Dead is not only one of the eldest sons of their High God, but also the first of all human beings to die in Kamchatka. This strengthens our impression that it would be well worthwhile to make further investigation into the hypothesis of Hermanns, that in Tibet also Yama represented primordial man, as a counterpart of the ancient Tibetan first man, Ye smon. In the present work Ye smon is not discussed, as he is rather a shadowy figure. Such a report as that quoted by Scherman, however, shows that in this case also the Buddhist façade might well hide fascinating ancient Tibetan ideas, or pre-Buddhist syncretism in the Bon religion (Iran?). With regard to the background of the intriguing combination of the yak bull, the woman, and Yama, the final word has not yet been spoken.

678 E. de Schlagintweit, *Le bouddhisme au Tibet*. Lyon 1881, p. 69f.

679 A. Grünwedel, l.c., p. 168, Fig. 48.

A. Wayman, L.c., p. 130, very rightly remarks that it is the yum and not Yama, as stated by Grünwedel, who is holding the trident. But for that very reason the yum is to be regarded as Tsamundi. It should also be remarked that according to Grünwedel the woman under the bull is a corpse. If she is really coloured a deathly white, Grünwedel is most probably right. This variation on the theme quite agrees with the theology of contempt for woman and the womb of which the Yellow Caps were great adherents, and with the symbolism of bull-and-woman as the primordial parents, also in a wider context with the concept of sexuality as the ultimate essential source of evil. In that case this variation, too, proves what liberties the Tibetan theologians and artists could take with the theme.

680 R. de Nebesky-Wojkowitz, l.c., p. 82f.

A. Wayman, l.c., p. 127f.

681 A. Wayman, l.c., p. 128.

682 F. D. Lessing, *Yung Ho Kung*. Stockholm 1942, p. 77, 114.

683 J. N. Banerjea, l.c., p. 525.

684 Naturally the course of development suggested in the text is hypothetical in several points. It seemed not only interesting, however, but also useful to order the information in this manner, as various facts and problems with regard to the iconographical and historical background

of Yama were not named or formulated before. That these problems are so far from a solution, is probably due in part to the fact that Yamāntaka's official position rather prevented Yama from being noticed as one of the greatest gods of Tibet's popular religion.

685 G. Tucci, l.c., vol. II, p. 594 ff.

686 G. Ch. Toussaint, l.c., p. 352.

687 R. de Nebesky-Wojkowitz, l.c., p. 86.
F. Maraini, *Geheim Tibet*. Amsterdam s.a., p. 136 en pl. 8, describes a fresco in a monastery of the Yellow Caps, depicting two skeletons in copulation. According to the author, who worked with Tucci on one of his journeys, these skeletons are the two servants of Yama, called *Shin kyong*. This seems highly probable. According to de Nebesky-Wojkowitz, for the 'Old Style' order the male skeleton represented a form of Yama himself. The fresco might be an important indication in support of the hypothesis, that the Yellow Caps changed the original brother-sister relationship into that of yab-yum. However this may be, the fresco not only illustrates the attitude of the Yellow Caps towards sexuality, it is also an impressive example of the typically Tibetan iron consistency leading to the devil or to Nothingness. Here Buddhism has turned Tibetan realism into X-ray realism.

688 M. Hermanns, l.c., p. 148.

689 S. Hedin, *Trans-Himalaya*. London 1909. Vol. I, p. 313.

690 Unless Bhattacharyya made a mistake, which seems extremely unlikely in view of his explicit and emphatic statement regarding sādhanamālā, which is confirmed by the Tibetan data. Reference has already been made to the considerable Śaiva influence, also in Tibet.

691 G. Tucci, *Indo-Tibetica*, III, 2. Roma 1936, p. 56.

692 id., *Tibetan painted scrolls*, vol. I, p. 218.

693 M. Hermanns, l.c., p. 127.

694 ibid., p. 190f. (Yama as Mahākālā).

695 In Fan-i-ming i-chi (no. 2131 of the Taisho edition of the Chinese canon p. 1085,3): information supplied by Prof. Dr. E. Zürcher.

696 M. Hermanns, *Die Familie der A-mdo Tibeter*. Freiburg 1959, p. 50.

697 S. Ch. Das, l.c., p. 326f.

698 Prince Peter of Greece and Denmark, *A study in polandry*. 's-Gravenhage 1963, p. 465-479, 568.

699 ibid., p. 429.

700 *The Blue Annals*, vol. I, p. 210, 218ff., 226, 229; vol. II, p. 610, 647, 914.
H. Hoffmann, *Quellen zur Geschichte der tibetischen Bon-Religion*. Wiesbaden 1950, p. 230f., mentions a brother-and-sister pair of the Bon po, which makes the problem of Za ma brother and sister still more difficult and intriguing. Although here too the sister seems to have been more or less eliminated, she is again the most important figure. Did the Bon borrow from Buddhism here or Buddhism from the Bon?

701 F. Sierksma, l.c., p. 163ff., 188, pl. 41. mistakenly identifies the bronze as Yama and Yamī. Interpretation of other points given there is also corrected here, it is hoped.

702 Yama always refers to the exoteric Yama, unless explicitly otherwise stated. The two other forms could be disregarded. For many readers they would have rendered the discussion unnecessarily complicated.

703 F. Sierksma, l.c., p. 163ff., 188.

704 The close link with the Terrifying Ones and with the vajra is highly significant. See also 702.

705 L. Jisl, V. Sis, J. Vanis, *Tibetische Kunst*. Prag 1958, pl. 46.

706 W. Y. Evans-Wentz, *The Tibetan book of the dead*[3]. London 1960, p. 127, footnote 4.

707 Dr. Pott subsequently most kindly supplied this authoritative information. The assumptions

we had made are hereby confirmed. The less esoteric meaning of this mudrā, the general religious interpretation of which was communicated to the author by the incarnate lama Ras-c'un sprul-sku 'jam-dpal kun-bzaṅ. He gave this gesture the Tibetan name *sdig-mdzub* (sdig pa = to threaten, mdzub = finger). The meaning he explained as follows: when a man prays to Vajrabhairava (= Yamāntaka), the god employs this gesture to say to the other (inimical) gods 'if you do not give this man his safety, I shall destroy you!' Thus a god may put a god under the ban of a threat by means of this mudrā, or a man may coerce a god or himself with it. It is a clear characteristic of Tibetan yoga in its aggressive aspect, carrying a reference to the Terrifying Ones.

708   Her striking ear ornaments also make it seem likely that she is Tsamundi. Cf.:
G. Tucci, *Tibetan painted scrolls*, vol. III, pl. 187.

709   F. Sierksma, l.c., p. 164.
The four bronzes are to be found (in the order in which they were observed):
Leiden: Rijksmuseum vor Volkenkunde; Inv. 2798-23.
Prague: L. Jisl, V. Sis, J. Vanis, l.c., pl. 82.
Philadelphia: Dr. A. Wayman writes that he has seen a similar bronze in the Philadelphia Museum of Art, Nepalese gallery.
Rotterdam: Museum voor Land-en Volkenkunde; Inv. 29934.
In contradistinction to the bronze of Yama and Tsamundi already discussed, the representation of complete yab-yum seems to be less rare than was supposed, although it remains unusual and contrary to the iconographical rules.

710   Technically, this appears from the fact that Yama's penis is practically the only support of Tsamundi, who is cast separately; without it, she would fall to the ground. The Leiden bronze is cast in one piece, so that one cannot really speak of two figures.

711   Museum voor Land- en Volkenkunde, Rotterdam; Inv, 29933.

712   F. Sierksma, l.c., p. 165.

713   M. H. Duncan, l.c., p. 225.

714   Human, animal or demonic figures trampled underfoot to either side of the representation of a deity or a divine pair, are often to be seen. But then there is no question of separating that which is otherwise sexually united. Particularly interesting is the representation of Śiva and his śakti, separated by Vajrapāṇi. A connection with the separation discussed here seems by no means unlikely:
E. Lamotte, *Histoire du bouddhisme indien*, etc. Louvain 1958, p. 762.
It should further be mentioned, that a woman under a bull is also found under Yamāntaka and his yum and under the goddess with the head of a pig, Vajravārāhī. In the first instance it may be presumed with some certainty that there is a secondary derivation from the Yama symbolism, in the second case it seems probable:
W. E. Clark, *Two lamaistic pantheons*. Cambridge 1937. vol. II, p. 45, 69, 235.
W. Filchner, *Kumbum Dschamba Ling*. Leipzig 1933, p. 110f.

715   A. Wayman, l.c., p. 126ff.

716   The problem of relative chronology is naturally very intriguing here. At any rate Yama with his magical associations and the Tantric Path of sexual practices do not seem to be younger in Tibet than the ideas revolving around Yamāntaka and Yamāri. The link between the Yama of the people and the national primordial parents must be primary, but whether the separation discussed here is older than that brought about by Yamāri is hard to decide.

717   G. Sandberg, *Tibet and the Tibetans*. London 1906, p. 107, states that in Ganden (dGa'ldan) 'a very old statue of Shinje' was worshipped.

718 L. A. Waddell, l.c., p. 519, 530 footnote.
The Blue Annals, vol. I, p. 149 (Roerich Yamāntaka = gŚin rje).
W. Filchner, l.c., p. 317 ff., 324, 416, 504, who practically always speaks of Yamāntaka where Vladimircov (whom he quotes in extenso) speaks of gŚin-rje. On rereading these data it became evident that definite attempts were made to give autocratic power to Yamāntaka, the god of the monks, and to eliminate Yama. In this respect also Yama provides a synopsis of Tibetan cultural history that covers every detail.
G. Schulemann, *Geschichte der Dalai Lamas*. Leipzig 1958, p. 115, also confirms the impression that Yama was afterwards pushed to one side.
A. Tafel, *Meine Tibetreise*. Stuttgart 1914, Bd. I, p. 236, calls the central figure of the Cham of Kumbum Tschüs dyal (= c'os rgyal) and regards him as Yama.

719 L. A. Waddell, l.c., p. 39.
D. L. Snellgrove, l.c., p. 229f., 263, 268f., 271.
A. Govinda, l.c., p. 132, 233, 239, 247.
W. Y. Evans-Wentz, l.c., p. XXX.

720 S. H. Ribbach, *Dragpo Namgyal*. München 1940, p. 229.

721 P. H. Pott, l.c., 1951, p. 34.

722 A. Govinda, l.c., p. 239.
Cf. G. Tucci, l.c., vol. II, p. 362.

723 Rijksmuseum voor Volkenkunde, Leiden. Inv. B 107-9.

724 ibid., Inv. 2740-40.
Cf. S. Hummel, *Geheimnisse tibetischer Malereien*. Leipzig 1949, p. 78, Abb. 4, which offers another variant (pregnant woman under bull ??).

725 S. Hummel, l.c., p. 2f.

726 A. Govinda, l.c., p. 250.

727 W. Y. Evans-Wentz, *Tibet's great yogi Milarepa²*. London 1958.

728 Besides the reproductions in the relevant books and illustrated works, a comparatively small number of thangkas were available for study.

729 H. Harrer, *Sieben Jahre in Tibet*. Wien 1952, p. 178.
Th. Illion, *Geheim Tibet*. 's-Gravenhage 1938, p. 127f., also leaves no doubt as to the fairly general homosexuality in the monasteries.
E. Kagawuchi, *Three years in Tibet*. Benares 1909, p. 292, 470, also mentions the matter, particularly as occurring among the soldier-monks.

730 E. Schäfer, l.c., p. 102.

731 A. Tafel, l.c., vol. I, p. 222.

732 T. Y. Pemba, *Young days in Tibet*. London 1957, p. 17, 25, 82, 118, 148, 156.

733 Ch. Bell, *The religion of Tibet*. Oxford 1931, p. 139.
A. David-Neel, *Textes tibétains inédits*. Paris 1952, p. 94, gives the French translation.

COMMENTARIES ON THE PLATES

As this book is not of the nature of an iconography, the following commentaries, in agreement with the text, are mainly addressed to the reader with a general interest, and iconographical detail is passed over. These details are only noticed when they have to do with the argument. A convenient systematic conspectus of the overflowing Tibetan pantheon, based only upon Tibetan texts with India in the background, is unfortunately still lacking, because a very great number of the texts still await the labours of the Tibetologist. Those interested in the characteristics by means of which one can identify the various deities, can easily find their way with the help of:

A. Getty, *The gods of northern Buddhism*[2]. Oxford 1928.

A. K. Gordon, *The iconography of Tibetan Lamaism*. New York 1939.

R. de Nebesky-Wojkowitz, *Oracles and demons of Tibet*. The Hague 1956, names the other chief sources on p. 22.

P. H. Pott, *Introduction to the Tibetan collection of the National Museum of Ethnology, Leiden*. Leiden, 1951, gives a more extensive list on p. 2 ss.

Meanwhile it will be clear from the last chapters of this book and from some of the pieces reproduced, which were little or not known, that Tibetologists still have much work to do before it will be possible not only fully to identify all images and pictures from the iconographical point of view, but also – which is of far greater import – to place them in their religious, cultural and historical context. G. Tucci, who has published important standard works for specialists (*int. al. Tibetan painted scrolls*, 3 vols., Roma 1949), has written a most lucid little book about the mystic unity in the midst of this confusing diversity. This exposé is useful for understanding the religious nature of the Terrifying Ones, their place in the scroll paintings, and scroll paintings in general:

G. Tucci, *The theory and practice of the Maṇḍala*. With special reference to the modern psychology of the subconscious. London 1961.

The following notes were written more than three years after the book was finished. On one or two points, therefore, the reader will find a slightly altered interpretation, as a result of the work since done by Tibetologists and by the author himself, or of the information supplied by Tibetan informants who arrived meanwhile.

1. **GŚIN-RJE GŚED** (Skt. Yamāntaka) yab-yum. *Bronze, some parts polychrome. Height 35 cm. Museum voor Land- en Volkenkunde, Rotterdam; inv.no. 29945.*

The god with sixteen legs and thirty-four arms, who conquered the god of death according to the mystic principle of *similia similibus*, is shown in mystic sexual union with his female partner. This is called *yab-yum* in Tibetan, *i.e.* father-mother. In the tantric Buddhism of India he entirely replaced Yama, the god of death, but in Tibet the latter again played an important part, particularly among the people, as *gŚin-rje*. He is a Protector of the Doctrine, but also of the order of the Yellow Caps. My Tibetan informant, who belongs to this order, never called this 'killer of *gŚin-rje*' by his Tibetan name, but always by his second Sanskrit name of Vajra-bhairava, pronouncing it in the Tibetan way. In theology, which distinguishes five Buddha-families, he belongs to the family of Vairocana, where he represents the terrifying aspect of the peaceable Mañjuśri. By concentrating entirely upon this god, the mystic can become aware that everything there is, is nothing but the semblance of sexuality and aggression, so achieving release from the chain of reincarnation.

2. ŚIVA. *Bronze. Southern India. 12th cent.* A.D. *Height 154 cm. Museum van Aziatische kunst, Amsterdam.*

This world-famous bronze shows the Indian god Śiva dancing his equally renowned cosmic dance. He is standing upon a demon and is surrounded by a circle of flames, two characteristics also often displayed by the Terrifying Deities of Tibet. In one of his hands he bears a little drum, in another a flame of fire. The drum is also found in Tibet, and likewise the snake we see winding round hsi foremost right arm. One of the ornaments in his hair is a death's head. In this statue also, then, we see signs of the great influence exerted upon tantric Buddhism by Śaivism. His wide-flowing locks symbolise the seven rivers of India, one of which is the Ganges, with the river goddess Gangā rising up from it.

3. VAJRAPĀṆI. (Tib. Phyag na rdo-rje). *Bronze. Nepal. Height 17,5 cm. Late 19th cent.* A.D. *Rijksmuseum voor Volkenkunde, Leyden; Inv.no. 2798-34.*

'Vajra-in-hand', as is his name in both languages, is highly characteristic of the development of Buddhism and of the Terrifying Deities in that religion. Originally he was a Hinduist popular god, a yakṣa such as most Indian villages had. Many who were converted to the new religion of Buddhism continued to worship ancient gods, including Vajrapāṇi, who was to attain to great importance and special significance. At an early period in Buddhist art he is already found in the company of the Buddha. The texts show that he was here taking the place of the constant companion of the Buddha, the gentle disciple Ananda. There is reason to suppose that this replacement of a disciple who was a monk by a popular god, was a sign of agreement between monks and laity, two groups between whom tension soon arose in Buddhism. From companion, Vajrapāṇi became Protector of the Buddha and his doctrine. Bu-ston relates that in the Mahāyāna he was particularly important for the sacred writings. The protectors of the faith became increasingly important in Buddhism and when its next phase, Vajrayāna, came into conflict with other religions, Vajrapāṇi the leader of the fearful defenders of the Doctrine became of the greatest consequence. He was the obvious choice to settle accounts with the chief rival god, with Śiva. As the bodhisattva of Akṣobhya, the buddha who presided over the family of terrifying gods, he was assigned his prominent place in the theological system, and included among the eight great bodhisattvas. In Tibet, so susceptible to Terrifying gods because it was so aggressive, his importance grew again. In a Tibetan biography of Padmasambhava he is called the only ruler of supreme esoteric wisdom. He was even received into the national religion, the Bon, as the Lord of the Mystery. In the earliest Buddhism of Tibet he was naturally in the first place the lord of magic. Thus many aspects of Buddhism and its history are united in this bodhisattva. According to Hummel his terrifying character is already expressed in the Magadha sculpture of India, but characteristically it is hardly anywhere but in Tibet that he is depicted as a fearsome demon (see no. 21). The present bronze shows him as it were in between peaceful and terrifying. He is an ordinary bodhisattva, beautiful and benevolent. But he has the third eye, and the vajra in his hand indicates the same demoniac possibilities. This statuette may therefore be regarded as a transition between the companion of the Buddha and the dread lord of the Tibetan exorcists, not only a theologically important, but also a popular deity.

4. TANTRIC MAGICIAN. *Bronze. Height 14,5 cm. Rijksmuseum voor Volkenkunde, Leyden;
inv.no. 3550-2.*

On the back of this statuette there is an inscription indicating that it represents Mañjuśrīmitra, a
pupil of the great Padmasambhava who introduced Buddhism into Tibet as a mixture of mainly
magic and sexual practices. It is reproduced here because the magician, who is dressed in the usual
habit of a monk, is holding the two most important ritual symbols of Tibet's Buddhism. In his
right hand he has the original weapon of the Indian god Indra, the vajra, *i.e.* the thunderbolt. In
Buddhism the vajra has become a sign of magic power, and also a symbol of the 'method', of active
and practical compassion. As such, its complement is found in the ritual bell, the symbol of insight
and wisdom, of the Void. The conjunction of the two symbolised the *unio mystica*, so that the vajra
had also a phallic significance. Like the word vajra, the Tibetan name *rdo-rje* means diamond. The
vajra of the peaceable deities has the classical Indian form of two joined five-taloned claws, the tips
of the talons being joined together. When the tips of the talons remain separated, the vajra is called
khro rdo-rje, which means that it pertains to the domain of the Terrifying Deities. Although this type
is passed over or but rarely mentioned, such a *khro rdo-rje* is in my possession and was recognised
and named as such by my informant. In his left hand the magician is not holding the ritual bell,
but the magic dagger by means of which the conquered spirits are held in subjection. This is quite
in agreement with the magical form of Buddhism introduced by Padmasambhava, which has
strongly marked Tibetan Buddhism. It is even not rare, in ancient portrayals of deities, for the
body of the god to consist of a magic dagger.

5. NAG-PO CHEN-PO (Skt. Mahākāla). *Scroll painting. Measurements 88 by 61 cm. Rijksmuseum
voor Volkenkunde, Leyden; inv.no. 3329-2.*

Nag-po chen-po, the Great Black One, is usually called mGon-po, the Lord, in Tibet, where he has
a prominent place in the pantheon. Another form is one of the most important Protector gods of
Tibetan Buddhism. Yet this Terrifying One comes from India, and there he plays a great part in
the charnel fields as Śiva, the Great Black One, together with his terrible consort, Kālī. One of
his most characteristic symbols is the trident, which in this image, too, he is holding in his left hand.
The trident was carried by wandering yogins in Tibet also. As Śaivism had a very great influence
upon Buddhist tantrism and consequently upon the Buddhism of Tibet, this god, who became one
of the eight great Protectors of the Doctrine, must not be omitted here.

The scroll painting which is reproduced here is a so-called Maṇḍala. Compare G. Tucci, *The
theory and practice of the Maṇḍala*. London 1961.

6. MAÑJUŚRI as DHARMADHĀTUVĀIŚVARA. *Bronze (Nepalese). Height 27 cm. Rijksmuseum voor Volkenkunde, Leyden; inv.no. 2739-60.*

The prominent bodhisattva as 'lord of the sphere of the divine word' is shown here because of the
original, non-sexual presentment of his female partner, who is seated on his left thigh.

7. BDE-MCHOG (Skt. Śamvara) yab-yum. *Gilded wood. Height 82 cm. Collection Verbert (photographic archives Koninklijk Instituut voor de Tropen, Amsterdam).*

Śamvara is the name of a pre-Aryan, thus autochthonous Indian god, but his Tibetan name,
meaning 'Perfect Bliss', already betrays the fact that he no longer retains the slightest connection

with his past. As a tantric god he is a depersonalised, so-called mystic Buddha of demonic character. With Heruka, Hevajra etc. he belongs theologically to that group of gods who are the terrifying aspects of the supreme Buddhas. One of these Buddhas is Vajradhara, who in one system is the highest of all. This image shows Vajradhara/Samvara *in coitu* with his expressively depicted partner.

8. KYE-BA RDO-RJE (Skt. Hevajra) yab-yum. *Bronze (school of Peking). Early 19th cent.* A.D. *Height 21 cm. Rijksmuseum voor Volkenkunde, Leyden; inv.no. 3433-1.*

This god is discussed at length in the present work with reference to the Hevajra tantra edited and translated by Snellgrove. Here he is represented with eight heads and sixteen arms, holding in his right hands eight skulls that contain the mounts of eight terrifying deities, whose peaceable forms are to be seen in the skull-bowls he holds in his left hands. P. H. Pott calls such a deity a multiple figure. One may agree with this and also share that author's respect for the tantric mystics, without agreeing with his thesis that Buddhist tantrism was originally a pure mysticism and theology, which afterwards degenerated. Actually, theology attempted to raise popular religion to a higher plane. De Jong has pointed out that there is remarkably little philosophy to be found in the tantras. The philosophy and the mystic gnosis (gnosis is the term very happily applied to this religiosity by Tucci) are found in the commentaries upon the tantras. The Hevajra tantra is indeed a fairly vulgar piece of religiosity, altogether corresponding to what Weber called 'Plebejerreligion', breathing a vindictive sense of injury and full of badly sublimated aggressivity and sexuality. To say that the god has eight hated gods 'in his pocket' would be more in keeping with the climate of this tantra than seeking a sublime gnosis in it, for only afterwards was the god turned into a profound symbol, in the same way as in Tibet they managed to make terrifying deities of deep meaning of a native mountain god or a Mongolian war-god. This god, who is a hypostasis, a Buddhistic production, proves once again that this mysticism cannot be isolated, but must be considered in the frame of the history of its religion, which had always to adapt itself to popular and even plebeian notions in order to remain alive, thus becoming highly ambivalent. Tshongkapa had very good reason to assign a place apart in the theological system to the tantras and thereby to such a god as Hevajra.

9. PADMASAMBHAVA. *Scroll painting. Measurements 47 by 31 cm. Rijksmuseum voor Volkenkunde, Leyden; inv.no. 2740-18.*

This is the foreign missionary – my Tibetan informant often called him by his Sanskrit name, though writing down the Tibetan name Gu-ru pad-ma 'od-'bar in describing this thangka – who aimed to introduce so deviating a form of Buddhism in Tibet that Hoffmann says he wanted to found a religion of his own. His name is connected with magic and sexual practices. He was fond of power, women and wine. On occasion of a drinking-bout he stopped the sun for seven days with his magic dagger, so that the feast might continue. His influence upon the religion of Tibet has been very great indeed, although he is more of a myth than a historical figure. His image was seen in nearly every temple. He is portrayed as an un-Tibetan type. It was, I think, Bacot who was the first to point out that it is striking how often Padmasambhava is depicted with the round eyes of a voluptuary, as is also the case on the thangka reproduced here. Whether this trait stems from friends or foes, it is clear that his preoccupation with sexual matters had already drawn the attention of the Tibetans themselves. The history of Tibet's Buddhism may indeed be characterised as a struggle for and against that which the name of Padmasambhava stood for. The Yellow Caps were able to eliminate this in part, and to regard him as a black sheep. It was remarkable, therefore, that my informant, a Yellow Cap and consequently celibate, would admit no semblance of opposition to

Padmasambhava, and repeatedly called him a very great man, perhaps fom a sense of need for Tibetan unity in oppression and exile.

10. PADMASAMBHAVA. *Scroll painting. Sven Hedin Collection, Statens Etnogr. Museum, Stockholm.*

This thangka shows Padmasambhava in his terrifying appearance, evident from the sword in his right hand and the skull-bowl of blood in his left. He is seated on a human skin with hands and skull still attached, in all probability the remains of an enemy of the Doctrine. His face too shows angry features, that form a fascinating contrast with his lascivious eyes (see note on previous illustration). He is by himself what the Terrifying Deities are in conjunction with their female partners:sexuality and aggressivity two-in-one.

11. YAB-YUM. *From F. Maraini, Tibet secret, Paris (B. Arthaud), 1952.*

Yab-yum, the physical symbolisation of spiritual two-in-oneness, the mystic unity of right action and correct insight, was originally only indicated in Tantrism. The śakti 'rode' upon her partner's hip. However, the Tibetans, being a realistic and drastic people in religion and art also, turned it into a *coitus*. The illustration is an example of this realism, which was sometimes pronouncedly sensual and voluptuous.

12. MAGIC DAGGER DEITY. *Detail of a scroll painting with a Heruka maṇḍala. Museum voor Land- en Volkenkunde, Rotterdam; inv.no. 47066.*

The magic dagger (Tibetan: *phur-bu*) as a ritual object in and as a symbol of the magical, aggressive Tantrism so very characteristic of the religion of Tibet, was referred to above, as also the depicting of gods whose body is a magic dagger, particularly in earlier times. One may say that in these cases the dagger has been deified, or that the god has come to coincide with the magical weapon that destroys men and demons. The reproduction shows an example of such a Terrifying One, a god who is piercing an enemy in the shape of a dagger.

13. CHARNEL FIELD WITH GODS. *Scroll painting. Measurements 94 by 60 cm. Collection Dr. A. W. Schwaninger-Caprani, Basle.*

This thangka shows a charnel field, as is evident from the upper border of skins, skulls, intestines, plucked-out eyes, etc. and the row of death's heads at either side. The charnel field itself is far less horrible than it is often depicted. This is a picture to be completed by the viewer, and only the attributes of the gods are shown (see note on no. 37). In the centre rides *dPal-dan lha-mo* or Lha-mo, as she is usually called. On one side she has a form of the Tibetan Mahākāla, on the other Beg-tse. The origin of the charnel field mysticism, of which this scroll painting is an expression, lies in the Indian Śaivaism. Not infrequently, one sees the triad Mahākāla, Kālī and Yama on such thangkas.

14. ACALA. *Scroll painting. Measurements 105 by 67 cm. Rijksmuseum voor Volkenkunde, Leyden; inv.no. 2798-1.*

Acala is a terrifying protector of the doctrine from India, who is rarely found in Tibet, though apparently more important in Japan. Above him the well-known Indian sage Nāgārjuna is depicted. Acala himself, surrounded by eight demonic figures, has four heads and four arms. He is standing upon two corpses, which one might also take to be a woman and a man, separated so that they can no more prolong the chain of rebirth. Below him, surrounded by four demons, we see the familiar Mahākāla, the Great Black One, in the shape of a brahmin blowing on a tantric flute of human bone. The scroll is a *mGon-khaṅ thaṅ-ka*, an impressive painting from the abode of the demons that was to be found in nearly all monasteries.

15. RMA-CHEN SPOM-RA. *Part of a scroll painting. Reprint from J. F. Rock, The Am-nye Ma-chen Range and adjacent countries, Rome 1956, by permission of the editor, Prof. G. Tucci.*

rMa-chen spom-ra, as he is called in most texts, but whom the local people know as *Am-nye rma-chen*, *i.e.* the great ancestor, is one of the mountain gods who played leading roles in pre-Buddhist Tibet and about whom R. A. Stein has recently written much of interest, which could not be included any more in this book. Naturally he appears here in Buddhist guise, but it is typical that his expression and attitude lack the gruesomely demonic aspect of the other Terrifying Deities. In this Protector of the Doctrine we can still see something of the ancient, benevolent ancestor. He is on horseback, like all mountain gods, and carries Buddhist symbols. He is one of the very greatest mountain gods (*ri-lha*). Speaking of these gods, my informant immediately and spontaneously named *rMa-chen sPom-ra*. His mountain lies in the North-east. The reformer Tshongkhapa, who also came from those parts, was well acquainted with his cult, and *Am-nye ma-chen* was worshipped as one of the tutelar deities of the first monastery of the Yellow Caps, Ganden. The ancient god was so respected there that his image was carried out of the monastery every evening, so that, as a married man, at night he need not keep to the decree of celibacy that ruled within in the monastery. Later on this carrying outside in effigy was omitted, but every evening a specially appointed monk would request the mountain god, in loud *but deferential* tones, to leave the monastery for the night. Respect for the old mountain god, once with his colleagues the centre of Tibet's religion, is very evident. In every region the health of men, cattle and corn, depended upon the mountain-god-ancestor. In their honour great New Year festivals were held, when tales of creation were recited and all kinds of sports took place. In recent times they were still worshipped with great reverence.

16. RTA-MGRIN (Skt. Hayagrīva). *Scroll painting. Measurements 112 by 77 cm. Rijksmuseum voor Volkenkunde, Leyden; inv.no. 1383-2.*

This well-known god with the horse's head showing among his dressed locks, is one of the eight great Protectors of the Doctrine. His neighing puts all enemies to flight, according to liturgical texts. Besides the horse's head and a few other specific symbols, he here displays some general characteristics of the Terrifying Deities: in the midst of spreading flames, mostly naked with an animal skin as covering, wearing a garland of death's heads and a crown of skulls, he is treading down two human beings, probably enemies.

17. BEG-TSE. *Meditation drawing in colour on a black ground. Measurements 43 by 32 cm. Rijksmuseum voor Volkenkunde, Leyden; inv.no. B 107-10.*

A meditation drawing of this kind will be discussed with reference to a similar portrayal of gŚin-rje (Skt. Yama), no. 36. Beg-tse is another of the eight great Protectors of the Doctrine. He is of Mongolian origin, however, and was not honoured in Tibet until the second half of the 16th century A.D. As a Mongolian god he is pre-Buddhist. He wears a cuirasse and a helmet of copper. This, together with the fact that he is riding a horse, indicates that he was originally a Mongolian warrior on horseback. As in texts referring to him it is stated several times that his abode is a mountain, he might be related to the benevolent, pre-Buddhist mountain gods of the Tibetans, or may have been regarded as so related. One text studied by De Nebesky-Wojkowitz, however, states that when Beg-tse is shown on horseback he is a 'wild *btsan*', a spirit of the air, who also rides over mountains. However this may be, it is interesting to see how even in recent times a pre-Buddhist god could be accepted into Buddhism and his character changed. As depicted here, he is most decidedly not an ancient mountain god or a wild *btsan*, not even a Buddhist defender of the faith, but a subject of meditation upon the charnel field, as is apparent from the border of entrails, eyes, etc. along the top. The two vultures feasting upon a corpse in the left lower corner leave not a trace of doubt in this respect. His horse, that sets one hoof upon the vagina of a beautiful naked woman, is an adaptation of the bull of the god of death, who does the same (see also no. 39). The zestful Mongolian warrior-god, likeness of Mongolian pastoralists specialised upon the horse, has become a divinity who must be visualised upon a charnel field in order to prove that man is merely blinded by lust of power and sexual lust, as life inevitably ends in death. The old nomad god would not recognise himself.

18. BEG-TSE. *Scroll painting. Measurements 48 by 36 cm. Collection Verbert 119.*

A description of this originally Mongolian god is given above (no. 17). The thangka shows him with eight companions. Although the foreground recalls a mystic charnel field and the master magician Vajrapāṇi appears above, one notices that the expression upon the god's face is not diabolic, but peaceful. The same trait is seen in portrayals of pre-Buddhist Tibetan mountain gods, who were originally benevolent rather than demonic figures.

19. DPAL-LDAN LHA-MO or LHA-MO. *Scroll painting. Measurements 70 by 52 cm. Rijksmuseum voor Land- en Volkenkunde, Leyden; inv.no. 2740-54.*

This goddess is one of the most frightening of the Dreadful gods, and thus she is depicted in an image of horror, ruin and death. To note a few points, she is riding through a sea of blood that enemies are trodden into. In her mouth she has a corpse, so she is a cannibal. In her right hand she has the skull of a child born of incest. She is accompanied by two female demons (ḍākinīs), one with a lion's head, the other with the head of a mythical monster. Two princes of the church sit all serene in the upper corners. Naturally this painting also may be explained realistically, or given an esoteric mystical interpretation. Let us only remark here that for the people *Lha-mo* was very real. In Sanskrit she is called Śrī-Devī or Kālī, but *Lha-mo* became a real Tibetan. She is the national goddess of Tibet and tutelar deity of the Yellow Caps, while her emanation is stated to be the principal patron goddess of Lhasa, the capital. Psychologically her pointed, aggressive breast is interesting. The same breasts – a sign of feminine aggressivity that also appears in other cultures – are displayed by her companions. Yet even without them it is evident that we have to do with 'bad mothers'. In one story Lha-mo killed her son, skinned his body and ate his heart, when she could not convert her husband and son to Buddhism. So this satanic protectress of the Doctrine has other than only mystic aspects.

20. BDE-MCHOG (Skt. Śamvara) yab-yum. *Scroll painting. Measurements 62 by 49 cm. Collection Verbert, 63.*

This god was already mentioned in relation with the image of Vajradhara/Śamvara (no. 7). Of the many iconographical details, for which the reader must be referred to the iconographical hand-books, one deserves mention because it is not included there. We notice that two figures are exerting all their strength to push the legs of the cohabiting pair as far apart as possible. As a man and a woman are lying under these feet, this detail strengthens the hypothesis advanced in the present work with regard to those representations of gŚin-rje (Skt. Yama) where the bull and the woman cohabit, and those where the bull and the woman are separated: when the mystic union has been achieved, there is an end of physical cohabitation, so that the turning wheel of birth is stopped. It is difficult to imagine any other function of the two vigorously pushing figures except to keep apart the man and woman under the feet of the deities. For a more aesthetic treatment of the union of a black yab and a white yum see H. Hoffmann, *Die Religionen Tibets*, pl. 10 opposite p. 113 where, besides, the partners are not many-armed.

21. VAJRAPĀṆI (Tib. Phyag na rdo-rje). *Scroll painting. Measurements 53 by 30 cm. Rijksmuseum voor Volkenkunde, Leyden; Inv.no 2798-8.*

The development of this bodhisattva gives expression to the increasing importance of the laity and the terrifying deities in Buddhism. On this scroll painting he is shown as a real terrifying deity, in contrast with his appearance in the bronze of no. 3. In his case also a few of the main characteristics are the expression of the face, the heavy build, the tiger's skin as loin-cloth and the streaming hair. Like some other terrifying deities, he is standing on a lotus. Though hardly a fine piece of work, the painting is reproduced here because the deity is depicted with noticeably heavy breasts, which led the director of the Rijksmuseum voor Volkenkunde, Dr. P. H. Pott, to suppose that this demonic bodhisattva might be intended for a female. If this supposition is correct, one might rather speak of bisexuality. A counter-argument is, that the union of the male and female is almost always expressed by representing the deity in yab-yum. Such depiction of the male deity in coition with his female partner is repeatedly discussed in the present volume, also in these notes. On the other hand, as pointed out in the discussion of Pl. 3, this deity has a curiously dual nature. Certainty as to the significance of the breasts (for they might also be an indication of the massive frame of terrifying deities in general) can, of course, only be obtained if there are relevant Tibetan texts. Vajrapāṇi's great importance as the leader of the terrible protectors of the doctrine in India was already pointed out. Characteristic of his part in the conversion of Tibet is a story about Padmasambhava. When this missionary was traversing barbarian Tibet, the native gods attempted to stop him. Among them was one of the chief and most popular mountain gods of the country, *gNyan-chen thang-la*. Thus the ancient order opposed the new, for the mountain gods may be accounted the most important representatives of ancient Tibet. The afore-said mountain god tried to make the Buddhist teacher retire by means of mist and snow-storms, but the latter set himself down in anger (!) and meditated upon *Phyag na rdo-rje*. All the gods became fearful, and the mountain god was subjugated and bound by an oath (De Nebesky-Wojkowitz, *Oracles and demons*, 205). The text this author translates gives the story as illustration of the thesis that the great mountain god is an emanation of *Phyag na rdo-rje*. Here again, then, we have the theological reconciliation of opponents who were once irreconcilable, and whose irreconcilability still remains visible, also in this deity.

22. DPAL-LDAN LHA-MO or LHA-MO. *Statuette. Sven Hedin Collection, Statens Etnografiska Museum, Stockholm.*

For commentary see no. 19.

274

23. DPA'-BO DUR-KHROD BDAG-PO YAB-YUM. *Fresco in the monastery of Dungkar. From F. Maraini, Tibet secret, Paris (B. Arthaud) 1952, pl. 5.*

This scene has been said to represent the Citipati from India, called in Tibetan *dur-khrod bdag-po*, masters of the charnel field. In the above-mentioned book (p. 165) Maraini also looks that way when characterising this pair as Shin-kyong (prob. *gŚin-skyoṅ*), though of course he did not overlook the yab-yum nature of this fresco. The Citipati, however, are two skeletons dancing arm in arm. Their drastic reinterpretation as two skeletons in coition can hardly be regarded as a slight variant. It is of particular importance, therefore, that a Tibetan text mentions such a macabre pair, that according to De Nebesky-Wojkowitz (*Oracles and Demons* etc., p. 86) is 'undoubtedly' a form of the god of death *gŚin-rje* (Skt. Yama) in conjunction with his female partner. Apparently the two acolytes of the god were changed into the god himself and his partner in this reinterpretation, and the consequences were not avoided. This form of the god of death has two names. The first is *Dur-khrod bdag-po lcam-dral*, the lord of the charnel field brother-and-sister, an incestuous appellation very appropriate to the Tibetan Yama. The second name is *dPa'-bo dur-khrod bdag-po yab-yum*, the hero, the lord of the charnel field conjoined with his female partner. That the relevant text only describes the male and not the female partner is not strange, as this god was only venerated by the ancient orders and the Yellow Caps may well have purified the text because of its incestuous connotations, though it is curious in this connection that this fresco was in a monastery of the Yellow Caps. However this may be, the main thing is that this pair is explicitly mentioned. The male partner is described as a white skeleton 'of a most frightening appearance', with a skull-club and a skull-bowl of blood in his hands, and finally the two gods are stated to 'reside in the centre of a vehemently blazing fire'. Our fresco displays these characteristics. The idea that it represents the Citipati or the Shin-kyong, then, is to be rejected. Everything points to its being the Tibetan Yama who is depicted here as the Hero, the lord of the charnel field yab-yum. This is not only iconographically important, it is also characteristic. Even allowing for a mystical interpretation, the deeply moving and disenchanting scene of two skeletons in copulation is characteristic of Tibet, for obsessed by death and eternity, Tibet tenaciously follows out the last consequence, crossing the ultimate frontier in a symbolism which is at once realistic and surrealist. Lacking medical training, one cannot judge whether certain anatomical peculiarities (*e.g.* the backbone, the right leg of the female skeleton) are ignorant faults in drawing, aim at a greater artistic effect, or are meant as mystic 'horror-jokes', to underline the complete meaninglessness of life *and* death. This last possibility is not to be excluded. The long toes, making the feet into more or less ape-like hands, might point in that direction. Be that as it may, this fresco is uniquely Tibetan.

24. RDO-RJE RNAL-'BYOR-MA (Skt. Vajra-yoginī or Sarvabuddhaḍākinī). *Bronze. Height 15 cm. Museum voor Land- en Volkenkunde, Rotterdam; inv.no. 29165.*

In late-Buddhist mysticism ḍākinīs are the female symbols of those inspiring forces in man which enable him to make the leap from temporality to timelessness. They are the incorporations of the knowledge of unshrouded reality, therefore they are naked. The most important of them is the Vajra-yoginī, symbol of the highest, ultimate insight. She must not be confused with the Kuṇḍalinī śakti of the Hinduistic tantras, for as a spiritual principle she is exactly the opposite of the natural sexual power of that Hinduist śakti, even if the latter be sublimated. The Vajra-yoginī symbolises insight and knowledge, not strength. 'The attempt to trace the Buddhist system of meditation to the Kuṇḍalinī Yoga of Tantric Hinduism is therefore as misleading as calling it Kuṇḍalinī Yoga' (A. Govinda). Others have also pointed out the difference between Hinduist and Buddhist tantrism in connection with the part assigned to the male and the female principle. Vajra-yoginī is, in Tibet, linked in particular with the ritual mysticism named gCod. The reader is referred to the chapter dealing with this matter: in gCod she is the symbol of the spiritual act by which the mystic drastically and aggressively realises the naked truth of the nothingness of the ego. In her right hand she has the knife of 'decapitation', in her left the skull-bowl. She wears a crown and a chain of skulls. (See chapter VI, page 142.)

25. KU-RU-KU-LE (Skt. Kurukullā). *Bronze. Height 11 cm. Museum voor Land- en Volkenkunde, Rotterdam; inv.no. 29157.*

When Buddhism accepted foreign gods under pressure from the lay population, the goddess Tārā was soon one of the favourites. She was believed to live in every good and pious woman. In Tantrism she also took on demonic shapes, of which the red Tārā, shown here, is one. She is the goddess of riches and was also worshipped by unhappy lovers. In Tibet this Tārā was demonic only, as clearly appears in this bronze.

26. MI-LA RAS-PA. *Scroll painting. Sven Hedin Collection, Statens Etnografiska Museum, Stockholm.*

Sometimes appearing-like a buffoon, sometimes deeply spiritualised was the wandering mystic and poet Milarepa. Every man of letters in Tibet knew the history of his life, while his poetry belonged to the popular repertoire. There is nothing of his clownish aspect to be discerned on this thangka, but then it is called 'Praise to the honourable Milarepa' and represents him as a deified being. Below his heavenly manifestation he is depicted in his most familiar earthly shape: with his right hand at his ear 'listening to the echoes of nature' as he himself expressed it. We see various episodes in the life of this national figure, beloved both by laymen and monks, who lived in the 11th and 12th century A.D. Several times he is shown in a cave, because he meditated in caves high in the mountains without food and almost without clothing and there found ultimate salvation.

27. TSHOṄ-KHA-PA. *Scroll painting. Measurements 78 by 55 cm. Rijksmuseum voor Volkenkunde, Leyden; inv.no. 2740-40.*

This scroll painting was explained down to the slightest detail by my Tibetan informant, but as the explanation would require far too much space, attention can only be drawn to the chief points of his explanation. In the centre the founder of the Yellow Cap order, Tshongkhapa, is depicted in the traditional manner, flanked by his two favourite pupils. He is seated upon a cloud, which above him merges into the paradise of Maitrreya. Below we see in the middle two monks who are engaged in the stylised theological debate that is a sign of their learning and their striving after salvation, and on the right a layman bringing gifts. Laymen were simply called gift-givers. This, we may say, is a kind of indication how life should proceed after and 'under' Tshongkhapa: the monks must study and be devout, the laymen, looking upon the great reformer, must proffer gifts intended for the monks. Below on the left we see the god of death, gŚin-rje, who is shown enlarged in a separate illustration (see for discussion no. 39). At the bottom, to the extreme right, are two horse-like animals, who with their raised ears are symbols of (devout) attention – at least my informant repeatedly stressed their attentive listening. Our usage affords no objection to calling the reformer thus portrayed a god. Tshongkhapa is sometimes represented with demonic traits as a Protector of the Doctrine.

28. TSHOṄ-KHA-PA. *Scroll painting. Measurements outside 144 by 77 cm, image 81,5 by 55,5 cm. Bernisches Historisches Museum, Berne.*

A scroll painting that differs from the previous one in several points. An interesting aspect is, that according to B. C. Olschak, *Religion und Kunst im Alten Tibet*, Zürich (Ars Tibetana) 1962, p. 59, the figure below on the right is the first Dalai Lama, and the whole thangka is to be regarded as a vision in his meditation. The corresponding figure in no. oo, my informant stated, is a layman, a gift-giver. According to Olschak the Terrifying Deity below on the left is Nag-po chen-po, but this should be gŚin-rje (Yama).

29. SPYAN-RAS-GŹIGS (Skt. Avalokiteśvara). *Scroll painting. Measurements 93,5 by 59,5 cm. Collection Dr. A. W. Schwaninger-Caprani, Basle.*

The bodhisattva who is essentially the bodhisattva of pity and compassion and whose name has become most widely known in the West, was known and loved in all the countries of Mahāyāna Buddhism. His Chinese female form, Kwan-yin, is characteristic and intriguing (cf. F. Sierksma, *The gods as we shape them*, London 1960, nrs. 27-31, pp. 154-159 and the literature listed on p. 187, particularly M. Th. de Mallmann, *Introduction à l'étude d'Avalokiteçvara*, 1948). In the four-armed shape depicted here he was, in Tibet, believed to incarnate in the Dalai Lamas. As such, he was of course an essentially national deity. His compassion was unlimited, which is expressed on this thangka by the fact that he is surrounded by the manifestations of the Buddha in the six worlds (cf. the Wheel of Existence, no. 36): the white Buddha in the world of the gods, the green Buddha in the world of the titans, the yellow Buddha in the human world, the reddish Buddha in the world of the tortured spirits, the blue Buddha in the animal world, the smoke-coloured Buddha in hell.

30. DGE-'DUN GRUB-PA. *Part of a scroll painting. Collection Verbert 118.*

dGe-'dun grub-pa was a nephew and pupil of Tshongkhapa the founder of the order of the Yellow Caps, who was the first abbot of the monastery Ganden (dGa-ldan). This nephew became the fourth abbot. He was a very gifted, but also very shrewd and ambitious character, who did all he could to strengthen the hierarchical system of the Yellow Caps and to extend the influence of the order. The famous monastery Tashilunpo (*bKra-śis lun-po*) was founded by him. It is assumed by some that he also developed the dogma of incarnation, which made possible the succession of Dalai Lamas and other incarnations. In any case he was afterwards promoted, with retrospective effect, to be the first in the series of Dalai Lamas. He lived from 1391-1478.

31. TIBETAN PRINCE OF THE CHURCH. *Gilded bronze. Height 18 cm. Rijksmuseum voor Volkenkunde, Leyden; inv.no. 3414-4.*

This statuette represents a Tibetan hierarch of the order of the Yellow Caps, the left hand lying open in the lap, the right hand raised in a gesture of argument and instruction. Such high-ranking and holy priests also belonged to the pantheon.

32. DEMONIC MASK. *Wood. Height about 50 cm. Rijksmuseum voor Volkenkunde, Leyden; inv.no. 2739-81.*

A wooden mask for dancing used in the *'cham*, which is also discussed in the present work. The '*cham* was a religious ritual dance, in which practically all the parts were those of Terrifying Deities, particularly the god of death. It is not known whom this mask represents.

33. ZA-BYED RDO-RJE MKHA'-'GRO. *Bronze. Height 16 cm. Museum voor Land- en Volken-kunde, Rotterdam; inv.no. 29166.*

I came across this statuette, which was strange to me, in the attics of the Museum mentioned above. It corresponds to the description of Yamāntaka as Vajrabhairava in the quotation given by Getty, 2nd ed., p. 164, and was identified accordingly by Dr. P. H. Pott. In this quotation, however, there is no mention of the god being portrayed in a sitting posture. Therefore it reminded me of the godling drawn in A. Tafel, Bd. I, p. 182, with which it is practically identical. The reliable Tafel informs us, that the god's mouth was placed against the mouth of a sick person, when the medicine was introduced into the mouth of the patient via the mouth of the god. Apparently this is a piece of folk religion. When the illustration was shown to two Tibetan informants, one of them immediately recognised the image, while the other said he had never seen one, but was acquainted with the god. Both called him *Za-byed mkha'-'gro*, *i.e.* the eating-ḍāka. *Mkha'-'gro* is the Sanskrit ḍāka, the male counterpart of the familiar ḍākinīs. The informant who knew of these statuettes related, that the 'prayer-name' was *Byin-sreg*, probably = *sbyin-sreg*, *i.e.* burnt-offering. This is in agreement with his explanation, that in worshipping this god seeds were burnt in the open mouth. The more learned of the two afterwards gave a fuller explanation. His written description, translated by Prof. Dr. J. W. de Jong, was: '*Za-byed rdo-rje mkha'-'gro*. Both his hands are in the mudrā of huṃkāra. He holds the vajra and the bell. His fox-yellow hair is turned back upwards. His mouth is wide open. His belly hangs down. His limbs are coarse. His right leg is stretched out.' This last detail does not accord with the bronze, whilst the description is obviously intended for a painting. At that time the informant was working upon the great collection of Tibetan books and manuscripts of the Rijksmuseum voor Volkenkunde in Leiden, and it is probable that he took this description from one of those works. He was most definite, however, in his oral description of the Eater. The statuette served for a particular meditation, which might also be carried out without the help of such an image 'in the mind alone', whereby the sins of man are eaten by the god, swallowed up and thus destroyed. This can only be carried out, he continued, by persons who have attained a very high degree of spiritual development. It may be added that the swallowing up of sins by a terrifying deity is also found in other connections in the Tibetan religion. If we put together these data, we find the god was used in three ways. He served for magic medicinal purposes. He was used in ritual and in meditation, symbolically to swallow up sins. For the latter purpose he was also used in a purely meditative fashion, *i.e.* visualised. Thus this bronze exemplifies the contrast between the people and the monks, and the contrast within monastic religion between ritualism and mysticism. The name Yamāntaka/Vajrabhairava is to be rejected. The two informants spoke not infrequently of Vajrabhairava, but never used the name in connection with this statuette. Iconographically one might think of Mahākāla, who as the protector of science was represented seated and with four arms, with a large head and wide open mouth and with his legs in more or less the same 'un-Buddhistic' attitude (Gordon, ill. between pp. 90-91). Later Prof. Dr. J. W. de Jong kindly drew attention to the Tibetan dictionary of *Chos-kyi grags-pa* (1957), where under *Za-byed* one finds: 1) mouth, 2) fire, 3) *fire-god (me-lha)*, 4) face, 5) demon, 6) vajra of Indra. It is to be noted that the Indian fire-god Agni was called hutāśa, that is eater of offerings, or hutabhuj, that is enjoyer of offerings. It is difficult to determine what have been the historical background and 'mergers' of *Za-byed rdo-rje mkha'-'gro*. That Mahākāla in the shape described above, or (also) Agni (*me-lha?*) were among his ancestors does not seem impossible. That he is a Tibetan creation or re-creation seems very probable. Further research regarding this unknown Tibetan god will not only be necessary, but also interesting, and clear up his exact relationship with Vajrabhairava both in India and Tibet. Finally, it is perhaps not without significance that the informant who knew not only the god, but also these images, was the incarnation pertaining to a monastery (*Ras-chuṅ phuk*) that really belonged to an ancient, unreformed order.

34. RNAM-SRAS (Skt. Vaiśravaṇa). *Bronze. Height 29 cm. Museum voor Land- en Volkenkunde, Rotterdam; inv.no. 29940.*

This god seems to be *rNam-sras*, the god of wealth and one of the eight great Protectors of the Doctrine. His three-headed, three-legged and ten-armed appearance is an enigma to me and to those I consulted. There are other statuettes or paintings of deities in Tibetan art that cannot yet be deciphered. The only thing there can be no doubt about, is that the god is a Terrifying One.

35. DUS-'KHOR (Skt. Kālacakra) yab-yum. *Scroll painting. Measurements 38 by 27 cm. Collection Verbert 113.*

Kālacakra means 'wheel of time' and is an insignificant, pale deity. Important is the fact, that Kālacakra (Tib. *Dus-kyi 'khor-lo*) is the name of the last theological system by means of which it was attempted to save a more and more decaying Buddhism with the help of still more foreign elements. It was introduced in India in 966 A.D. and in Tibet in 1026. According to Hoffmann, from whom these data are taken, the system is founded upon astronomy and astrology, and its starting-point is the strict identity of macrocosm and microcosm, of universe and man. It comprises many tantras, divided into mother-tantras, whose subject is the highest insight, and father-tantras dealing with active compassion. Characteristic of a pervading sense of doom is, I think, the strong eschatological element in the system: after a catastrophe, Buddhism will arise in new glory. The new system designed to make Buddhism more attractive was unable to save it from downfall in India, but had a great influence in Tibet and formed an important basis for the theology of the Yellow Caps. The god, who is therefore a hypostasis of the system and not a Terrifying Deity, is depicted here in yab-yum sitting on a lotus throne.

36. SRID-PA'I 'KHOR-LO (Skt. Bhavacakra). *Scroll painting. Collection H. Froelich, Brugg and Kathmandu.*

If the previous deity, the Wheel of Time, was a late and anaemic creation, the Wheel of Existence – a literal translation – shown here belonged to early Buddhism, and was more widely disseminated in Tibet than in any other country. It was to be seen in every temple and monastery as a visual synopsis of the doctrine. It was also called 'the actions and their fruits' (*las dang 'bras*). In the small circle at the centre we see the urges to action: the hog (ignorance, stupidity), the cock (passion and desire), and the snake (hatred). By either obeying these three *origines mali* or conquering them to some extent, one may descend or rise higher in the six worlds depicted in the great wheel of existence. The three upper segments show the comparatively happy spheres of existence: above that of the gods and to right and left those of titans and men. The three lower segments show the world of the animals, that of the tortured spirits and that of those tortured in hell. All these forms of existence are temporary, including that of the gods. That is why a monstrous being holds the wheel in its claws. Some deny that this is the Tibetan god of death, *gŚin-rje*, but there can be no doubt that in this demon the people and many monks recognised the god of death, who in this instance is the

Tibetan equivalent of the Indian Māra, the demon who tempted the Buddha. Not only human existence, then, all existence is transient and subject to death, so that true salvation can only consist in liberation from temporality, even the temporality of the gods. This is only possible through the complete liquidation and elimination of the three fundamental evils, sometimes named the three poisons.

37. GŚIN-RJE (Skt. Yama). *So-called meditation drawing in colours on a black ground. Measurements 43 by 32 cm. Rijksmuseum voor Volkenkunde, Leyden; inv.no. B 107-98.*

Pictures are only used in the elementary classes of mysticism, so to say. Mastery of meditation is only achieved when, without material resources, one can systematically, bit by bit, visually 'build up' a deity, and then systematically 'break him down' again. A meditation drawing such as this one is for the service of those who have progressed half-way. Only the attributes are shown of the god of death and of his female partner Tsamunthi. One is supposed, as it were, to 'fill in' the gods visually. Such drawings at the same time afford expression to the conviction, that ultimately the deities are projections of ours. The upper border of entrails, eyes, etc. shows we are on a charnel field. The bull and the woman and other details also indicate the semblance of reality. This seeming reality of sexuality, aggressivity and death is visible to our unenlightened eyes, divine reality is invisible and can only be seen with the mystic eye, that is: produced by the mind ... and unbuilded again.

38. GŚIN-RJE (Skt. Yama or Yamarāja). *Bronze. Height 17 cm. Museum voor Land- en Volkenkunde, Rotterdam; inv.no. 29933.*

Here the god of death is standing alone upon a bull that is copulating with a woman. As protector of the order of the Yellow Caps he wears the wheel of the Doctrine on his chest. His protective nature is perhaps also expressed in this bronze in the position of his hands (karaṇa-mudrā, according to a Tibetan informant sdig-mdzub in Tibetan = threatening fingers) discussed in the present work. My two Tibetan informants could tell me no more of him than that he is Yamarāja and that his female partner, if such be present, is named Tsamundi. The main informant, who had both the ordinary theological and the tantric degree, showed a marked disinclination to speak of this god. Wishing to be helpful, however, he offered to transmit my written questions to the greatest contemporary theologian of Tibet, whose name he did not mention. The answers sent by this theologian were either non-committal or contained information that has long been current in the West. Curious, however, was the following answer to the following question, translated as literally as possible by Prof. Dr. J. W. de Jong: 'One sees that the buffalo is copulating with the female demon. What is this? Out of the heart of the buffaloes the buffalo is trodden down. This mode of being is not trustworthy (or: not well-founded).' Quite literally, the last sentence reads: 'This mode of being is not of a pure source (khuṅ-dag).' This cryptic answer makes the impression of an evasion. One might hazard the guess that (similia similibus!) from out the essence of the bulls, that is from out Yama with the bull's head as quintessence of all that is bull, the bull is destroyed and that the cohabiting, *i.e.* the ordinary human way of life, is of impure origin in the mystic domain of truth and has no foundation. One might also guess, that in the copulating of bull and woman one bull destroys the other 'bull', that is to say that sexuality destroys itself and thus is an untrustworthy way of living. The only thing one can conclude with some certainty from this answer, is that sexual ty is aggressively destroyed and that Yellow Caps do not like to speak of the subject to outsiders. This confirms the hypotheses advanced in the last chapter of this book, which was already finished when the two informants arrived. In connection with this depiction of the god of death without a partner, one more of the afore-mentioned written questions and answers may be added for the sake of completeness: 'In some cases the Dharmarāja (= Yama) is accompanied by the yum, sometimes he is not. What is the difference? During the worship of Yamāntaka (*'Jigs-byed*) it is customary for the Dharmarāja, the yab, to be alone.'

39. GŚIN-RJE (Skt. Yama) and Tsamundi. *Detail of a scroll painting. Rijksmuseum voor Volkenkunde, Leyden; inv.no. 2740-40.*

The way the god of death is represented here with his helpmeet Tsamundi differs in two important points from other depictions. Tsamundi is more or less 'riding' upon his hip, which in former times symbolised their union, that was afterwards depicted as a sexual reality. In the second place the bull and the woman are not separated, neither is the bull copulating with the woman, but he has thrust his hind foot into her vagina, causing a bloody wound. The first trait points to aversion for incest and condemnation of sexuality, the second to condemnation of sexuality and contempt of women. My Tibetan informant insisted on calling the woman a *bgegs*, that is a demon or devil. He was not willing to call her a woman, nor to recognise the evident femininity of this devil and her mutilation by the bull, with whom in other instances she cohabits absorbedly. At first he confined himself to four words only: 'Yamarāja (= Yama king), Tsamunthi, *ma-he* (= buffalo, bull), *dgra-bgegs* (= hostile demon).' See also no. 38. On this thangka of Tshonkhapa the wheel of the doctrine on *gŚin-rje*'s chest shows besides that this form of the god is the property of the Yellow Caps, who condemned sexuality and women more strongly than the old orders. In a celibate order, which also set Yamāntaka far above Yama, the tendency was more easily indulged to set sexuality, aggressivity and death on a level in this way. The mentality of the other portrayals of this god in the present work is entirely different. See also the final chapter of this book.

40. GŚIN-RJE (Skt. Yama) and Tsamundi or Yamī. *Bronze. Height 25 cm. Museum voor Land- en Volkenkunde, Rotterdam; inv.no. 29934.*

In all probability this bronze, which I found in the attics of the above Museum and described for the first time in *The gods as we shape them*, no. 41, is unique. In the final chapter of the present work it is discussed more fully and, I hope, better. Iconographical specialists were unable to provide an explanation. No relevant texts were to be found. One can only, then, make a supposition referring to as many data of religious history and iconography as possible. Regarding this bronze once again, one might also wonder whether it is not one of a series, representing a particular phase of a gŚin-rje meditation. It is known that the mystics had first to visualise the god, then his partner, then their union and so on. Then this bronze might represent the moment before the unio mystica of gŚin-rje and Tsamunthi. In the case of a Tibetan deity one must not only ask in what form he is shown, but also in what religious milieu he played a part. Here the god lacks the 'wheel of the doctrine', so he stands outside the milieu of the Yellow Caps. We may therefore think of a mysticism of sexual hue. As far as her appearance goes, the god's companion might be his sister Yamī, particularly as she is handing him a skull-bowl full of blood (see De Nebesky-Wojkowitz, *Oracles and demons*, p. 82). The sexual nature of the scene conflicts with this, while it would also be probably the only representation of Yamī together with Yama. Therefore one must perhaps choose for Tsamundi. Only new texts can supply the correct answer. For further discussion see the final chapter.

41. GŚIN-RJE (Skt. Yama) yab-yum. *Gilded bronze. Height 14,5 cm. Rijksmuseum voor Volkenkunde, Leyden; inv.no. 2798-23.*

Here the god of death is united with his female partner, Tsamundi (trident in right hand). It is significant, that the bull and the woman under their feet are separated, while in other cases, when the god and his yum do not cohabit, the bull and the woman do. The unio mystica undoes the life that is serf to passion and reproduction. See also the final chapter of this book.

42. GŚIN-RJE GŚED DMAR (Skt. Raktayamāri)? *Bronze. Height 14,5 cm. Rijksmuseum voor Volkenkunde, Leyden; inv.no. 2714-3.*

Not only his female partner, long called Yamī, who must now with a probability verging upon certainty be named Tsamundi or Tsamunthi (sometimes Ekajāti), but also *gŚin-rje* (Yama) himself has caused iconographical difficulties, and still does so. At any rate, I have been unable to identify this bronze with all the means at my disposal. The specialist at the Museum called it Yama with his śakti. Objections to this, however, are the human face and the woman and bull with the woman lying on top of the bull. According to Getty Yamāri, a form of Yamāntaka, stands on a woman (or corpse) and a bull, the woman (the corpse) lying on top, but has no female partner, while the bronze in our case has. Grünwedel, however, (*Mythologie des Buddhismus* usw., 172, 174) describes and depicts a pair of deities yab-yum, who are almost entirely identical with the bronze reproduced here. The only difference is, that in Grünwedel's indistinct drawing the right arm of the female partner is not raised, while the right hand seems to be empty, and the left hand seems to hold some other object. As all other characteristics, including the most important ones, are the same, it is highly probable that we may regard our bronze as representing *gŚin-rje gśed dmar* (Skt. Raktayamāri), that is the red Yamāri, not Yama but Yama's conqueror (compare P. H. Pott, *Introduction* etc., p. 102). The difficulties of iconographers in such matters result from a shortage of available texts, but also from the fact, that when in magic and mysticism the principle of similia similibus is applied and death is conquered by (super)death, distinctions are difficult to make. Confusion with regard to Yama and Yamāntaka was already mentioned in this book.

43. GE-SA. *Scroll painting. Measurements 83½ by 58 cm. Musée Guimet, Paris; inv.no. M.G. 23.081.*

The story of the warlike and fierce king Gesar, whose name alone is derived from the Roman Caesar, the Greek Kaisar, may be regarded as the national epic of Tibet. We now have detailed knowledge of its contents and backgrounds, thanks to R. A. Stein's *L'épopée et le barde au Tibet*, which appeared after the present work was finished, so that it could only incidentally be made use of. Although according to Stein it must have been written by a Buddhist monk, being a mixture of the old religion and Buddhism, it has now become almost exclusively the property of the people, and is sung by bards. The Yellow Caps at any rate will have nothing to do with it. My informant regarded it as a collection of childish inventions. The vicissitudes of Gesar's life even included the defeating of a god like *Pe-har*. This divine king was warrior, magician, 'divine trickster' and protector of Buddhism, who crushed enemies as an 'enemy-god'. With the aid of a thangka or image representing him, one could practise a current form of divination. The thangka reproduced here is a painted biography of the great king. (In R. A. Stein, *La civilisation tibétaine*, an enlarged detail is to be seen opposite p. 231). The familiar black tents of the Tibetan nomad herders and the great number of horses catch the eye. Just as the face of the ancient mountain gods is often very little demonic or even decidedly benevolent, so too the expression of the beloved Gesar is very friendly here, however fierce and bellicose he might be and however much he is a protector of religion. This matter deserves further examination, the more so as there is some reason to regard him as a relation of the mountain gods. Many Tibetans expected an apocalyptic return of the mythical national hero Gesar, who at the end of time would destroy the enemies and bring about a glorious resurrection of Tibet and its religion. Perhaps now many are expecting him still.

ACKNOWLEDGEMENTS

Acknowledgement is made to the following museums, private organizations and individuals for their permission to reproduce photographs: Museum voor Aziatische Kunst, Amsterdam: 2. Musée Guimet, Paris: 43. Bernisches Historisches Museum, Berne: 28. Museum voor Land- en Volkenkunde, Rotterdam: 1, 12, 24, 25, 33, 34, 38, 40. Rijksmuseum voor Volkenkunde, Leyden: 3, 4, 5, 6, 8, 9, 14, 16, 17, 19, 21, 27, 31, 32, 37, 39, 41, 42. Statens Etnografiska Museum, Stockholm, Sven Hedin Collection: 10, 22, 26. Collection H. Froelich, Brugg and Kathmandu: 36. Collection Dr. A. W. Schwaninger-Caprani, Basle: 13, 29. Collection Verbert (photographic archives Koninklijk Instituut voor de Tropen, Amsterdam): 7, 18, 20, 30, 35. F. Maraini, *Tibet Secret*, Paris (B. Arthaud) 1952: 11, 23. B. Ch. Olschak, *Religion und Kunst im alten Tibet*, published by the Swiss Aid to Tibetans, Solothurn und Wahlwies a.B.: 10, 13, 22, 26, 28, 29, 36. J. F. Rock, *The Am-nye Ma-chen Range and adjacent countries*, Rome 1956, by permission of the editor, Prof. G. Tucci: 15.

Thanks are also due to Mr. C. Zwanenburg, photographer of the Rijksmuseum voor Volkenkunde, Leyden, for the photographs of objects in this museum and Nrs. 24, 25, 33, 34, 38, 40, and to Mr. L. P. Scholten, photographer of the Museum voor Land- en Volkenkunde, Rotterdam, for the front cover photograph.

This book was designed and produced at Mouton & Co., publishing house. The blocks for the black and white illustrations were made by L. Th. Boelaars & Zn., N.V., The Hague; those for the colour illustrations nos. 1, 5, 16, 19 and 37 by Koningsveld & Zn., N.V., Leyden; those for the colour illustrations nos. 10, 13, 22, 26, 28, 29 and 36 by Otto Immer-Zulauf & Söhne, Zürich. The paper for this book was supplied by G. H. Bührmann N.V., Amsterdam. Text and illustrations were printed by Mouton & Co., printers at The Hague. Binding by Van Rijmenam N.V., The Hague.